TREASURE HUNT

TREASURE HUNT

Shipwreck, Diving, and the
Quest for Treasure in an Age of Heroes

Peter Earle

THOMAS DUNNE BOOKS
ST. MARTIN'S PRESS ⚬ NEW YORK

THOMAS DUNNE BOOKS.
An imprint of St. Martin's Press.

TREASURE HUNT. Copyright © 2007 by Peter Earle. All rights reserved. Printed in the United States of America. For information, address St. Martin's Press, 175 Fifth Avenue, New York, N.Y. 10010.

www.thomasdunnebooks.com
www.stmartins.com

Library of Congress Cataloging-in-Publication Data

Earle, Peter, 1937–
    Treasure hunt : shipwreck, diving, and the quest for treasure in an age of heroes / Peter Earle. —1st ed.
        p. cm.
    "Thomas Dunne Books."
    Originally published: London : Methuen, 2007.
    Includes bibliographical references and index.
    ISBN-13: 978-0-312-38039-7
    ISBN-10: 0-312-38039-9
    1. Treasure troves—History. 2. Shipwrecks—History. 3. Salvage—History.
4. Explorers—History. I. Title.

G525 .E17 2008
622'.1909—dc22

2008013311

First published in Great Britain by Methuen Publishing Ltd

First U.S. Edition: July 2008

10 9 8 7 6 5 4 3 2 1

Contents

List of Illustrations

1. Jacob Rowe's driving engine. Reproduced by permission of the National Maritime Museum, London.
2. 'An English East-Indiaman, c. 1720' by Peter Monamy. Reproduced by permission of the National Maritime Museum, London.
3. Working the tongs from a small boat. Illustration from the logbook of William Evans.
4. Blowing up a wrecked collier in the mouth of the Tyne (SP 29/336). Reproduced by permission of The National Archives, UK.
5. The supposed location of the treasure buried by the Spaniards on Ireland Island, Bermuda (MS. Rawl. A.305, fol. 1r). Reproduced by permission of The Bodleian Library, University of Oxford.
6. The VOC wharf at Middelburg from an aquarelle by J Arends.
7. Captain Thomas Dickinson's 158 feet long derrick (ADM 7/498). Reproduced by permission of the National Archives, UK.
8. Chart drawn in 1687 for *The West-India Pilot* showing the 'Plate Rack' – the wreck of the *Concepción* which had been discovered by William Phips earlier in the same year. Reproduced by permission of The British Library. Copyright © The British Library Board. All Rights Reserved.
9. Chart drawn for the VOC to show the location of the wrecks of the *Vliegent Hart* and *Anna Catharina*.

10. Engravings on a silver tankard made to celebrate John Lethbridge's success in salvaging treasure.
11. Divers' tongs of various sorts drawn in 1734 for Märten Triewald's book *The Art of Living Under Water.*
12. John Rennie's improved diving bell. Reproduced by permission of The British Library. Copyright © The British Library Board. All Rights Reserved.
13. Semi-atmospheric diving apparatus made by William Tonkin for John Braithwaite. Reproduced by permission of The British Library. Copyright © The British Library Board. All Rights Reserved.
14. Portrait of Sir William Phips (artist unknown).
15. Chart showing the wreck site of the *Concepción.* Reproduced by permission of The British Library. Copyright © The British Library Board. All Rights Reserved.
16. Edmond Halley's diving bell of 1691. Reproduced by permission of The British Library. Copyright © The British Library Board. All Rights Reserved.
17. Swedish diver working with tongs on the guns of the royal warship *Vasa.*
18. Royal Navy Sailors working from a diving platform (reproduced by permission of The Royal Society, London. Copyright © The Royal Society.)

Endpapers: reproduced by permission of The British Library. Copyright © The British Library Board. All Rights Reserved.

The author and publishers have made every effort to trace all copyright holders of illustrations contained in this publication. It is hoped that those not yet traced will be acknowledged in subsequent editions of the book. The publishers would be grateful for any assistance in tracing copyright holders.

'We all dribble a little at the thought of gold and silver, and make lust respectable by sermonising about concern for the past. Nonsense. It's not Anglo-Saxons or medieval sailors people are interested in – it's money, cash, guineas, pieces of eight, sovereigns, ingots, stuff you can run your hands through and count and feel the weight of and stash away under the bed.'

Moon Tiger, Penelope Lively (1988)

'That's what it was – the sort of silliness gentlemen will get up among themselves to play at adventure. A treasure-hunting expedition. Each of them put down so much money, you understand . . .'

Victory, Joseph Conrad (1963)

'The "treasures of the deep" have at all times been the subject of much visionary exaggeration, and the accounts of the exploits of divers equally extravagant.'

'Diving', *Chambers' Encyclopedia* (1908)

Preface

'A man who will not fight for a galleon, will not fight for anything'. Admiral Sir Charles Wager.[1]

Much of English naval history rests on the fact that most English sailors would fight for a galleon only too happily and had often done so successfully since Elizabethan times. Some were pirates, some privateers, and some sailors in the Queen's navy, but all were motivated by a passionate desire to seize Spanish ships and Spanish treasure and make themselves rich or at least richer, with little thought of their own safety, a passion for unearned gold and pieces of eight that was an integral part of the English psyche. Dreams of Spanish treasure were indeed almost a national obsession and many men also lusted after the vast quantities said to lie at the bottom of the sea in the wrecks of Spanish galleons, treasure which could be acquired without fighting if only one could find the wrecks and dive down to them.

Such treasure, however, continued to be just the stuff of dreams, given the contemporary state of diving technology, until the day in June 1687 when a ship dropped anchor in English waters after a voyage in which the bounds of the possible had been expanded almost beyond belief. It seemed almost incredible that her captain, William Phips, had brought home nearly forty tons of silver and gold, a treasure said to be worth a quarter of a million pounds sterling, a simply colossal sum by the standards of the day which needs to be multiplied by several hundreds to give some idea of its value today. This treasure in coins and bullion had been raised by naked divers, unaided by any breathing equipment, from the *Concepción*, a Spanish galleon wrecked over forty years before on a coral reef in the middle of the ocean. 'The money fished up has caused great excitement and has awakened the spirit of many to engage in similar enterprises, which were previously thought impossible', wrote the Tuscan envoy in London to his masters in Florence.[2] The great British treasure hunting boom had begun.

Stories of sunken treasure had always circulated and had multiplied in recent years as colonization in Bermuda, the Bahamas and Jamaica brought Englishmen closer to the homeward-bound routes of the famous Spanish treasure galleons. Many of these galleons were known to have wrecked and many sailors and other travellers knew or pretended to know where the wrecks lay. It seemed that Captain Phips' example would be easy to follow and those ambitious and wealthy enough to fit out an expedition to 'go a wrecking', in the contemporary phrase, were bound to be successful. There were to be many such adventurers, most of whom sought a grant from the crown to search for Spanish or other wrecks in specific areas, grants which theoretically gave them a monopoly in that area in return for handsome royalties to be paid if they were successful. Most of these expeditions were based on extremely dubious information provided by yarn-spinning sailors and they were promoted by the men known to contemporaries as projectors, some fairly honest but many of them tricksters and cheats skilled in drawing in the gullible and relieving them of their money.

Those drawn in were a cross-section of the great and good of late seventeenth and early eighteenth-century society, the king and queen themselves, dukes and other noblemen, generals, courtiers and officials of state departments such as the Admiralty and the Treasury, as well as lesser and more practical men such as sailors and divers and men convinced that they and they alone knew where a treasure lay. The first two chapters of the book set the scene by discussing the whereabouts and possible value of the many wrecks of Spanish galleons and the technology available to those who sought to find them. Chapter Three describes the voyages by Captain Phips and others in search of the *Concepción*, and the book then goes on to describe the promotion and progress or lack of it of several of the treasure hunting expeditions which followed his amazing success. All these expeditions carried the hopes and dreams of large numbers of investors and nearly all were complete failures for, as the poet and projector Aaron Hill put it in 1715, 'a thousand families have been since undone, by sending their estates a diving after shipwrecked treasure'.[3] Such failures make good stories and include a lively and often bizarre cast of characters whose antics tell us much about the society and the age in which they took place. They provide, for instance, a fascinating insight into the greed and gullibility of a society notorious for its love of gambling and famous for its creation of many of the institutions of modern finance and the modern economy. It is certainly no accident that the boom in treasure hunting with its focus on vast profits, risk, invention, adventure and, hopefully, achievement, should coincide with the early years of the Financial and Industrial Revolutions. Gambling and treasure hunting are closely connected to the birth of modern capitalism.

Running parallel with and closely connected to this surge in interest in treasure hunting from 1687 onwards was a boom in the development of diving technology which mainly took the form of new equipment to enable divers to work longer and more effectively under water, equipment which will seem very crude and dangerous to those familiar with modern diving technology. This really took off in the early 1690s, the years which saw the first great promotional and stock market boom in English economic history. These were also years of warfare on the grand scale and it is not surprising to find that military and naval inventions led the field in this promotion boom but, amazingly, diving inventions and diving companies came a close second with fifteen to twenty separate applications for patents of invention in the years 1691–3. The boom collapsed after this flurry of excitement, and some of the applications lapsed, but there were to be some further improvements in diving equipment in the second and third decades of the eighteenth century. The process by which people were granted patents of invention in this period was very different than it is today and involved little in the way of checks on so-called inventors' claims to originality. It was indeed an invitation to dishonesty and trickery and some of these inventions and company promotions were simply scams designed to defraud those who invested in them. Others seem bizarre today but were promoted with serious intent, while a few were of great importance in the history of diving technology, such as the improvements to the diving-bell made by the astronomer Edmond Halley whose paper 'The Art of Living Under Water' ensured that he would be famous in the history of diving as well as in the history of comets.

The last six chapters of the book describe the period from 1715 to the early 1830s during which a new breed of diver emerged. Divers and their backers were still interested in treasure hunting and getting rich, but repeated failures of well-publicized expeditions made them more cautious, and interest tended to focus more on the salvage of ships which had wrecked recently and whose location was reasonably well-known. Most of these were outward-bound English and Dutch East-Indiamen which nearly always carried a large 'treasure' in coin and bullion to finance their purchases in Asia. The book concentrates on salvage expeditions carried out by the most famous men in English eighteenth-century diving history, John Lethbridge, Jacob Rowe, William Evans and the Braithwaite family, using wherever possible fresh evidence from such documents as lawsuits and logbooks. These divers had considerable success in recovering bullion and other valuables from wreck sites all over the world, from South Africa and the Atlantic Islands to the Shetlands, Hebrides and West Indies. This work was done with great skill and courage, sometimes in very difficult conditions, and their story provides a counterpart to the often ludicrous failures encountered in some of the earlier chapters.

Interspersed with these increasingly professional salvage enterprises will be descriptions of ventures into pure treasure hunting, such as Jacob Rowe's attempt to recover the so-called Tobermory treasure in the Isle of Mull or the endless attempts to raise treasure from the Spanish galleons and French warships sunk in 1702 in Vigo Bay in Galicia after a devastating battle in which the entire

Franco-Spanish fleet was captured or destroyed by the English and the Dutch. Both these treasure hunting ventures were total failures, but the book finishes with one of the greatest success stories of this early phase of diving history, the salvage by Royal Navy sailors of the treasure sunk in HMS *Thetis* off the coast of Brazil in 1830. This treasure was recovered using a diving-bell, the most important technological advance made during the period covered by this book, and it is a logical point to end the story as it was the last important use of a diving-bell to salvage treasure. New and more effective technology was developed, which would evolve into the standard helmet diving dress so familiar from illustrations of late nineteenth-century and early twentieth-century divers, and the days of the divers in the heroic age described in this book were over.

My thanks are due to the libraries and record offices where I have done my research, especially the National Archives and the British Library. Many thanks too to Geoffrey Harris, Henry Horwitz and Nikolaus Graf Sandizell for references and information, to William Braithwaite, direct descendant of the diving Braithwaites of the eighteenth and early nineteenth centuries for information on his ancestors and the chance to look at their surviving logbooks. Very special thanks also to John Bevan who read the book in typescript and whose vast knowledge of diving and its history saved me from many errors. And, finally, my especial thanks as usual to my friend and colleague David Hebb who provided me with ideas, references and encouragement during the two years in which the book was researched and written and then read the completed work in typescript and made many valuable suggestions for its improvement.

As this book was in its final stages of preparation news came in that a wreck had been located some forty miles off Land's End by Odyssey Marine Exploration and much treasure has been recovered. It is thought that the wreck was the *Merchant Royal*, referred to in Chapter One. Congratulations to Greg Stemm and his team.

CHAPTER ONE

Sad Newes from the Seas

CHAPTER ONE

Sad Newes from the Seas

'She had in her 300,000 pounds in readie boloigne [bullion]; 100,000 pounds in gold, and as much value in jewels, besides each man's adventure, and the whole cargoson, or rich lading of the ship, all of which was sunke in the sea, nothing saved.'

Sad Newes from the Seas was the title of a pamphlet written in 1641 to describe and bemoan the loss 'of that good ship called the Merchaunt Royall, which was cast away ten leagues from the Lands End'. This unfortunate vessel was sailing from Cadiz to Antwerp when she foundered and was carrying a treasure in gold, silver and jewels valued by contemporaries at somewhere between half a million and a million pounds sterling, a simply colossal sum by the standards of the day and a serious treasure by anybody's reckoning.[1]

Such a loss was certainly sad news for the merchants and ship-owners concerned, and very sad news indeed for the families of those who drowned, but such disasters were very good news for the treasure hunters and salvors who are the main subject of this book. Such men liked nothing better than a rich shipwreck, especially one from which nothing had been saved. In this case, however, little could be done about it, since salvage in deep water so far from land was impossible in the seventeenth century and so this huge treasure still lies somewhere between Land's End and Ushant, possibly the richest wreck ever to sink in English or near English waters. Estimates of its value in today's money start at £20 million and go up to £100 million or more, enough to attract the most sophisticated and well-equipped treasure hunters in the world, three teams of which were combing the seabed of the Channel Approaches for the *Merchant Royal* while this chapter was being written.[2]

There were, however, many other wrecks lying on the bottom of the sea which could in theory have been discovered and salvaged by a seventeenth-century adventurer. Some ships foundered, like the *Merchant Royal,* and were lost in the open sea, others (very few in fact) were sunk in battle and some were consumed by fire, an ever-present danger on a wooden ship. But the great majority of ships were lost as a result of hitting reefs, rocks or the coast which normally meant that they sank in fairly shallow water close to land, or actually on the shore, or in among the reefs which had destroyed them. The contemporary state of the arts of diving and salvage will be examined in the next chapter but, in very general terms, wrecks in less than seven or eight fathoms of water (forty to fifty feet), could (just about) be salvaged in the seventeenth century if conditions were very favourable. Such good conditions would include the presence of some competent divers, the absence of people intent on preventing them from diving, good weather, good visibility underwater, an easy lie for the goods to be salvaged so that treasure and other desirables were not still deep inside the wreck or under sand and rocks and, perhaps above all, a lot of luck.

The seas were not as crowded with shipping in the seventeenth century as they were to become in later centuries, but they were already quite busy as the maritime states of Western Europe expanded their horizons and began to develop trade throughout the known world. The ships employed were poorly equipped, badly maintained and often seriously overloaded. Navigation was still very primitive, with no way of determining longitude except by dead reckoning (which can roughly be translated as guesswork), so that no sailor could be certain where he was unless known landmarks were clearly visible and sadly what was 'known' sometimes turned out to be a mistake. The sailors themselves were often drunk or incompetent and even the most sober and best qualified of captains was not immune from making serious errors. As a result, shipwreck was a common hazard, even more frequent than it was to be in the eighteenth century and it is probable that at least one in twenty of all the ships that went to sea perished.[3]

The great majority of these wrecks were, however, of no great value and were certainly not worth risking one's life to salvage, as they carried only foodstuffs, raw materials and other mundane cargoes or goods, such as sugar and pepper, which had little value once they had spent a few days in sea water. Many other wrecks of high and low value were thrown on the coast and were easily salvaged from the shore once the storm which wrecked them had subsided. But, in addition to this multitude of low value or easily salvaged wrecks, there were, by the second half of the seventeenth century, a few potentially very valuable ones with unsalvaged cargoes of gold and silver and jewels scattered across the seabeds of the globe, some of them worth as much, or more than, the *Merchant Royal.* Such ships have attracted the attention of treasure hunters almost from the moment they sank and many men have searched for them, both in the seventeenth century and even more since the Second World War when the development of SCUBA equipment and other technological advances opened up the seabeds of the world to serious investigation.

Some of these valuable wrecks reflected unusual circumstances, as indeed was true of the *Merchant Royal,* since very few ships sailed in English waters with such a treasure. But most of them were the wrecks of ships sailing on regular bullion or treasure carrying routes which had been unfortunate enough as to hit a reef or otherwise founder. Geography, and well-established trading habits, ensured that there were familiar patterns to shipping throughout the world and, by 1650, a well-informed contemporary would have been able to identify several of these routes on which some ships carried large cargoes of bullion and other treasure and there was no reason why these very valuable ships should have been less prone to shipwreck than their poorer consorts. Some of these routes were completely inaccessible to the salvors and treasure hunters based in Western Europe and America who will be the main subject of this book. There were, for instance, regular exports of treasure from Japan to China and from Arabia to Persia and northern India which were vulnerable to attack by European pirates but, when such ships wrecked as they did from time to time, they were unlikely to attract European divers and salvors who would have found their presence very precarious in the face of hostility from local rulers.

The same was true in the Pacific where there were many very rich shipwrecks but little chance of foreigners salvaging them in the face of Spanish antagonism. There were, for instance, several shipwrecks in the Armada del Sur, the fleet which brought silver north to Panama, from Callao in Peru, on the first stage of its long journey to Spain. Shipwreck was also a fairly common phenomenon for the Manila galleons which carried vast quantities of silver from Acapulco in Mexico to Manila in the Philippines and brought oriental luxuries back. These were very long and terrible voyages and many of these galleons wrecked, in California, in Japan, in the Marianas Islands and above all in the Philippines themselves, where the tortuous navigation between the many islands was always dangerous. But such places were far too remote for anyone except the Spaniards themselves to think of trying to salvage these rich galleons and other Europeans, especially the British, confined themselves to trying to capture them and were occasionally successful.

Such considerations meant that nearly all the valuable shipwrecks which were likely to arouse the cupidity of European and Americans were located on just two major bullion-carrying routes. One of these was the route from Europe to India, for virtually every ship that sailed to the east had several chests of treasure aboard since it had quickly been discovered that, although Asians had little taste for European manufactures, they found European and American gold and silver more than welcome. So East-Indiamen carried treasure, from £5,000 to £50,000 on a typical ship. These ships were all Portuguese until near the end of the sixteenth century, but in the seventeenth and eighteenth centuries English, Dutch, French and later Danish and Swedish vessels joined in the lucrative business. Many of these rich ships were wrecked, some just a few miles from home, in the sandbanks of Holland and Zeeland, the English Channel or the Tagus in Portugal, but most of them scattered along the regular route, in the Scottish Islands, where many Dutch and Scandinavian East-Indiamen were lost, in the Atlantic Islands of Madeira and the Cape Verdes, on the coast of South Africa, around the islands of the Indian Ocean and so onwards, in India, Persia, Indonesia and the South China Sea. Many of these wrecks would be out of bounds to salvors from Europe, but some of them were accessible as we shall see.

Valuable as these wrecks of East-Indiamen were, they pale into insignificance when compared with the richest of all treasure ships, the Spanish vessels, mainly galleons, which brought home the gold and silver of America to Cadiz and Seville. Spain was a very bureaucratic nation and from an early date everything connected with the *Carrera de Indias*, as the treasure fleets were officially called, was governed by rules which covered everything down to the most minute detail, rules which were not, of course, always observed.[4] Two fleets were normally despatched each year, one to Vera Cruz, the port of Mexico, and the other to Tierra Firme, the mainland of South America, with its terminus in Porto Bello. In America the ships discharged their European cargoes and awaited the arrival of the goods to be carried home to Spain. In bulk these consisted of such mundane articles as sugar, hides, tobacco, dyestuffs and other colonial goods, but in value, treasure, mainly silver, but also some gold, emeralds and pearls, made up over ninety per cent of the return cargoes. The Tierra Firme fleet normally completed its lading at Cartagena de Indias in Colombia, the richest and best fortified city in the Indies, and then made its way to Havana in Cuba, where it often joined up with the fleet returning from Mexico before sailing home to Spain, with any luck before 20 August which traditional wisdom decreed was the last safe date to sail before the hurricane season.

The scale of the enterprise was quite staggering, with over one hundred ships making the journey in many years. And, needless to say, a great number of them were lost, some five or six hundred in the century between 1550 and 1650. So there were plenty of Spanish wrecks lying at the bottom of the sea. But not many of these would be of any interest to a salvor. Only a few of the best-armed and most powerful galleons carried substantial quantities of treasure, and indeed there was a tendency for the treasure to be concentrated in fewer ships as time went on, so that the rich ships became even richer. It was unusual for a galleon to carry more than half a million *pesos* in the middle of the sixteenth century, though even this was the equivalent of about £100,000 and so twice the value of the richest East-Indiamen. Spanish treasure ships were simply in a different class and by the first half of the seventeenth century many of them carried well over a million *pesos*, and some four or more millions, while in the eighteenth century one can find figures of six, seven and eight millions being carried on a single ship.

So wrecked galleons became progressively more attractive to the treasure hunter, though only a comparatively small number of these rich shipwrecks would ever become a potential target. The Spanish were astonishingly good at salvaging their ships, even in these days of very primitive diving technology. They had developed the business of transferring treasure from a galleon foundering in mid-Atlantic to a sturdier sister ship to a fine art, rarely dropping even a single chest into the ocean. And any ship which wrecked in shallow waters near a Spanish shipping centre was likely to be salvaged carefully and thoroughly, often over several years, which allowed the salvors to choose the most propitious weather and tidal conditions to do their business. The west end of Cuba, for instance, was the crossroads of the whole treasure shipping business and its dangerous waters were a graveyard for many rich galleons, but nearly all of these were salvaged from Havana, some of them 'to the last nail' as one captain boasted in a letter to his King. And even if these ships had not been salvaged, no foreigner would have dared to organize a treasure hunting expedition right under the noses of the Spanish in such well-protected waters. If they wanted silver from the seas near Havana or Cartagena or other Spanish strongholds, they would fight for it and not dive for it.

This did not mean that there was a lack of rich Spanish ship-wrecks to attract treasure hunters. For they did not always wreck their ships conveniently near their major settlements or in places where it was easy and safe to conduct salvage operations. And so there were enough rich wrecks to satisfy anyone's greed, if only they could be found, in the reefs of the Caribbean on the passage between Cartagena and Havana, in the reefs on both sides of the Straits of Florida, the normal passage out of the Caribbean for the silver-laden galleons, in the Bahamas and Bermuda, neither of which were settled by the Spaniards, and in many other remote places. To give some examples, we will look at five major disasters. These involved a total of nine lost galleons, all carrying very large quantities of treasure. Every one of them is a treasure hunter's dream and some of these dreams have come true.

The first case study relates to one of the greatest mysteries in the history of the Spanish treasure fleets, the disappearance, in September 1563, of the *capitana* (flagship) of Juan Menendez on its way home from Havana. Juan was the only son of Pedro Menendez de Avilés, a famous man in Spanish colonial history and the head of a very powerful clan which completely dominated the shipping business between Spain and America in the late 1550s and 1560s. Juan Menendez' *capitana* (unnamed in contemporary records) was carrying half a million *pesos* (pieces of eight) on the King's account and probably at least as much again for merchants and other private individuals, a very substantial treasure for that date. He set sail from Havana in command of thirteen ships on 13 August (this double thirteen being seen as a bad omen) and made a successful passage of the Straits of Florida but then, on 10 September, the fleet was hit and shattered by a storm somewhere near the island of Bermuda.[5]

In the following weeks, Spanish colonial officials were able to determine what had happened to the fleet after the storm. Seven ships made it safely to the Azores and one sailed directly to Spain. Two, badly damaged, managed to reach the north coast of Hispaniola, and they reported seeing two other ships sink, from one of which they had been able to rescue some of the crew and most of the treasure. This left just the *capitana,* unaccounted for and indeed her fate was never discovered as was reported in 1591, twenty-eight years after her disappearance. 'Up to today no one knows anything about it.'[6]

The last sighting of the *capitana* had been reported by the master of one of the ships which reached the Azores. While running helplessly before the storm he had seen the *capitana* dangerously low in the water, as though she was leaking badly, but where he was when he made this last sighting he had no idea. Modern shipwreck books tend to place the *capitana* of Juan Menendez in the waters of Bermuda since survivors said that was where the storm started, but there is really no evidence that this is correct. Indeed, if she was leaking badly, it seems far more likely that she would have tried to make a passage through the eastern Bahamas in order to reach Puerto Rico or Hispaniola where she could have been repaired, as two other stricken ships in the fleet managed to do.[7]

Pedro Menendez de Avilés thought that his son and the crew of the *capitana* might have escaped to some island or to Florida and asked King Philip II for permission to fit out two ships to go to Bermuda and the coast of Florida, 'coasting it, jumping ashore in various places to ask the Indians by signs if there were men with beards in that land or in some island nearby, since the Indians have no beards'. The King gave permission but, in the event, urgent political necessities prevented the despatch of this search party and the only searches that were made seem to have been along the coasts of Hispaniola and Puerto Rico. But nowhere was there any sign of the lost ship.[8]

People did not forget the *capitana* of Juan Menendez; her loss was too dramatic for that. But the story became just one of many stories of lost ships which dreamers and adventurers would have liked to find. And then, some thirty years after her disappearance, there was a sudden revival of interest as no less than three applications were made to search for a treasure which sounds suspiciously as though it might be the treasure from the lost *capitana*. The most intriguing story was that told by Hernando del Castillo, a Cuban who, in 1598, fought a lawsuit in Seville against Gieronimo Martín, cosmographer, pilot and citizen of Seville, both men seeking exclusive right to search for the treasure from a wreck in the Bahamas. Castillo claimed that in the previous year he had been captured while at sea by an English ship which had later wrecked in a storm off the island of Inagua in the south-eastern Bahamas. The survivors, including Castillo, reached the shore and he remained on the island two months before managing to escape with two companions by stealing a boat. 'We went to a cay which is a league and a half from the island and on the next day we went to another cay and from that cay three days later we passed to a certain place where we found a great quantity of money in bars of silver, pieces of gold, silver coins and other things.' On another occasion, Castillo told the Council of the Indies in Seville 'that on a cay near the island of Inagua there is a great quantity of bars of silver and gold and money and sixty guns'.[9]

Castillo's evidence is vague in the extreme, though you could hardly expect him to present the Council with a map showing the exact location of his treasure. Such limited information is typical of treasure hunters who want to tempt investors into backing them but do not want to give too much away. In fact Castillo was a bit of a blabbermouth and the basic outline of his story was known in Mexico and Cuba as well as in Seville where his opponent in the lawsuit, Gieronimo Martín stole the story and embellished it in the hope that his greater social distinction would win him the case and the required royal permission to search for the treasure. Martín claimed that the treasure on the cay came from ships wrecked there more than thirty years before, which would more or less fit the *capitana* of Juan Menendez, and that he had seen signs of it while travelling in those parts, a claim which was successfully challenged by Castillo.

The story is further complicated by the fact that a third party, Pedro de Arana, had already received a contract in 1592 allowing him to search for treasure in the Bahamas for eight years. His application referred back forty years (i.e. to the early 1550s), when 'two ships coming from the Indies loaded with silver . . . were lost on a certain island, near to Hispaniola, where the people got ashore and saved the money which they placed in a *corral* made of stone divided in half and in each part placed the treasure of one of the ships'. They then made a boat out of the wreckage and sailed for Cuba but were wrecked on the way 'and everyone was drowned except one sailor and a negro woman from whom came this account'. Such sources of information, where just one or two people are left to tell the tale, are very common in treasure hunting applications, but it is intriguing that the Spanish name for the

Hogsties, a dangerous collection of reefs and cays a little to the north of Inagua, is Los Corrales.[10]

None of these applications for search licences said specifically that the treasure they were interested in was from the *capitana* of Juan Menendez and it is clear that the ship that Arana sought was of an earlier date. Much more specific information is, however, contained in a printed memorial of 1618 which recounts the voyages made in 1613 by the Venetian Thomas de Cardona, a well-known explorer and entrepreneur. Cardona was mainly interested in finding and developing new pearl fisheries, but he maintained an interest in finding old shipwrecks as a sideline. He clearly knew the Inagua story and he despatched one of his vessels to go through the Old Bahama Channel (along the north of Cuba) to search Inagua and neighbouring islands 'where it is conjectured the silver of the galleon commanded by Juan Menendez lies'.[11]

None of these searches for treasure in the south-eastern Bahamas was successful, nor indeed was another one which set out in 1621 'to look for a ship full of silver which was lost returning from New Spain to the metropolis sixty years ago on an island . . . called Inagua', a description which can only refer to Juan Menendez' galleon.[12] Nevertheless, it seems probable that there was not simply wishful thinking behind these applications. It is true that tales of treasure piled up on cays by shipwrecked sailors, and glimpsed by passing mariners who had no chance to pick it up, are rather common in Spanish sources. But this does not mean they are all untrue. After all, what else were survivors to do with the treasure as their wrecked ship sank into the sea? In any case such stories, true or not, were just the stuff to excite the optimists who populate the pages of this book.

For one galleon to disappear without trace in a storm was not all that unusual. For four to do the same was quite extraordinary. But this is what happened to four galleons from the fleet of seven, a cargo ship and a small advice boat which set sail from Cartagena de Indias in Colombia for Havana on All Saints' Day 1605, under the command of Luis Hernandez de Córdoba. This well-travelled route was safe enough in fine weather, but presented hazard after hazard in a storm since it was necessary to find a safe passage through a whole string of shoals and reefs, such as Serrana and Serranilla Banks, Pedro Shoals, Quita Sueño (Quit Sleep) and many others, in the south-western Caribbean.[13]

It was then somewhat alarming for the sailors in the fleet when, after five days of easy sailing with a pleasant following breeze, the wind increased to gale force and then veered round to the north-east in the night. A veteran seaman was to say later that he had never seen so strong a wind nor such high waves. 'Like mountains they crashed into us as we looked up at them and held on for dear life.' Visibility was virtually nil in the darkness and driving rain, but survivors believed that the fleet was then somewhere east of the Serranilla Bank, a long chain of coral heads, reefs and rocks twenty-four miles long, which were known to Spanish sailors as Las Viboras (the Vipers) because of their menacing and deadly appearance. The stricken ships occasionally saw each other fighting the storm as best they could, but, for the most part, it was every galleon for herself as masts and rigging crashed to the decks and water levels in the hold rose to dangerous heights. Two bedraggled vessels and the cargo ship made it to safety in Jamaica, bringing with them some survivors from the advice boat which had capsized and sunk. And one galleon turned back the other way and managed to make port in Cartagena, being towed in for the last few miles by a galley. But of the remaining four, including the *capitana* and *almiranta*, and most of the treasure, there was no sign.

Two parties were sent to search along the reefs early in 1606, one from Jamaica and the other from Havana, and people throughout the Spanish Caribbean were instructed to keep their eyes open for wreckage or survivors. Some things were found including some masts and rigging floating in the sea and a large carved figure from the poop of *San Roque*, the *capitana* of the fleet. Wreckage was even found on the central American coast, carried there by the prevailing currents. But not a single survivor, or even a corpse, was found, a real mystery since the storm blew itself out quite quickly and the sea was calm on the morning following the disaster. In such circumstances one would have expected at least a few people to have survived, if only on planks and other floating wreckage, but there were none.

Some rather intriguing information was reported by an officer in the treasure fleet which left Cartagena de Indias on 20 August 1606. While they were sailing through shoal waters on the south-west side of Serrana Bank, one of the sailors shouted out that he could see the complete wreck of a ship on the bottom of the sea, which at that point was some nine fathoms (54 feet) deep. Another confirmed this sighting and a third said that he had seen something black but was not sure what it was. Officers asked the captain if they could turn around and search the area again, but he refused to believe the sailors' story and ordered the ship to continue on its course. Many things, such as rocks, look like black shadows through the gin-clear waters of the Caribbean and Spanish sailors had vivid imaginations, so the captain probably made the right decision. His orders were to sail as quickly as possible to Havana and not to risk his precious galleon and cargo of treasure chasing dreams in shoal waters. The sailors' supposed sighting of the wreck was taken more seriously in Havana where the Governor arranged for another search party to be sent out, complete with black pearl divers who were said to have the best underwater vision in the Caribbean. But this party, like the others, had no success.

Córdoba's galleons, as they are usually known, naturally attracted the attention of contemporary treasure hunters, though some of these seem to have exploited the royal search licences for their own nefarious purposes. A small fleet which had set out in March 1607 to the Serrana and Serranilla Banks in search of the lost galleons was later discovered to have actually been engaged in contraband trading in Jamaica and Cuba. This was quite a common motive for seeking a treasure hunting licence from the Crown, since once out at sea in a well-equipped ship, there was little the authorities could do to exert any control. In 1613, Thomas de Cardona, whom we met earlier searching for the *capitana* of Juan Menendez, had a go at finding Córdoba's galleons. He acquired a pilot from Jamaica (which was still Spanish at this time) who had the reputation of knowing more than anyone else about the reefs, and then 'we went in search of the Vivoras, Serrana and Serranilla which are the places where it is known that Córdoba suffered the storm and lost the galleons'.[14] Cardona claimed to have some new invention to help him but whatever this was it brought him no success. Nevertheless, this and other attempts to find the remains of the lost galleons kept the story alive, so that it was still intriguingly current when the English began to settle Jamaica after their conquest of the island in 1655. Everyone knew it was a good idea to keep one's eyes open when fishing or turtling near the reefs and shoals.

No salvage was possible on Córdoba's wrecks because they were never discovered and the Spanish Crown was not prepared to go to any further expense after the failure of the search parties. But, when galleons were lost near a major shipping centre like Havana and there were survivors who knew where the wrecks lay (or thought they did), then the Crown was prepared to spend large sums of money to recover some of its losses. This was to be the case with *Santa Margarita*, a treasure galleon sailing with the Tierra Firme fleet of 1622 and *Nuestra Señora de Atocha*, the *almiranta* of the same fleet. These two vessels were officially carrying about one and a half million *pesos* of treasure between them, and no doubt much more clandestinely, so it made good sense to try to recover some of this huge sum.[15]

As often happened, a number of misadventures had delayed the sailing of the fleet and it finally set out from Havana for Spain on Sunday 4 September 1622, a desperately dangerous time to sail since it was well into the hurricane season. 'God blinded the eyes of those in charge', wrote a contemporary, and the results of this blindness were very soon apparent. On the very next day a terrible storm broke out which did enormous damage on the west end of Cuba, blowing down houses, uprooting trees and destroying the plantations. And the storm was even worse at sea, striking the fleet at one of the most dangerous parts of the whole route, the southern entrance to the Straits of Florida where there was very little room to manoeuvre. That Monday night the wind swung round into the south and drove the galleons, many of them already dismasted or otherwise damaged, towards the reefs, a terrifying helter-skelter made worse by the ominously large numbers of grey sharks that followed in their wake. Most of the fleet did, in fact, manage to find its way west to the comparative safety of the Gulf of Mexico, but at least four ships were to be lost on the Marquesas and the Dry Tortugas, the very last of the Florida Keys, way to the west of Key West and almost directly north of Havana.

The *Santa Margarita* was swept by the waves across a reef in the Marquesas and grounded and broke up in the sandy shallows beyond. Her captain was one of the sixty or so survivors and he was able to see for himself the fate of the *Atocha* which struck the reefs about a mile away from him. As she sank, the last thing to be seen of her hull was the beautifully painted image of Our Lady of Atocha on her poop. And then that too was gone and there was only her mizzen mast showing above the water. Clinging to it were five bedraggled figures, one sailor, two teenage apprentices and two black slaves, the only survivors from the 265 people who had set sail from Havana only two days before.

The survivors from the two galleons were picked up by a launch from another ship in the fleet and taken back to Havana. Here it was decided that salvage should be attempted promptly before the ships completely broke up or enemies came and salvaged for themselves. A fleet of five small vessels was quickly put together under the command of Captain Gaspar de Vargas, a veteran seaman whose career went back to the Spanish Armada of 1588. He fitted his flotilla with the utmost despatch and it was ready to sail for the Florida Keys on 16 September, just two weeks after the shipwreck. He carried several survivors with him and they were able quickly to locate the mizzen mast of the *Atocha* which was still sticking out of the water. She lay in nine or ten fathoms depth of water (fifty-five to sixty feet), which was deep but not impossible for the naked Indian and black slave divers who plunged to the bottom clutching a stone to speed their descent. In the short time that they were able to spend on the wreck before their lungs gave out, they ascertained that it would be impossible to enter the storerooms where the treasure lay since the hatches were still firmly locked and the decks still in one piece. The salvage party had rather foolishly come out without equipment suitable for breaking up the decks of a sunken ship so, after recovering a couple of small guns, they sailed further west to seek the remains of the *Santa Margarita*. But nothing could be seen of her, so quickly had she broken up and her remains covered with sand. So they sailed still further west to Loggerhead Key in the Dry Tortugas where a third galleon, *Rosario,* had been stranded. The survivors who had been huddling together on the windswept key for three weeks, with little food or water, were picked up and comforted and the ship which was lying in shallow water was thoroughly salvaged, access to the storerooms being achieved by burning the upper decks down to the waterline.

Gaspar de Vargas was joined the next year by Nicolas de Cordona, an expert salvor from Mexico, and between them they employed large numbers of skilled divers from Cuba, Mexico and the pearl-diving island of Margarita, near Venezuela, which was said later in the century to have five hundred or so divers, 'the best in the world'. These men worked hard but had only very limited success and so the official attempt to salvage the two lost galleons was given up in 1623, after 100,000 *pesos* of royal money had been spent to very little effect. The way was now open for a private salvor to make an *asiento* or contract with the representatives of the Crown and this opportunity was seized by Francisco Núñez Melián, a native of Havana, a politician, gambler and inventor, and the epitome of the adventurous and self-promoting entrepreneurs who have been attracted to diving and the salvage business from those days to our own. He made a contract with the Crown in 1624, by which both of them were each to receive one-third of the goods recovered and the remainder was to be put aside to meet the expenses of the expedition, a generous concession since *asentistas* usually had to meet their own expenses.

Operations did not start until 1626 when Melián set out with a flotilla of small vessels and frigates to protect them from the enemies and predators who might be expected. Like his pre-decessors he took with him large numbers of free Indian and slave divers and, as an incentive, he vowed to give the first slave to locate and recover a silver bar his freedom, a promise which was duly honoured. 'Now I swear by Our Lord you shall have your liberty', proclaimed Melián to Juan de Casta Bañon, the fortunate diver. One bar of silver led quickly to others and this was to be a very successful season with 64,000 silver coins, over 300 silver ingots and eight bronze guns recovered from the wreck of the *Santa*

Margarita in the three months between June and August 1626. But nothing was recovered from the *Atocha* which had now been lost again in the shifting sands.

Melián was to return to the wreck site every year for the rest of the 1620s, but he was never to have the same degree of success. There was plenty of treasure remaining, but much of it was covered by sand and it was much harder to reach than during the first season. His success had also attracted several attacks from the Dutch, with whom the Spanish were at war, and also from hostile Indians and English and French pirates. In 1629, his last diving season, he claimed that there were more than twenty-five enemy ships hanging around his salvage vessels, waiting for a chance to seize what they had brought up or to explore the wreck themselves. But, despite this disappointing end to his campaign of salvage, Melián had won for himself not just riches but fame and he was rewarded with the office of Governor and Captain-General of Venezuela, a position which could well be just as profitable as diving for treasure. His contract was taken over by Juan de Anuez who continued to salvage with little success, on and off until 1641, the very year when yet another great treasure galleon disaster set people's eyes looking in a different direction.

This ill-fated vessel was *Nuestra Señora de la pura y limpia Concepción*, commonly known as the *Concepción*, the *almiranta* or vice-admiral of a fleet which left Vera Cruz for Havana and Spain in July 1641. The fleet had spent over a year rotting in the tropical heat of the Mexican port and the *Concepción* was in a very bad state, overcrowded, overloaded and leaking badly but still thought capable of carrying four thousand miles across the ocean some five hundred passengers and crew and a treasure, in silver, gold and emeralds, which was valued by Francisco Granillo, the *contramaestre* or mate who had supervised its stowage, at four million *pesos*. Attempts were made to repair the leaks in Havana which took time and carried the fleet even further into the hurricane season. So it was not until 20 September that they finally set sail for home, a full month after what was considered the last safe date to set out on the homeward passage. 'The sea which was waiting for them would not have come as a complete surprise', wrote Pierre Chaunu, the great French historian of the Spanish silver fleets.[16]

All went well at first and after a week of easy sailing they were clear of the Straits of Florida and had turned north-east towards Bermuda. But now, in very much the same sea area as the *capitana* of Juan Menendez, they were struck by a fierce storm which was 'the strongest that had ever been experienced or seen at sea'. Admittedly most storms were described in similar terms, but this one was certainly a terrible experience for the *Concepción* which very nearly capsized and whose hurriedly repaired leaks burst open again, so that at first seven and a half, and then ten, feet of water were reported in the hold. 'Each person said goodbye to his companions', wrote a survivor. 'Not even the bravest had any hope of life', this despair reaching its nadir when the image of Our Lady of the Conception, the patroness of the ship, was swept away from the poop by an enormous wave.

The mainmast was cut away and several guns cast overboard to lighten the ship and some measure of control was achieved as the storm abated, but the galleon was in no condition to cross the Atlantic to Spain. It was determined instead to try to reach Puerto Rico, about a thousand miles to the south-east, where it would be possible to make full repairs. The course was changed and, after three weeks of slow progress, the pilot Bartolomé Guillen announced on 23 October that they were now due north of Puerto Rico and prepared to give the order to sail south. Every other person aboard with experience of the sea, including the *Concepción*'s commander Don Juan de Villavicencio, felt sure that Guillen was wrong and that they had not gone nearly so far to the east. Many believed they were north, not of Puerto Rico but of the Abrojos (literally 'open your eyes'), a dangerous area of shoals and reefs some fifty miles north of Hispaniola. But, in the *Carrera de Indias*, it was the pilot who had the last word in navigation and so orders were given to sail south. In a dramatic gesture, Don Juan dissociated himself from the decision. He called for a silver bowl of water to be brought to him on the poop deck and then, in full view of the assembled crew and passengers, he washed his hands of all responsibility.

A week of calm weather followed the change of course but then, on 30 October, the wind got up from the north-east and the galleon's speed increased. On the evening of the next day, in fine weather, a sudden violent shudder ran through the ship as she scraped on sunken rocks below. Moments later she hit a submerged coral reef with such force that the bottom of the vessel was torn out. Their situation was now desperate as they lay jammed in amongst coral heads which rose forty or fifty feet from the sandy sea bed, a beautiful but desolate final resting place in the midst of a long crescent of sunken reefs and the occasional rock which dried out at low water.

Where were they? Their attempts to determine their latitude, quite an easy task for a competent sailor, demonstrated some appalling incompetence in navigational skills, with estimates ranging from under twenty to twenty-two degrees North, a full two degrees or 120 miles difference. They had even less idea of the longitude in which they lay entrapped. Some still believed they were north of Puerto Rico. Others thought they were north of Anegada in the Virgin Islands, even further east. The better sailors aboard were still convinced that they were north of the Abrojos. From east to west such discrepancies covered a range of some 350 miles and from north to south over a hundred. They were well and truly lost!

There was nothing for it but to abandon ship and sail south in the longboat, the only boat still seaworthy, and on rafts made from the wreckage. The longboat carried just thirty-three men, far below its full capacity, and was the first to leave the wreck site with Don Juan himself and many other distinguished people aboard, a shocking case of officers and gentlemen first. Once they reached land they knew exactly where they were, Puerto Plata on the north coast of Hispaniola, a long way from Puerto Rico. Three of the eight rafts which later followed in the wake of the longboat were never seen again and many men on the others were lost, either washed overboard, dead of exhaustion or the prey of sharks. The biggest party of 120 people, including all the people of distinction still left, went on two rafts which were much better built and stronger than the rest, but this did not prevent them from having a most unpleasant landfall, being captured by an English pirate in sight of land. The pirate captain asked them where they had been wrecked and was amazed to be told that it had been on reefs north of Anegada. 'Drunkards', he retorted, 'that wasn't Anegada where you were lost. Those were the Abrojos.' The pirates did no physical harm to the shipwrecked men on the rafts. They just relieved them of their fine clothes and personal adornments and, according to evidence given later in Hispaniola, half a million *pesos* worth of treasure. It seems probable that this would have consisted of very high value, low bulk items such as gold, emeralds and other jewels, so that this was a very lucky pirate crew indeed.

Don Juan de Villavicencio was to make many abortive attempts to get together an expedition to search for his lost galleon, a sorry tale of incompetence, mismanagement and arguments between the various parties involved. Eventually he gave up but such a rich wreck was not to be forgotten. The Crown was besieged by private applications to search for and salvage the *Concepción* and several of these expeditions actually sailed to the Abrojos, but they failed to find any trace of her. These potential salvors had plenty of information from survivors, many of whom were so frightened by their experience that they vowed never to go to sea again and settled in Hispaniola, and from local fishermen and sailors who knew the currents and shoals north of Hispaniola. They had eyewitness descriptions of the reefs where the *Concepción* had been lost, marks which could identify the wreck site, and details of the course taken by the longboat to reach land and much else. Antonio Petri y Arce who applied for a search permit in 1672, thirty-one years after the wreck, claimed to have been a great friend of Francisco Granillo, the mate of the lost ship, who had left him 'very particular information and descriptions of the place where the silver is located' before he died. But this particular information, like all the rest, proved to be mistaken and the last resting place of the *Concepción* remained a mystery, an exciting challenge for the French and Spanish who lived on the coast of Hispaniola and for English settlers and drifters who, from the middle of the seventeenth century, were getting to know well the waters of the Bahamas and of the Turks and Caicos Islands, not far to the north-east of the Abrojos or the Handkerchief Shoal as it was known in English.

The last shipwrecked Spanish galleon that will be considered in this section is the *Nuestra Señora de las Maravillas,* the *almiranta* of the Tierra Firme treasure fleet which was lost early in 1656 at Los Mimbres on the Little Bahama Bank. She was commanded by Mathias de Orellana and was carrying a very large treasure since there had been no shipments from Peru for three years before she made her final fatal voyage. Just how much that treasure was is, as usual, difficult to say with complete conviction. Robert Marx who rediscovered the wreck of the *Maravillas* in 1972 stated authoritatively that she 'was the second richest ship ever lost in the Western Hemisphere and carried gold and silver then valued at over $50 million'. Or perhaps we can follow the estimate of Padre Diego Portichuelo de Ribaneyra, a chaplain from Lima cathedral who was one of the few to survive the shipwreck. He later wrote a book describing his adventurous journey home to Spain and in this he stated that the *Maravillas* was carrying 'five millions . . . in gold and silver', not to mention her rich cargo of tropical staples.[17]

The return of the treasure galleons from South America was delayed for a long time by the presence of an English fleet in the Caribbean which had been sent out by Oliver Cromwell to make conquests in the West Indies at the expense of the Spanish. After a rather humiliating rebuff in Hispaniola, the English seized Jamaica as a consolation prize and so acquired for themselves a base right in the heart of the Spanish Indies which was to cause ceaseless trouble for the Spanish colonists for the next twenty years or so. The English fleet left behind a well armed force of adventurers to hold the island and then set off for home, a fact learned by the commanders of the Spanish treasure fleet on 25 August 1655. They now felt it safe to sail from Cartagena to Havana from whence, after several weeks of careening, repairing and provisioning the ships, they set sail for home on New Year's Day 1656, 'with such favourable weather that we all promised ourselves a very happy voyage'. All was still well three days later when, on the evening of 4 January, the continuing good weather promised an early exit from the dangers of the Straits of Florida and the passengers were looking forward to celebrating this important moment in the voyage home with 'games and *fiestas*' on the following night. But, sadly, this was not to be.

At ten at night, the lookout in the *Maravillas,* the leading vessel in the fleet, shouted a warning that the water ahead was turning white, a sure sign that they were in very shallow water with a sandy bottom. This was soon confirmed by a heave of the lead and it became immediately clear that they had somehow drifted dangerously close to the eastern side of the Straits. The *almirante,* Don Mathias, ordered the helmsman to change course away from the banks and at the same time ordered a gun to be fired as a signal of danger for the rest of the fleet. But this was unfortunately misunderstood. The result was complete confusion in the fleet which ended with the flagship ramming the *Maravillas* with its bowsprit. It took half an hour to separate the two galleons and then the *capitana,* under the command of the Marques de Montealegre, sailed away, not realizing, or at least claiming not to realize, that the *Maravillas* had been severely holed below the waterline which proved to be a fatal wound.

Since the galleon was clearly sinking and there was no hope of saving her with the pumps, Don Mathias, the *almirante,* did the only thing possible and tried to run her aground in some place where her treasure and crew could be rescued by the other ships in the fleet later. But this manoeuvre was to prove totally unsuccessful. While Padre Diego from Lima was kept busy confessing as many men as he could in the short time available, including Don Mathias himself, the *Maravillas* struck repeatedly on a coral reef and then sank to a sandy bottom with her fore and sterncastles still clear of the water, though not for long. The freshening wind smashed the already stricken galleon to pieces, leaving the survivors clinging desperately to the foremast, which was still proud of the water, or to hatches, planks and other wreckage floating in the sea. Only about forty-five out of 600 survived the ordeal, to be picked up the next day by the *Jesús María* and, according to Padre Diego, the Peruvian cleric who has left for posterity a graphic description of the shipwreck, many of these few survivors were heretics and some of them Moors and so were presumably of little account. It was certainly an unpleasant experience for a man who had been looking forward to a *fiesta*.

Gaspar de los Reyes, assistant pilot of the *Jesús María* and later to become a famous treasure hunter, buoyed the two main pieces of the wreck and then carried the survivors back to Havana. Here it was decided that there was a good chance of recovering at least some of the treasure and so a very large salvage expedition under the command of Juan de Somovilla Tejada was prepared. This consisted of six well-armed frigates, since there was danger of attack because Spain was still at war with England, and large numbers of divers, many of them from the pearl-fishing island of Margarita near Venezuela. The island's Governor had been ordered to supply Somovilla with forty Indian divers, 'the best that you have in that island', and if he was not able to find enough he was to make up the number with negroes. In the event he succeeded in finding thirty-five Indian divers who were paid twenty *pesos* per head 'for the maintenance of their families' and five black slaves, 'very good divers'.[18]

When this expedition returned to the wreck site they discovered that the marker buoys left by Gaspar de los Reyes had been washed away, but the forepart of the wreck was fairly quickly located by dragging the approximate area with long weighted cables and an impressive amount of treasure and guns was brought up by the divers before the approach of a hurricane forced them to close down for the season. But the salvors found that even this soon, just a few months after the shipwreck, much of the wreckage and treasure was already covered by sand and this was to be a continuing problem. Not that this stopped the salvage efforts. Divers continued to work on the wreck of the *Maravillas* throughout the rest of the 1650s and then intermittently until 1678, twenty-two years after the wreck, when the Spaniards at last seem to have given up. But even that was not the end, for a hurricane in October 1680 uncovered part of the wreck from its covering of sand and for the next few years adventurers from all over the Caribbean and the North American colonies hastened to the site to try their luck. As the Spanish historian Fernando Serrano Mangas has written, 'the *almiranta* lost in Los Mimbres in 1656 is perhaps the most dived upon ship in the history of the world' and he was just referring to the diving that went on in the seventeenth century.[19] But there was to be plenty more diving in modern times. For, during the treasure hunting boom that started in the 1950s, the wreck of *Nuestra Señora de las Maravillas* was one of the main targets and even after its discovery by Robert Marx in 1972 there was still more of its treasure left in those shifting sands and some of this was recovered in the 1990s.

By the 1670s and 1680s there were fairly large numbers of British and Irish settlers in Jamaica, Bermuda, the Bahamas and the North American colonies who were interested in such wrecks as the *Maravillas* and the *Concepción* and the other Spanish wrecks in the waters they frequented. But there were also Spanish wrecks much closer to home, the lost ships from the ill-fated and storm-tossed Spanish Armada of 1588. Fifteen of these, maybe more, were scuttled or wrecked on the coast of Ireland, all the way round from Antrim in the north to Dingle and the Blaskets in the south-west. These stricken ships were welcomed by the local population, who watched with glee 'a most extreme wind and cruel storm . . . which put us in very good hope that many of the ships should be beaten up and cast away on the rocks'.[20] Wrecking was a strong tradition on these impoverished coasts and plundering began immediately, many of the survivors being slaughtered and stripped of their clothing and valuables as they came ashore. But much of what the galleons held sank below the waves and its value was to increase in people's imagination as the years went by. The very word Spanish implied great wealth in sixteenth- and seventeenth-century minds and the value of these sunken galleons soon became legend. Every galleon was thought to carry vast quantities of gold to fund King Philip II's conquest of England, while the noblemen aboard had naturally brought their own personal treasure to enable them to present a dignified appearance when they took possession of their English estates.[21]

The Spanish wrecks in Ireland were long to attract treasure hunters, but what really gripped the public imagination was the ship lost in Tobermory Bay in the island of Mull off the west coast of Scotland, 'the prize in the greatest and most enduring treasure hunt in British history', as Alison McLeay describes it in her book *The Tobermory Treasure*.[22] This battered ship sought Tobermory as a haven from the storm, but she was not to ride safely for long. A few weeks after her arrival she sank at her moorings following a terrible explosion. Whether this was an accident or the result of sabotage is still debated, but one thing is certain. Once the Tobermory galleon had sunk beneath the waves, the value of her treasure was to escalate in the public imagination until it had reached fabulous proportions.

The wreck lay sixty feet deep at low water so salvage was not easy but, by the 1640s, attempts were being made to reach it and some guns were successfully raised. By 1676, the great ship had acquired a name and a value, as is reported in a memorandum of the Earl of Argyll who had jurisdiction over the wreck site. 'The Spanish wreck ship . . . is reputed to have been the *Admirall of Florence* in the Armada of 1588, a ship of fifty-six guns, and there was aboard 30,000,000 of money.'[23] Millions are very rare in English sources at this date and even if these were Scots pounds, one-tenth the value of English ones, this was an enormous amount of money; indeed one might well say an absurd amount, but it certainly appealed to the imagination. Seven years later, Archibald Miller, who had been working on the wreck, was able to produce, or nearly produce, documentary evidence and so confirm the value of the treasure on board. 'The ship's name is the Florence of Spaine . . . I saw one paper of lattin extracted out of the Spanish records that there was thirty millions of cash on board the said ship.' And if that was not enough to pull in the investors, he had another juicy little item to titillate whoever might read his report. 'I found a Crowne and Diadem and had hooked the same, but . . . it fell amongst the timbers. This Crowne is also in ye Spanish records.'[24]

There is something very modern about Miller's report with its nod to archival research. Just why or how he was able to peruse this exciting paper of Latin extracts he does not say, maybe wisely since the Spanish records at the time were kept in Castilian and not Latin. But such claims have always been part of the weaponry of the treasure hunting promoter. Today, such claims may well rest on fact, since treasure hunting researchers, as well as historians, are allowed to work in the Spanish archives. But, sadly, what they have found would have brought no joy to the many, many expeditions which have sought to raise the treasure of the Tobermory Galleon. For the ship lost in Tobermory Bay was not the Florence of Spain or any other of the great ships of the Armada. It was instead a very large but relatively humble cargo ship from the great shipping centre of Ragusa (Dubrovnik) in the Adriatic which had been requisitioned by the authorities in Sicily and chartered for the Enterprise of England. It was packed with soldiers, food, drink, weapons and all the paraphernalia of war, but there is no evidence that it was carrying any substantial treasure at all. But this sad news from the archives was not confirmed until the early 1980s and so was not available to deter the innumerable expeditions whose divers had sought the treasure in vain during the preceding four hundred years.[25]

Chapter Two

Men Under the Sea

Chapter Two

Men Under the Sea

'He fell like a diver from the well-made chariot, and the life left his bones . . . this man could feed a large number with the oysters he could find, diving off a ship, even in rough weather, to judge by his easy tumble to the plain from his chariot.'[1]

Homer employs the image of a diver in the *Iliad* on two separate occasions and this seems pretty good evidence that the occupation has had a long history. Indeed it is probable that men learned to dive almost as soon as they learned to swim. In the quotation above, Homer's diver is after oysters and the acquisition of such delicacies of the table as shellfish and octopus was certainly a major motivation for the pursuit. But there were many other things of value at the bottom of the sea. Archaeological sites are scattered with objects which could only have been acquired by diving, such as pearls, mother-of-pearl ornaments, various types of shell and red coral, while sponge-diving is another underwater occupation which has been carried on in the Mediterranean from ancient times to the present day. Divers were also employed in Greek and Roman times in underwater construction work, in warfare and of course in the recovery of treasure from wrecks.[2]

Homer's diver is used as a simile for rapid descent, an image which suggests that these ancient Greek divers were using the same technique to reach the bottom fast as the negro and Indian divers employed by the Spanish in the seventeenth century. These men (and occasionally women) clutched a large stone and leapt over-board, or sometimes held a stone or lead weight above their heads and dived headfirst into the sea, thus maximizing their time at the sea bottom. Such divers often had a rope around their waist, so they would know where their boat was and could signal for assistance when it was time to return to the surface. They normally dived naked, except perhaps for a belt to carry a knife and a 'goody-bag' to place their spoils in. No one is really certain whether they wore goggles or not. From the sixteenth century, there is evidence of the existence of such aids to underwater sight, most of them made of transparent horn or turtle-shell, but it seems unlikely that many divers used them since the pressure on their eyes as they descended could have been dangerous. It is more likely that they used some form of water-glass, such as the glass-bottomed buckets still used by octopus fishermen in the Mediterranean. Held just below the water these would enable the diver to identify his objective and aim his dive accordingly.

The key to a successful free dive was, of course, the length of time that the diver could stay underwater and so work on the bottom and there have been some extraordinary stories told about the endurance of the divers of the past. The native pearl-divers from the Bahamas, who were considered by the Spanish to be the finest divers in the New World, were said to be able to dive to a hundred feet and stay underwater for up to fifteen minutes. Similar descriptions can be found of the pearl-divers of the Indian Ocean and the sponge-divers of the Greek Islands. Such seventeenth-century tales should obviously be taken with a pinch of salt, but there is no doubt that these men or women who were forced by circumstances or inclination to dive for their livelihood could perform remarkable feats. Nevertheless, it seems probable that a depth of sixty or seventy feet and two, possibly three, minutes underwater were closer to the norm of a diver's endurance in the seventeenth century. Such dives repeated several times in a day put an enormous strain on the divers who seldom lived long and often rose to the surface, after a particularly strenuous dive, with blood pouring out of their ears and nose and even their eyes.

The limitations of the unaided naked diver posed a challenge to virtuosi who could see enormous benefits to themselves and to mankind if some method could be devised to lengthen the time spent at the bottom by divers. Some very ingenious devices were suggested, most notably by Leonardo da Vinci, but these were, for the most part, completely impractical and showed ignorance of the reality of life underwater. One common device, for example, was some sort of helmet with a pipe leading from the diver to a float on the surface, through which he could suck air down into his lungs. But such devices could only have been of any use in very shallow water, since a diver cannot breathe through such a pipe if his lungs are more than two or three feet below the surface, so great is the pressure differential even in shallow depths. Even a powerful bellows blowing the air down from above would not enable a seventeenth-century diver to go very deep using such an appliance.[3]

There was, however, one important technological development in underwater salvage which was probably of great antiquity, but not much used before the seventeenth century. This was the diving-bell or, as it was sometimes called, the diving tub. This device depended on the fact that a glass or similar container will retain air in its enclosed end when it is inverted and plunged into water. The diving-bell exploited this principle by making something big enough to hold one or two men inside who could breathe the trapped air when the open end was weighted with lead and lowered into the water. A bell was a convenient, but not necessary, shape for such a device and a much cheaper version could be made from a large wine cask.

John Winthrop, the Governor of Massachusetts, described a bigger form of the same device which was used in 1642 by one Edward Bendall to salvage the wreck of a ship which had blown up in Boston Harbour, an accident which was caused, according to the Puritan Governor, by the crew's blasphemous scorn for his religion. Bendall made 'two great tubbs, bigger than a butt [wine barrel], very tight, and open at one end, upon which were hanged so many weights as would sink it to the ground. It was let down, the diver sitting in it, a cord in his hand to give notice when they should draw him up, and another cord to show when they should remove it from place to place, so he could continue in his tub near half an hour, and fasten ropes to the ordnaunce [guns], and put the lead, etc., into a net or tub.' These last tasks might be done from within the tub or the diver if brave could hold his breath and crawl out from the open bottom to work for a minute or two before returning to his air supply.[4]

The most famous, and technically most difficult, feat of salvage achieved with a diving-bell in the seventeenth century was that carried out on the great Swedish royal warship, *Vasa*, which capsized and sank near Stockholm in August 1628. Many attempts were made to salvage the ship from the surface but she lay too deep, over a hundred feet, for any of them to have any success. All this changed however in 1663 when a Swedish army officer, Hans Albrekt von Treileben, teamed up with Andreas Peckell, a German salvage expert. Peckell's divers worked from a bell but one of completely different design from that used by Bendall, as we can learn from the fortunate coincidence that the work was described by Francesco Negri, a contemporary Italian traveller.[5]

The bell was, in fact, shaped more like a huge inverted pudding basin than a bell. It was about four feet high, made of lead, and attached by four cables to a square lead platform some eighteen inches below on which the diver stood. This meant that only the diver's head and the upper part of his body was out of the water and he had to wear a very bulky, watertight, leather suit to combat the cold. Once lowered to the bottom, the diver's first task was to use tongs, or a wooden stave with an iron hook, to catch onto and clear the debris which littered the wreck, either by himself or by attaching a rope from the surface. This work of clearance was slow, as time at the bottom was limited to just fifteen minutes by the cold and by the great depth which restricted the amount of air trapped in the bell. By the end of the winter, the way was clear for more profitable salvage and, on 1 April 1664, the first of over fifty brass cannon, each weighing one or two tons, was raised to the surface, a remarkable achievement which prefigured that other remarkable achievement, the raising of the whole ship some three hundred years later.

Both Peckell's bell and Bendall's tub had one obvious disadvantage however. The men working in them would have had great difficulty in seeing very much since, even on the brightest day, the equipment above them would have obscured the light. This problem had, in fact, been overcome in 1626 by Francisco Núñez Melián, the enterprising man who took over the search for the two treasure wrecks of the 1622 fleet after the official salvage parties had given up. He had a bronze diving-bell cast to his design in Havana, but this had windows which would enable the man or men inside 'to see the most hidden things . . . something never seen before'.[6] This was probably not true as there is a record of a bell with windows being used in Italy in the sixteenth century, but Melián's bell may well have been the first one with windows to be used in the New World. The expense of having the bell made quickly paid off and it was an important factor in his success, enabling the divers who descended in it to see the scattered treasure more easily and to spend much longer picking it up from the sea bottom. From this time onwards, most major Spanish salvage teams would take a bell with them as a necessary part of their equipment, though it is probable that not all of these had windows since locating glass which could combine transparency with sufficient strength was not easy before technical improvements in glass manufacture in the late seventeenth century. It also required very skilled workmen to be able to fit the windows into the bronze or wooden shell so that the bell remained watertight.

The diving-bell was a very valuable aid to salvage, but it suffered from many disadvantages and was not always practicable to use. It could not be used in very deep water, since the further down it was taken the more the air inside was compressed by the pressure of the water. Eleven fathoms (sixty-six feet, i.e. three atmospheres total pressure) was generally considered the maximum effective depth and no one else seems to have emulated the salvage of the *Vasa*'s guns at a hundred feet. At eleven fathoms the bell would be two-thirds full of water, leaving only just enough room for the diver to get his gulp of air. Some divers also complained that the air at the top of the bell became unbearably hot after half an hour or so under water. This is unlikely to have been literally true since, although compression as the bell descended and exhalation by the divers would have raised the temperature of the air in the bell, this would not have generated enough heat to be unbearable. Divers may well have been experiencing a growing contrast between escalating cold at the bottom and fairly constant warmth at the top. This warm air would also, of course, have become increasingly unpleasant to breathe as the divers continually inhaled and exhaled the same air trapped in the bell, leading to dangers of carbon dioxide poisoning and hypoxia (lack of oxygen). Whatever the correct explanation, the air sooner or later became unbearable to breathe and the divers had to be raised to the surface.[7]

Time at the bottom could be extended by using a bigger bell which trapped more air, but this solution brought its own problems as the larger the bell the more it cost and the more difficult it was to manoeuvre. A large-size bell also needed a big launch or ship above it to be able to lower and raise it and the divers within. Even a small one needed a pretty stout support vessel. But shipwrecks very often occur in places where it would be quite impossible to operate safely with such vessels. It was, for instance, generally impractical to use a bell in reef waters or very near the coast, situations where safety normally dictated that a canoe or small oared vessel rather than a decked ship should be employed. It was also difficult to work from a bell if the sea bottom was very uneven or cluttered up with boulders. And it was, of course, dangerous to use a tub or a bell in rough water since it was liable to swing about underwater and might even overturn. All these problems meant that, although bells were taken on more and more salvage expeditions as the seventeenth century progressed, they often remained in the hold of the salvage ship since, once at the wreck site, it was obvious to everyone that conditions were not suitable for the safe use of a bell.

Diving and divers were common in many parts of the world, in the sponge-diving islands of the Eastern Mediterranean, in pearl-diving centres such as Gujurat and Coromandel in India, in Japan and in the South China Sea, in the Pacific where in places such as the Mariana Islands the native culture was heavily dependent on the development of skills both on and under the water. Here visiting Europeans could amuse themselves by watching the natives dive to great depths for nails and other iron objects which were greatly desired as fish-hooks. But nowhere were the arts of diving and marine salvage so well developed as in metropolitan Spain and in her colonies. Most Spanish ports would have divers and salvage equipment available in the event of a wreck and the galleons were required to carry 'a diver, to discover where any ship leaks, in case it cannot be found on the inside'.[8]

These divers were well paid, receiving ten *escudos* a month, only a little less than the mate or the ship's carpenter, and two and a half times the wages of an ordinary seaman. And the Spanish colonies, as has been seen, had so many slave and free Indian divers that it was possible to put scores of divers to work on a really valuable wreck. Free Indian divers normally got some sort of contracted payment to compensate them for the time away from home and they would also be likely to receive some inducement to work hard. Juan de Somovilla Tejada, who commanded the salvage team working on the wreck of the *Maravillas* in 1656, agreed with his divers to pay them five *pesos* for every large bar of silver brought up and fifty for every bronze gun and such payments were the normal way of rewarding and encouraging divers all over the world. Little is known, however, about the rewards received by the slave divers. One writer believes that the freedom offered in 1626 by Melián to the first slave to bring up treasure from the wreck of the *Santa Margarita* became common practice thereafter, which is a nice idea but not one supported by much evidence.[9] Nor do the documents show slaves being given pro rata payments for each bar, gun or whatever was recovered. But they probably were, since otherwise it would be difficult to explain why they tried so hard. Slaves were employed in other maritime pursuits, as sailors, even as members of pirate crews, and they were nearly always allowed to retain some part of their wages or loot by their shore-based masters and the same is probably true of the slave divers who recovered so much treasure for Spain. At least one hopes so.

Most of this book will be about diving and salvage conducted by people from Great Britain and her colonies overseas. British waters are of course much colder and have much worse underwater visibility than those of southern Europe, and these may have been factors in discouraging both swimming and diving. Whatever the reason, the evidence suggests that there were very few divers at work in British waters before the 1680s. Indeed, during the whole of the first three-quarters of the seventeenth century, only three divers appear with any prominence in the English public records. Since these men were usually referred to by the definite article, 'the diver' rather than 'a diver', one might be forgiven for thinking that they were the only divers during their period of prominence. There are sufficient brief or passing references to other divers to show that this would be an exaggeration, but it does seem clear that in this period Englishmen preferred to salvage ships with their feet dry by using drags and grapples and hooks from the surface to bring up objects from the seabed.

The first of our pioneers was usually called simply 'Jacob, the Diver'. His proper name was Jacob Jansen, anglicized to Johnson, and he was a native of Enkhuizen in Holland, although he later became an English subject. He learned his trade in the Low Countries and had already acquired a formidable reputation as a diver and salvor before he came to England in 1620 'to doe service in recovering sunck ordnance, wrackt [wrecked] goods and money upon his Majesty's coasts of England and Ireland . . . by a playne and manifest way of dyving deepe under water'.[10] Jacob was to dive off the English and Irish coasts for the next fourteen years or so, mainly on English and Dutch East-Indiamen, but also on merchant ships from Venice, Spain and Hamburg, on a Spanish galleon captured by the Dutch which was lost in Castlehaven Harbour on the south coast of Ireland and on Spanish Armada wrecks reputed to lie in the sea off Broadhaven in County Mayo.

The sources which provide our knowledge of him arose mainly from his litigious and rather greedy nature which led to confrontation with other like-minded people, such as the men who set him to work and were reluctant to pay him, the landlords and others who claimed jurisdiction over wrecks on the coasts where he worked and other salvors whom he felt had infringed his warrant or authority. From the lawsuits and exchanges of correspondence which arose from such disputes, we can see that the law was far from certain as to who owned the rights to wrecked goods on the coasts of England and Ireland. Local landowners often claimed such rights over goods washed ashore but some, like the town of Dartmouth in Devon with whom Jacob was in dispute in 1630, were less certain about goods sunk in the sea, 'the invention of getting such things out of the sea' being too recent for the law to have adapted to it, further evidence that diving was unusual in England at this time. The town worthies finally decided that such things did not lie within their jurisdiction, a satisfactory decision for Jacob since the guns he was diving for were 'there in the sea without the Castle'.[11]

Salvors like Jacob were very vulnerable once they had raised valuables from the seabed in this period, since the power of the King and the Lord High Admiral and other great men for whom he worked was far from being very effective at any great distance from the capital. In places like Cornwall or Ireland there was little to stop local authorities and their forces of armed men from confiscating what he had recovered or preventing him from diving at all, as happened in 1628 when he attempted to dive for silver from a Dutch ship which, after sailing from San Lucar in Spain, had been wrecked at Polpeor Cove near the Lizard in Cornwall in 1619. Some of this treasure had been recovered by Cornishmen, under the command of the powerful local landlord Sir John Killigrew, and they 'threaten death to all persons who attempt to seek after the remainder'. There was even less chance of royal authority being acknowledged in the wilds of County Mayo in north-west Ireland. When Jacob arrived in Broadhaven in July 1631 and flourished his royal commission to search for Armada wrecks he was told by Ellen Cormick, the spirited wife of the local strong man, that 'for ought she knew it might be made under a hedge'. And when he sailed to some islands nearby to try to get some information from the locals about the whereabouts of the wrecks, he met a wall of silence, orchestrated once again by Ellen Cormick. She relented eventually, since she did not know how to dive, and consented to tell him where the wrecks lay if he agreed to give her husband £20 for every brass cannon salvaged. But, when he did raise a gun, his boat was boarded by Cormick's men and the gun carried away into his castle. It was generally held that taking the

Cormicks to law would do Jacob little good for 'they will sweare downe the Dutchman and all his partie'.[12]

Despite these setbacks, Jacob Johnson was a very successful diver and he was able to exploit his unique position to negotiate very favourable terms for himself. In 1624, for instance, he was hired by the Duke of Buckingham, the Lord High Admiral, to dive on the wreck of a warship from Dunkirk which had been lost off Deal. He was offered half of what he recovered as his reward which in Spain would have been considered very reasonable terms. But this was not enough for Jacob. He claimed that when he was in Holland he used to get two-thirds of the value of brass guns raised and three-quarters of iron guns and anchors 'and whatsoever else he hath taken out of the sea by diving'. This insolent bargaining infuriated Buckingham who ordered Edward Nicholas, his secretary, to find another diver who would do the work cheaper. Nicholas made enquiries both in England and Holland but the experts he consulted knew 'but one [diver] who is your man'. Jacob Johnson really was *the* diver.[13]

The sources do not tell us what secret methods Jacob had to establish for himself such a strong position. One might have thought he was using a bell or some such device to give him an advantage over other divers. But there is no mention of this in any document connected with him, nor of an 'engine' or a 'machine', words often used by contemporaries to refer to diving-bells or indeed to any ingenious manufactured object. What evidence exists suggests that, in fact, Jacob was simply a much better natural diver than anyone else in northern Europe at this time. A witness in a lawsuit relating to the *Campen*, a Dutch East India wreck which Jacob dived on in 1628 at the Needles off the Isle of Wight, said that he saw him dive to the bottom of the wreck and hook up four anchors which the witness saw lying upon a chest, 'the water being clear'. Jacob was to make several other dives on this wreck and recovered two more anchors, five guns, some lead and about five thousand pieces of eight in total.[14]

Gold and silver coins and bars were always the most attractive find for divers, but anchors and guns were also a very useful source of income. They were usually easy to see from the surface and fairly simple to salvage with a rope looped round the anchor flukes or the trunnions which projected on each side of cannon. And, in the first half of the seventeenth century, most cannon on English warships were made of very valuable and slow to deteriorate bronze instead of iron as they were to be later. It was such bronze guns that were to be the main preoccupation of our second diver, Robert Willis, a man from New England where he had been 'very instrumental in weighing [raising] severall gunns and other goods that were sunke in five or six fathoms where also there came a considerable tide. He is not a man of art, but of experience.'[15]

Early in 1655 Willis was recommended as a suitable man to raise the guns of the *Liberty*. This great ship had been launched in 1633 as the *Charles*, one of the finest ships in the navy of King Charles I, but was renamed the *Liberty* by the Commonwealth government early in 1650 to symbolize the change from royal tyranny to republican freedom. This ideological gesture was, however, to backfire when the forty-four-gun ship ran aground on a sandbank off Harwich a few months later and was lost. Willis was employed by the Navy to dive on this wreck every summer season from 1655 to 1658 and he also worked on two other naval wrecks, the forty-four-gun *Sussex* which had blown up off Portsmouth in December 1653 after loose gunpowder had been accidentally ignited and the fifty-gun *Laurel* which ran aground and was lost on a sandbank off Great Yarmouth in May 1657, due 'to the great negligence of her chief officers'. But of the three it was the *Liberty* which offered the greatest likelihood of success and so it was at Harwich that Willis concentrated his efforts.[16]

Willis was based at the naval dockyard at Deptford where his diving vessel called, suitably enough, the *Diver Hoy* was fitted out at the beginning of each season, a hoy being the generic term for a particular sort of small coastal vessel. He and his crew were paid wages by the navy and Willis urged his employers to offer above the standard rate as he was having trouble in getting men to serve with him, 'the vessel being so small, and the employment so short and dangerous, having to lie day and night among the sands'. These men would have been equipped with sweeps, grapples and hooks and the other equipment used by salvage crews. But they also seem to have had a diving-bell or tub aboard to help with the work, since in October 1655 Willis received £30 on account of his wages 'and to make engines' and a bell would be the most likely 'engine' for him to make.

Raising guns from the shifting sands off Harwich was certainly not easy and the work was arduous and sometimes dangerous, although at the beginning of Willis' campaign everything seemed simple enough. In the spring of 1655 the water was clear and he could see some of the guns from the surface and decided, rather foolishly, to leave them until the summer when he thought that the water might be even clearer. But, when summer did come, strong winds from the south and west had thickened the water so that visibility was no longer good and when 'once in a fortnight . . . he did see downe hee found that these winds had covered them [the guns] with sand'.[17] Willis learned his lesson about salvaging guns in shifting sands the hard way, since the good conditions of spring 1655 were not to reappear for a couple of years. In the meantime, continuous bad weather meant that in his first two seasons he managed to bring up only a copper kettle and a saker (a small bronze cannon) for which (and for all subsequent bronze raised) he received payment of twenty shillings a hundredweight on top of his wages.

Willis did better in the 1657 season. In May the *Liberty* could 'now clerely be discovered upon the shelfe whereon she lies as a wrack'. The guns were not yet visible but by July he had found two and was 'in hopes of recovering more, but they must be gained by waiting an opportunity'. Such opportunities occurred and in September 1657 'a trew account' showed that Willis had raised four more guns of a total weight of 101 hundredweight. In 1658 he was slow to show any progress but was, as usual, confident. 'As yett', he reported on 7 June, 'I have got never a goon [gun] by reason of soe much blowing weather. I am not yett without hopes for I have been once downe [in the bell?] . . . and with an iron felt two or three goons in the sand, but the recovery of them depends upon the Providence of God in calme weather.' A week later, the navy's agent at Harwich was also optimistic and thought that Willis was 'likely to do much good on the guns, if fair weather presents. He made his gear fast to a great one yesterday, but in heaving it up, his gear gave way three times, so he sent in for better ropes', such comments being all that exists to suggest just how difficult this work was. Weather conditions improved later in the season and Willis raised two anchors, a copper furnace and at least five bronze guns, four culverins and one huge cannon of two and a half tons, which at twenty shillings per hundredweight provided him with a welcome sum to support his family who had been left in New England.[18]

Robert Willis and the *Diver Hoy* disappear from the official records at the end of the 1658 diving season, but it seems probable that he remained ready for duty at Deptford and he may have been on hand to help when the diarist John Evelyn went down river with other members of the Royal Society for some entertainment in July 1661. 'We tried our diving-bell, or engine, in the water-dock at Deptford, in which our curator continued half an hour under water; it was made of cast lead, let down with a strong cable.' The members of the Royal Society were interested in just about everything and developments in the technology of working and breathing under water were certainly on their agenda. They conducted experiments on breathing in a confined space and under water with birds and animals; they asked the great scientist Robert Hooke to 'procure glasses fit to see under water, as far as the thickness or turbidity of the water would permit'. And they seem to have had regular demonstrations of the diving-bell. When Samuel Pepys was unanimously elected a member of the Society in February 1665, his useful connections with the navy were recognized and he was almost immediately asked 'to bespeak a man, at Deptford, for diving'. Pepys was pretty busy this year and he seems to have neglected to carry out this commission, for a few months later 'the President was desired to put Mr Pepys in mind of the diver for the diving experiments in this season'.[19]

In August 1662, Robert Willis, still described as 'the diver', makes a reappearance in the public records in a letter to the Navy Commissioners. He was back up at Harwich, working on the same wreck as in the 1650s, now subtly renamed again to reflect the Restoration of King Charles II. Willis reported that he 'swept the track of the *Charles*, but the sea has been so turbulent that he has not dared to lie over her'. The next year too he was to have trouble with the weather and he had to report no success in recovering the guns of the *Charles*, and was afraid that 'the hand of God or the power of darkness is against him', this pessimistic comment suggesting that his New England Puritan background was getting to him. Indeed, the man who had seemed so confident and competent, if unlucky, in the 1650s, now seemed to have lost his nerve. 'Yesterday there came a strange dreadful fish and swam round about the hoy . . . it had long gray whiskers, five or six inches at the least, and some say it had long hair hanging down to the shoulders; but it looked gasfully [ghastly].'[20] This is the last we hear of Robert Willis and no one else seems to have replaced him at Deptford as a regular navy diver, though one would have thought that such an appointment would have been a useful one.

The last of our three divers, Edmond Custis, was born in 1623 at Cirencester in England, but was brought up from an early age in the Low Countries. He earned his living there as a merchant in partnership with his brother Thomas and also as a spy reporting to the English government on Dutch affairs. There is no indication that he had anything to do with diving or marine salvage until 1668, when he was forty-five years old. But he was to make up for lost time during the next six or seven years after which he disappears from the records and seems to have retired.

During the Second Dutch War, which ended in 1667, the English government had found it convenient to remit subsidies to their ally, the Bishop of Munster, by shipping hundreds of tons of tin in blocks from Cornwall to Ostend where it could be converted into cash at better rates than in England. But, in 1665, three of these ships sank in the sands between Ostend and Nieuwpoort in Flanders. Some of the tin lost was quickly recovered, but much was left in the sand and English agents in the Low Countries were ordered to contract with someone to raise as much as possible. The agents were instructed to offer the salvors half of all the cargo recovered.[21]

Edmond Custis, described as a merchant of Flushing [Vlissingen], was successful in securing this contract against considerable opposition, mainly by offering to pay King Charles II £1,000 over and above his moiety if he should raise 120,000 pounds weight (over fifty tons) of tin. The royal agents were also hoping that Custis could be persuaded to pay the 'rewards' that had to be paid out to the Mayor of Ostend and his under-officers to allow the salvage to go on at all. Custis and his men worked on the wrecks in each of the three summer seasons from 1668 to 1670 with considerable success. There is little detail in the sources used on their methods of salvage except to say that it was difficult operating in the sand, as might be expected, and that local fishing boats were employed to do the work. The work itself was always described as 'fishing' and the men who did it 'fishers'. These were common contemporary expressions for salvage work done from the surface and it seems probable that the large number of blocks of tin raised were brought up with hooks, grabs and tongs and other traditional tools.

Whatever the salvage methods used, it is clear that Edmond Custis had impressed King Charles and his brother James, who was Duke of York and Lord High Admiral of England. The royal brothers were always on the lookout for ways to increase their income and, in 1670, the Duke of York made the first of what were to be many royal treasure hunting contracts in the years to come. The Duke believed, with some justification, that he had rights over all wrecks on the coasts of England and Ireland and he contracted with Custis to split equally the profits from any such wrecks that he should work on with Custis bearing the expenses. The Duke also empowered him to search for wrecks in the West Indies and Bermuda. This was the first of many such agreements that we will come across. In this case the Duke was to retain one quarter and Custis three-quarters of the profits. Custis owed these contracts to the good offices of Matthew Wren, the Duke's Secretary, and in March 1671 he agreed to pay Wren five per cent of his profits on English and Irish wrecks, 'one full and entire twentieth part . . . of my moiety of all such ships, vessells, guns, anchors or any ships' furniture, goods, treasure and marchandize which I shall recover by wreck fishing and whereof His Royal Highness hath the other moiety'. In 1675, he was to offer Samuel Pepys the same terms when he replaced Wren as Secretary on the latter's death.[22]

No details have been found of Edmond Custis' success or

otherwise in fishing for wrecks in partnership with the Duke of York. But it seems certain that he did, in fact, set out an expedition, for a petition to the Duke from Lieutenant Peter Edwards of the *Blessing* smack states that in 1671 he had been appointed to inspect the wreck fishing activities of Edmond Custis and make sure that a good account was kept of what was raised.[23] It seems, too, that Custis was planning to employ hitherto unknown methods of salvage for, on 16 March 1672, he was granted a patent for 'a new way . . . of discovering and takeing upp of goods out of wrecks and ships sunck in the sea, or upon the coasts, that have been sunck long ago, with several tools and engines never before made use of (in these parts) for that end or purpose'. Unfortunately, the wording of this patent, which gave him fourteen years' exclusive rights to his invention from 11 July 1670, was just as deliberately vague as most patents in this period before proper specifications were required. However, the mention of the word 'engines' may give some hint as to what was involved, while the emphasis that the invention was only new 'in these parts' suggests that the patent covered some form of diving-bell.[24]

The spring of 1672 was not, however, a good time to go treasure hunting on the coasts of England. The Third Dutch War was just about to begin, Lieutenant Edwards was recalled to normal naval duty and Edmond Custis reverted to his old role of passing on to the English government news of the movements of the Dutch fleet which he received from his brother, Thomas, in the Low Countries. But, Dutch War or not, the reputation of Custis as a diver remained public knowledge and early in the following year he was to receive a summons which showed that he was considered uniquely competent in England in the business of solving very difficult underwater problems.

The problems lay in the mouth of the River Tyne, the all important outlet for the Northumberland and Durham coal ships whose cargoes were vital for heating the houses of London and for the many coal-fuelled manufactories which had developed in the great capital city. December 1672 had been cold in the north-east and the hills on both sides of the upper Tyne were covered with a 'greate snow'. But, on 18 and 19 December, a warm wind and much rain from the south brought on a sudden thaw, 'which caused a fresh (as they terme it here) or sudden flood in this river'. The raging waters rushed through Newcastle, causing damage to warehouses and coal stocks on the river banks, and then struck the great fleet of colliers which were lying at anchor at North Shields near the mouth of the river. Eight ships were completely wrecked and, although six of these were cleared away fairly easily, two very large colliers had completely blocked the passage in and out of the Tyne, one of England's busiest rivers. 'The two wrecks were absolutely fixt for ages to continue, and that harbour like to be lost for ever.'[25]

Several attempts were made to clear the river but to no effect and, on 14 January 1673, the Government agent in Newcastle, Anthony Isaacson, advised his masters in London that the only person who could solve the problem was Edmond Custis. 'There's nothing yet effected as to the clearing the river of the wrecks, and I believe nothing will be done, unlesse Mr. Custis come downe.' Given this recommendation, the King ordered Custis north 'with all speed' and advised the now desperate town government of Newcastle that he was 'a person soe well versed in matters of that kind, that wee noe way doubt his success there'. Custis himself was full of confidence in his abilities and, when he arrived in the northern city, was determined to take full advantage of his powerful bargaining position. He eventually contracted with the town to do the work for his expenses and a reward for the huge sum of £5,000 if he was successful and nothing if he was not, what contemporaries called 'no purchase, no pay', a contract favoured by privateers and buccaneers.

Conditions had to be absolutely right if Custis was to have any hope of success. No recent rain to bring down more 'freshes', not much wind, not too great a swell and, above all, no 'neddee or whirle of water [which] would without great pains and care overturn the engine from its designed place'. At last, on 8 March 1673, he was satisfied and at low water he descended in his 'engine' some fourteen feet to the largest of the two sunken coal ships. He then placed under her side a chest containing seven barrels of gunpowder, to which had been firmly attached a hollow mast long enough to clear the surface of the river. Exactly how the powder was ignited or how Custis managed to get away to safety is not quite clear. All we know is that 'a Fire-Ball' was conveyed through the mast to the chest of gunpowder. This, as its name implies, was a ball filled with combustible or explosive material, often employed as a projectile by both the armies and navies of the period. It certainly did the trick.

A huge crowd had gathered to watch the fun, in boats on the Tyne itself, standing shoulder to shoulder on both shores of the river and on the hill below Tynemouth Castle to the north of the wreck site. These people had watched with growing excitement as Custis made his preparations and then with amazement as the powder chest exploded, sending high up into the air a great shower of water, smoke and pieces of the ship, the power of the explosion being such that 'those that stood a mile off upon the hills felt the ground shake under them at the blow'.[26]

The trade of Newcastle was saved, as the Government agent reported. He 'hath had very good successe, having shaken a great part of the vessell, and broke away a great part of the sterne, so that if fair weather continue, he doubts not soon to remove the whole, either by powder or engines, and what he cannot doe in good weather, bad (there being a breach) will doe for him'. Custis claimed that what he had done 'was never known, or at least not known to be practised in any country by any nation whatsoever before'. This seems to have been true. The Spaniards had attempted in 1657 to blow up some heavy timbers impeding access to the silver in the wreck of the *Maravillas*. They sent divers down to place a small barrel full of powder under the obstruction, to which was attached a metal tube made of arquebus [a sort of musket] barrels welded together. But they were forced to give up after several failed attempts to get fire down the tube to ignite the powder.[27]

Edmond Custis never received the reward he was due for his amazing achievement, the town of Newcastle being inclined 'to undervalue a thing now they see it done . . . which at first they would have paid any rate for, the too usuall fault of corporations when once their owne ends are served'.[28] This is sadly only too true and, after a flurry of letters of support from the King and the Lord

Lieutenant of Northumberland among others had been ignored by the 'corporation' of Newcastle, Custis had to settle for less than his due and he slips out of the public records and so out of our ken, and no other man seems to have replaced him as 'the' diver in England for the rest of the 1670s. But, although there may not have been very many divers in England at this time, this was not true of the colonies in the New World whose waters not only held or were reputed to hold much treasure but were also much warmer and more welcoming to divers.

England's first successful colony in the Americas was Bermuda, first settled in 1609, and the Bermudians quickly became notorious for their skills in boat building, sailing and finding and ransacking wrecks. There were plenty of these to work on, for Bermuda lay athwart the homebound route of the Spanish galleons, was only 240 feet above sea level at its highest point, was often covered in cloud and was surrounded with barrier reefs on which many a Spanish ship had perished. Jamaica, conquered by the English in 1655, was another place well-known for the small-boat skills of its inhabitants and these were put to many uses, privateering and buccaneering, illicit trading with the Spaniards, fishing, turtling, diving and, when the opportunity arose, wrecking.[29]

Jamaica and Bermuda were to be in the forefront of English diving and salvage work in the Americas, using mainly Indian and black slave divers but also whites who had acquired the necessary skills in their warm waters. But it was the Bahamas, settled by people from England and Bermuda from the late 1640s, which were the home of the most notorious beachcombers and wreckers. The Bahamas were virtually devoid of government, and the authorities at home were alarmed to hear that the young men of the islands were not interested in planting cotton and tobacco, like other colonists, but preferred to 'runn a coasting in shallops [small boats] which is a lazie course of life'. These lazy, amphibious fellows pursued or looked for whatever might show a profit or provide a bit of fun, whales, ambergris, tortoiseshell, wrecks, or anything else which attracted their attention on or under the water.[30]

By the early 1680s, the Bahamas were attracting 'all kinds of dissolute fellows', including several former buccaneers who combined wrecking with drinking and the occasional bit of piracy. Their most profitable source of wreck at this date was the Spanish treasure galleon *Maravillas*, part of whose cargo had become visible once again as a result of shifting sands. The English salvors, like the Spanish before them, used a diving-bell, or rather tub, on this site, said to have been invented by a Bermudian, who puts it 'perpendicularly into the sea so that it does not fill, but he can put his head into it when he wants breath, by which means he stays three-quarters of an hour under water'. Most Englishmen revelled in this new and relatively easy way of getting hold of Spanish silver, though there were exceptions such as Sir Thomas Lynch, the hispanophile Governor of Jamaica who, in 1682, wrote to the Governor of New Providence, the most populous island in the Bahamas. 'It is known that your islands are peopled by men who are intent rather on pillaging Spanish wrecks than planting, that they carry on their work by Indians kidnapped or entrapped on the coast of Florida . . . The sea ought to be free and the wrecks [belong to] the Spaniards.'[31] Few other Englishmen agreed with such sentiments however and the early 1680s saw a growing interest in Spanish wrecks amongst the colonists and a determined effort to locate some new ones to dive on. By now the English had been sailing, fishing, fighting and trading for several decades in the West Indies, the Bahamas and the coastal waters of North America and they had begun to acquire quite a lot of useful information from other sailors, talkative Spaniards and anyone else with a good yarn to spin. These stories were told and retold aboard ship and in sailors' bars and some, suitably embellished, ended up in letters written back to England by merchants or colonial governors.

One story which was often repeated concerned the *almiranta* or vice-admiral of the homebound fleet from Mexico some forty years before which was said to have been wrecked somewhere on the shoals to the north of Hispaniola, a ship which we can see with hindsight was the *Concepción* whose wreck was discussed above,[32] though no Englishman ever seems to have learned her name. There should be no great surprise that Englishmen knew something about the wreck of this ship. An English pirate ship had captured and interrogated two raft-loads of the survivors and had even told them on which shoals they had been wrecked. And, since then, innumerable English traders, fishermen and pirates had landed on the north coast of Hispaniola where they would be quite likely to meet survivors of the shipwreck or at least someone who knew the story.

Needless to say, such promising sources of information were not entirely reliable and the story told often varied with the teller. Some thought the wreck had occurred in 1643, others in 1645. Some said it was on this reef, some on that. Some thought there was just one wreck, others confused it with stories of other lost galleons and believed that there were several wrecks in the same place. But, vague though all this information was, there was no doubt in anyone's mind that there was some truth in these often repeated stories. Somewhere on the reefs and shoals to the north of Hispaniola lay a great treasure waiting for someone to find it. And that someone could only be an Englishman, according to James Farmer of Bermuda. He claimed to have heard that people of other nations had gone in search of the lost galleon and its cargo of treasure, 'but were diswaded by a kind of Demonical prophet who said it should never be brought away but by some of ye English nation'.[33]

Chapter Three

Captain Phips' Wreck Project

Chapter Three

Captain Phips' Wreck Project

"Witness Sir William Phips' voyage to the wreck; 'twas a mere project, a lottery of a hundred thousand to one odds, a hazard, which if it had fail'd, every body wou'd have been asham'd to have own'd themselves concern'd in . . . but it had success, and who reflects upon the project?"[1]

Serious English attempts to fulfil the prophecy and find the wreck of the *Concepción* began in the summer of 1682 when two men came to London and gained an audience with Sir John Narborough and Sir Richard Haddock, two influential admirals who had the ear of King Charles II. Their visitors were Sir Richard White, an Irishman with strong links to Spain, a well-known fixer and go-between who turns up in a lot of odd places in the history of this period, and Captain Isaac Harmon, a Dutchman with some interesting information. He claimed that 'he had been a prisoner in Cadiz with the pilot [of the *Concepción*] who knew where the ship was sunk' and had given him before he died a document which became known as 'the Spanish directions'. This purported to give the exact latitude in which the wreck lay, a general description of the reef where it was located and the course which 'ye galloone's boate steered and fell in with Port Plate [i.e. Puerto Plata in Hispaniola]'.[2]

No treasure hunter could expect better information than this, however dubious its provenance. Admiral Narborough became very excited, for he had been obsessed by the story of the wreck ever since 1657 when, at the age of seventeen, he had first served in the West Indies. He was able to impart his enthusiasm to the King who agreed to finance an expedition to search for the wreck and to split the profits fifty-fifty with the adventurers. The *Bonetta*, a shallow draught naval sloop, was chosen as suitable for such an expedition and fitted out under the command of Captain Edward Stanley, a fine seaman who was accompanied by his brother, Peter, a former buccaneer who knew the seas to the north of Hispaniola as well as anyone alive, as pilot. They set sail in April 1683 with orders to search for a 'rack' in the 'Abroxes', as the English called the Abrojos.

Stanley was hardly clear of English waters before another adventurer and treasure hunter was knocking on Sir John Narborough's door. This was a man who was truly larger than life, a man who was 'tall, beyond the common set of men, and thick as well as tall, and strong as well as thick'.[3] His name was Captain William Phips and he was a Boston sea captain who had acquired a reputation for 'continually finding sunken ships'. He claimed to know where the wreck of the *Concepción* lay, having 'a strong impression upon his mind that he must be the discoverer of it'. He seems to have completely swept away both Sir John and the King by the sheer force of his personality and he, too, was provided with a royal ship, the *Rose of Algier*, in order to find out if his instinct was correct. He set sail in September 1683 for a voyage to Boston and so to the Bahamas, 'for the obtaining . . . all such plate, silver, bullion, gold and other riches . . . out of any wreck or wrecks, lying or being amongst the Bahama Islands or in any other place or places thereabouts in any of his said Majesty's, the King of England's, dominions'.[4]

Captain Stanley was some four months ahead of Phips in his quest and, on 5 July 1683, he saw the breakers of the Abrojos for the first time. Captain Harmon was sent off in a boat 'to give instructions to find ye wreck' and everything looked as though it was going to be very easy.[5] But any early optimism soon evaporated and Stanley became disillusioned as voyage after voyage from his base in Jamaica to the Abrojos ended with absolutely no sight of the *Concepción*. He rapidly lost confidence in Harmon who kept changing his mind as to which part of the shoals the wreck lay in and he seemed confused too about the marks which were supposed to distinguish the wreck site. At first Harmon said the location was marked by 'three great spotts which appeared to have but little water', but later it was 'a rock which appears like a boat keel up'. After more than a year of this Captain Stanley confided to his journal: 'I have noe hopes of finding ye wrack, Captain Harmon vareing in his opinion.'

Stanley might have lost confidence in Harmon, but he still had a firm belief in the wreck. He was however becoming more and more convinced that it could not possibly lie in the Abrojos, so thoroughly had he and his crew searched the reefs. Could the *Concepción* have wrecked on another reef? Spanish and English charts of this period show no reefs east of the Abrojos (also called Handkerchief or Mouchoir Bank), but they were incorrect. There is, in fact, a large area of shoals and reefs about thirty-five miles south-east of the Abrojos which is now called the Silver Bank and was to be known in the late seventeenth century as the Ambrosian Bank. Many sailors who knew the region were aware of this, including Captain Stanley's brother Peter. The likelihood of this being the last resting place of the *Concepción* was increased by a piece of information in the 'Spanish directions' which had consistently puzzled Stanley. The directions said that the galleon's boat had steered south-south-west to make its landfall in Puerto Plata. This direction more or less fits the Silver Bank, but not the Abrojos which are due north of Puerto Plata.

Confirmation that his thinking was on the right track came from an extraordinary story told to Stanley in Jamaica by a sailor called Thomas Smith. He claimed that his ship had accidentally found itself in reefs south-east of the Abrojos. And, in the midst of these, they had seen a flat rock on which were 'severall sows and piggs [different shapes of bars] of silver heaped up one upon another, and allsoe one barre of gold; and within forty foot from that rocke whereon ye silver lay they saw ye hull of a ship, which lay upright wedged in between two rocks'. Sailors had been seeing treasure heaped on rocks in the middle of reefs for many a year, as has been seen, and Smith was probably just a confidence trickster who hoped to get a share of the treasure if his guess as to its location was correct. But both Stanley and the Governor of Jamaica were convinced by the story, especially when the daring sailor said that he was prepared to enter 'into articles to be hanged if he did not show them the wreck, provided they brought him to the ledge of rocks before mentioned'.

So Captain Stanley set sail again, in fact twice more, this time to the reefs south-east of the Abrojos. He confirmed their existence, but still had no success in finding the wreck as he was driven away by bad weather which nearly claimed his life. He set sail back to England in April 1686 a very disappointed man, after three years of unsuccessful wreck hunting. His journal shows him to have been a superb sailor, whose persistent attempts to find the wreck in dangerous reef waters and very often in appalling weather can only be admired, but he lacked the one attribute necessary to any successful treasure hunter: luck.

Captain William Phips by contrast was a lucky man, as will be seen, but this was far from apparent on his first voyage to look for the *Concepción* in the King's ship *Rose of Algier*. Indeed, he seemed barely competent as a captain, totally unable to maintain discipline among his men, and more interested in boasting about his new status as the captain of a royal ship than in making a profit for the royal master who had entrusted him with it. Phips' crew seem to have been a very wild bunch who enlisted for shares rather than wages on the old buccaneers' contract of 'No Purchase, No Pay', and they behaved more like buccaneers than sailors on a royal ship. While the ship was in Cork completing its stores, members of the crew were roaming around the countryside shooting sheep and poultry to enhance their shipboard diet. Later, the royal agent on board, John Knepp, discovered that large quantities of brandy and wine had been stolen from his private store. The noise of drunken carousing soon told him where it had got to but, when he remonstrated with the men, 'they said God damn them they would swear and be drunk as often as they pleased'.[6]

This bad behaviour continued in Boston where Phips had gone, ostensibly to pick up more crew and diving tubs, but really to show off his rise in status to people who had previously snubbed him in his home port. While he strutted about insulting the good citizens of Boston, his men were drinking, fighting and generally abusing the local inhabitants, so it was with relief that they saw him sail away 'on the King's private business' on 14 January 1684. Phips' first call was in the Bahamas where he hoped to pick up some treasure from the *Maravillas* to provide him with working capital. But his hopes were to be frustrated, as the wreck had now been worked for several years by a succession of salvors and there was very little visible treasure left to be recovered.

Phips' men, who were on shares, were naturally disappointed, to say the least, and it can hardly have surprised Phips very much when they mutinied. The men 'approach'd him on the quarterdeck, with drawn swords in their hands, and required him to join with them in running away with the ship, to drive a trade of piracy in the South Seas'. But Phips had greater things in mind and was not tempted. He may have been a poor disciplinarian on a day-to-day basis, but the giant captain knew how to deal with a mutiny as we learn from his contemporary biographer, the famous puritan divine Cotton Mather. 'He rush'd in upon them and with the blows of his bare hands fell'd many of them and quell'd all the rest.'[7]

The *Rose of Algier* now made its way to Jamaica where Phips discharged all but a handful of loyal members of his crew and hired new men in Port Royal to replace the mutineers. His stay in the Jamaican port overlapped that of Captain Stanley in the *Bonetta* and it seems more than likely that he would have acquired information about Stanley's cruise in the Abrojos either directly or from gossip in the local bars. Useful information would have included the fact that the Abrojos were now seen to be a dead loss and that the wreck was probably on reefs further east. He probably also learned the details of 'the Spanish directions' as every sailor on the *Bonetta* would have known them and it would have been a poor treasure hunter who could not get them to talk for drink or money.

Captain Phips was now ahead of Stanley when he set out from Jamaica late in 1684 for the eastern reefs. He had with him as consorts to work in close to the reefs two shallow-draught sloops whose captains, William Davis of Bermuda and Abraham Adderley of the Bahamas, were old friends whom he could trust. Phips called first at Puerto Plata in Hispaniola, where he 'fished out of a very old Spaniard, [or Portuguese] a little advice about the true spot where lay the wreck', and then sailed north-east. He soon struck 'a new bank' which he named the Ambrosian Bank and spent some time searching for the wreck, but he was no more successful than Stanley was to be and did not 'exactly hit upon it'. Nevertheless, Phips was confident that he was looking in more or less the right place, but was none too certain of the men whom he had picked up in Jamaica. They seemed 'too ill a crew to be confided in' and rather too likely to mutiny if his venture should prove successful. He therefore decided to return to England and come back on a second voyage with new and more trustworthy men to finish the job.

Phips had originally hoped that the King would once again back his new voyage but, in his absence, King Charles II had died and his brother, King James II, who succeeded him was an expert on naval affairs who was far from impressed by the way that Phips had mismanaged his command of a royal ship. King James was just as interested in making money out of treasure hunting as his brother, but was not prepared to spend any more of his royal income on it. As with his previous contract with Edmond Custis, the King would confine himself to collecting a royalty on anything that was brought home. This meant that Phips had to raise the considerable investment required from private investors and he needed to do this fairly quickly, as by now too many people in the West Indies, America and England could have made the same deductions as him as to the likely whereabouts of the *Concepción*.

England in the 1680s was, in fact, a pretty good place for the projector with a good story looking for money. There were many wealthy men, but a distinct lack of stimulating investment opportunities, especially of the type which might attract the courtier or wealthy man-about-town rather than those for whom business was itself a profession. A story of a fabulous treasure lying beneath the seas in a place known only to this impressive, fast-talking Boston sea-captain might well tempt money out of hands that would otherwise have spent it at the races or on the back-gammon board. Nevertheless, progress was slow, and 'this project went a begging for a great while'. It was too fantastic for most.

'Bless us! That folk should go three thousand miles to angle in the open sea for pieces of eight.'[8]

It was once again Sir John Narborough who really got Captain Phips' new wreck project off the ground. He had always been fascinated by the story of the *Concepción*, as has been seen, and from his privileged position in the Admiralty he was able to read for himself the reports and journals of both Phips and Stanley. Since these more or less agreed with each other as to the whereabouts of the wreck, Narborough felt certain that the project was a viable one and decided to back it with his own money and with his considerable influence among the great and the good. He was a wealthy man himself, from accumulated prize money and an immensely rich second wife, and he was able to persuade a real grandee, Charles Monck, 2nd Duke of Albemarle, to head the syndicate and put up a quarter of the capital. Once such a great man as the Duke of Albemarle had lent his name and his money to the project, it was comparatively easy to raise the rest of the capital which was divided into eight parts, Albemarle holding two and the other six investors one each. These included a fairly representative sample of wealthy businessmen and courtiers, though the final one-eighth was taken up by a somewhat humbler man, the merchant John Smith, as payment for his 40-ton sloop the *Henry* which was to act as consort to the syndicate's main vessel, the powerful *James and Mary* of 200 tons and twenty-three guns.[9]

On 18 July 1685 the King gave Albemarle an exclusive warrant 'to search for, seize, and take-up all wrecks as shall bee by him or them [his substitutes] found in ye seas to ye windward of ye north side of Hispaniola or about the islands or shoales of Bahama near the Gulf of Florida in America'. And a fortnight later articles of agreement between the seven partners and Phips were drawn up and signed. Phips had no investment but was to command the expedition and was to use 'his uttermost skill for the owners' benefitt and advantage'. In return he was to receive one-sixteenth of the treasure, 'one-tenth part of the whole being first taken out for the King's Royalty and the whole charge of the voyage being first paid and satisfyed'. This may seem a small potential return for his initiative, but there is no way that he could have located and salvaged the *Concepción* using his own resources and he had to make the best terms that he could with the investors.

Phips seems to have done rather better this time in selecting the seventy men who crewed the two ships. They were paid wages and not shares and, judging by the logbooks of the two vessels, there was no repetition of the bad behaviour of the previous voyage. Five of them had been amongst the loyal men on the *Rose of Algier* and so were familiar with the waters where they were to search and these included Francis Rogers who was to command the sloop *Henry*. In addition to the sailors Phips took just four native American divers with him. This seems an incredibly small number when one considers the scores of divers employed by Spanish salvors or indeed by the English and Americans who had worked the wreck of the *Maravillas*. The equipment needed for salvage is not specified in the ships' accounts, but it certainly included at least one diving tub as well as dredges, rakes and grapples and the normal lifting equipment carried by any ship. All was ready by the autumn of 1685 when, on 12 September, the *James and Mary* and the *Henry* 'set sail for the fishing-ground which had been so well baited half an hundred years before'.[10]

The voyage across the Atlantic of the two ships, 'both in pursuite of a Spanish wreck', was fairly uneventful and by mid-December they were in the harbour of Puerto Plata where they intended to trade with the local hunters and the Spanish. This diversion was designed to provide the syndicate with at least some profit if all else failed and it also enabled then to stock up with fresh meat killed by the hunters. There was nothing much for the *Henry* to do in Puerto Plata, so Phips decided to send her out to make a preliminary search for the wreck. On 12 January 1686, her captain, Francis Rogers, welcomed aboard William Covill, the second mate of the *James and Mary*, who had been his shipmate in the *Rose of Algier* on Phips' previous voyage to the banks, and three of the Indian divers.

The logbook of the *Henry* has survived and so it is possible to follow Rogers day by day on his momentous voyage. It is obvious that he knew exactly where he was going. He sailed east along the north coast of Hispaniola for five days and then, at Cape Cabron, 'steard away due north for ye banke'. Early in the morning of 18

January they could see the east end of the reef, now known as the North Riff, which forms the northern edge of the Ambrosian Bank (i.e. Silver Bank). The weather was very calm and Rogers anchored for the night about three-quarters of a mile south of the reef.

Next morning, the weather was still good and they set out to search the reef, this being done by peering through the water between the coral heads as they progressed and sending a diver down if there should be something of interest to inspect more closely. Rogers was in the sloop's boat with one diver, and William Covill in a canoe with the other two divers, and they spent the whole day searching some six miles along the north side of the reef. Visibility through the water was excellent, but they saw nothing that could possibly be the remains of a wreck. On the following day, 20 January 1687, they repeated the exercise on the south side of the reef and this time their 'peeping among the boilers' [the coral heads which rose from the seabed] was to bring success to William Covill and his two divers, 'for which blessing wee returne praise and thankes to Almighty God . . . She lyes in ye midst of reife . . . Most part of her timber is consum'd away, and soe overgrowne with coral that had itt not been for her guns shee would scarce ever been found, itt being at least 45 yeares since shee was lost and ye richest ship that ever went out of ye West Indies.'[11]

How was it that William Covill and his two divers should find the wreck so easily on the second day of searching, after so many other expeditions, both Spanish and English, had failed to find any trace of it? They could just have been lucky, of course, and they were certainly fortunate with the weather which was ideal for 'peeping among the boilers'. But it seems likely that they were also in possession of a fairly good idea of where to look from the 'Spanish directions'. Everyone had naturally assumed that these referred to the Abrojos or Handkerchief Bank, since this is where the galleon was traditionally said to have wrecked, but, of course, the directions did not fit this reef as this assumption was incorrect and it is therefore not surprising that Captain Harmon should have become so confused. But when applied to the Silver or Ambrosian Bank they would make perfect sense and this is probably how Rogers and Covill knew exactly where to start their search with such happy results.

The three divers worked hard for the next two days after the discovery of the *Concepción* and raised eight bars of silver and some three thousand silver coins of different denominations, but they then had to break off as the sky 'begann to looke suspicious' towards the north. They buoyed the wreck, so they could find it again, and sailed back to tell Captain Phips the good news, not without some difficulty as they got entangled in another reef on the southern edge of the Ambrosian Bank, the South Riff, whose existence had not previously been known. Contrary winds and the need to evade a possible pirate were to delay them further, so it was sixteen days after leaving the *Concepción* before they were safely back in Puerto Plata. Rogers seems to have had a sense of humour for at first he disappointed Phips by pretending they had tried hard but found nothing, but then he casually pushed a bar of silver onto the table between them. 'Why? What is this? Whence comes this?', Phips cried out in amazement. 'And then, with changed countenances, they told him how and where they got it. Then, said he, Thanks be to God! We are made; and so away they went, all hands to work.'[12]

There was some delay before all hands could in fact set to work, as both vessels had to be careened and stocked with wood, water and hogs and bullocks sufficient to make them independent of the shore for a couple of months. So it was not until 21 February that the *James and Mary* got her first glimpse of the wreck site and the reef, 'which appeared like to a halfe moone', and the next day she was joined by the *Henry* which was a very slow sailer. Both ships anchored and made themselves snug for a long stay, the *Henry* 'as near the reef as conveniently she could without danger'. This was about two miles from the wreck, a rather long journey for the divers and sailors to travel to work each day.

Phips was lucky in that the decking which had originally covered the store rooms where the silver was stowed had virtually all gone, either ripped off by the survivors or by storms as the ship broke up or eaten by the worms which made short work of a wooden ship in those waters. 'Not the least plank or hull of the ship appeared; for the ship being broke to pieces on the rock, the parts were either driven away with the violence of the waves, or consumed by the worms which in those seas will eat through the thickest plank in some years time.'[13] The silver was therefore fairly easy to access, though it had been overladen with coral in many places which had to be cleared away by the sailors with the long-handled rakes and dredges which they operated from the surface. Phips did not dare use the diving tub as this would have meant anchoring the *Henry* directly above the wreck, a very dangerous manoeuvre which he was not prepared to risk. This meant that practically all the work below was done by the divers in the short time that they could hold their breath. This was standard practice for Spanish salvage expeditions, but they normally had scores of divers. Phips, as we have seen, only had four.

These four Indian divers must have been incredibly tough men. They did several dives a day to depths of between five and seven fathoms (thirty to forty feet) and, while below, filled baskets with loose coins or pieces of silver plate or fixed ropes to larger items which could then be hauled up. Phips spent fifty-eight days on the wreck site, including the day he arrived and the day he set sail, and the divers were to work on forty of them, losing only nine days to bad weather, eight Sundays on which Phips, a good New Englander, was not prepared to work, and one day when the divers, who were poorly on several other days, were seen to be too sick to work. But ill or not, they were back at work the next day.

In the first five full days' work on the wreck, the divers brought up a total of just over 20,000 pieces of eight in dollars and half-dollars, about 1,000 pieces of eight per diver per day. They also raised four hundredweight of silver bullion and three guns. This may seem a lot, and indeed it was, since it was sufficient to cover the complete costs of the expedition. However, if Phips was to salvage the wreck completely, he had to think in terms of tons of silver, not thousands of pieces of eight. No one knew how much was on the sunken galleon, but it was a reasonable assumption that it would have been some three or four million *pesos* of silver, in other words well over a hundred tons. But twenty thousand pieces of eight, though itself a small fortune, did not even weigh one ton.

The rate of salvage was soon to get much faster with the arrival at the reef, presumably by prior arrangement, of the two sloops commanded by Abraham Adderley and William Davis which had sailed with Phips on the previous expedition. They contracted to work for Phips and were to make a real difference since they brought with them more divers, exactly how many is not known but sufficient to greatly accelerate the rate of recovery. The work of the divers also began to be much more productive as they hit on one of the main treasure storerooms of the ship. It was no longer a question of putting a few loose coins in a bag. Now the divers were able to fasten their ropes to 'whole chests of 2,000 dollars together, for though the chests were rotted off and consumed, yet the dollars, with rust, were grown together as one lump', a clustering which is often found by treasure hunters today. Then, beneath the chests of coins, they got into a section rich in bullion and productivity shot up. On twenty-four working days between 4 March and 11 April 1687 they never raised less than half a ton of silver; on eight different days they collected over a ton, and on two remarkable days at the end of March they brought up nearly four tons, mainly in bullion.

When progress in early March had been slow Phips was determined to try the diving tub to improve recoveries. On 7 March, a day of fair weather and smooth water, William Davis was persuaded to take his sloop well into the reef and anchor her, 'head and sterne with two chains and grapnells' directly over the wreck. The tub was lowered from the sloop and the divers got to work in much more comfortable conditions. Over a ton of silver and two brass guns were recovered but the experiment was to last for only one day. That night it looked 'likely to blow hard' and it did, blowing the anchored sloop off her moorings and onto a shoal. Not much damage was done, but no further attempt was made to use the tub.

On 13 April the divers reported that they had completely emptied the great storeroom which they had mined so effectively. Next day was a day of exploration. 'Having clear'd ye roome where they workt before, our dyvers spent their day in finding a new one', but they had no immediate success in this and after a few days Phips decided to take what he had got and sail for home. He had now raised over twenty-five tons of silver, seven guns and a few bits and pieces, including a little gold. It was obvious that this was only part of the total treasure, but it was still worth an enormous amount of money in seventeenth-century England. He was running short of stores, his divers were tired and there was a danger, if he stayed on the reef much longer, that he might attract the attention of pirates who were active in many parts of the West Indies at that time.

There was also the danger of trouble from his own men who 'when they saw such vast litters of silver sows and pigs, as they call them, come on board them at the Captain's call, they knew not how to bear it, that they should not share all among themselves, and be gone to lead a short life and a merry'.[14] Phips talked down the potential mutiny by promising the men that they would be fairly rewarded, a promise which was to be honoured. But it was clearly time to sail for home. He sailed to the Turks Islands for wood and water and then, on 2 May, left for England. He dropped anchor in the Downs on 6 June, a nine-month round trip which was to make Captain William Phips famous for ever and keep England buzzing with excitement for years into the future. The news soon spread. 'Letters from Deal of the 7th advise the arrival of the *James and Mary*, Captain Phips, from the West Indies, who went in search of the Spanish galleons that were cast away 42 years since, one of which she found and got treasure to the value, it is said, of £250,000.'[15] A quarter of a million pounds sterling! It was unbelievable.

Phips sailed into the Thames and anchored at Deptford where admiring Londoners came to sing his praises. And there were also visitors from the Royal Mint to weigh and value the treasure and take away the royal tenth. Their final official valuation was just under £210,000, rather less than the quarter of a million being bandied about by popular opinion, but still a very large treasure indeed. The King received just over £20,000 as his tenth, Phips got £11,000, enough to sustain a very dignified life in New England, and each of the syndicate's eight shares was valued at £20,703 15s 0d, a rather attractive fifty-two-fold return on an investment of just £400. No one had ever made such a return on an investment before and Phips' treasure was to expand the bounds of the possible in late seventeenth-century England.[16]

The King was delighted with Captain Phips' achievement and he knighted him 'in consideration of the service done by him, in bringing such a treasure into the nation'. A few weeks later Phips was granted the post of Provost-Marshal of New England, just one step away from the summit of his astonishing career, the governorship of Massachusetts. Sir William Phips, like Francisco Núñez Melian, the salvor of the *Santa Margarita* in the 1620s, was thus able to convert treasure hunting success not just into riches but into worldly honours. What the King of Spain, the nominal owner of all this treasure, thought we do not know, but his ambassador in London, Don Pedro Ronquillo, felt obliged to claim the recovered treasure for his king. 'His master', he said, 'might let his money lie at the bottom of the sea as long as he pleased', though this was just bravado as the Tuscan envoy noted in a letter home to Florence. 'There is no doubt that the Spanish ministers do not expect to succeed in their enterprise.'[17]

During the summer of 1687 a second expedition was being prepared under the overall command of Sir John Narborough who was determined to see for himself the wreck which had obsessed him for so long. He sailed in the royal frigate *Foresight*, which was to provide naval protection for the salvors, and he took as his first lieutenant Edward Stanley, another man with a real interest in seeing just where the wreck of the *Concepción* lay. This expedition was on a much bigger scale than the first one and there were five vessels altogether in the flotilla, two of them commanded by Phips and Francis Rogers. Diving equipment, boats and divers were provided on a similar generous scale and the total cost was £16,000, five times the cost of the first venture.

Delay followed delay in the fitting-out and despatch of the expedition which did not sail until 3 September 1687, six weeks later than planned. Ironically, much of the delay was caused by the Duke of Albemarle who as head of the syndicate would have wanted the salvage team to get back to the wreck as quickly as possible. He was himself supposed to be travelling with the expedition on his way to the West Indies to take up a new post as Governor of Jamaica, but he fell ill after over-indulging at his farewell party. Departure was postponed for several weeks, awaiting his recovery, but finally Sir John Narborough decided that he could wait no longer and sailed without him, to be followed by the Duke a month later in the royal ship *Assistance*. These delays seemed likely to be costly since, almost as soon as news arrived in England of Phips' success, there had been reports of ships fitting out to go to the wreck from England, France, Holland and Spain and it must have seemed very probable that some of the scores of colonial sloops and divers who had worked on the *Maravillas* would also home in on this new source of riches.

And so it turned out. As soon as Sir John arrived in Barbados on 29 November 1687, after a very slow passage, he heard 'that several vessells are at worke on ye wreck and have taken up all the upper silver to a considerable value'.[18] When the *Foresight* arrived at the wreck site on 15 December, she met with an amazing and very discouraging sight. According to Stanley, there were altogether eight ships and twenty-eight brigantines, sloops and shallops anchored in the clear water to the south of the reef, one small shallop anchored directly over the *Concepción*, working the wreck with a diving tub, and about twenty boats and canoes full of divers also working on the wreck. They were to learn that another eighteen vessels had already taken what they wanted and gone home to Bermuda and Jamaica, while there were still more enterprising colonials on their way. It seemed as though all the men and all the ships and boats in the English colonies were either on the Ambrosian Bank or on their way there. Most of these vessels cleared off when Narborough arrived, not wanting to face the wrath and firepower of this official salvor with a royal licence, but 'some stayed that had no money', hoping to get work for themselves and their divers.

When Captain Phips had dismissed the two sloops which had assisted him the previous season, their crews had been pledged to silence and promised more work when he returned with the second expedition. But to keep such a secret was virtually impossible in the tight-knit and gossipy maritime world of the colonies. Cotton Mather said that the person who gave the game away was the cabin boy employed by Abraham Adderley who was 'spirited away' by certain Bermudians, 'to tell them the exact place where the wreck was to be found'. Whether this was true or not, it was obvious that someone had passed the word on and the result was now plain to be seen. News of the discovery of the wreck had reached Bermuda by late June and Jamaica in the first week of July, so this swarm of colonial fortune-hunters had been gleaning Phips' harvest for at least five months. No one has left a description of what happened during these months of unlimited private enterprise, but it must have been a fairly horrific scene, particularly under water. On some days there must have been well over a hundred Indian and black divers, working on shares, struggling to grab the biggest pieces of silver for themselves. How much they grabbed altogether is not certain, though Sir John Narborough thought it was a quarter of a million pounds sterling, more than Phips had brought home from the first expedition. Sir John's figure was based on the wreckers' own gossip and it may well have been near the truth.[19]

If Sir John's estimate was right, it did not necessarily mean that his expedition would be a complete disaster. Maybe half a million pounds sterling had been taken out of the wreck by Phips and the colonial scavengers together, but that was still only half the treasure if there had really been four million *pesos* (about £1 million) shipped out of Vera Cruz in 1641, as the Spanish ambassador in London had recently asserted. Narborough himself was, like most fortune hunters, ridiculously optimistic as to the amount of treasure still left in the wreck. In a letter to Lord Falkland, who held one of the eighths in the syndicate, he said that 'our information says there was 12 millions of pieces of eight [circa £3 million] lost in her, most was in barrs, and by all accounts there hath not binn taken up above ye value of three millions of pieces of eight'. And, in a letter to Samuel Pepys a week later, he wrote that 'according to reports we have had from Spain there is not ye one fourth parte taken up that was lost in her'. So, in his opinion, there was still a job to be done and his wreck squadron got down to the business of doing it.[20]

Sir John had no shortage of hands for the work. There were nearly four hundred men on the five ships of his squadron, and, in addition, he was employing huge numbers of divers, forty-five to start with and two hundred for the last few weeks of salvage, some brought out from England but most of them hired from the sloops. This was far more than were ever employed by the great Spanish salvage teams which had worked on the wrecks of the *Santa Margarita* and the *Maravillas,* and a simply staggering number when compared with the four divers available to Phips at the beginning of the first expedition. The sloop crews and divers whom Sir John hired were encouraged to work hard by being offered shares in the silver salvaged, at first just a twentieth but in the end a quarter of everything that they brought up. These were very generous terms, but sadly they were not going to make anyone very rich. Day after day the divers hacked away with pick-axes to clear the wreck right down to her bottom, while the sailors in the boats above them hauled up not treasure but tons and tons of ballast and pieces of coral. There was some silver scattered about in the wreckage or encased in the coral which was smashed on board the ships with hammers, but it was a good day when fifty pounds weight was raised. After three months of this underwater labour just over a ton of silver had been raised, a quantity which Phips had quite often brought up in a single day on the first expedition.

Sir John's men believed that they had now completely cleared the forepart of the wreck and he turned his attention to the stern which was invisible under a thick casing of coral. Underneath here should be the poop of the galleon with its great cabins full of who knew what marvellous treasure. And then there were the after plate rooms. Sir John's Spanish informants on the island of Hispaniola had told him that most of the *Concepción's* silver lay aft of her mainmast, so he was still confident that 'there is more treasure in ye wreck than what hath binn taken up'. The problem was to get at it, to remove the great weight of coral which was preventing the divers from earning their reward. It was a dilemma which would have been difficult to solve even with the benefit of modern underwater technology, but Sir John was not a man to give up easily.

At times he had sixty divers working below together, 'as many as cann work on ye after part'. They were able to loosen with their pick-axes some of the coral rocks which could then be hauled up with the tackle of the ships' boats above. But they were still just scratching at the great mass of rock and soon there was no more that the Indian and black divers could move. They had tried everything. The longboat was equipped with a spar forty feet long with an iron crow-bar attached to its end, but this was no more effective than the divers working with pick-axes below the water. They tried to break off the coral by fixing grapnels to the rock and hauling on the long-boat's tackle, but the strain was too great and the grapnels broke. This was all very dangerous work for naked men to be doing while holding their breath under water and one suspects that there would have been plenty of accidents. These were not reported, but the Royal Navy logbooks do report two deaths without giving any details, Sancho, 'an Indian diver', who died on board the *Foresight* on 27 January and 'a negro man' who was 'drownded at ye wrack' on 15 February. Captain Stanley also remarked in his logbook that on their first dive 'most of ye divers did bleed at ye nose which is usual at first working' and this has been reported by other observers.[21]

There remained only one way to break into the stern. They would have to blow up the coral with explosives and Sir William Phips believed that he could do this with the materials he had to hand. He waited for a completely calm day, 9 April 1688, to make his attempt. The fuse was led down through forty feet of cane tubing to a waterproof chest packed with gunpowder. Divers placed the chest under the coral and quickly swam away, while Phips' gunner lit the fuse in the longboat above. The flame raced down the cane tubing but, before it had got halfway to the chest, the heat split open the cane and water poured down, 'soe that ye powder in ye chest was damnafied'. Five days later 'Sir William Phips try'd his fire chest againe but could not fire itt'. He never tried again and Narborough was forced to report to the Duke of Albemarle in Jamaica that we 'have used all our endeavours to get up ye rocks abaft but find them too strong for us'. If only they had had Edmond Custis and his fireballs with them!

There is an ironic coda to this frustrating story of Narborough's attempts to break through the coral into the potentially rich stern section of the *Concepción*. On 30 November 1978, an American expedition led by the diver Burt Webber was successful in emulating Captain Phips by once again finding the wreck of the *Concepción*, after many other expeditions had failed to do so. During the many months that Webber and his divers were working on the wreck, they carefully mapped everything they found and soon came to a startling conclusion. The stern of the galleon had never been in the great mass of coral which Sir John's divers had so energetically attacked with their pick-axes. It had instead broken away from the rest of the ship soon after she wrecked and had then ricocheted through the reefs to a completely different resting place. All the effort expended by the divers and Phips' hazardous attempts to blow up the coral had been a waste of time.[22]

Defeated by the coral on top of the so-called poop, Sir John turned his attention to another possibility of making the expedition a success after all. While in Hispaniola he had been introduced to 'an ancient Spaniard at Puerto Plata who was in her [*Concepción*] when lost'. There seem to have been quite a few ancient Spaniards at Puerto Plata with stories to tell to inquisitive and gullible strangers and this one was no exception. He told Narborough that 'before quitting the wreck they had taken out all the gold and chief riches which were left and laid them on top of a broad rock about three yards under water and about eighty paces from the wreck'. There were many rocks which more or less fitted this description and boat crews searched them all but without success.[23] As has been seen, this was a story often told about Spanish treasure wrecks and it was almost certainly completely untrue, since what evidence does exist suggests that 'the gold and chief riches' were taken on the two big rafts which were captured by the pirates.

Sir John was naturally disappointed though still unwilling to give up, but human weakness and the *Concepción* was to beat him in the end. A fever was raging through the *Foresight* and, on 18 May 1688, the Admiral caught it and died just over a week later. On the afternoon of his death, Stanley 'gave him as honourable a funerall as the time and place where we were would allow'. He took the corpse into the pinnace and rowed towards the reef, followed by all the sloops and boats in the fleet. As he struck the pinnace's flag and lowered Sir John's body into the sea, the *Foresight* fired three volleys of musket shot and forty guns, at which signal all the other ships and boats honoured their dead admiral with a salute. And so, Sir John, who had sought the treasure of the *Concepción* since he was a boy of seventeen, was buried on her wreck site.

Chapter Four

The Great Treasure Hunting Boom

Chapter Four

The Great Treasure Hunting Boom

"Though the money brought into England from the first wreck was very considerable, yet much more was lost on projects of the same nature. For every silly story of a rich wreck was credited."[1]

'The money fished up from the Spanish galleon in America has caused great excitement', wrote Francesco Terriesi, the Tuscan agent in London, after Phips' arrival back in England in June 1687 with his almost unbelievable treasure. 'It has awakened the spirit of many to engage in similar enterprises, which were previously thought impossible.' Terriesi was an intelligent and perceptive commentator on English affairs and he was absolutely right. In the six years following Phips' success there were at least thirty expeditions planned and many of these actually set out to try and emulate the Boston man's achievement. 'This wealth that was fetch'd out of the sea . . . was trumpeted all over the world and set men's heads at work to get more', wrote the anonymous author of *Angliae Tutamen*, a pamphlet published in 1695 to provide the public with a 'fair and clear discovery of many crafty cheats and villainous knaveries'. 'Patents were obtain'd from the Royal Fountains for the sole fishing of wrecks on the coasts of America, Spain, Portugal, Ireland, Scotland, England etc. and societies form'd of merchants and gentlemen to manage this affair in several kingdoms.' The great treasure hunting boom had begun.[2]

First off the mark was Louis Duras, Earl of Feversham, a

Frenchman who commanded King James II's army and a big name who would draw in lesser men to invest in a project which had gained his approval. On 15 August 1687, just two months after Phips' return, he and his partners were granted by the King the right to search for and salvage 'all and every such wrecks, jetsam, flotsam, lagan, goods derelict, riches, bullion, plate, gold, silver, coyne, barrs or piggs of silver, ingotts of gold, merchandizes and other goods and chattels', treasure in short, which had been lost at any time in the past or should be lost in the next three years on the rocks, shelves and shoals 'on the north side of the coast of the mainland of America between Rio de la Hacha [in Colombia] and Chagres [in Panama]'.[3]

Very few of these grants give any indication as to which wreck was to be the target, but there was certainly plenty of Spanish silver lying on the bottom of the sea along this coastline, though whether the Spanish authorities would look kindly on divers in English pay searching for treasure in the heart of their empire was of course another matter. But they seemed to think they could dive for Spanish treasure wherever they liked and these treasure hunting grants or patents merely specified the geographical area in which the grantees would have monopoly rights or, rather, would be the only Englishmen allowed to search. The grants also asserted the King's right to a share of anything recovered, in this case one-eighth. This was a fairly common royalty for wrecks in American waters, though fractions from a quarter to a tenth can be found in other contracts. Not that it mattered very much since few of these expeditions ever sailed and even fewer found anything to share with the King.

King James II appears to have granted only one other patent for wreck hunting in 1687, to Thomas Harford, master of a sloop from Bermuda who had been one of the many who had worked on the *Concepción* after Phips' departure in May 1687, he and his consorts raising twelve brass guns from the Spanish galleon. Now he was mainly interested in acquiring a monopoly of whale fishing in 'all ye Bohemian Islands [i.e. Bahamas]', but he also asked for 'a certaine wrack . . .which lay within five leagues of the aforesaid islands' to be included. A much more ambitious application was made in February 1688 by Robert Brent, a well-known projector who was the front man for another syndicate. He was given a three-year grant to search for wrecks 'on or near the coast of America between the Bermudas and Porto Rico or between Cartagena and the Havanna', a large sea area which, together with the grants given to Feversham and to Narborough and Phips for their second expedition, meant that most of the western Caribbean and virtually the whole area north of Puerto Rico and Hispaniola was now covered by this web of paper grants spun in London.[4]

There is no evidence that any of these planned treasure hunting expeditions ever came to fruition, except, of course, for that commanded by Narborough and Phips whose second expedition found very little in the early months of 1688. With so many men and vessels at his disposal, Narborough also followed up a number of other reported wrecks in the vicinity of Silver Bank. In January 1688, for instance, he sent to the Duke of Albemarle in Jamaica a man called Henry Glassen, 'a person of sober life and an able seaman' who would tell him what he knew of wrecks in the Bahamas. Glassen claimed to have seen six brass guns in the sea near Crooked Island, a likely place for a wreck since it lay on the edge of one of the major passages through the Bahamas. Other informants said that the guns were from a ship lost twenty years previously but, although several sloops went out to search for this wreck, no one found anything. In May, Narborough ordered Captain Stanley to follow up a story of a reef of rocks sixteen leagues east of Silver Bank which were said to have treasure lying on them. Stanley was given just ten days to 'search well ye said reefe of rocks for treasure of gold, silver and wrecks', but though he found a reef he found no treasure.[5]

A lawsuit of 1692 shows that English treasure hunting adventurers were looking or at least thinking even further afield in the late 1680s. A syndicate headed by Lord Falkland, the Treasurer of the Navy and a one-eighth investor in Phips' wreck project, was suing an Irish sea captain and merchant called Thomas Hewetson in the Court of Chancery. They claimed that in 1688 they had raised £32,000 to fit out four vessels under Hewetson's command to trade in the West Indies and from there to sail to the Pacific coast of South America where they had heard that a good trade could be carried on with the Indians of Chile. They had also been informed 'by persons of known ability and integrity that great quantityes of gold and silver and other treasures and commodities might be recovered out of the seas near St Helena in the South Seas which had been cast away and lost by shipwreck'. This did not refer to the island in the South Atlantic, but Punta Santa Elena on the northern side of the Gulf of Guayaquil in Ecuador. However, nothing came of this exciting project since Hewetson had made no attempt to find the wreck but had instead sold off the ships and the trade goods and absconded with most of the adventurers' investment.

Hewetson naturally denied all this. He had indeed been told in 1687 about the gold and silver cast away near Punta Santa Elena in a Spanish ship trading from Lima to Panama, this being the first stage of the long journey made by Peruvian silver on its way to Europe. He had applied to King James II for a patent to possess himself of this wreck and his application had, at first, met with a very favourable response. But pressure from the Spanish ambassador and from merchants trading to Spain had caused the King to refuse the warrant, despite a thirty-fifth share being given as a bribe 'to a particular favourite then at court', this being the Earl of Sunderland who was Secretary of State. Hewetson then claimed that Falkland had tried to get him a French commission for the voyage, but this too had come to nothing and so he had finally confined himself to a trading and privateering voyage in the West Indies.[6]

Hewetson obtained his knowledge about the wreck from 'Joseph Curtis and others', while Falkland's informants were said to be 'persons of known ability and integrity'. There were, however, much better sources of information about wrecks on the Pacific coast of South America, some available to anyone who could read and the rest easily accessed by a man who was Treasurer of the Navy. All this arose from a remarkably well-documented buccaneering expedition in 1680–1 led by Bartholomew Sharpe. He and his men had marched across the isthmus of Panama, helped themselves to canoes and from these had captured Spanish merchant ships which they converted into men of war. They had then marauded up and down the Pacific coast from Mexico to Chile. These were the first Englishmen to raid these areas since Sir John Hawkins had been captured off Ecuador by the Spaniards in 1594 and they had a rare old time. One of their greatest successes was the capture in July 1681 of the Spanish galleon *Rosario* which had on board among other items of significant value 'a great book full of sea charts and maps'. This was treasure indeed for the charts covered the whole of the Pacific coast, an area hardly known at all to the English. On his return home early in 1682 Sharpe presented these maps and charts to the King who arranged to have them copied and translated for the use of the Admiralty. Sharpe also encouraged the cartographer William Hack to make annotated copies for sale so these charts quickly got a wide circulation.[7]

The information added to the copies of these charts was enough to make a treasure hunter go crazy with excitement and so it is no surprise that people should be thinking of treasure hunting expeditions to South America in the late 1680s. 'In the year 1631 the Almiranta of the King of Spain was cast away on this shoal, in her was abundance of treasure', it says on a map of the Pearl Islands in the Gulf of Panama. Further south, near the northern border of modern Ecuador, there was 'a shoal with rocks . . . on which was cast away . . . a great pilot of this sea with the ship Clarius in the year 1594. In the said ship was a vast treasure and many rich ships have been also cast away on the same shoals'. And there were many more, eight rich wrecks in all, including further south still, off Punta Santa Elena, the 'rock of Colanche on which was cast away a ship with a vast treasure.' And all of these with the wreck sites actually marked on the chart. What a joy! What a wonderful way to sell charts![8]

In addition to these lovely maps, there was the very lively (and inventive) account of the voyage of Bartholomew Sharpe written by his shipmate Basil Ringrose. This was published in 1685 and, among many other remarkable assertions in his book which would interest a treasure hunter, was his description of the Isle of Plata (Isla de la Plata off the coast of Ecuador). This island was called Drake's Island by the buccaneers and they claimed it was given that name because it was here that Sir Francis Drake had shared out the great treasure he had captured in 1578 from the Spanish ship *Cacafuego* during his circumnavigation of the world. 'This island receives its name from Sir Francis Drake his shareing of his plate by bowlefulls which he tooke when he robbed their armada in this sea.' Ringrose took this story a stage further, stating that Drake had captured so much silver that he was 'forced to heave much of it overboard, because his ship could not carry it. Hence was this island called by the Spanish themselves the Isle of Plate [i.e. silver].'

This story is absolute nonsense, quite apart from the unlikelihood of a pirate dumping his treasure in the ocean. Drake, in fact, never went to this island and, even if he had, he had plenty of room on the *Golden Hind* for the silver that he captured. But it makes a good story and would certainly have been believed in the 1680s and indeed it is still included in modern treasure hunting guides. Shortly after his discussion of Drake's treasure, Ringrose lets his imagination rip once again, this time with rather more substance behind the exaggeration. 'They say that a ship was fitted out of Lima in the time of Oliver Cromwell of 70 brass guns, having thirty millions of dollars on board . . . which was lost in keeping the shore along in the bay of Manta', once again in Ecuador, about a hundred miles north of Punta Santa Elena.[9]

Hewetson may have been persuaded not to search for these treasures, but this did not stop other people from having a go. On 1 November 1689 the ship *Farewell* set sail from Plymouth for the Pacific coast of South America under the command of Captain John Strong. She carried a trading cargo and also a privateering commission against the French with whom England was now at war. Strong also had instructions to search for 'a rich wreck or two, at or near to St. Helena . . . about 2 degrees south' and for this he had several 'good divers' aboard and 'bombs and carkasses [fireballs] to work on the wreck if there should be occasion to blow up rocks'. Strong reached Punta Santa Elena in August 1690 and spent a few days searching around the point before becoming discouraged when all the Spaniards he spoke to said 'that there had been no wreck thereabouts, but one ship that was cast away four years before that time, carrying a cargo of cloth'.

A few days later he got some rather more exciting information from the captain of a Spanish merchant ship who told him that the rich wreck he was seeking was eight leagues beyond the point and in four fathoms of water about half a mile from the shore. She was 'the Vice-Admirall of the South Seas in which were twelve million of pieces of eight, besides a great quantity of plate'. The Spanish had salvaged some of her treasure, but had then been defeated 'by the breaking in of the sand' and so abandoned the wreck. Strong spent a week or so searching the area with his boats in a rather dilatory fashion, but 'could find no sign of any wrack'. So he gave up and set sail for home, 'by reason there is no prospect of finding ye wrack and little likelyhood of any trade nor any hopes of meeting a Frenchman', a comprehensive burst of pessimism which neatly sums up the voyage. The *Farewell* arrived back in England in June 1691, having lost her owners the substantial sum of £12,000.[10]

The wreck which Captain Strong failed to find was one of the richest in the annals of treasure hunting. She was the *Jesus Maria de la Limpia Concepción*, the *capitana* or flagship of the Spanish South Sea fleet (Armada del Sur), which wrecked on the Chanduy Reef near Punta Santa Elena on 26 October 1654. Her captain, Don Francisco de Sosa, made heroic efforts to salvage her with the aid of over fifty divers from Guayaquil, Lima and Panama, and they recovered one and a half million *pesos* of treasure. Later salvage expeditions brought the total recovered to about three and a half million, creating a major scandal since the ship's register recorded a cargo of only three million *pesos* altogether. Much of what was brought up was indeed unregistered and so it was anyone's guess how much was left when the sand and mud eventually defeated the Spanish salvors. Some say the total aboard was ten millions, but it might just as well have been the twelve bandied about by Captain Strong's informants or even the thirty millions in the account of Basil Ringrose who was almost certainly referring to the same wreck. Whatever the real figure, it was certainly a lot and people have been searching for the treasure ever since or at least until 1996, when a team led by Herman Moro claimed to have found the long-lost shipwreck, though they found very little and some people have questioned whether they really had been working in the right place. There is one final irony about the silver salvaged from the *capitana* of 1654 as the ship is usually called. The recovered treasure was brought up to Panama and was carried by mule-train across the isthmus and so on to Havana in Cuba where it was loaded on a galleon which set sail for Spain on New Year's Day 1656. And this galleon was the ill-fated *Nuestra Señora de las Maravillas* which herself was wrecked just three days later in the Bahamas.[11]

These South Sea wrecks must certainly have seemed promising to treasure hunters, but it was in the Caribbean south-west of Jamaica that the greatest efforts were to be made in the years following Phips' success. The story is rather complicated but it can begin with a letter written in March 1689 by Laurens de Graff, a Dutch buccaneer now in French service, to the French Governor of the colony of Saint-Domingue (modern Haiti). De Graff had captured a small pirate vessel and on board was a Spanish royal pilot with an interesting tale to tell. The pilot said, after interrogation, that some four years earlier he had been sent by the King of Spain to search 'for a galleon lost on the Serranillas eighty years ago on which there was a lot of silver', a date which fits almost exactly the loss of the four ships commanded by Luis Hernandez de Córdoba in November 1605.[12]

Spanish interest in the Serranillas had been aroused by a story which had reached Madrid from Cuba. This was, in fact, the old, old story of salvaged silver being piled up by survivors inside a ring of rocks 'on one of those little islands of the Serranillas'. But then, in time-honoured fashion, a hurricane blew up and destroyed their boat and provisions so that all the survivors died of hunger except one who managed to reach Cuba on driftwood to tell the tale. De Graff was understandably intrigued by this story and persuaded the Spanish captain to help him by promising to make him rich enough 'to be happy all his life if he would show us this place'. They needed to hurry as it was common knowledge that the English from Jamaica had been searching for this wreck for many years, 'furnished with all the machines and instruments necessary to fish silver out of the sea'. Many had given up, but there were still three or four sloop crews not at all discouraged by other people's failures who hoped 'that they might be as lucky as those who found the galleon near the Abrojos, north-north-east of Porto Plata, where they had raised so great a fortune'. Armed with the information supplied by the Spaniard, de Graff was confident that the next Captain Phips would be him and not a subject of the king of England.

He got together a search party of four small vessels and some two hundred men and arrived at the Serranillas on 12 April 1689. A Jamaican ship which had been working on the wreck tried to escape de Graff into the night, but was captured with four brass cannon of great antiquity aboard. De Graff took these and, setting to work himself, recovered three more brass and one iron cannon. It all seemed very promising, despite the absence of a great pile of silver in a ring of rocks, and he sent back to Saint-Domingue for more provisions and another fifteen or twenty divers, since he only had three and they were not very good at their job. Ideally he would have liked to have had Indian divers from the coast of Florida, 'who surpass all others in diving', an opinion which he shared with Sir John Narborough who had the use of some kidnapped Florida Indians during his salvage of the *Concepción* in 1688.

The presence of de Graff in the Serranillas was soon known back in Jamaica where the local wreckers were outraged that Frenchmen might profit from what they considered 'their' wreck, a sentiment which could only be strengthened by the fact that King William III had declared war on Louis XIV on 7 May 1689. This view was shared by the Jamaican authorities who sent the royal frigate *Drake* to chase de Graff away. The frigate then remained near the reef as protection for the flood of Jamaicans who sailed out in their sloops to work the wreck, encouraged by a proclamation issued by the Governor of Jamaica 'that any of their Majestie's [i.e King William and Queen Mary's] subjects belonging to that island might go in the search and discovery of any wrecks in the American seas and to fish and dive on any such wreck', provided they paid a royalty of one-tenth of what they found. This proclamation completely ignored the many other grants of wrecks which had been made by the Crown in the Caribbean and also the rather larger royalties which were being demanded for these grants, but it had the required effect. By May 1690 there were twelve or thirteen sloops with large numbers of divers working on the wreck. There were indeed so many men at the

Serranillas that when a new Governor arrived in Jamaica at the end of May he found that the wreck had rendered 'Port Royal very thin of seamen'. However, the weather had been bad and 'very little treasure has been recovered so far', just 'twenty-three dough boys or lumps of silver, some broken plate and golden beads'.[13]

'By a ship arrived lately from the West Indies', wrote the splendidly named Narcissus Luttrell in his London newsletter for 17 August 1690, 'we have an account of a new wreck discovered there, where £15,000 had already been taken up.' There was a buzz of excitement in the metropolis as people wondered whether this could be the next great wreck project. But such hopes were doomed to disappointment, despite the belief of Thomas Spragg, captain of the escorting frigate HMS *Drake* that the wreck 'is to be imagined to be very rich'.[14] The French had found it very difficult to work the wreck and believed that most of the treasure had sunk down beneath the sand and rocks. And the English, though they did recover some silver, were not finding it much easier, being unable to break through the ballast to the treasure which they hoped lay below. 'She is so overgrown with rocks that the divers cannot make their way through without crows of iron of forty pounds weight.' Sir Hans Sloane, the physician and natural historian whose collections and library were to form the nucleus of the British Museum, was very interested in wrecks and the way in which they disintegrated and disappeared over time and he described the process in 1707 in words which will ring a bell with modern divers. 'Though there have been lost divers [several] ships laden with money on many shoals of the West Indies such as the Serranillas . . . yet in most parts there is such a vegetation of coralline matter out of the sea-water, as that the bottom of the sea is incrustated with it, and the wrecks hid by them . . . It is not only from this, but also sand driving by the winds and currents, or earthquakes that happen at the bottom of the sea, that wrecks may be covered and past finding.' The divers from Jamaica found all this to be only too true and mention of the Serranillas wreck in the documents of the time soon dwindles away to nothing and one must assume that the salvage attempts were abandoned.[15]

There are occasional references to other wreck hunting

expeditions to the Caribbean in the 1690s, but most, or all, of these seem to have been unsuccessful. In October 1691, for instance, the same Spanish pilot who had helped de Graff promised to take the French to another Spanish wreck 'on a rock called La Misteriosa unknown to geographers', but they were prevented from reaching it by a hurricane and so the rock retained its mystery. A year later, Luttrell reported that three ships were fitting out for the West Indies, bound for the Bay of Mexico, 'having the King of Spain's pass, where they are to fish for an extraordinary rich wreck, divers of our nobility having engaged therein'. The Spanish were allies of the English in the 1690s but, even so, it seems unlikely that they would have allowed foreigners to dive for treasure in Mexican waters, so maybe Luttrell was misinformed as he was in many of his more sensational stories. In any case, we hear no more of this expedition nor of another one in 1694 which was reported by John Houghton, a pioneer of economic journalism and advertisement whose newspaper strongly supported virtually all the projects of this projecting age. 'I am informed that there is great hope of gain from a Spanish wreck, as yet very little talked on; and I am desired to let the world know it', a good example of the puffery and promotional activity needed to arouse public interest in this plethora of wreck hunting projects.[16]

Meanwhile projectors and adventurers were beginning to carve up the coasts of the British Isles. The great popular excitement about wrecks and treasure naturally aroused fresh interest in the Tobermory galleon. In May 1686, King James had granted Richard Pendarves, William Farrington, Cornelius de Gelder and Samuel Sawton a fourteen-year contract to work on this and other wrecks on the Scottish coast. The last three of these men were inventors and were the proprietors of a patent granted in 1681 for 'a new invention, being several tooles, engines, or instruments (to be wrought without diveing) for the weighing or recovering from under water of ships' guns or goods'. With the help of these tools and engines they worked on the wreck for the next three summers and were reported to have raised 'twelve brass gunnes and other things of no great value', before abandoning the site in 1688. Their place was taken by William Sacheverell, a romantic young man visiting the island on a tour of the west of Scotland. He got together some divers and a bell and, during a period of clear and serene weather, thought that it would be difficult to imagine anything 'more beautiful and diverting than to see the divers sinking threescore foot under water, and stay sometimes above an hour, and at last returning with the spoils of the Ocean'. But he soon deserted the wreck site when the weather became more typical of Mull, 'bleak, stormy, rainy, windy', and set off to enjoy the justly celebrated ruins of St Columba's church on the nearby island of Iona.[17]

There were new hopes too of finding Spanish silver in the Armada wrecks off the coast of Ireland. In January 1691 the projector Robert Baden said that he had been granted permission in 1688 by King James II to search for wrecks on the west coast of Ireland. He also claimed that he had been at great expense in carrying out such searches, though it seems unlikely that he would have been able to achieve much in the years 1688–90 when Ireland was in a state of virtual civil war. Now he wanted this grant confirmed by the new monarchs of Ireland, a petition which was granted on 19 October 1691 when he was given rights over all wrecks on the west coast of Ireland 'between 51 and 57 degrees', paying one-fifth royalty to the Crown on all goods recovered except guns, which he was to deliver to the Ordnance Office who would pay him 'one third part of the value thereof', some indication of the reputation for durability of Spanish brass guns since any ordnance recovered from an Armada wreck would have lain in the sea for over a hundred years. Not all Irish wrecks were on the west coast and, almost simultaneously, Henry Wallop, Vice-Admiral of the coast of Leinster [east and south-east Ireland] was granted a seven-year patent to search for wrecks 'upon or near the coast of the Province of Leinster'.[18]

Hopes of profitable recovery from wrecks in England were focused on the south coast and especially on the coast of Cornwall. The fortunate recipient of royal favour in this area was Philip Ford, a merchant and shipowner of London who had been involved in 1687 in recovering some of the silver taken from the wreck site of the *Concepción* by the colonial sloops. Now he wanted his own treasure and, in September 1688, he signed an indenture with King James II, only weeks before the latter was driven out of his kingdom by his nephew and son-in-law William of Orange. Ford was granted a seven-year patent to search for wrecks 'upon or near the English coast from the North Foreland [in Kent] to the westward of the Lizard, including the rocks, shelves, shoales, seas and banks upon or near the islands of Scilly', paying a royalty of one-fifth to the King and a further one-fifth to Sidney, Lord Godolphin, for wrecks in the Scilly Islands of which he was the proprietor.[19]

Philip Ford was unique among this procession of treasure hunters who made contracts with the Crown in the years following 1687, in that he was the only one to recover silver and so pay the King the royalty which was so hopefully inscribed in all these indentures. We first hear of this in August 1689 when the Lords of the Treasury are in dispute with the Bishop of Exeter who, as Vice-Admiral of South Cornwall, claimed half of what Ford's men had recovered, regardless of his contract with the Crown. This echo of the problems that Jacob the Diver had experienced in Cornwall in the 1620s was eventually resolved in Ford's favour and so the 'four piggs of silver conteyning by estimation 3,055 ounces [later revised to 3,310] . . . which were taken up near the Lizard' were divided between Ford and the officers of the Mint who received 662 ounces 'of silver recovered out of the sea at the Lizard' as the King's fifth.[20]

The sources are silent as to which wreck near the Lizard this silver came from, but it may well have been that of the Genoese ship, *Santo Christo de Castello*, which sank near Bumble Rock in October 1667 with a large quantity of silver. This wreck and a Dutch ship from San Lucar which had foundered in nearby Polpeor Cove in 1619 with £100,000 worth of silver aboard were perennial favourites for divers in the late seventeenth and eighteenth centuries, so much so that diving here became an accepted means of demonstrating the prowess of both the diver and his equipment. Robert Davis, shipbuilder, diver and brother-in-law of the writer Daniel Defoe, laid on such a demonstration on 25 September 1704, as is attested by seven local inhabitants who watched him at work. 'We, whose names are hereunto set . . . do certify that Mr Robert Davis did, in his diving engine, go down in the sea several fathoms deep under water, at a place called Purpeare [Polpeor] Cove, and did sing the hundredth Psalm under water, and afterwards go several times under water in his said engine at the Bumble Rocks, where were taken up several bars or pigs of silver some years ago [by Ford?]' The hundredth psalm was of course a very suitable choice for this amazing feat of singing, since it is very short and starts, 'Make a joyful noise unto the Lord'.[21]

The fact that Ford's divers had actually recovered four bars of silver off the Cornish coast focussed attention on this area and the potential profits that might be gleaned from his grant. In June 1691, the Governor of the recently chartered Linen Company petitioned the Crown to be granted the royal fifth on any future recoveries from Ford's salvage operations for a rental of 20 nobles per annum. The Company claimed that this hypothetical flood of silver into its coffers was necessary if it was not to 'sink for want of a seasonable support during its minority', a choice of words which much amused W.R. Scott, the pioneering, and normally rather dry, historian of joint-stock companies, who chuckled at the idea of 'a homoeopathic remedy of upholding a sinking industry by the raising of foundered ships'. Queen Mary was 'graciously disposed' towards the petition, being supportive of anything which might help the ailing linen industry and so 'reduce the power of France, employ many thousands etc.', but the Treasury was not so enthusiastic and rejected it.[22]

This was mainly because the Linen Company was almost immediately outbid by Thomas Neale, the greatest projector of this projecting age. In his petition of 8 August 1691 he claimed that, during the three years since the grant had been awarded, Ford and his partners 'have ever since tried, at very great charge, to raise the said wrecks, but with so little success that the parties concerned had often some thoughts to leave it off'. Neale, however, a famous gambler as well as a projector, was more sanguine and had lately bought one half of Ford's grant for £1,000 and was 'still in hopes of a hit'. He claimed that he had laid out £5,000 in working the site and was now applying for the reversion of Ford's patent when it expired in 1695 and half the Crown's royalty on the existing patent for a down payment of £400 or all of it for £800. Such figures rather overshadowed the Linen Company's timid offer of twenty nobles, £6 13s 4d, a year and so it is no surprise that a cash-strapped treasury should accept Neale's offer though not before upping the ante a little to £500 for a half-share of the Crown's royalty. Neale also got a seven-year reversion of Ford's patent which included an extension of its limits at both ends, from the North Foreland to Landguard Fort at Harwich, thus covering the whole Thames estuary, and from Land's End to Barnstaple in north Devon. Thus were Thomas Neale's 'good and faithful services' rewarded.[23]

Neale was a Hampshire landowner and Member of Parliament whose career was an increasingly frenetic attempt to become really rich in an age when people in England were for the first time beginning to think in seven figures. It was a venal age in which money could buy office, power and influence and Neale bought himself into Court and government circles in the 1670s by purchasing the reversion of the office of Master of the Mint and by paying £6,000 for the office of Groom Porter. This was a nice job for a gambler, since it involved the general oversight of all billiard tables, bowling alleys, dicing and gaming houses, a task which naturally provided him with plenty of bribes and fees while more money could be made by organizing gambling sessions for the great and good in his own lodgings. These two offices enabled him to get to know everyone worth knowing and were the platform for his astonishing career as a projector.

Before 1688, he was best known for building projects, including the development of Shadwell in London's docklands and Tunbridge Wells in Kent. But, despite his striking physical resemblance to the deposed James II, it was after 1688 that Neale really blossomed, being involved in no less than thirty-nine separate projects in the next four years. These ranged from the development of fishing, mining, postal services and street lighting to more property development including that of Seven Dials near Covent Garden, ingenious schemes for increasing government revenue and several intriguing inventions such as his 'new sort of dice cut perfectly square by a mould' to prevent cheating. Some of Neale's projects prospered, but many failed and he was lampooned in 1696 as a man 'whose life all parts of Fortune's wheel hath seen'.[24]

It is hardly surprising that such a man should have been interested in treasure hunting. This seems to have started in October 1687 when he purchased a 3/32 share in the syndicate working the wreck of the *Concepción*. This, like many of Neale's ventures, was a losing investment since his share was in the disastrous second voyage to the Silver Bank which recovered treasure worth less than half the cost of the expedition. Nothing daunted, Neale returned to the treasure hunting business in September 1690 when he petitioned for a licence to search for wrecks in Bermuda, 'being lately informed of some wreck in those parts by a person come thence who had made him believe he does know very near the just place where it is'. There were a lot of knowing people like this to be found in London in the 1690s. The petition was referred for advice to William Blathwayt, another man with several different offices, including that of Secretary for War. But it was as Auditor General of the Plantations that he said that he had examined the petition 'and do conceive it may be for their Majestie's service that such a grant as is desired by Mr Neale may pass unto him', an opinion which led to Neale being given a grant of all wrecks cast away 'within twenty leagues of the Isle of Bermudas'.[25]

Neale had now really got the treasure hunting bug and in the next couple of years he was to be involved in no less than nine further wreck grants. Three of these were for Irish wrecks. The first, granted in April 1691, was for wrecks within ten leagues of Broadhaven in County Mayo, the same place where Jacob the Diver had had so much trouble with the Cormick clan in the 1630s.[26] A few months later he is again showing an interest in Spanish Armada wrecks on the west coast of Ireland, 'in some of which 'tis likely much treasure was lost, which if narrowly looked for could perhaps be found and tooke up'. This time his point of focus was in south-west Ireland, 'between Cape Clear and Baltimore' where he asked for a seven-year grant, 'without infringing any grant made already'. Since both Broadhaven and Cape Clear did, in fact, fall within the grant to Robert Baden of west coast wrecks 'between the latitudes of 51 and 57 degrees', one suspects that Neale was in some way involved with Baden, perhaps as a partner or simply making use of Baden's contacts to promote his own application for a suitable fee or share. This was certainly true of the wrecks on the coast of Leinster which were granted to Henry Wallop, Vice-Admiral of Leinster, in September 1691. Neale's name does not appear in this application, but just four months later we learn that it was, in fact, Neale who obtained the royal warrant 'in the name of Henry Wallop Esq. who is lately dead' and was now asking for the name of his brother John Wallop to be inserted in the indenture.[27]

Neale was also busy carving out a paper shipwreck empire for himself on the other side of the Atlantic. In October 1691, he reported that he had been told 'of a wreck of good value, lost forty years ago, lying between Cape Henry in Virginia and the Spanish coast in America, and is desirous to recover it at his own charge'. In June 1692, he was granted a seven-year extension of his Bermuda grant, in return for £450 paid into the Exchequer, 'and further to grant him all treasure trove or treasure of what nature or kind soever formerly hidden in the ground . . . in the little island called Ireland near the said island of Bermudas'. This was the only application in this period for treasure hidden ashore rather than lost in the sea and Neale was duly granted permission for the same seven-year period 'to search for, digg up, take and bring away any such treasure trove or treasure hid as aforesaid', on payment of a one-fifth royalty to the Crown.[28]

Neale was the only treasure hunting petitioner who realized that practically anything would be granted if a small payment was made into the royal coffers and, just a week after the renewal of his Bermuda contract, he was paying out another £450 for a grant of all wrecks 'between the city or town of Carthagena [Cartagena de Indias in Colombia] and the island of Jamaica in America or between either of those places and the city of Havana or within the space comprehended within three right lines joining the said three places', a rather difficult triangle to draw since these three places lie very nearly on a straight line. And, just to complete the picture, in February 1693 Neale, in partnership with John Tyzacke, a well-known contemporary inventor, was granted all wrecks within thirty miles of Sable Island near Nova Scotia and once again Neale secured his contract by advancing money to the Crown, in this case £200 to buy out the Crown's rights to any royalty. What wreck Neale and Tyzacke hoped to find in these northern latitudes is not stated in the grant, but the fogbound seas round Sable Island have always been a notorious place for shipwrecks.[29]

The only treasure hunting projects initiated by Neale for which much information has survived are the two grants for Bermuda, one for wrecks within twenty leagues of the islands and the other for treasure hidden in the ground on Ireland Island. Neither of these projects seem to have made anyone rich, but they provide interesting insights into the problems and methods of treasure hunting. Neale's syndicate appointed three Bermuda men as agents to push forward the wreck project in the islands and they seem to have encountered nothing but trouble. The main agent was Thomas Walker, described as gentleman, who sailed from London with the patent and arrived in Bermuda on 22 May 1691. The next day he paid a visit to the Governor, Isaac Richier, to whom he showed the patent and a letter from the patentees granting the governor one-twentieth of everything recovered in return 'for his encouragement, aid and assistance'. At first Richier seemed quite happy with this arrangement and he ordered the island's clergymen to publish the patent in their churches and 'to encourage the people of these islands to make known their discoveries to Walker or the other agents'.[30]

This honeymoon period lasted a few months during which Walker collected what information he could about local wrecks and was joined by another agent, Captain Robert Hall, owner and master of the forty-gun *Rebecca*. But now, on reflection, the Governor began to think that if there was money to be made out of wrecks in Bermuda he wanted more than five per cent of it. In conjunction with Henry Fifield, the Sheriff of Bermuda, he conducted a reign of terror against Walker and Hall, ridiculing their patent, seizing Hall's ship, and threatening them both with prison, court martial and physical violence. Meanwhile, he claimed that as Vice-Admiral of Bermuda any wrecks discovered belonged to him and he threatened with imprisonment anybody who gave information about them to Walker. This sorry story ended with

Walker being tried and acquitted for the murder of the sheriff Henry Fifield who had unwisely provoked Walker into a fatal sword fight.

One suspects that there was more to all this than appears at face value in the documents, but it is clear that conditions in Bermuda were not ideal for searching for wrecks. Walker later claimed that Richier's threats had effectively silenced two men, one who 'had formerly seen some guns much like brass' in the sea and the other who 'had seen and discovered a very large and as he supposed rich wreck'. And, when Walker did find a ship to work on, the process of search and salvage was brought to a halt by one Captain Bare, 'a known pirate' who 'did by force of arms take away from the wrecks a whale boat, sixteen divers and three white men, all in the wreck service'. These men were later recovered from Barbados where they had been taken and the black slave divers rehired from their owners for thirty shillings each a month, but there was no doubt that doing business in remote, pirate-infested colonies was not quite as straightforward as it might have seemed in London.

Matters improved somewhat when Richier was replaced as Governor by Colonel Goddard and Walker was free to get on with his business. In January 1694, it was reported that Walker had been 'as industrious in the discovery of wrecks (by the general account of the inhabitants here) as any man could possibly be'. However, all this effort was to little purpose and there was no hope 'of anything considerable. What may be done in some other wreck entombed I know not, but I declare (without manner of reservation) I would not exchange shares with any of them upon equal terms.' This pessimistic assessment was made by John Dudgeon who had shares in the other Bermuda project, the Ireland Island treasure, for which he was the local agent. The patent for this had been granted to Thomas Neale in June 1692 and a draft prospectus drawn up a few weeks later enables us to see what it was all about. Neale had got hold of a story that a Spanish galleon had been cast away on Bermuda shortly before the English took possession of the islands in 1609. The survivors had built a boat out of the wreckage and had buried in the small island of Ireland, to the north-west of the main island, 'very great quantities of bullion and coyne, both gold and silver', leaving marks so that they would be able to find the treasure again. But, when they returned in the following year, the English had arrived and fired on their ship. The Spanish, 'supposing no inhabitants there, were very much frighted, and said 'twas the Devil that guarded the treasure, and went home again without it'.[31]

Neale was 'willing that others may be partners with him' and he planned to split the grant into a thousand shares, some of which would be retained to cover expenses and to reward those who might be of assistance including himself. The rest were put up for sale. To facilitate this he collected a number of affidavits as to the truth of the story, including one from our old friend Captain Edmond Custis who 'can give great information of the truth of this matter, being once going upon it, in the time of King Charles the Second, but was by some accident hindered'. This has not survived, but an affidavit by one Captain Richard Long was sworn before a London notary on 22 October 1692 and is, in its way, a classic example of a treasure hunter's deposition. Long said that he had often heard of the Ireland Island treasure but did not become absolutely convinced of its truth until some nine years previously, when he met an old Spaniard in Algiers while they were both the slaves of the Barbary corsairs. The Spaniard had told him repeatedly of the treasure and had emphasized that it was 'a very vast quantity, he expressing himself in Spanish three times that it was 'abundancia, abundancia, abundancia.' Unfortunately, Long did not have the exact details of the treasure's location as he had been ransomed before the Spaniard could tell him any more.[32]

Thomas Neale now vanishes from the story and one must assume that the affidavits of Long and others had done the trick and created a market for the shares in the reputed treasure, for the next we know is that Neale had sold out and assigned the patent to Samuel Weale, another well-known projector. Weale and the other 'Proprietors of the Treasure Trove' appointed John Dudgeon, a merchant with links to Bermuda, as agent. He was probably a bit of an operator himself as he was described in 1700 as 'a sort of stock jobber for thirty years', an epithet which was not very complimentary at that time.[33] His orders were to sail to Bermuda, if possible in company with Colonel Goddard who was replacing

Richier as Governor, and once there to organize a survey of Ireland Island, to negotiate with the island's landowners for permission to search and dig on their land, and to bolster the market for shares in the project by obtaining another batch of affidavits, this time from local 'persons of repute and antiquity'. Weale had doubled the number of shares to 2,000 of which Dudgeon was to receive fifty as agent (and £50 in cash) and he was to be allowed to dispose of another forty to anyone who seemed likely to forward the project in the islands.

Dudgeon arrived in Bermuda on 10 August 1693 and he carried out these instructions to the letter. He commissioned John Rowe, a former surveyor of Jamaica, to survey Ireland Island and in November Rowe produced a beautiful chart with sufficient markers to the location of the treasure to excite the dullest punter, including a dotted line running from Spanish Point on the main island through Cross Island to the very narrowest part of Ireland Island where 'people do imagine they hid their treasure'. The owners of land on the island said that they were perfectly happy to let Dudgeon's men 'digg and search for the said treasure', as long as they left the land as they found it and gave fifty shares to the proprietor of any land in which treasure was found. Dudgeon had a little difficulty in collecting affidavits from 'ancient' people, as a terrible period of sickness had 'carried off most of the old men' and there was now no one on the island aged over 75. However, he eventually got together eleven witnesses, some ancient, some 'of repute' and some both, who all swore to the truth of what they said before Governor Goddard and their affidavits were given added authenticity by attaching the island's splendid seals to them.[34]

These affidavits provide an intriguing insight into what was felt necessary to get people to believe a tall story. Old people in the 1690s were still respected and were expected to know more and be more trustworthy than the young. So the witnesses themselves were chosen for their age and would often gain even greater credence by claiming to have heard the story as a lad from another very old man. Even better as a source of authority would be a very old Spaniard. Two deponents told the story of Mrs Ellin Burrows, 'an antient woman' who when in England had met an ancient

Spaniard 'with a white beard' who claimed to have been on the ship when it wrecked and also in the party who were frightened away by the English guns. Thomas Walker, the wreck agent for Thomas Neale whom we met above, also gave evidence and he told of meeting 'an antient gentleman', a former minister called Sampson Bond who during the Third Dutch War was captured by a Dutch privateer and taken to Corunna, the naval base in north-western Spain. Here he met many local sailors who had heard the story from their fathers and grandfathers who told them that many people had tried to return to the 'Devil's Island' to recover the treasure, but had been foiled 'by accidents and misfortunes'.

Nearly all the deponents mention markers which had been left by the Spaniards 'for the better finding their treasure again', a cross, a yellow-wood tree, an iron bolt driven into the rocks, 'a post with a brass hand upon it' or 'three heaps of stones curiously piled up in a triangle'. And at least half of those consulted thought that the reason that the treasure had never been found was because it was enchanted and protected by 'fire drakes' [dragons] who could often be seen rising up from the site or flying about from place to place. Others had seen phantom ships sailing where there was not sufficient water to float them and then suddenly disappearing. Dragons were not the only supernatural defences. One man who tried to look for the treasure 'was possest with a panick feare' and dared do no more. Another group of searchers were told by 'an eminent astrologer' that if they started to dig, 'they would for a small time be struck blind, upon which all the diggers left off and would not worke any more, saying they would not trust the devil with their eye sight'. Many people claimed that those who tried to land on Ireland Island to search for the treasure were forced back and thwarted by wind, rain and mist, and there was a general belief that searching for the treasure would lead to 'great stormes and endanger the lives of many persons'. But, lest such depositions should lead to the projectors giving up in despair, there were others who denied the enchantment of the treasure or said that it was no longer effective.

Dudgeon sent all this rather astonishing material back to Weale in London and seemed generally optimistic about finding the treasure, though he was even keener on another treasure which he had heard about at Crooked Island in the Bahamas. Nevertheless, one suspects that this whole business of taking affidavits on the island was simply a way of exciting interest in London and pushing up the price of shares. It seems rather odd, for instance, that in January 1694, five months after his arrival, Dudgeon should write to Weale saying that he had no equipment and asking to be sent 'five dozen of pickaxes and as many shovells well shod . . . at the receipt of which my utmost pains will not be wanting to exercise them'. What serious expedition would send a man to dig up a treasure three thousand miles away without a single shovel? Whatever the truth, the treasure disappears from the records some time in 1694 and the only further news we have of John Dudgeon concerns his ultimately successful attempt to become Secretary of Bermuda, a potentially more profitable position than agent for the Ireland Island treasure though maybe not quite so much fun.

The considered judgment of Sir Hans Sloane can serve to bring to a close this strange story of treasures in Bermuda. 'There was one ship lost amongst the rest, said to be very rich, near Bermudas, which was divided into shares and sold. It was said to be in posession of the Devil, and they told stories of how he kept it. I do not find the people who spent their money on this . . . got any thing by them.'[35]

The private papers of Thomas Neale have not survived and so it is not possible to find out exactly what he was up to in the many other treasure hunting enterprises in which his name appears as petitioner and projector. One suspects, however, that nothing is quite as it seems and that the bland wording of the petitions and grants is concealing some complicated double dealing. There is no evidence that Neale did, in fact, organize expeditions to search for any wrecks except those in Bermuda and, possibly, those in Cornwall in which he bought a half-share from Philip Ford. In many cases he clearly seems to be acting as agent, presumably on commission, and no doubt with an agreed share in any successes which should arise from the patents he had helped to obtain. But the shipwreck game was such that there did not have to be any successes for its promoters to be successful.

There were, in fact, two different reasons for going to the considerable expense of acquiring a royal grant to search for treasure in a particular area. Some people, Albemarle and Narborough for example, genuinely believed that they possessed information which would enable them to find a wreck and were quite prepared to fund an expedition to do so out of their own pockets, though they might well hedge a little by selling on part of their share. The object of a royal grant in their case was simply to register their claim and to protect their investment from interlopers. But in an age mad about wrecks, treasure, gambling and projecting, there was another and rather less noble motive for seeking a royal grant. The process is outlined in 1692 by Captain John Pointz who claimed in his petition to have been 'for thirty-six years well skilled in taking up anything out of the sea'. He referred to the many letters patent for the taking up of wrecks which had been granted in recent years to 'persons who never designed, nor yet began to recover the same . . . but have only divided their said patents into shares and sold them at extravagant rates, by which their Majesties' intentions are frustrated, the purchasers losers and those that would have taken up the same wrecks hindered'.[36]

Such operations would normally be conducted in two stages. At first there would be just a small group of people whose task was to obtain a saleable asset in the form of a royal treasure hunting patent for a particular geographical area. Shares would be apportioned between these original partners who would normally include the adventurer who had thought up the idea, some monied men who could fund the process of getting a patent, a character like Thomas Neale with an inside knowledge of just how to manipulate courtiers and, if necessary, bribe them with free shares in the project, and usually 'a Noble Lord who will be usefull in the management of the business', bribing noble lords being a necessary part of getting anything done in the corrupt world of the 1690s. And then, armed with the patent, the original partners would divide it up into several hundred, sometimes several thousand, shares, and promote the project by all means possible, emphasizing their exact knowledge of the wreck site and the authenticity of the information they had received, blowing up the potential treasure to be won to hundreds of thousands or millions of pounds, in coffee-houses, on the Exchange and everywhere else where men met and talked. This process was often facilitated by giving away several shares to the great and the good whose reputation and standing in society would ensure that their well-advertised involvement in the project would draw in hordes of dupes and cullies in their wake. And so the shares would be sold, a market would develop to trade in the shares and the promoters would get rich.

This process was very much more effective at making money quickly and surely than the long, tiresome and very expensive business of fitting out a ship or ships, buying 'engines' and other equipment, hiring or buying divers (slave divers from Madeira were selling at over £70 a head), hiring, feeding and paying a crew at inflated wartime rates of pay and all the rest of the expense necessary to set out an expedition which, at best, might find nothing but sell a trading cargo at a profit and, at worst, be captured by the French privateers who swarmed through the seas during this decade of war. This was so self-evident that the projector Samuel Weale had to emphasize in one of his many prospectuses that it was not only possible, but probable, to make more money by finding wrecks than by stockjobbing, citing as the norm, as did many other promoters, the exceptional profits made by the investors in Phips' great voyage to the Silver Bank. 'That which most persons have in their eye on such undertakings as this is to get money by the buying or selling of shares, but the excellency of this undertaking lyes in this, that there is far more profit to be gotten working the wrecks than by buying or selling of shares, though shares might be sold for £50 a share. As for instance if a proprietor having 100 shares sells at £50 per share that makes but £5,000, but supposing there be but £200,000 gotten by one expedition, the product of the 100 shares [out of a total of 2,000] amounts to £10,000, double as much profit for just one voyage. And £200,000 is a very low computation for a summer's voyage on the wrecks.' Such delightfully creative arithmetic lay at the very heart of the great treasure hunting boom and is, of course, still employed today.[37]

Educated public opinion was very hostile to this business of stockjobbing, as it was called, and in 1703 it is interesting to note that William Blathwayt tried to persuade the Treasury to demand proof of the reality of the wreck that some promoters claimed to be seeking before granting a patent. 'But whereas the pernicious trade of stockjobbing ought to be discouraged . . . I humbly offer that before the passing of this grant your Lordships be satisfied by good proofs of the truth of the information [about the value and whereabouts of the wreck], lest some of the petitioners be surprized by the others into a society of stockjobbing instead of a real and well grounded undertaking.'[38] But, since even the Lords of the Treasury were not above benefitting from the receipt of such information, such a requirement does not ever seem to have been imposed and so the stockjobbers flourished.

By 1694 the momentum had gone out of the great treasure hunting boom, as project after project ended in disappointment with only stockjobbers making any profit. People with money to invest found alternative and more remunerative homes for their savings, such as the Bank of England whose capital was raised with the utmost of ease in July 1694. Even more suitable as an investment for frustrated treasure hunters was the Million Adventure of the same year whose object was to raise a million pounds for the war effort. This, the first English lottery, was based on a Venetian example and was promoted by none other than Thomas Neale who by now was tired of wreck hunting projects. The attraction of the lottery was that the punters could not lose, since the million raised was in effect a loan to the Government for sixteen years. All who bought tickets received a modest rate of interest on their investment, while the winning tickets provided sufficient income for the lucky recipient to live like a lord.[39]

A lottery ticket on which you could not lose was certainly more attractive than a share in a treasure hunting project in which you were almost certain to lose, but it still leaves unanswered the question of why all these post-Phips treasure hunters were so unsuccessful. Sometimes, as has been seen, it was because the speculators were dilatory, incompetent or did not even set out an expedition. But it was also because it was incredibly difficult with the equipment available to find and salvage a wreck which had lain for any length of time at the bottom of the sea. Sometimes fortunate circumstances would uncover part of a ship sufficiently for valuables to be seen by the naked eye, as with the *Maravillas* and the wreck in the Serranillas. But sooner or later these wrecks would be covered in sand or coral and, in the absence of electronic search tools such as magnetometers and metal detectors, there was little chance that a late seventeenth-century treasure hunter would find anything.

The real point here is that Captain Phips was incredibly lucky. He found his wreck easily. It lay at a manageable depth and his divers almost immediately broke into a huge treasure room where they could raise the treasure day after day with ease and the weather was fine and so on. It was, as a contemporary remarked, a gamble of 'a million to one against . . . but they succeeded against all prospect of probability, and were enriched by the accident; and the consequence of this was, that a thousand families have been since undone, by sending their estates a diving after shipwrecked treasure'.[40] It was asking too much that Phips' luck should be duplicated, though it was of course human nature to hope for the best and we will see later that, once peace made conditions easier and safer for treasure hunters, more people would be sending their estates a diving with just as much optimism as they had done in the late 1680s and 1690s.

Chapter Five

Diving-Engines of Divers Kinds

Chapter Five

Diving-Engines of Divers Kinds

"And then came up Diving-Engines of various make, some like a bell, others like a tubb, some like a compleat suit of armour of copper, and leather between the joynts, and pipes to convey wind, and a Polyphemus eye in the forehead to give light."[1]

The 1690s were a rather remarkable decade in English history, a period not just of treasure hunting but also of revolution, warfare on a scale never before seen and the creation of many of the fundamental institutions of modern British society, such as parliamentary democracy, the rule of law, the Bank of England and the National Debt. It was a time of optimism and inventiveness, despite the threat of invasion by the French, a rising burden of taxation and great misery amongst the poor. And it was above all a time when all ranks strove to get richer, maybe by gambling on billiards or the throw of a dice at backgammon, on cockfighting or foot races or on such minutiae of the war as the date that such and such a foreign city would surrender to a besieging army. These forms of gambling were however to be challenged in the 1690s by something new and very modern, the development of a stock market which would burst forth ready-made with all the paraphernalia of brokers and jobbers, bulls and bears and a press providing listings of current prices, most of this being derived from the more precocious example of the Dutch.

Prior to 1688 there had been little for such people to speculate in, since virtually the only shares available were those in the great chartered trading companies, such as the East India and Royal African Companies, who took some trouble to ensure that undesirables did not buy their shares. These companies remained the most important speculation on the new Stock Market but, by the early 1690s, it was no longer seen as necessary for a joint-stock company to be chartered by the Crown or Parliament and a host of new companies were set up on the basis of simple articles of association, several of which were established to exploit the patents granted for wreck-hunting, discussed in the previous chapter.

There was plenty of money available to invest in such companies, for the war had reduced the opportunities for investment in foreign trade and merchant shipping. 'A great many stocks have arisen since this war with France', wrote the economic journalist John Houghton. 'For trade being obstructed at sea, few that had money were willing it should lie idle.' Heavy losses to French privateers in the early years of the war made many feel 'a sensible ebb of their fortunes', as Daniel Defoe, himself a loser to the French, remarked. 'These, prompted by necessity, rack their wits for new contrivances, new inventions, new trades, stocks, projects and any thing to retrieve the desperate credit of their fortunes.'[2] The result was the first great company promotion and stock market boom in English history which saw the number of joint-stock companies increase from eleven to around a hundred between 1689 and 1695. 'In the short space of four years', wrote the Victorian historian Thomas Babington Macaulay in his famous *History of England,* 'a crowd of companies, every one of which confidently held out to subscribers the hope of immense gains, sprang into existence: the Insurance Company, the Paper Company, the Lutestring Company, the Pearl Fishery Company, the Glass Bottle Company' and many more.[3]

This growth, in turn, largely depended on a simultaneous increase in the granting of patents for invention in the years 1691 to 1693 during which years, according to one account, there were sixty-four such patents granted and, according to another, sixty-one. Whatever the exact figure, this was a lot of patents by the standards of the day, over a quarter of all patents granted in the second half of the seventeenth century and the largest triennial number until the inventions of the early Industrial Revolution began to make their mark after 1760. This boom itself is rather a remarkable occurrence, but even more remarkable is the nature of the inventions patented. In a period of warfare it is no surprise that the leading field for invention should be in the supply of military and naval equipment of various kinds which accounted for twelve patents. But, second in line, were eleven for various types of diving-engines and diving equipment and these were, in fact, the survivors of seventeen petitions to be granted a patent for something to do with diving, six of which lapsed or were rejected by the Government. 'Oh, a patent gives a reputation to it, and cullies in the company', wrote the author of *Angliae Tutamen* in 1695, and it was indeed this reputation or publicity which was the main attraction of patents. They provided little legal protection, were expensive and required lengthy attendance in London to ensure success, so that it is more than likely that there were other non-patented inventions in addition to these seventeen.[4]

It seems almost incredible that inventions of diving equipment should play such an important role in the economy, but this was, of course, just a by-product of the treasure hunting boom which was discussed in the previous chapter. It may seem even more incredible that people could think up seventeen (or more) different sorts of diving-engine or diving apparatus in just three years, but there they are in the petitions to the Crown and, for most of them, in the final grant of letters patent giving their proprietors a monopoly of their use for fourteen years, in accordance with the provisions of Section 6 of the 1624 Statute of Monopolies which allowed 'the sole working or making of any manner of new manufactures within this realm to the true and first inventor'.[5]

This material is, however, not quite as useful for a history of diving as one might expect, as the patent system of the late seventeenth century was very different from what it was to become later. It was in effect merely a system of registering new inventions, not of examining them, and proof of originality rested almost entirely on the word of the inventor, the government giving applications far less scrutiny than England's two great economic rivals, the Netherlands and France. There was no need as yet for a full description of the invention and it was, in fact, in the inventor's interest to keep the information given to the minimum to deter imitators. Specifications were not required until 1711 and carried no real weight until the 1760s. It was all a very long way from Lord Mansfield's famous judgment in 1778 on what a patent should be. 'The law requires as the price the patentee must pay to the public for his monopoly that he should, to the very best of his knowledge, give the fullest and most sufficient description of all the particulars on which the effect depends.' He later defined what he meant by 'most sufficient'. 'You must specify upon record your invention in such a way as shall teach an artist [i.e. craftsman], when your term is out, to make it, and to make it as well as you, by your directions; for then at the end of the term the public shall have the benefit.'[6] However, English law was not interested in such matters in the 1690s and considered that it was 'the patentee's hazard' whether his invention was really new. And if anybody wanted to challenge his claim to originality, he was at liberty to fight it out in the courts.

The patent system of the 1690s was in essence a system for extracting money from so-called inventors and their backers in return for a 14-year licence to exploit their inventions and the general public as they pleased. The applicant for a patent had to steer his proposal through ten separate stages, a 'maze of writs, seals and docquets', each of which required a fee to be paid, a procedure which cost between £70 and £100 and could take up to six months to complete. The only stage where there was any possibility of an informed opinion being given on the invention by an outsider was when, fairly early in the proceedings, the petition from the inventor was referred to the Attorney-General or Solicitor-General or, if it was a matter of naval or military interest, to the relevant officers for a demonstration. Sometimes these references throw up interesting material, but usually they simply repeat the wording of the original petition and say that as far as they can tell the information contained in it is true.[7]

Despite these very real problems of interpretation, it is still possible to acquire some information about contemporary diving equipment from these applications for patents of invention. The wording is very vague, but it does tell us something and does at least indicate what it was that inventors thought would be worth patenting. As has been seen earlier, the only real improvement on natural, unaided diving before the 1690s had been the diving-bell and this was, in fact, the subject of one of the earliest patents of invention for diving equipment granted in England, although it would be difficult to discern this from the patent which was granted to Richard Norwood on 2 April 1632. His invention was described as 'a special meanes to dive into the sea or other deepe waters, there to discover, and thence by an engine to raise or bringe upp such goods as are cast awaie by shipwracke or otherwise'. This is hardly giving much away but, fortunately, we know from other sources that Richard Norwood was reputed to have invented in 1612 the form of diving-bell known in the English colonies as the 'Bermuda Tub', this being simply a large open-ended wine cask, heavily weighted at its open end, which was inverted and lowered into the water, thus trapping air in its closed end.[8]

Some of the inventions patented in the 1690s were trying to improve on this basic diving tub, by improving visibility under water, by making the tub more mobile, or by increasing bottom time by the introduction of a method of renewing the trapped air which soon got unbreathable. Others were striving towards some primitive form of the diving helmet of the nineteenth century which would give the diver mobility on the bottom and send down to him a constant supply of fresh air. Yet others seem to be anticipating the caisson, a large watertight case or chest which was being used in laying the foundations of wharves and the piers of bridges by the middle of the eighteenth century.

Two applications in 1693, one by George Ball and the other a month later by Francis Ball, presumably some relation, seem to bypass the laws of physics since they both claimed to have invented a method by which divers could remain under water for half an hour without any assistance whatsoever. George Ball, gentleman, claimed to have found a new invention to improve 'natural' diving, whereby a man may 'without any habit [clothing] or enclosure' remain above ten fathoms under water, 'for half an hour or more, having the free use of his limbs'. Francis Ball, merchant, and his partner Cornelius de Gelder 'with great paines, study and expence' had invented 'a way whereby persons may dive and live under water with freedom at eight or ten fathom depth, for the space of half-an-hour or more, and to come up again without the help of any engine or instrument, which invention being never found out before will be of great use for recovery of ships, goods, treasure, guns, merchandize'. A warrant at a later stage in this application describes the invention as 'a way whereby persons may dive and live under water, naked' which sounds similar to the patent granted to Henry Ayscoghe, gentleman, in 1687. His new invention consisted 'of teaching persons to walk and remain under water for ye space of one, two, or three hours without any covering over their head or body, ye water coming both round and next their naked skin'. These inventions sound a bit fanciful, though, of course, some key factors such as an aqualung may have been left out of the description, and indeed both the Ball applications lapsed and neither received a patent.[9]

The joint application with Francis Ball was the second time that Cornelius de Gelder had appeared in the English patent records for, in March 1681, he and two partners had been granted a patent for 'a new invention, being several tooles, engines, or instruments (to bee wrought without diveing) for the weighing or recovering from under water shipps' gunns or goods, by accident shipwreckt or lost in the harbours at sea'.[10] Such improvements in lifting devices were of course an essential part of the salvage which the work of divers should ideally lead to and the very first application in the diving equipment boom was of this nature. This patent was granted in November 1689 to Francis Smartfoot, a prosperous citizen of London with just the right sort of surname for a projector. He had petitioned in July for 'letters patent for the sole working of a new invention or sea crabb for working in the sea, for fishing and taking up of ships, gunns, goods, lost and forsaken with more facility than hath yet been obtained by any'. There is no further description in the petition and it would be nice to imagine a mechanical crustacean with huge claws cleaning up the debris of shipwrecks from the bottom of the sea. But, alas, a 'crab' was simply a portable capstan in contemporary nautical terminology and a 'sea-crab', as defined by the *Oxford English Dictionary*, was either one of many slang words for a sailor or 'a crab used at sea'.[11]

Whatever the particular advantages of Smartfoot's invention over existing equipment, the Privy Council thought that it might be useful and referred it to the Commissioners of the Navy for their opinion. This was the only piece of equipment invented during this boom which was inspected by the Navy which seems to imply a surprising lack of interest in diving and diving equipment. Be that as it may, the Commissioners reported on 9 September that 'some of them have lately viewed the engine mentioned in the said petition by the name of Sea Crabb and are humbly of opinion that it is a new invention and that it may be usefull', giving absolutely no details, and they recommended that the Privy Council go ahead with processing the application.[12]

A week later Smartfoot asked for an extra clause to be inserted, allowing him and his partners to work and use his engine in 'all the seas under his Majestie's dominion', except the south coast which, as has been seen, had been licensed to Philip Ford a year previously. It was agreed that royalties on goods recovered should be one-fifth on everything taken up from depths up to ten fathoms (60 feet) and nothing for recoveries from deeper waters, these being 'for the sole benefit, incouragement and advantage of the inventor and towards the supporting of the charge of vessells and working the said engine'. All this was granted in Smartfoot's letters patent, though a year later the unusual and, in fact, unique royalty schedule was revised to give the Crown one-tenth, however deep the water.[13]

Francis Smartfoot's invention seems to have been a useful one and one finds mention of it from time to time. In March 1692, for instance, there was a notice inserted in the *London Gazette*, the official newspaper, reporting that 'the patentees of the engine called the Sea-Crab' had been given permission by Trinity House to lay a red buoy over the wreck of the *Loyal London* which had blown up in the Thames estuary. 'These are to give notice thereof, that none may remove the same', a notice which was probably designed more as an advertisement that the patentees were actively in business than for the stated reason. In 1695, a Colonel Chantrell was thought to be planning to infringe Smartfoot's patent and was warned off. And in November 1702, with just a year of the patent left, 'the Patentees of the Seacrab Engines' wrote to the Queen's Most Excellent Majesty offering to send a vessel to take up the treasure and guns which had been sunk as a result of the great battle of Vigo Bay a month earlier, in which an Anglo-Dutch fleet had completely destroyed a Franco-Spanish one. They claimed that they were able to give 'very effectual proof of their great usefulness to break up ships and recover guns etc.', but, unfortunately, the victorious English fleet had already returned and so they were forced to leave the salvage of the Vigo treasure to other men, some of whom will be met in a later chapter. The patentees took the opportunity to 'acquaint your Majesty that wee have such usefull engines and that wee are now most ready and willing to serve your Majesty upon any occasion you shall please to command'. The petition was signed Wynne Houblon & Company which suggests that Smartfoot had either died or sold out to these connections of the powerful mercantile and banking family. Queen Anne was duly impressed and ordered that the petition be transmitted to the Lord High Admiral, who happened to be her husband Prince George of Denmark, with a recommendation that his officers use the 'engine therein mentioned when any occasion shall offer'.[14]

Francis Smartfoot applied for a patent for another invention in addition to his sea-crab. This, too, was referred to the Admiralty whose inspectors reported 'that they have also seen another invention of the petitioners for a man's breathing under water in a pair of lungs fixt to his back as he swims, and do humbly conceive the same may be of use to the said engine [i.e. when using the sea-crab]'. As usual no detail is attached, but the idea of a diver using an inflated and weighted goatskin or similar container for air has a very long history indeed and was one of the diving devices suggested by Leonardo da Vinci who posited a diver with a breathing tube attached to an air bag.[15]

We hear no more about Smartfoot's 'pair of lungs', so maybe they did not work too well, but many of the other applications demonstrate a desire for a mobility under water which was difficult to achieve with the traditional diving-bell. The best documented is the invention of the Londoner, John Overing, who was in partnership with the Duke of Leinster, a general and one of King William's foreign favourites who had acquired a huge treasure hunting grant which will be discussed in the next chapter. Overing petitioned for letters patent in July 1692, claiming that he had 'found out a new engine to convey air into pipes by new contrived bellows, with plates covered with leather for securing the head and retaining the air about the upper part of the body, which gives liberty for a man to see, walk, and work for a considerable time many fathoms under water'. This is a bit vague, but it seems to be a crude prototype of what historians of diving call semi-atmospheric diving apparatus. This is equipment in which the diver's head and part or all of his body is in a receptacle which is sealed off from the water and so remains at atmospheric pressure when lowered into the sea, while the diver's arms or arms and legs are free to move under water and so are subject to increasing pressure the deeper he goes. That this was the sort of 'engine' that Overing had developed is given some support from a contemporary description of the equipment being used in a demonstration on the Thames a couple of weeks before the letters patent were issued.[16]

The Thames at this date was even more of a venue for splendid displays than it is today. Richard Lapthorne of Hatton Garden described for the benefit of his patron in Devon a magnificent fireworks display which took place on the river on the night of 21 July 1688. 'I heare but of one that was killed. There were as I am informed above 100,000 spectators. It lightned exceedingly all the while.' In October 1692, Narcissus Luttrell reported a display which seems to have anticipated the river of fire produced for the Millennium celebrations. A barge with a brick roof was 'to be rowed from London Bridge to Whitehall and is to appear in flames all the way with variety of fireworks to issue thence'. And a few months later he described a pleasure boat which the Queen boarded at Whitehall 'and heard a consort of musick, vocall and instrumentall: it was built for entertainment, having twenty-four sash windows [a recent innovation], and four banquetting houses on top'.[17]

They might not have been able to compete with entertainment

like this, but the makers and inventors of new diving equipment saw the Thames as an ideal venue for the demonstration of their wares and had done so since at least the early 1620s, when the Dutch inventor Cornelius van Drebbel arranged for his prototype submarine to make a submerged journey from Westminster to Greenwich, propelled by twelve oarsmen fifteen feet under the surface of the river and watched by several thousand spectators.

John Overing's invention was not quite in this league, but was still impressive enough to draw a crowd. 'Yesterday', wrote the indefatigable Narcissus Luttrell on 8 September 1692, 'the Duke of Leinster's engine for working of wrecks was experimented on the Thames, where one Bradley, a waterman, walkt at bottom under water till he came to Somerset House, and discours'd by the way out of a leather pipe, and a boat went before to blow air to him: he had a tin case fastened about his neck with two leather pipes.' One of these pipes was designed to receive air blown down from a boat and the other doubled as an exhaust and a speaking tube, as Luttrell later explained to his readers. 'The wreck engine had two pipes fastened to the case; one of them fastened to a boat, into which a man blowed constantly with a pair of bellows: he walked from Whitehall to Somerset House, taking up sand, stones, etc. from the bottom, where one of his leaden shoes falling off, he called to them through the pipe, so was taken up: may prove a usefull invention.'[18]

A few months later, Overing inserted a piece in the *London Gazette* in which he referred to the great approbation with which the trial of his machine in the Thames had been received. Apparently, some of the many rogues who flourished in London in the early 1690s had used the publicity to sell fictitious shares in the invention and Overing warned them off. 'These are to give notice that Mr John Overing of Dunstans in the East, London, is the true and real inventer of this engine, who hath a patent under the Great Seal for the sole use thereof.' There is no evidence as to the success or otherwise of Overing's invention, though the fact that we hear nothing of it in future years suggests that it was found to be impracticable. There were two obvious problems. As has been seen, there were strict limits to the depth that air could be blown to a diver by the use of bellows. And, wearing such clumsy equipment, the diver must have had great difficulty in keeping his feet. The waterman Bradley was certainly wise to signal to be hauled up when he lost one of his leaden shoes.[19]

Several other inventions during these boom years seem to have involved various forms of semi-atmospheric apparatus. The most explicit description is contained in a grant given on 31 May 1692 to Isaac Thompson and his partners. Thompson, described as 'engine-maker to their Majesties', had invented 'a new engine, whereby a man may be let down under water . . . by the assistance of a certain diving-habit which does well secure them from the pressure of the water, and leaves their arms and legs naked and at liberty; with the help of another engine for pumping air, the said person so let down may safely continue for an hour at least under water, with great freedom and clearness of sight'. John Tyzack and John Stapleton, both well-known inventors and projectors of the period, seem to have invented similar equipment though the descriptions are too vague for certainty.[20]

None of these applications specify how water was prevented from entering where the diver's arms and legs emerged from the sealed 'engine' (probably some sort of barrel or cylinder), though solving such a problem was certainly within the bounds of maritime skills and ingenuity of the period. Nor do they give much information about the engines 'for pumping air'. Air supply to divers by means of powerful pumps on board the support vessel was to become the norm in the first half of the nineteenth century, but in the 1690s there were no really efficient and reliable pumps available though some improvements had recently been made by the French physicist Dr Denis Papin.[21]

In addition to the inventions mentioned above, it is possible that there was another application for a patent for some sort of semi-atmospheric machine. This was the engine invented by the Cornishman, Joseph Williams, described as a tinner, and his three Cornish partners John and Nicholas Honychurch and James Trefusis. In their application of 20 August 1691, their invention was described as 'an engine consisting of covering vessels and pipes whereby they are enabled to work several fathoms under water for divers hours together without any want of air'. This description could apply to virtually any of the types of diving-engine, but the equipment is described in a lawsuit by Rice Jones, one of the shareholders, as 'an engine, suit or garment' for diving under water which sounds rather similar to Isaac Thompson's 'diving-habit'.[22]

Joseph Williams' petition for letters patent was referred by the Privy Council to Sir John Somers, the Solicitor-General, whose report was cynical but witty and much more quotable than the usual bland rubber-stamping of these official reports. He did not actually get to see the engine, since he did not leave his office, but he had been told by the petitioners 'that they have severall experiments thereof with very good success. And in particular the petitioner Joseph Williams says that by the help of this engine he himself continued severall fathoms under water for near an hour, without being sensible of any want of air at the time when he thought fit to come up. And as far as I can inform myself the invention is new, and if it should succeed to such a degree as the petitioners believe it will, it may be of very generall use, and may deserve to be encouraged. And in case it failes, I do not find that any body will suffer besides themselves.'[23]

Joseph Williams and his partners have had a bad press over the years, for one of those who bought shares in his invention was none other than the famous writer Daniel Defoe, at that date plain Daniel Foe who, in his 1697 book *An Essay upon Projects,* informed his readers that 'I could give a very diverting history of a patent-monger whose cully was no body but my self'. He gave no details, but detective work by his biographers has dug up cases in the Court of Chancery which show that it was Joseph Williams to whom he was referring. Williams and his partners had agreed 'one with another that the said invention or engine should be divided into four hundred parts' and these shares were sold at £20 each to some fifty separate 'cullies'. Defoe himself was desperate to make money at this time and he bought ten shares for £200 and, because of his energy and skill in bookkeeping, was made secretary-treasurer for the syndicate.[24]

The initial public enthusiasm for the project soon waned, when it seemed that nothing was being done with the shareholders' money, and the court case arose when the syndicate tried to raise more money by levying a further ten shillings a share. Most of the shareholders refused to pay up, suspicious that the whole scheme was simply a means of extracting money for a merely paper project. John Skeate, one of the defendants, admitted to paying £20 for 1/400th part of the invention, having been 'persuaded, deluded and prevailed upon through the many and dayly importunities and perswasions of the said Joseph Williams'. But he would not pay any more as Williams had agreed that there would be 'noe further costs or charges . . . other than what should grow due from the first day in which the same [engine] should be sett on board in order to worke'. There was no sign of this so he refused to pay.[25]

This lawsuit, typical of the 'Projecting Age', as Defoe called it, gives the impression that the diving-engine of Joseph Williams was, like many other contemporary inventions, a mere figment of the imagination of the so-called inventor and his partners. But, in fact, it seems to have been real enough if we can believe a notice posted in the *London Gazette* in February 1693 which, like that from John Overing quoted above, was designed at once to deter imitators with the threat of prosecution and to advertise the quality of their engines. 'Which engine hath several times been tryed betwixt Chelsey and London-Bridge, and at Limehouse-Reach where the inventor was six hours at a time under water without any want of air, to the great satisfaction of many persons then present; two of which engines are now sent to work upon one of their Majesties ships.' It seems unlikely that either of these statements would have been placed in the government newspaper if they were completely untrue. The engine was still in existence ten years later when James Trefusis, one of the patentees, petitioned for a seven-year extension of the patent. He said he was the only one of the patentees 'who has worked the said engine and has as yet made no profit out of it, though he has had costly experiments,' a statement which suggests that the engine was real enough but not very practicable.[26]

The words diving-bell or tub appear in none of the applications for letters patent, but it is probable in some cases and, in one case certain, that improvements to the bell were what the inventors were interested in. Samuel Wimball, for instance, was promoting 'a new invented engine of brass, lead, iron and other metalls by which one or more persons may descend twenty fathom and stay there 24 hours'. The persons inside the machine were 'safely secured from any pressure or inconveniency of the water, and have perfect freedom of air and breathing, and likewise free liberty of seeing whatever is in the water, and of using his or their hands or bodies, whereby any thing may be fastened to whatever is on the bottom'. Twenty fathoms (120 feet) would have been very deep for a contemporary bell and there is no indication as to how sufficient air was supplied to the divers to enable them to stay at the bottom for twenty-four hours, but this certainly seems to be referring to some sort of improved bell.[27]

Captain Edmond Custis, whom we met in Chapter Two blowing up colliers in the river Tyne, seems to have come out of retirement to take part in the diving boom of the early 1690s. He, too, had invented a new engine which would take a diver down to twenty fathoms and enable him to stay there 'at the bottom of the sea' for a whole day. Once at the bottom, the diver could use a compass so as to 'direct those above deck what course to steer to any wreck he shall find and thence to take up all that is not perished'. His speciality, not surprisingly given his Newcastle adventure, was breaking ships up so that the divers could get at the cargo, 'if need be in a way not yet used to break up with powder [i.e. gunpowder] such ship'.[28]

Custis advertised his skills in the *London Gazette* at the end of April 1693. He reported that his own diving company, together with their 'maritime engines', had now joined up with a company called Donnills and Hollinsheds, neither of these names appearing anywhere else in the records of the 1690s. Together, they undertook 'to take up guns, merchandize, treasure etc. and to blow up, or break to pieces, ships in competent depths, and then take up the lading. Such therefore as are proprietors of any wrecks recoverable by the arts aforesaid, or discoverers of old wrecks, may please to have recourse unto the said company, on Tuesdays and Fridays in the evening at the Merchants Coffee-house in Cornhill, London, where they shall be treated with all suitable encouragement.' Custis is the only one of these diving entrepreneurs to show any detailed knowledge of what the salvage of a wreck involved and, given his previous record, one has a certain confidence in his ability to do what he claimed to be able to do, though not perhaps at twenty fathoms depth.[29]

The best-known and best documented of all the new diving inventions in the 1690s boom was the improved diving-bell invented by Edmond Halley, the famous mathematician and astronomer who accurately predicted the reappearance after 76 years, of the comet that now bears his name. One of the most brilliant men of his very talented generation, he was described by Isaac Newton in 1687 as 'the most acute and universally learned Mr. Edmond Halley'. Halley was a very active Fellow of the Royal Society and he spoke at their meetings on many different subjects, one of which was diving whose problems and challenges had intrigued him ever since he like everyone else had been astonished by the success of Captain Phips' expedition to the Silver Bank. In a paper read before the Society on 28 January 1691, he spoke with admiration of the Indian divers who had worked on the Spanish wreck and were able to stay under water for several minutes. 'But in this case the diver is obliged to do all he does holding his breath, which must needs take away the liberty of action, and grows still more and more uneasie till such time as he can endure it no longer.' Halley was therefore determined 'to contrive a means to be under water and move there breathing all the while'.[30]

His most important contribution to the improvement of the bell was the development of a system of supplying fresh air to the divers. This was done with a pair of barrels, weighted with lead so that they would sink, and fitted with bungholes at top and bottom, the top one having a leather hose with a tap attached. The barrel was filled with air and then plugged and lowered to the bell where one of the divers would take the end of the hose, place it below the bell and open the tap, while another diver opened a cock in the top of the bell. The water pressure forced the fresh air in the barrel into the bell and this drove the stale air out through the top of the bell, causing impressive turbulence in the water above. The barrel was then raised to the surface and refilled with air so that they could start all over again. Using two barrels in sequence, it was possible to keep a constant supply of fresh air and at the same time maintain the level of water in the bell to a minimum. The barrels also provided a means of communicating with the surface. 'By the return of the air-barrels he sent up orders, wrote with an iron pen on small pieces of lead, directing where the bell was to be moved.'[31]

Halley first spoke of this ingenious system in January 1691 but he did not, in fact, invent it, since something very similar had been used by Andreas Peckell in his salvage of the guns of the *Vasa* in the 1660s and it had also been discussed in 1672 by George Sinclair in his description of the 'Diving-ark', a sort of bell, in his book *The Hydrostaticks*. 'If a man were necessitated to tarry a pretty while below, fresh air might be sent down from above, in bottles or bladders.' Sinclair must have been just about the first writer to suggest diving as a leisure pursuit, when he recommended 'the ark for pleasure and recreation as well as profit'. Halley, who was exceptionally well read, probably knew this work, but like many inventors he was reluctant to acknowledge his debts and it is always his name which is associated with this important innovation.[32]

Soon after he gave his paper to the Royal Society, Halley was to have a chance to test his theories. On 4 April 1691, the *Guinea Frigate*, a ship belonging to the Royal African Company, was wrecked at Pagham near Chichester in Sussex. This Company's main business was the shipment and sale of slaves to the West Indian planters, but the wrecked ship was not a slaver and had sailed direct to England from West Africa with a cargo valued at £100,000 of which £20,000 was in gold. The crew were saved and so was the gold which was sent up to London with an armed escort and there sold to the Mint who turned it into golden guineas. But the rest of the cargo, redwood, beeswax and no less than forty-two tons of ivory or elephants' teeth, was lost.[33]

Halley approached the committee set up by the Company to negotiate with potential salvors and persuaded them that he would be able to salvage the wreck with the help of a new type of bell which he had invented. By the end of May this bell was completed and was demonstrated on the Thames. 'There was tried this weeke an experiment of a new engine for diving for wreck, the inventor exposing himself in person in the first essay . . . The figure which encloses the diver is in the form of a bell and an expedient to convey with it barrells of ayre for the divers' better subsistence in the deepe.' The bell was then taken down to the wreck but, on its first trial, the hawser which was to lower it into the sea was found to be defective and 'the casks [i.e. air barrels] likewise prove not so well as expected'. When these teething problems had been overcome the bell was successfully lowered and Halley himself, a man in his early thirties, went down in it to inspect the wreck.[34]

Halley described his invention in detail in a paper called 'A Relation of the Diving Bell' which was read to the Royal Society on 23 September 1691. The bell was five feet deep and five feet in diameter at the bottom and three at the top and was weighted with sufficient lead to balance the displaced water and so make its movement in the water relatively easy. It had a stage slung on ropes thirty inches below for the men to stand on when they were working and a bench inside on which they could sit, dry-shod, when they were cold. There was a window in the top of the bell made of very thick but clear glass 'which let in light so effectually that, being in the bell, he could read the small print of the advertisement of a *Gazette*'. There was also a small cock 'to let out the hott and effete air unfitt for further respiration'. At this stage Halley seems to have used only one barrel of air, capable of holding forty gallons, coated with lead, and fitted with a bung hole underneath and a cock above. 'By this means', he boasted, 'I have kept three men an hour and three-quarters under the water and in ten fathoms deep without any the least inconvenience and in as perfect freedom to act as if they had been above.'[35]

Staying down at that depth for so long would have made the divers liable to the bends or decompression illness. But this condition was unknown in Halley's day and any resulting discomfort would probably have been attributed to rheumatism. The only drawback of diving which Halley mentions was the 'forceable and painful pressure upon our ears' as the bell was let down, 'which grew worse and worse till something in the ear gave way to the air to enter', a sensation familiar enough to regular air travellers. The means of circumventing the cold in the waters off the Sussex coast was 'a costume of waxed canvas lined with fur', as we learn from a letter written by Constantyn Huygens to his brother Christiaan, the famous Dutch physicist. Halley also told him how clearly he could see under water which had enabled him 'to encounter every sort of fish which could be found in those parts'. Halley was intrigued by the two types of light in the bell, pale sea green 'by reflection from the water under the bell' and a pale cherry colour when bright sunlight shone through the window above. He had absolutely no doubt as to the efficacy of his innovation which, if made larger, would be able to maintain any number of men 'for as long time and at as great a depth as shall be desired'.[36]

Papers to the Royal Society, a demonstration on the Thames before an invited audience of fine ladies and gentlemen, and the general buzz of interest as to what the famous Edmond Halley was doing down in Sussex, all provided an ideal background to the patenting and marketing of the invention, since even a Fellow of the Royal Society is not necessarily immune to an interest in making money. Halley acquired three wealthy backers headed by Sir Stephen Evance, a goldsmith-banker who was one of the most prominent promoters of the age with interests in mining, both in England and the colonies, privateering, the fisheries and government loans. On 31 August 1691 the syndicate applied for a grant for 'a certain new engine, never yet known, whereby, by conveying of air into the diving vessel, they can maintain several persons at the same time to live and work safely under water, at any depth, for many hours together'. The letters patent were granted on 7 October and Halley and his partners immediately turned the invention into a joint-stock company with six hundred shares. This company, incorporated by the name of 'The Governor and Company for recovering of wrecks in England', was one of five whose shares were quoted and traded on the fledgling London Stock Exchange in the first half of the 1690s, the others being companies exploiting the inventions of John Williams, Joseph Williams, John Tyzacke and John Overing.[37]

Halley's diving-bell, as described above, was to be used with some modifications into the second half of the eighteenth century. The same is probably not true of two other improvements to the bell which he suggested at the same time. The first was a method of making the structure more mobile by fitting it with 'four wheels of brass and lead' and making the bell and all its equipment of such a weight that 'when put under water [it will] be very near equiponderate [of equal weight] with it, and consequently be moveable there with a small force'. No more is heard of this and all the bells on which there is information before the second half of the eighteenth century were moved from above in response to signals from the divers and not by the divers themselves. The other invention was intriguing and appears in almost every illustration of Halley's bell. This was 'the capp of maintenance', a small open helmet worn by the diver down to below his shoulders when he wanted to work outside the structure. Air was supplied by a pipe from the diving-bell to the diver's cap. Although it would certainly have been a very useful innovation if a diver working outside no longer had to hold his breath, it seems unlikely that the cap of maintenance could have been very effective, since air could only pass upwards under water and so 'the travelling diver', as Halley called him, would have to be above the water level in the bell. This is a rather unlikely scenario, though it might be feasible for a diver working on the deck of a sunken ship with the bell on the sea bottom. One certainly never hears of such a mini-bell being employed in later years and divers who emerged from bells under water were still having to hold their breath in the 1820s.[38]

Halley's design was to be a great success and have a long life, but it was not successful in salvaging the *Guinea Frigate*. Halley told Sir Hans Sloane that, when they had first gone down on the wreck in the bell, they had a perfect view of the ship and all about it. But they were unable to get at the cargo and 'in a very short time [the wreck] was almost covered with sand and oase [ooze, i.e. mud or slime], so that the project of recovering the teeth was frustrated'. Halley, or more often his employees, were to work on the wreck without success every summer season until 1696 when the Royal African Company sought to agree with other divers to salvage their goods. They contracted with no less than seven different companies, two of which, those of Francis Smartfoot and Francis Ball, have made an appearance in this chapter. None were successful and, on 16 August 1698, 'the wreck of the Guynie Frigate lost near Chichester with 42 tuns of elephants' teeth' was knocked down at auction for £400. The wreck was to remain a challenge to divers for decades to come but, despite much effort to locate them, those teeth are probably still there, deep in the Sussex sand and mud, the product of a very large number of elephants who had probably not been killed by men, but had died in elephants' graveyards which were periodically raided by native traders who went into these desolate places to pick up 'the elephants' teeth which lay scattered up and down there'.[39]

Only one of the seventeen applications in the 1690s diving-engine boom was submitted with a drawing. This was the invention of John Williams of Exeter, not to be confused with the Cornishman Joseph Williams, which has been described by three different historians of diving as 'a diving tower', a 'mobile well' and a prototype 'caisson'. It consisted of a rectangular wooden chamber which rested on the seabed and was connected to the surface by a narrower wooden tube with a ladder inside and open to the air at the top. The chamber had four portholes and eight armholes fitted with leather gauntlets through which the operators could hopefully do some work, using hooks and other tools lowered down outside the apparatus. This seems a rather clumsy and impractical piece of equipment which would only work successfully, if at all, in shallow and very calm water, though Williams with the usual exaggeration of the inventor claimed that four men could work in the chamber for twelve hours 'fifteen fathoms [90 feet] and more under water in the sea'.[40]

John Williams was almost certainly one of the many fraudulent projectors who hoped to profit from the public's gullibility during the patent boom. In 1695, a linen-draper called Ebenezer Dunston complained in the Court of Chancery that he was being wrongfully sued for payment of a bond that he had given to John Williams who pretended 'to be a skilful engineer in the art of diveing and takeing up wrecks out of the sea'. Williams, like Halley, had divided his patent into six hundred shares which he sold for £20 each and he was busily engaged in trying to raise more money on these shares, even though he had made no attempt to improve or to use the engine and had absconded. Williams' London agent, a goldsmith, was also not very impressed and he gave evidence that the patentee had been a merchant of Exeter 'of good credit and esteem', but his diving engine had 'turned to a very bad account'. The historian Zélide Cowan quotes a piece from the *Flying Post* which suggests that the invention had, in fact, been put into operation. 'John Williams . . . did take up great quantities of guns, bar-iron and other goods, but being chased, twice sunk and three times taken by the French, had been forced to desist from any other attempts during the war.' But this ludicrous piece of puffery was surely just John Williams' attempt to excuse his failure to make his invention a reality.[41]

The dishonesty of inventors such as the two Williams, and no doubt others whose financial trickery is now lost in the great archival morass of the records of the Courts of Chancery and Exchequer, gave the whole patent system a bad name. Daniel Defoe, though a passionate advocate of some innovation, complained of those projectors who 'cry up an empty notion to that degree that people have been betrayed to part with their money in a New-Nothing; and when the inventors have carried on the jest till they have sold all their own interest, they leave the cloud to vanish of itself'. Later he mocked the gullibility of the public. 'The diver shall work at the bottom of the Thames . . . till funds are raised to carry it on, by men who have more money than brains, and then good night patent and invention, the proprietor has done his business and is gone.'[42]

The anonymous author of *Angliae Tutamen* described the whole process of deception in a splendid piece of polemic written in 1695. His wonderful description of the different types of diving-engines appears as the epigraph at the head of this chapter and he goes on to describe the process of getting the letters patent, and then 'about making the engines they went, and after several alterations and amendments, which took up two or three years . . . they divided the whole project into four, and afterwards as many hundred shares, and presented some to people of note and figure, to give reputation to the affair, and these doughty names were subscribed to play the part of a shooing-horn . . . to bring their friends and acquaintance to see the engines, who were tickled in the ear with the vast wealth of gold and silver that should be taken out of the sea with these tools; and being led by an avaricious desire of growing rich on a sudden, they came in and were engaged, paid down their money, and had the pleasure to see . . . expeditions sent forward . . . up and down upon our coasts; and the mighty achievements they performed, was taking up a few iron-guns, chimney-backs, and ship's-tackle, which answered not the end . . . and stopped the further prosecution of the affair. So these fine diving-engines lie by the walls, are at rest, and, for ought I know, may never more disturb the world with their noise and nonsense.'[43]

There was clearly much truth in this spirited attack on the projectors. Booms will always attract tricksters eager to defraud the gullible. But not all inventors and not all projectors were dishonest and not all diving-engines were left propped up against walls. Some of the inventions, most notably Halley's bell and Smartfoot's sea-crab, were to have long and useful lives and the diving-engine boom was to lead to a huge increase in the number of divers and diving companies in England, as can be illustrated by the seven separate companies who applied to work on the wreck of the *Guinea Frigate* after Halley's men had given up. This could not have happened before 1690 when there were few people in England who could dive at all, let alone have any chance of recovering anything from a wreck.

In the 1690s, when there was an opportunity there were divers and salvors ready to rise (or rather sink) to the challenge. On 6 August 1695, for instance, Narcissus Luttrell reported the loss of the *Henry* East-Indiaman off the Irish coast and, two days later, he wrote that 'several persons, with diving engines, are gone for Ireland to endeavour to recover the lost goods of the *Henry* from the East Indies; they are to have for their pains a 4th part of what they gett up'. And this was not just journalistic puffery, as can be seen from the records of the East India Company which reported that the owners of the ship were 'using all possible means for the recovery and getting up of the goods . . . sunk in Dingley Bay' and much was, in fact, later recovered.[45] Salvage of this kind was to be the main employment of divers and diving-engines in the future, but not just yet. The lure of treasure hunting had not yet lost its attraction, despite many disappointments.

Chapter Six

A Long Story

Chapter Six

A Long Story

"You are to saile, wind and weather permitting, without loss of time, to such place or places in America where you know or shall judge such treasure and wrecks may be or are most likely to be found, and there use your best endeavour for discovering and recovering the same."[1]

The end of war with France in 1697 brought a renewed interest in treasure hunting, given that there was no longer any danger of salvage vessels being seized by a French privateer. Peace also meant there was less strain on the nation's naval resources, making it possible for two royal ships to be employed in treasure hunting on the model of the men-of-war which had been engaged to search for the wreck of the *Concepción* in the 1680s. Both these ships were to operate within the search area granted in February 1693 to 'Our Right Trusty and Right Intirely Beloved Cousin and Councillor Mainhardt, Duke of Leinster', a vast area which covered all wrecks in America between the latitudes of ten degrees south and forty degrees north, with the exclusion of such areas 'where grants of the like have been already made'. Since these limits went from just north of Lima, in Peru, to just south of New York, 'by computation one thousand and forty leagues or 3,120 miles', the Duke was certainly justified in describing his search area as 'a considerable quantity of sea room to fish in for wrecks'.[2]

The fortunate recipient of this amazing grant was one of King

William III's military favourites, Meinhard Schomberg, later Duke of Leinster and Schomberg, son of the 1st Duke of Schomberg, one of the most distinguished European soldiers of the late seventeenth century. Father and son were military adventurers who had served in the armies of Portugal, France and Prussia before coming over to serve King William III in Ireland where the father was killed at the Battle of the Boyne in July 1690 and the son was distinguished 'by the fury by which he sought to avenge his father's death'. 'He is one of the hottest, fiery men in England . . . brave, but capricious', wrote John Macky, spy and keen observer of his fellow men. He was also far from well off and, when he was made Duke of Leinster, Queen Mary graciously reduced the fees payable by half 'on account of the smallness of his fortune'. No doubt the Queen expected to be more than repaid from the royal tenth payable on all recoveries made within the Duke's vast treasure hunting grant, since the world had been assured that 'there are no lesse than twenty millions of plate and of gold and silver . . . computed to be in those wrecks already discovered within the limits aforesaid'.[3]

Treasure hunting might be expected to appeal to a man who was capricious, hot-tempered and short of money and the Duke straightaway set about exploiting his grant. A committee was appointed to manage the affair and this was headed by Sir James Houblon, a wealthy Huguenot merchant with Spanish connections who had influence at the Admiralty and in the banking world. These managers advised the Duke to divide his grant into 1,600 shares, reserving 608 for himself, while the rest were distributed to partners or sold off for £20 a share to those who made their way to the Black Bull in Cornhill on Thursday afternoons, where 'his Grace's trustees and managers' were pleased to receive 'all persons that desire to be interested in the said wrecks, or have anything to offer relating thereto'. The money thus raised was used to buy and fit out two ships for an expedition to work on the wrecks. Either the Duke, or his committee, also acquired an interest in John Overing's newly invented diving engine which, as has been seen above, was demonstrated on several occasions in the Thames 'to the great satisfaction of the Duke of Leinster'.[4]

All must have seemed very promising to the Duke, his managers and the shareholders, but alas they were to be disappointed. Before the ships despatched on the expedition could get started on any of the wrecks, they were captured by 'some French men of war and hereby and by the continuance of the war the working on these wrecks hath been suspended, whereby the shares fell from £20 to £5 a share'. The Duke must have been pleased that it was not his money invested in the expedition and even happier when, in November 1696, Parliament granted him the huge income of £4,000 per annum out of the revenues of the Post Office, 'being the interest at 4 per cent of £100,000 awarded to his father in consideration of his great services'. Grants from Parliament were a far more reliable way of shoring up a Duke's resources than searching for treasure.[5]

Now assured of a handsome income, the Duke and his advisers decided that in future they would not go treasure hunting in their search area themselves, but would license others to do so in return for a percentage of the recoveries. The first person to submit a successful proposal was Captain Richard Long, a man already known to the Duke's management committee, since in April 1695 he had been assigned one twentieth of all treasure which should be recovered as a result of information given by him about the location of wrecks. Nothing seems to have come of this but, in May 1697, Captain Long reappeared on the treasure hunting scene, having persuaded King William of 'the probability hee had of discovering where gold might be found in America, in a part where no Europeans have ever settled upon, as also that hee was credibly informed where two plate wrecks lay in the West Indies, and hee had good hopes of recovering great part of their treasure'. The King was sufficiently impressed to order the Treasury to draw up a contract with Long and the Admiralty to supply him with a sixth-rate frigate.'[6]

Richard Long was a man who turns up in a number of curious places in the records of the late seventeenth century. He has, in fact, already appeared in this book as one of those who gave evidence in 1692 as to the reality of the Ireland Island treasure in Bermuda. At that time he said he was 36 years old, so was born about 1656, and he was described as the Quaker master of a trading ship. He claimed to have obtained his information about the Bermuda treasure from an elderly Spaniard whom he had met while a slave in Algiers in 1683. Prior to that there is evidence of him trading on the Caribbean coast of central America in the late 1670s and, during this period of his life, he seems to have acquired a good understanding of Spanish and a very good knowledge of the coast and the haunts of the buccaneers, though being a Quaker he probably did not fight with them himself. Many people were to say rude things about Richard Long, but no one doubted his knowledge and skill as a navigator, a reputation endorsed in 1701 by Admiral John Benbow, commander-in-chief in the West Indies and one of the most respected admirals in the navy, who recommended Long as 'a very knowing man in those parts'. Long also prided himself on being a 'conjuror' and he was known as 'Conjuring Dick Long'. This is a difficult word to interpret, as it had several different contemporary meanings, but it was most commonly applied to someone who could predict the future as a result of 'conjuring' the Devil. This would certainly have been a useful skill, but it seems unlikely that Long would have behaved as he did if he really had been able to predict his future, so maybe the verdict of someone who met him in the course of his expedition was correct. 'We could by no means find him the Conjuror he gives himself for.'[7]

This then was the man who signed very impressive articles of agreement with the representatives of King William III on 6 July 1697. There were two different aims for Long's proposed expedition, the 'mines of gold and silver or other treasure in America not possessed by Christians' and 'certain wrecks in America', and these were treated as separate ventures in his articles of agreement. In return for the provision of a ship, the King was to have the first £10,000 arising from the mines project and then, for the next seven years, 'nine parts of the whole discovery, the remaining tenth part to be reserved to Richard Long, and after seven years the King to have the whole'. The King would also receive one-tenth as his royalty from any treasure recovered in the wreck project, while Long had agreed for his own share with the trustees for the Duke of Schomberg and Leinster and was to be given one hundred of the 1,600 shares, or one-sixteenth, exactly the same share that had been granted to Captain William Phips in July 1685. This was no doubt intentional, since such shares were normally governed by precedent and one must hope that Richard Long was contented with the deal he had made.[8]

The ship supplied by the Admiralty was the *Rupert Prize*, a fairly small, shallow-draught frigate which had been captured from the French in 1692. She was armed with eighteen guns and had a crew of seventy men and Long assured the King's officers that, despite his religion, 'if any did stop me I would defend myself and keep the ship in order fitt for it'.[9] While fitting out in England, Long changed his surgeon's mate for 'another who is likewise a chymist and understands mines' and he also made sure he had what he needed for the wreck project, taking aboard divers, tongs, drags and an unspecified 'engine'. He asked for and received permission to go ashore during his expedition 'with as many as twenty armed men, besides two artists in metals', in order to search for the mines, and he was also granted the power to give commissions to Indian chiefs, 'knowing that the name of a commission from the King of England would buoy up their fancyes to assist me in this gold design'. Long seems to have been trusted completely by the King and his ministers. Unusually for an expedition of this sort, he had no agent from the Treasury aboard to keep an eye on him and his accounts and he was given complete freedom to do as he pleased. 'The King leaves the Contractor free to pursue his voyage in such manner as he thinks best.' As usual, fitting out and all the necessary arrangements took a long time and it was not until 10 May 1698 that James Vernon, the Secretary of State, forwarded the King's instructions and wished Long 'a good voyage, and all success in your intended expedition'. And it was nearly a month later, on 4 June, that the *Rupert Prize* actually sailed from Spithead for Madeira and the West Indies.[10]

Although Long had a commission to exploit wrecks as well as mines, there is no doubt that, in his mind, it was the latter, and especially gold mines, that took priority. Indeed, it would be fair to say that he was obsessed with central American gold mines and was determined that England, and so himself, should profit from them. This was by no means an empty fantasy for this region had been famous for its gold, both alluvial gold from the rivers and gold dug out of mines, since the very beginning of Spanish settlement in the Caribbean. Two areas attracted Long in particular, the Cape Grace de Dios river [Cabo Gracias á Dios now modern Coco River] which is now the boundary between Honduras and Nicaragua and, best of all, the Isthmus of Darien, the wild mountainous land between Panama and Colombia which, to the intrepid, offered a passage between the Caribbean and the Pacific.

There was certainly plenty of gold in Darien. In 1620 the Spanish traveller Antonio Vázquez de Espinosa described the mines along the Rio Chocó in Darien as the 'richest in gold in the Indies'. Later in the century it was those of Santa Maria which attracted attention. These were also described as the richest in the Indies and were high up in the mountains on the river of that name which flowed into the Gulf of San Miguel on the Pacific side of the isthmus. There was a settlement here for the Spanish soldiers who guarded the mines and the Indian and black miners and here too, in the dry season when the waters were low, other Indians would bring gold dust which they had panned from the many gold-bearing rivers in the mountains. Such a place was an obvious target for predators and the mines of Santa Maria were seized by the buccaneers, under Captain Bartholomew Sharpe, as they crossed the isthmus in April 1680 on their way to maraud in the Pacific. No doubt they made a terrible noise as they laboured through the mountains and so gave warning to the Spanish for, when they arrived, they learned that just three days previously a boat carrying three hundredweight of gold had made its way down the river to Panama and there was very little left for them to loot.[11]

As a trader in the Caribbean and a frequent visitor to Jamaica, Richard Long would have been familiar with the story of this buccaneer raid on the mines of Santa Maria and he probably had a very good idea of just where they were sited. However, there were others, much easier of access from the Caribbean, which were to become his first interest. These were the mines of Canea or Cany, later to be called the 'Golden Mountain', which were discovered in 1687 by an Indian who unwisely gave the secret away to the Spaniards. By the time of Long's visit there were said to be five in total, 'the biggest thereof employs eight hundred negroes, and one or two hundred a piece in the two lesser. The others they have not opened for want of hands to worke in them.' Long was not certain where these mines were, but he believed they lay up one of the tributaries of the Rio Grande del Darien (modern Atrato), the great river which flowed into the Gulf of Darien and so into the Caribbean.[12]

On 8 October 1698 the *Rupert Prize* dropped anchor at the eastern end of the San Blas archipelago, a major rendezvous for the buccaneers and a place giving easy access to the isthmus of Darien. Long was to remain on this coast for nearly two months, slowly making his way further south and east to the Isle of Pines and the Gulf of Darien. His objectives were to find out more about the whereabouts of Canea and other mining areas, to determine the political divisions amongst the local Indian chiefs and to make friends with those who seemed most powerful or likely to be useful to him. Judging by the one-sided evidence of his journal and report, this was very easy to do. The Indians of Darien were volatile in their political affiliations, but had been inclined to be friendly with anyone who was hostile to the Spanish since the days of Drake in the late sixteenth century and Long was to find them still friendly, more so indeed than when he had paid a visit there in the late 1670s and been fired upon as he tried to come ashore. The only really hostile tribe were apparently the Chuckoes, a people also singled out as dangerous by the buccaneer travel writer William Dampier. According to Long's informants, they were at war with all the other Indians 'and sometimes come down the great river by moonlight nights and kill them by surprise'.[13]

But there was no such trouble with any other tribe and Long spent much of his time making visits ashore, two days here, three days there, in which he plied the locals with presents and huge quantities of liquor, pumped them for information, and assured them of his love and of that of the King of England. Such visits were reciprocated by the Indians, some of whom brought their wives and children aboard with them, and the *Rupert Prize* often rocked to the drunken parties and assurances of mutual trust and affection which ensued. The most important of the local chiefs was

Captain Ambrosio, 'a valiant Indian', whose power-base was inland from where Long had made his first landfall. Long got on well with him, as he later informed his masters in England. 'This Indian showed me abundance of respect when I was there, often takeing me in his arms and it was with him I first made the peace.'[14]

Even more important to Long's plans was Captain or Prince Diego who commanded five thousand men in the lands at the head of the Gulf of Darien. Friendship with him was essential if the English were to have passage through his territory to the gold mines of Canea and this was achieved during a four day visit to his 'town' at the beginning of November. Diego was very hostile to the Spanish and agreed to rise against them with all his men if Long would bring fifty armed men from his ship. This agreement was confirmed at the end of the month when Long went ashore with four people from his crew, two of them a married couple, who were to remain as hostages. Captain Diego showed them a good place for an English settlement by the river and Long himself cut down the first tree, before departing to rejoin his ship, leaving Midshipman William Trenwith, 'of good sense and the fittest person I had with me for such an undertaking', to raise the ensign of St George and take command of this lonely English outpost in the wet and mosquito-ridden wilds of Darien. Long was later to interpret this minute settlement as English 'possession' of Darien, an act of pre-emption which he believed would be sufficient 'to prevent any design of the French' on the area, though it seems doubtful whether the French (or indeed the Spanish) would have shared his interpretation of international law.[15]

The establishment of this small settlement was the last thing Long did before he set sail on 3 December 1698 along the coast of the Spanish Main and then north to Jamaica. He claimed later in letters and in his report that he left Darien because of the danger from the Spanish Armada de Barlovento (Windward fleet), the squadron which had the unenviable duty of clearing the coasts of Spanish America of pirates, buccaneers, clandestine traders and other miscreants. This is probably true, but it seems unlikely that Long had ever seriously envisaged making a raid on the mines himself. If he had really sent fifty of his men, as promised to Prince

Diego, that would have left just twenty to guard the ship, an unacceptable risk for a man who had been loaned a royal ship for private purposes. What he probably hoped was that, armed with his new knowledge of the mines and his 'treaties' and friendship with important Indian chiefs, he would be able to persuade people in Jamaica or elsewhere to send out an expedition with him as guide and major shareholder. But that, as we shall see, was never to be.

Richard Long's visit to Darien was complicated by the coincidence, if it was one, that he was there at the same time as the ships and men of the ill-fated Company of Scotland. The Act of Union with England was some years off and the Company was Scotland's misguided and poorly conceived attempt to emulate her southern neighbour's wealth by setting up as an imperial trading power. Ships were purchased to create a powerful merchant fleet to compete with the East India Companies of England, France and Holland, and a colony was to be established in Darien, a place described by William Paterson, the main promoter of the idea, as 'this door of the seas and the key of the universe', the vital link between Pacific and Atlantic in Scotland's projected worldwide trade.[16]

Sadly this scheme, which was crazier than anything that floated about in Richard Long's brain, caught the imagination of the people of Scotland and the Company was able to finance itself with their meagre savings, all of which would be lost, and to raise over a thousand men and women to settle in Darien, most of whom would die in the ships or in the rain-sodden, insect-ridden and feverous place where they decided to make their settlement. The Company of Scotland was doomed from the start and its history is a sorry story of ill-informed decisions, poor leadership and internal disputes, but its end was also speeded by understandable Spanish hostility and by the fairly predictable refusal of the English government to do anything to assist this potential trading competitor.

The five ships of the Company's first fleet reached the coast of Darien on the evening of 28 October 1698, some three weeks after Richard Long and the *Rupert Prize* had made their landfall. Long took them, at first, for the Spanish Armada de Barlovento and kept out of their way, but he soon realized that they were the Scots who, despite rather pitiful attempts to maintain secrecy as to their plans, had been expected. Long paid two courtesy visits to the Scottish ships and these were reciprocated with a visit by some of the Scots officers to the *Rupert Prize*. The Scots were naturally puzzled as to just what Long was doing on the coast. Was he, for instance, a spy sent by the English government to report on the Scottish colony?[17] Liquor flowed freely during these shipboard visits as each side tried to get the other drunk enough to give away important information. Long could claim to have won these drunken contests since his reports contained more accurate information about the Scots than theirs did about him. They seem, for instance, to have believed his assurances that he was mainly interested in searching for wrecks and, although they knew about Long's treaties with the Indians and the existence of the gold mines, they did not put two and two together and realize that the idea of raiding the latter was Long's driving passion. If they had they might well have joined him, since such a plan promised a much greater chance of success than trying to establish a colony in Darien.

Long may have fooled the Scots but he certainly did not impress them, despite his report that 'ye Scotch gentlemen treated me very nobly in respect to his Majesty's commission'. Hugh Rose, the Secretary of the Company of Scotland, was certainly respectful of Long's commission, but had doubts as to why he had been granted it. 'What others have found or may think of Lang [*sic*] we know not, but he appears to us to be of no great reach.' The Commodore of the Scots fleet, Captain Robert Pennecuik, was more explicit in his journal. 'Whatever the King or Government of England may have found in Captn Long we know not, but to us in all his conversation he appear'd a most ridiculous shallow-pated fellow, laught at and despis'd to his very face by his owne officers and continually drunk . . . He has a very large and ample commission, which oblidges all Governors of islands, Captains of ships etc. to be aiding and assisting to him in case he finds any wrack. This he gives out to have been his principall designe.'[18]

Long arrived back in Port Royal, Jamaica in January 1699 and, drunk or not, proceeded to careen his ship and get her ready for his principal design of wreck hunting. He also took the opportunity to write two lengthy letters back to England, one to the Board of Trade and one to the Duke of Leeds, Lord President of the Council, reporting quite favourably on the Scots and praising himself for his foresight in pre-empting both the Scots and the French by making treaties with the Indians in Darien.[19] He then sailed to Blewfields in south-west Jamaica where Rear Admiral Benbow and three ships of the English West Indian fleet were at anchor. Benbow had a good opinion of Long and was one of the few people in authority who considered the idea of raiding the mines a good one, though he thought it wise to wait until England was at war with Spain which seemed likely to happen fairly soon. In the meantime, he ordered Long 'to look after a wreck' which lay on a reef 'fifty-five leagues S ½E of Blewfields in the latitude of 15.45 degrees north'. Long reached this reef on the evening of 20 February 1699 and he spent just one day searching for the wreck in his longboat in conditions which he considered 'very rocky and dangerous . . . but I could not find any thing'. Judging by the latitude and the direction he sailed, this reef was probably the Serranilla Bank and the wreck may be the same one that had foiled the Jamaican sloop men in 1691. It is obvious, however, that it did not hold much interest for Long and, having done the very minimum consistent with Benbow's orders, he set sail for the place where he had been 'credibly informed . . . two plate wrecks lay'.[20]

In the papers relating to Richard Long's application for a wreck hunting commission, there is no information given as to which two Spanish 'plate wracks' he wanted to search for. So it is in a spirit of discovery that we follow his voyage in his logbook, from the Serranilla Bank to the Cayman Islands where some repairs were done to his boats, past Cape San Antonio on the west end of Cuba and so towards Florida along the normal homeward path of the galleons from Havana. Long went ashore on the east coast of Florida, looking for wood, water, information and possibly divers, and then headed south and west along the Florida Keys to 'Markees Kees' (Marquesas Keys or Cayos del Marques). This destination provides the clue for his target since these keys west of Key West

were named after the Marquis of Cadereita, the commander of the
ill-fated 1622 treasure fleet, who set up camp here during the search
for the *Santa Margarita* and *Nuestra Señora de Atocha* and their
treasures. These ships are never named by Long, and we do not
learn how he had discovered the approximate location of the two
wrecks from which 'hee had great hopes of recovering great part of
their treasure'.[21]

Long was to spend most of April and May 1699 searching
intermittently for these wrecks, though his journal does not give
much detailed information. The work was done by parties of ten
or fifteen men in the longboat and two canoes who spent periods
from four to fourteen days on the banks, with occasional visits back
to the anchored *Rupert Prize* for food, water and, most
importantly, rum and sugar for their punch. The actual searching
was done mainly by the two canoes dragging a weighted cable
between them, a technique known as 'sweeping', with divers ready
to investigate anything they snagged. Hopes were high on the
weekend of 20–21 May when Long made his most 'diligent search
upon ye bank', but there was to be no success even though he
assured whoever might read his journal that 'if there had been a
shilling in the way, there was none with me but might have seen it
both Saturday Sunday and Monday'. On the following day Long
upped anchor and set off on the next stage of his odyssey, leaving
the wreck of the *Atocha* to be found on 20 July 1985 by the
American Mel Fisher and his salvage company Treasure Salvors.
Fisher, whose catch phrase was 'Today's the day!', took sixteen years
to find the 'mother lode' of the *Atocha* with the sophisticated
equipment available in the second half of the twentieth century.
Long spent about five or six weeks in 1699 on the same task but, try
as he would, no day was ever quite his day. Both treasure hunters
had faced the same overriding problem, a common one in the
search for wrecks. 'I have miscarry'd on the Marquisse wreck on
which I had so much dependance', wrote Long after his arrival
back in England a year later. 'The truth may be proved by the
records of Spaine that such a wreck lyes on ye shoals of Florida
which place I know myself to be well acquainted withal, but it is a
shifting sand whereof every storme drives the bancks one way the

next another way which is undoubtedly the cause of my miscarriage.'[22]

The last task which Long wanted to complete before returning to Jamaica, and so home, was to visit the lands of the Moskito Indians, on the coasts of Honduras and Nicaragua, to find out if there were sources of gold there as well. The Moskitos had always been friendly to the English and Long had no trouble in going ashore to pay visits and collect information. He received the most help from King Jearimia who controlled the lands around Cabo Gracias á Dios on the borders of modern Honduras and Nicaragua. From him he received optimistic reports as to the presence of gold up the great river which ran inland from the Cape, now called the Coco or Segovia river, and he made arrangements for a journey into the interior.[23]

On 11 August 1699, Long and thirteen men from his crew set sail up the river in the longboat 'upon a discovery', in company with the friendly King Jearimia. No journal exists for this expedition and Long has little to say about it in his surviving correspondence and reports. The truth is that it was such a terrible journey that he had no wish to remember it. His bald summary given to the Admiralty was that he had gone over three hundred miles up the river 'till floods prevented further passing'. The master of the *Rupert Prize*, John Twitt, remained at the mouth of the river, keeping communications open with Long by canoe until 9 September when he sailed to a safer anchorage, 'to secure ye ship by reason ye north time is coming', by which he meant the terribly destructive winds known as northers which blew down from the Gulf of Mexico at that time of year. A very sick Captain Long and his party eventually arrived back at the ship on 12 October, after two months absence; 'all had been sick at times by reason of the bad weather they had up the river and the great rains'. Two weeks later, they said farewell to King Jearimia and the *Rupert Prize* set sail for Jamaica where she arrived on 4 December 1699 after a terribly hard passage. Long and most of his men were still sick as he explained on his arrival home at Spithead on 12 May 1700 after his two years of unprofitable treasure hunting. 'The last time at Jamaica I did not write when I had an opportunity, for my selfe, clerk and most of

my men were sick. I had but four men in health at one time.'
Doing business in central America was not as easy as it might seem,
as the Scots, who had already abandoned their colony in Darien for
the second and final time, had also discovered.[24]

Back in England and with his health improved, Long set out on
a campaign to try to persuade someone in authority to back him
on a second voyage to Darien. He really did try hard, petitioning
the King, the Admiralty, the Board of Trade, the Speaker of the
House of Commons and the Duke of Leeds amongst others.
Petitions, letters and personal approaches were supported by copies
of his journal, complete with a very favourable account of just how
nice a place Darien was for a settlement, and a very beautiful map
of the Gulf of Darien which he had drawn himself and dedicated
to King William III. This map is replete with exciting annotations.
'Prince Diego's towne . . . who told me that the gold mines of
Canea were about four days journey off' and, at the top of the map,
'as neare as I can judge, the gold mines of Canea are hereabouts'.
But no one was interested. Richard Long had, after all, just proved
in a very expensive way that he was a failure and, in any case, the
disaster of the Scots had given the isthmus of Darien a bad name.[25]

The only man of authority with any time for Long was Admiral
Benbow in Jamaica and it was by his recommendation that Long
was commissioned in May 1701 as master of HM hulk *Lewis Prize*,
a sort of floating dockyard with sixteen shipwrights in her crew, in
which he sailed back to Jamaica, arriving there early in 1702. This
was a rather lowly command compared with the *Rupert Prize*, but
it was a command and it enabled him once again to get Admiral
Benbow interested in a raid on the gold mines. According to Long,
Benbow was so keen that he said he would go himself 'with the fleet
. . . as soon as warr was proclaimed. Then he would go in person
himself with 500 or 1,000 men . . . to take those gold mines.' We
only have Long's word for Benbow's enthusiasm, but it has the ring
of truth. Benbow was an adventurous man and all admirals in the
West Indies hoped to come away with plenty of money and what
could be better than the Admiral's share of a raid on a gold mine?
But Benbow's aggressive instincts were, in fact, to prevent him
joining in Long's proposed adventure. News of the declaration of

war against both France and Spain, in what was to be called the War of the Spanish Succession, reached Jamaica in July 1702 and a month later Benbow set sail to engage a French squadron in one of the most notorious actions in British naval history. Four of Benbow's seven captains refused to engage the enemy and two of them were later shot to death for cowardice, their funk being celebrated in a popular song:

> Says Kirby unto Wade: 'We will run; we will run',
> Says Kirby unto Wade: 'We will run.
> For I value no disgrace, nor the losing of my place,
> But the enemy I won't face, nor his gun, nor his gun.'

Benbow himself was as brave as ever, but was to die from wounds suffered in the battle which is usually known as 'Benbow's last fight'. And so Long lost his one and only patron. 'The Admiral's misfortune prevented his putting the [gold mines] design in execution', he was later sadly to reflect.[26]

Long's frustration was redoubled by the irony that, while Benbow was dying and he himself was piloting a royal ship to the Spanish city of Cartagena, nine sloops full of privateers from Jamaica had sailed to the Gulf of Darien on their way to take the mines of Canea. These men were nothing more than now respectable buccaneers who, the moment news of war reached Jamaica, had received commissions from Colonel Peter Beckford, Lieutenant Governor of Jamaica, to make war against the French and Spanish. They set sail on 24 July 1702 and on 19 August commenced their march to the mines in company with several hundred Indians, armed with lances, bows and arrows, exactly the plan that Long had proposed. The march into the interior was extremely arduous and required cutting their way through a dense forest, fording many fast-flowing rivers and climbing up and over several steep mountains, the highest of all being such 'as I thought Man could not be able to get up', recorded the privateer Davis who has left an account of the raid. 'Some of our men imagined it to be within a stone's throw of heaven, and would willingly have tarry'd there . . . supposing they should never come again so near the blissful region.' After eleven days of such hardship they reached the mines and the town which served them as a settlement. These were taken easily with much slaughter but, as in the buccaneer raid on Santa Maria in 1680, the absence of complete surprise meant disappointment in the amount of loot they were able to seize. They 'brought away about sixty-four pounds of gold', wrote Long who was well-informed as two of his former shipmates from the *Rupert Prize* were in the raiding party. 'They had not the expected success through their ignorance of the right methods to manage it', something which would not have happened if only he had been in the party.[27]

Long was certainly disgruntled not to have played a part in the raid, but he did not yet give up his hopes of getting something out of Darien. In November 1703, his frustration breaks through in a report to the Admiralty. 'I am still grieved to lye here upon a hulk and possessed of this belief that I know where several tunns of gold lyes, and [could] goe to the place to work upon it.' He informed his masters that he intended to lay his plan before the Earl of Nottingham, Queen Anne's Secretary of State, but he, like every-one else, was not interested.[28] Next year Long petitioned Prince George of Denmark, Queen Anne's husband and the Lord High Admiral, asking to be given another ship to complete his Darien design. He now had fresh information on sources of gold. 'There is a lake in Darien . . . there lies in it a great vallue of gold and it is yearly washed down from the mountains.' Later in the same petition he is at it again: 'There is a hill in Darien; it is not above six miles from the sea side, and there is a great many good reasons to be given that it is rich in gold.' But the Prince was no more interested in all this gold than the Secretary of State or Admiral William Whetstone, Benbow's replacement in Jamaica, who dismissed the tiresome Long from his command in September 1705. 'This day came aboard Capt. James Adlington with a commission by an order from Admiral Whetstone . . . having no manner of hearing why I should be turned out, so this is the end of my voyage in her Majestie's hulk Lewis Prize . . . now I design for England . . . if God permits.'[29]

Long still did not give up. In September 1706, back in London, he wrote to the Secretary of the Admiralty, full of plans as usual, and told them that he was just putting the finishing touches to a new map of Darien which he proposed to present to Prince George. Long was getting a bit crazy by now and said that 'if his royall hynes gives me his word I will show him upon the mapp [where] some tonns indeed of gold lyes'. Prince George gave no such word and so the map, an even more beautiful revision of the 1700 map, does not contain this information. However, in his dedication, Long promised once again to provide it 'if your Royal Highness shall please in person to demand it of me'. Meanwhile, the Prince had to be content with the exact location of the gold mines of Canea, the island behind which the Jamaican privateers hid their sloops when they went ashore and the, suspiciously straight, path which they travelled along to get to the gold mines.[30]

Two years later, Long was petitioning the Board of Trade again[31] and then, early in 1709, he played his last card with an approach to the Duke of Marlborough, Britain's great military hero whose victories over the French at Blenheim, Ramillies and Oudenarde led Long, and nearly everybody else, to imagine that peace between the warring nations was near at hand. Long was now earning his living as a merchant trading to the Low Coutries, but he had not of course forgotten Darien whose virtues he described in two letters to the Duke, in hyperbolical language worthy of the Company of Scotland. His plan now was for the Duke to include the British annexation of Darien in the peace treaty, humbly referring it to his Grace's wisdom, 'whether her Majesty has not a just right and title to that most valuable country, by what I transacted there'. Although 'my commission was to look for treasure', Long told the Duke, 'yet ye Gulf of Darien was the treasure I aimed of'. But Marlborough was no more interested in Darien than anyone else and so this treasure remained in Spanish hands, while Conjuring Dick Long was left with just memories and regrets to sustain him for the remaining eight years of his life.[32]

Chapter Seven

Captain Hunter's Treasure Hunt

Chapter Seven

Captain Hunter's Treasure Hunt

"Captain Hunter having given solemn assurances that he has actually been upon the place where there was a very considerable Spanish plate wreck . . . we conceived we had good ground to make humble application for a man of warr to go upon an expedition likely to be of nationall benefit."[1]

When Captain Long sailed into Port Royal, Jamaica, on 4 December 1699, he found five English men-of-war in the harbour. One of these was the HMS *Dolphin*, the second royal ship commissioned to search for treasure in the brief period of peace between the two great wars against the France of Louis XIV. She was commanded by Captain Collin Hunter who, after prolonged delays, was just about to start his treasure hunt as Long finished his. The two ships remained in Port Royal for nearly three months until, on 28 February 1700, they set sail together with five other men-of-war, Long on his way home and Hunter 'bound up ye north side of Hispaniola to look for a rack [wreck]'. And yet, in all this time, judging by their logbooks, reports and surviving correspondence, these two captains never met to discuss their mutual affairs. This indifference might be explained in Long's case by his illness, but Hunter was perfectly well and one can only surmise that this aloofness was a good indication that Captain Collin Hunter was a very strange man.[2]

Little is known of Hunter's background although he later claimed to have served in the Navy during most of the 1690s, 'in most stations till I had ye command of a machine'. A 'machine' was similar to a fireship, a small auxiliary vessel, and Hunter's machine the *Grafton* was very small indeed, a former merchant ship with no guns and just four men, so that promotion to command the *Dolphin*, with 32 guns and a crew of 90 or 100 men was a big step up.[3] Apart from this, all we know of Hunter is that he was familiar with the West Indies and that he had a suspicion of other people bordering on paranoia.

One man whom Hunter suspected of malice from the start was his own First Lieutenant, Nathaniel Champneys, a man with a more distinguished naval record than his captain, having been Lieutenant of other royal ships for seven years before his appointment to the *Dolphin*. He later claimed that he had received from Lord Orford, First Lord of the Admiralty, 'particular private orders' to keep an eye on Hunter and there could be some truth in this claim since he was summoned to the Admiralty shortly after taking up his post. Champneys was keen to emphasize that Hunter had been given command, not on account of his proven ability but because of the distinction of his backers. 'The said Captain [Hunter] is not knowne to the Admiralty on his own account, but on the account of other gentlemen whose honour is in a great measure pawned for the security and well doeing of his Majestie's ship.'[4]

These honourable gentlemen were headed by Charles Gerard, Earl of Macclesfield, the current head of a prominent Whig family who had suffered in the previous reign by their virulent opposition to King James II. They had been restored to all their honours by King William, but the Earl was still short of cash and so ready to listen to Samuel Travers, a shipowner to whom Collin Hunter had spun a typical treasure hunting story. Hunter had given Travers 'solemn assurances that he has actually been upon the place where there was a very considerable Spanish plate wreck and had received Spanish papers containing other great discoveries of the same kind, of all which he made affidavit before a Master in Chancery'. Contemporaries placed great value on affidavits sworn on oath in

Chancery and this plus the 'Spanish papers' were sufficient to establish Hunter in business. Money was raised to fit out an expedition, a contract was made with Sir James Houblon acting on behalf of the trustees of the Duke of Schomberg's treasure hunting patent, and the King was persuaded to instruct Lord Orford 'that it is his Majestie's pleasure a fifth-rate frigate go to the wreck which the Earl of Macclesfield is concerned in and proposes the *Dolphin* for that service'.[5]

Captain Hunter was busy fitting out his ship and testing some diving engines when we first hear of someone trying to upset his plans, a recurring theme of the Hunter saga, either in reality or in his imagination. On 29 September 1698 he wrote from Portsmouth to the Admiralty informing them 'that there are several mallitious reflections thrown upon my undertaking' and asked permission to come up to town to vindicate himself. A month later he was still busy justifying himself and had pinned the blame for the slander on one Captain Pollard who of course 'has deny'd that ever he said any thing'. What this is all about is not spelled out in Hunter's correspondence with the Admiralty, but it seems probable that he was being branded as a man who planned to use the King's ship for piracy once he was clear of home waters. The newswriter Narcissus Luttrell, for instance, reported inaccurately on a ship 'that was fitting up to fish upon a wreck in the West Indies' being arrested on 'suspicion she also designed to pyrate', and on at least two further occasions in the course of Hunter's expedition such suspicions about him were to be reiterated. Nothing could have seemed more likely in the second half of 1698, a period of almost epidemic piracy with Captain Kidd at large in the Indian Ocean, other pirates marauding in the Cape Verde Islands, the West Indies and along the North American coast and an attempted mutiny aboard HMS *Speedwell* at Barbados in August 1698. The mutineers had planned to kill the senior officers and sail for Madagascar, 'a place fitt for pleasant living for such as were pirates'. Who could say that Captain Hunter, in command of the King's fine frigate, did not have a similar pleasant life in mind? [6]

Hunter was able to clear himself of the pirate slander, but the authorities did not believe he could be completely trusted. In strong contrast to the freedom of manoeuvre granted to Captain Long, Hunter had to take aboard two minders or three if we include Lieutenant Champneys. Mr William Mill (or Mills) was appointed to look after the interest of the Earl of Macclesfield's syndicate and Mr Henry Oake was chosen by the Treasury as 'his Majestie's officer or agent to inspect the fishing for wrecks'. He was to keep strict accounts and to keep them secret from Captain Hunter 'or any other person' and for his 'care and trouble in the performance of this service' was to receive one per cent of the King's ten per cent interest in the undertaking. And in the event of Hunter's death, 'which God prevent', Oake was to take possession of the secret papers relating to the undertaking so that he could instruct whoever was appointed as Hunter's successor. Hunter's orders, which he received on 14 February 1699, required him to carry these two men as supernumeraries and 'permitt them quietly to do their business.' He was also ordered to sail to Barbados and then 'to use the best of your endeavours to find out and take up such wrecks', as described in his affidavit, 'and afterwards such other wrecks as you shall receive intelligence of'. It must have all seemed very simple as he set sail from Spithead for Madeira and Barbados on 21 February 1699, four and a half months after he had first reported his ship fully victualled and manned, thus setting a pattern of procrastination and delay which was to be maintained.[7]

Captain Hunter had some trouble with pirates near Madeira and he contrived to lose both his longboat and a small yacht intended as a consort on his way across the Atlantic, but his troubles did not really start until he arrived in Barbados where he was to spend no less than five months. At first all went well, as the *Dolphin* was careened and had her bottom cleaned in preparation for her treasure hunting expedition. But all this hard work could not disguise the growing antagonism between the Captain and Lieutenant Champneys. This came to a head early in May 1699 when Champneys complained about Hunter in a petition to the Admiralty which he copied to the Governor of Barbados. His main point was that his captain was dishonouring the Navy and the King by his failure to enforce the King's regulations and by his shockingly lax discipline which Champneys insultingly described as 'privateer methods'. Captain Hunter's 'private undertaking', he concluded, 'does not commissionate him to break the rules that all other King's Captains must obey'. The Lieutenant claimed that this petition was on behalf of 'the rest of the officers of the said ship', but the only two whose names appear were the purser James Cresswell, later dismissed for embezzlement, and the master Thomas Allin who was able to excuse himself on the grounds that 'they kept him fuddled ten days' until he signed the petition.[8]

Nearly two years later, Champneys' petition was deemed to be 'very seditious' at a court martial of the former purser. And it certainly seems rebellious, if not mutinous, to the neutral observer. Hunter naturally interpreted it this way and reported to the Admiralty that Champneys was puffed up with 'ambition, pride and malice'. 'His designe does plaine appear, he wants the command out of my hand.' The Lieutenant, he claimed, was planning to get control of the ship by killing both him and also William Mills, the agent of the syndicate who had financed the expedition. But Mills was not someone to trifle with and, on the evening of Sunday 7 May, he worsted Champneys in a sword fight ashore and the Lieutenant died of his wounds on the following day. Hunter was naturally very pleased at this removal of a serious obstacle to the progress of the voyage, but he did not thank Mr Mills for very long. 'That very day he [Champneys] came on shore, he engaged with Mr Mills who killed him', he wrote later in his report to the Admiralty. 'I have reason to believe (by the following transactions of the said Mills) that their chiefest quarrell was who should be Captain after they had turned me out.'[9]

Hunter was now to waste weeks in Barbados formally justifying himself to the Governor and Council against the aspersions in the petition, a process which took 'a great deal of time . . . because of their formal wayes of proceeding'. He also had to wait while Mills was tried for homicide, another long-winded process which ended in his acquittal on the grounds of self-defence. Hunter toyed with the idea of sailing and leaving Mills behind, but was checked by a friend who 'said that if I went away without the Company's agent, there would be great cause for people to believe what Mr Champneys had alledged, that I intended to runn away with the

King's shipp . . . soe that since it was but a week longer I promised to stay'. So it seems that the Lieutenant accused his Captain not just of behaving like a privateer but also of planning to turn pirate, the same malicious slander which had pursued him in London.[10]

One might have thought that, with the agent freed, the ship ready for sea and a brigantine acquired to replace the lost yacht as consort, the *Dolphin* would have now set out to look for treasure, but that was not the Hunter way. Rumours of pirates on the coast persuaded the Governor of Barbados that Hunter would be better employed in pursuing them than chasing wrecks and so he was sent off on a pirate hunting cruise. No pirates were seen or captured, but Hunter did seize a ketch running French brandy into Barbados contrary to the Navigation Acts. This he was entitled to do as a Royal Navy captain and he would have been hoping to earn some prize money from his seizure, but all he got on his return to Bridgetown was to be arrested himself at the suit of the master of the ketch and 'am here detained contrary to the express orders of . . . his Majesty'. Such arrests, even of the captains of royal ships, were not unusual in the West Indies but it was in Hunter's nature to see a plot behind his misfortune, though he was not quite sure where to place the blame. Was it the Governor seeking 'ye prize for himself' who was at fault? Or Mr Mills who thought he could take command of the *Dolphin* while Hunter was in prison? But, on reflection, Hunter was convinced that he had been the victim of a plot laid by a rival treasure hunting syndicate who 'the better to prevent my interfering with or molesting them used their utmost interest (though very villainous) to keep me here'.[11]

This may or may not have been true, but there certainly was another vessel in search of treasure in the eastern Caribbean at this time. This was the *Carlisle*, a powerful 36-gun ship fitted out by the Earl of Carlisle and other north country and Scottish lords and gentlemen. Her captain was John Breholt and, while Hunter was languishing in a Barbados prison, he had set sail from the same island on 11 August 1699 in company with two English men-of-war to engage in a hunt for Captain Kidd who was said to be seeking a safe haven in the Caribbean. Breholt joined in an exciting chase after pirates in the Virgin Islands and then parted from his naval consorts and sailed for Jamaica. Here he was well received by Admiral Benbow who arranged for the *Carlisle* to be escorted by warships on her way to Cuba where Captain Breholt 'was going on a wreck which was cast away about two years since off the Havana with great treasure'. One can conclude from this that Breholt was better than Hunter at getting on with the job, but it is difficult to see why he should have wanted to delay the *Dolphin* since the treasure she was seeking was certainly not on Cuba.[12]

After six weeks in custody, Captain Hunter 'made shift to get out of ye prison [i.e. escaped] and happily got on board' and his long enforced stay in Barbados at last came to an end. It was an undignified departure for the captain of a royal ship, with no time to revictual or water the *Dolphin* since the Provost Marshall had a 'posse to raise ye country to take me'.[13] He was able to take on water at St Lucia, where he arrived on 26 September 1699, but his plans to try and make up for lost time by sailing directly for the place where he had 'certain knowledge' of a wreck were thwarted by the refusal of merchants and officials in Antigua, Nevis and other islands to sell him any provisions on credit. This was not a particular slight on Hunter, but simply the result of reluctance to give credit to any royal officer, since the English government was notoriously slow in paying its debts. No credit meant hungry sailors who 'began to mutiny and would not stir', until Hunter was fortunate enough to get two weeks provisions from the captain of another royal ship. He used these to feed his crew as far as Jamaica where he arrived on 1 December 1699 and felt certain that Admiral Benbow would honour the royal orders and assist him.[14]

Communication between London and the West Indies was very slow, but it did exist and royal officials and Hunter's backers were becoming increasingly alarmed at the continuous delays incurred by HMS *Dolphin*. Matters came to a head on 1 November 1699 when a letter dated 22 August from Hunter in Barbados was read out at the Board of Admiralty. The letter reported the Captain's detention for seizing a merchant ship and the Lords of the Admiralty resolved that it should be laid before the King so 'that His Majesty may see how little service has been yet done, or probably will be done, by a ship which he is at the charge of maintaining'. So began the process of recalling the *Dolphin* and replacing Hunter as her captain, but it was a very slow process. The Duke of Schomberg had to be consulted and of course the Earl of Macclesfield and his syndicate who were the only people in either England or the West Indies to have a good word for Hunter. Macclesfield told the Admiralty Board on 25 November that he had been offerred 'a considerable sum of money for his shares in the wreck which Hunter is gone to look after, but that he thought him a very good man and would not sell. And Mr Travers said the like.' What the Board thought of such a foolish investment decision is not revealed.[15]

Macclesfield's support for Hunter delayed the Captain's recall and ensured that if Hunter was actually working on a wreck, he would be allowed to continue. But the Admiralty themselves had no more time for Captain Hunter. 'The account we have received of the present captain gives us such jealousy of [anxiety for] the safety of the ship, that it is our opinion the said ship should be forthwith called home and that a Captain should be sent from hence to take the charge of her.' But this was easier said than done. The Admiralty did not have the absolute authority over its captains that it was to have in later years and no less than three captains were offered but declined this duty, in the case of Captain Edward Chant over a month after he had previously accepted 'this or any other servis you please to command me'. These refusals, it is sad to say, were not out of any feeling of solidarity with their brother captain but because of the uncertain length of the command, the possible expenses to be incurred and the extremely unhealthy reputation of the West Indies. Such delays meant that it was not until April 1700 that Captain Edward Acton was finally persuaded to take on this disagreeable duty. He sailed out as a passenger in HMS *Fowey* and on 17 July arrived in Jamaica where he remained until the evening of 7 August when Hunter sailed into port in the *Dolphin* and 'at ye same time I went on board and took possession thereof'. It took a long time to sack a captain in these days before telegraph and wireless and in the meantime Hunter had been able to get on with his somewhat idiosyncratic life.[16]

Captain Hunter knew nothing of these plans to remove him from his command, but he must have had a pretty good idea that he was in trouble after wasting so much time. To counter this he wrote an optimistic letter to the Admiralty on 7 December 1699, a week after his arrival at Jamaica, saying that he was almost ready to set sail 'to fish on the wreck off Hispaniola' and was 'in very great hopes of sucksess'. But this, like many of Hunter's letters, was misleading and it was, in fact, to be nearly three months before he left Port Royal. Shortage of money was one problem, making it difficult to provision the ship and almost impossible to hire 'diving negroes' from the Jamaican slave-owners who wanted a hefty down payment for their men, 'for fear I should runn away with them and ye King's ship', that old piracy canard again. In the end Hunter was only able to raise the money to hire the divers and purchase other necessaries by selling the brigantine which had been intended as a consort on his treasure hunting expedition. The *Dolphin* was also plagued by sickness for the first time in her cruise. At one time over a third of the crew were incapacitated as an epidemic struck the ship and, when the men recovered, some were seduced away from the service of the ship by the offer of higher wages which Hunter could not match.[17]

This decline in numbers was a great worry since Hunter desperately wanted more men not less as a result of rumours of pirates operating in the area where he planned to sail. 'I understand [we are] particularly threatened by Captain Breholt whom I am informed is upon the piraticall account.' Breholt, who, in fact, was in South Carolina at this time, was not the only old enemy to reappear in Hunter's correspondence during his stay in Jamaica. Yet another real or imaginary cabal against his command was detected, this time led by William Mills, the investors' agent, and supported by Henry Oake, the Treasury agent, and Lieutenant Westcombe, the officer who had replaced the slain Champneys. This dispute, like the similar one in Barbados, wasted a lot of time and was eventually laid before Admiral Benbow who obviously had serious doubts about a captain who could alienate every senior officer on his ship. He was tempted to replace Hunter with Mills, but in the end he compromised, leaving Hunter as captain but enhancing Mills' power aboard ship, so creating a state of dual authority which was almost bound to cause trouble.[18]

It was then not a very happy ship which set sail in the first week
of March 1700 along the north coast of Hispaniola, 'being bound
to ye Turks Islands where it is ye wreck lyes'. It may seem
unbelievable, but HMS *Dolphin* was actually just about to start
treasure hunting after eleven wasted months in the West Indies.
Well, perhaps one should say she was almost about to start, for
Captain Hunter spent the rest of March chasing pirates off the
coast of Hispaniola. The most promising one got away in the night,
but two other possibles were seized, one of which turned out on
examination to be not a pirate but a pirate's prize and the other a
sloop which had been trading with the pirates. Hunter sent one of
his captures back to Jamaica, but kept the other as a replacement
for the brigantine he had been forced to sell to retrieve his credit. 'I
was glad of the opportunity', he wrote later in his report, 'as not
being able to doe anything upon ye wreck without such a small
vessel as they were.'[19]

The *Dolphin* and the sloop now sailed to the Turks Islands where
Hunter was certain he would find his wreck. Its name is never given
and there is no obvious Spanish shipwreck anywhere near the
waters he searched, but it is clear that he had acquired from
somewhere 'Spanish directions' with similar information to those
which had helped Phips find the *Concepción*. The two vessels
anchored near Seal Cay south-east of the Turks Islands on 7 April
1700 and the next day Hunter set out in the captured sloop 'in
pursuit of a rack lost on ye shoales of these islands'. He clearly did
not expect to take long to find the wreck and was almost
immediately optimistic. 'When I had come in amongst the islands
I was then assured it was the place I looked for.' His confidence was
further boosted when one of the sailors thought he had seen timber
in 'a pretty shallow spot'. Hunter anchored the sloop and looked
around and soon convinced himself he was in the right place. 'I
found my soundings exactly the same [as in his Spanish paper] and
the bearings of the three keys to differ but very little, so that
nothing disagreed but the distances. Nevertheless, I was satisfied it
was thereabouts.' Bad weather forced him to buoy the spot and
seek out safer moorings for the night, but next morning he was
back again and, 'having a man on board the sloop that could dive',

sent him down to investigate. The diver brought up some coral 'that by all appearance might a been growing upon wood. I was very joyful of this discovery.'[20]

Hunter now sailed back to report his good news to the men aboard the *Dolphin*, though it is clear that at least some of them shared the reader's suspicion that their captain was deceiving himself. The master, James Knowles, reported the sloop's return 'with pretence of having found her', while Mr Mills was very reluctant to let Hunter make use of the negro divers. Nevertheless, both vessels returned next morning to the 'pretended' wreck site and 'all our divers went down, but they brought up but little incouragement'. Hunter's immediate reaction was to suspect that the negro slave divers, like almost everyone else, were trying to cheat him (possibly on the orders of Mills). 'They were no sooner down, but they were up again', he complained later, 'soe that they could have no tyme to search for anything although it was not above 4½ fathoms [27 feet] at ye deepest'. Hunter therefore ordered his 'own servants who were young ladds' to dive down and 'check on the miserable, cheating negroes'.

In his report, Hunter said that these lads 'brought up more materiall signes than the divers and stayed longer under water', but this seems to have been wishful thinking and it convinced neither Mr Mills who 'concluded it was nothing but a rock', nor the very sceptical master who refers repeatedly in his journal to the 'pretended wrack' and thought that Hunter had found 'nothing but a shoale'. His entry for 12 April was particularly damning. 'This forenoon about 10 o'clock our sloop went on ye pretended wrack to make a farther sartch into ye matter, Capt. Hunter being positive of its being a wrack, every one else that hath seen it to be nothing but a rock, hundreds of ye like to be seen all round there for miles every way. Capt. [sic] Mills for ye better satisfaction hath sent our second mate, a midshipman and one of our quarter masters hue [who] are divers sufficient to attest ye truth of itt, ye negro divers being suspected of ye truth in saying it is no wrack but a rock. At ½ past 2 after noon returned with a full account of no wrack being there but a rock.'[21]

Hunter was to make one last attempt to prove his assertion,

'either with ye diveing engins or ye divers', but this was to end in a painful farce. He set out once again for the supposed wreck site in the sloop, but 'before we got halfway I was seized with ye loss of my limbs and a violent pain all over my body'. The sailors, fearing he was on the point of death, returned to the *Dolphin* where the captain was attended to by the ship's doctor and confined to his cabin. Mills now took command and sailed back to Jamaica, after assuring the other officers that Hunter had feigned his sickness because he knew that he would make no further discovery. And so the great Turks Islands treasure hunt was abandoned after exactly one week in the vicinity and 'we came to saile bound for Jamaica with God's leave, ye sartch of our pretended wrack being given over'.

The *Dolphin* now spent a month in Jamaica where Captain Hunter, once recovered from his mysterious illness, was again forced to combat attacks on his honesty and motivation. Mr Mills, now often styled Captain and still keen to take full command, naturally gave everyone the worst possible interpretation of Hunter's failure to find the wreck in the Turks Islands, 'since he finds the oaths he took [in the Court of Chancery] about finding the wrecks proves false'. A man who could perjure himself in this way was capable of anything and soon the miserable Hunter was faced with the piracy slander again. 'I cannot express the trouble I am in about the malitious report I hear is spread abroad of my being turned pirate', he wrote from Jamaica to the Admiralty on 10 May 1700 and the story was being told in London a month later in Narcissus Luttrell's newsletter. It was clearly time to go, and five days later Hunter set sail again, this time for the Spanish Main, to search for 'a wreck discovered by one Captain Moon who had taken money out of her betwixt ye Grand and Little Brew [Baru], a little to the westward of Cartagena'.[22]

Followers of Captain Hunter's expeditions will not be surprised to hear that this voyage was also a total failure. He took with him a pilot who claimed to have 'actually been upon the wreck with the said Moon', but this did not help Hunter and all he says in his report to the Admiralty was that 'after I had been a month in search could not find it'. The master of the *Dolphin* had a little more to say in his journal. This shows that Hunter anchored off the island of Grand Baru on 25 May 1700 and left the area for good on 6 June, not quite 'a month'. On five of these twelve days either Captain Hunter or his Lieutenant went in the ship's boat with the pilot 'to sartch for a wrack which he had been upon but fifteen months before, but could not find her'. Hunter then went to Cartagena de Indias, where he tried unsuccessfully to negotiate the release of a captured English ship, and then engaged in some equally futile pirate chasing along the Spanish Main before returning to Jamaica on 7 August, 'where I no sooner arrived but Captain Acton came on board and took possession of ye ship by virtue of your Lordships' commission, which my dewty obldged me to submitt to'.[23]

Hunter's woes were to continue. He left Jamaica for England by the first available merchant ship, having been warned that the agent Mills was trying to have him arrested. On his way home he somehow contrived to lose a chest and several boxes containing money and all his private papers and journals and so, on arrival in London late in 1700, the penniless captain was forced to seek sanctuary from his creditors lest he be confined to a debtors' prison. Since he claimed to have lost his journals, the Admiralty ordered him to produce from memory a report on his voyage and this was delivered on 18 February 1701. 'This narrative', he wrote in a covering letter, 'will show what ill practises hath been used against me (to retard my designe) from the beginning to the ending of the voyage'.[24]

This indeed is the main, almost the only, theme of the report which has been used with caution in writing this chapter. But, if Captain Hunter believed that this piece of special pleading would put him in good favour with the Admiralty, he was to be disappointed for the report condemns him in his own words and shows him to have been a pitiful, whining, ineffective man who should never have been given a command in the first place. It is therefore no surprise that the Lords of the Admiralty and their Secretary, Josiah Burchett, should have ignored Hunter's letters begging for the command 'of some small friggott or fireship'. He had been tried and found wanting.[25]

Chapter Eight

A New Way of Diving

Chapter Eight

A New Way of Diving

"Being, in the year 1715, quite reduced, and having large family, my thoughts turned upon some extraordinary method to retrieve my misfortunes."

Letter written by John Lethbridge in 1749.[1]

The complete failure of the expeditions of Long and Hunter and the renewal of the war against France in 1702 dampened further enthusiasm for treasure hunting, and there seems to have been only one new venture in the first decade of the eighteenth century. This followed the pattern of the expeditions of the 1680s and 1690s. The syndicate was headed by an aristocrat, Thomas Fairfax, 5th Lord Fairfax of Cameron, the grandson of Cromwell's general and himself a dashing cavalryman who had been a very active supporter of William III. According to family history, he 'inherited an extravagance characteristic of his race' and so was a ripe target for the creative imagination of one Peter Dearlove, a ship's carpenter who was in the Marshalsea Prison on a charge of piracy. 'The said Dearlove being reduced to great want', a former shipmate deposed, 'he framed a pretence that he knew of a rich wreck called the *Bon-Jesus* in the West Indies and could find the very place where the same lay. By which stratagem he drew in the Lord Fairfax to support him and gett him bayled out of prison.' The wreck was said to be worth 'two million sterling, besides perishable goods', a typically huge sum, so the impressionable

Fairfax had no difficulty in setting up an equally gullible consortium to look for it.[2]

Lord Fairfax was granted a patent on 10 January 1704 to search for and recover wrecks 'between 6 and 36 degrees of north latitude', yet another vast search area which covered the whole of the West Indies and Bahamas and the American mainland as far north as North Carolina. The original grant was for four years, with the normal provisions for inspection by a government official, and Queen Anne was to receive one-eighth as her royalty. The Queen was also the first name on the subscription list opened in June 1704, her treasurer Sidney Godolphin subscribing £500 'in the Queen's name and by her Majesty's commands'. Her husband, Prince George of Denmark, was second on the list and this royal patronage was sufficient to bring in a number of other noblemen and gentlemen and so raise the £25,000 considered necessary to buy ships, hire sailors and whatever else was necessary to get the show on the road. Narcissus Luttrell reported Lord Fairfax 'fitting out ships with engines and other materials' in June 1704 and on 9 September said that his three ships would be ready to sail out of the Thames in a fortnight. This claim proved to be a little premature since the war and the great danger of capture by privateers delayed the departure of the expedition for nearly two years. Three ships implies a powerful (and expensive) expedition and it seems probable that the syndicate hoped to supplement the proceeds from treasure hunting by privateering, since the terms of the subscription refer to the rules of division of 'all prizes or captures which shall be seized or taken'.[3]

Little information survives about this expedition, but it clearly did not have any success since, in January 1707, Lord Fairfax was petitioning successfully to have his patent extended until October 1711, having met 'so many discouragements and disappointments by reason of the present war'. His agents, he said, 'are now in the West Indies pursueing the discoveries of the wrecks there and he hath hopes of success'. Fairfax's hopes however, like so many before, were to be dashed and, in December 1709, he was forced to go into hiding to escape his creditors. He died the following year. In his will, he singled out from the rest of his chaotically indebted estate his shares in 'a certain West India wreck in which he had an interest'. These shares were lovingly left to his children, his brothers and sisters and other relations, but these scraps of paper were to do them little good since they 'never brought in one farthing'.[4]

A new interest in treasure hunting arose with the approach of the expiry date of the huge twenty-year grant given to the Duke of Schomberg and Leinster in February 1693. Prominent here was the ever-hopeful promoter Samuel Weale whom we last met failing to find the treasure on Ireland Island in Bermuda. Weale's ambitious scheme involved finding a suitable nobleman to seek 'a grant from the Queen in reversion of the present grant which any . . . man of good interest at court may have for asking'. Money would then be raised to fit out two powerful ships crewed by two hundred men to set out on this 'great and noble undertaking' and then how the profits would roll in.

According to Weale there was an estimated £20 million worth of plate, gold and silver in wrecks already known to be in the area of the Duke's grant. And one could add to this Spanish ships 'sunk in fights at sea during the war by Commodore Wager and others'. Weale was referring here to the *San José*, the Spanish treasure ship sunk off the coast of Colombia by Commodore Charles Wager in 1708 which is generally thought by today's treasure hunting community to be the richest of all undiscovered Spanish wrecks. And, just in case all this was not enough to bring in the punters, Weale claimed that the new syndicate would be able to acquire 'a much larger discovery' of wrecks both past and future from the shipwreck registers in the Court of Spain, 'which is no losse to them, because they never allow any of their subjects to work on wrecks, lest it should put them under a temptation wilfully to make wrecks'.[5]

But the Spanish court did not keep such registers and, if they had, they would certainly not have handed over the information contained in them to the English. And Lord Clarendon, who was the noble lord chosen by Weale to turn his fantasy into reality, refused to see him or have anything to do with him. And so Weale's plan collapsed, despite all his efforts which included a scheme to make his money-grabbing proposals more acceptable to the clergy and 'her most sacred Majesty' by handing out shares in his treasure hunting company to such good charitable institutions as the charity schools and the Societies for the Propagation of the Gospel and for the Reformation of Manners.[6]

Weale may have failed, but other men were still interested in getting hold of all, or part of, the Duke of Leinster's concession and there were four successful applications for grants in the years 1713 to 1715. The recipients of this royal favour were Edward Harley, 'commonly called Lord Harley, son and heir apparent of Robert Harley, Earl of Oxford', Morgan Randyll Esquire, Colonel Andrew Becker (or Bekker) and Windsor Sandys Esq., of Brimsfield Park, Gloucestershire. Their grants all covered very large areas of the sea defined by latitude and they seem to have been carelessly drafted since there was considerable overlap in their search areas. This, however, did not matter very much since, when the officers of the Treasury investigated these four grants in February 1721, they found that they had not given rise to much activity. In a succinct note it was observed that 'Harley's never attempted, Becker's did but without success, Randyll attempted at ye Land's End, Sandys never attempted'.[7]

The most interesting of these four grantees was Colonel Becker, an army officer with a German, or possibly French, background. He was granted the right to search for wrecks in American waters between 6 and 36 degrees north, but his main interest was in getting permission to use a 'new invented machine' on recent shipwrecks on the coasts of England, Scotland and Ireland. King George I was advised in November 1714 that he might 'lawfully grant to the petitioner [Becker] the sole use of this his new invention and he may therein agree with the owners of ships wrecked . . . for the raising of the same, or if he shall raise them without such agreement he will be intituled to a reasonable reward therefore called salvage to be ascertained by your Majesty's Court of Admiralty'.[8]

The legal concept of salvage has a long history, but this is the first time that the word had been used in relation to such a petition and as such marks a transition in the prime interests of the growing diving community. Most claims for grants prior to this date were concerned with what can be called 'treasure hunting', a concept quite different from 'salvage'. 'If the ship and goods perish in the sea, and the owners do totally forsake her and so she becomes a meer derelict', wrote Charles Molloy, the leading authority on maritime law, 'in that case the first possessor that recovers her or any part of her lading, gains a property.' A ship lost at sea could be therefore considered 'a meer derelict . . . if claim be not made within a reasonable time', and Molloy gave, as an example, the silver recovered by Sir William Phips from the *Concepción*, 'most apparently a derelict, and free not only for the undertakers to recover and possess but to keep as a property justly acquired by them'. The King of Spain might not agree with Molloy's law, but it was the legal basis of nearly all the treasure hunting expeditions which had set out from the mid-1680s onwards.

By contrast, salvage applied either to the recapture of a ship taken as prize or as payment by the owners for saving a ship and its effects from danger or for recovering the goods of a ship that had been lost. Such payment could be agreed by the owners by prior contract with the salvor or could be ascertained after the event by arbitration or, if necessary, by the High Court of Admiralty. English law provided for no fixed payment for salvage, except for recaptured prizes, though it was a general principle that reasonable compensation should be made to the salvor and this could vary from one-tenth to two-thirds of the goods recovered depending on such factors as the labour involved, the difficulty and the danger. One-third of the value recovered was the most common payment.[9]

To conduct such salvage Andrew Becker had invented a new machine which had been demonstrated on the Thames at the end of August 1715. The *Weekly Packet* recorded that King George I and 'a numerous concourse of nobility' were present to watch a diver 'walk under water three quarters of an hour, but by reason of the low tide, could then not go any further than from Whitehall to Somerset-Stairs'. 'But on the next day, upon a second tryal, he went much farther.' The journalist was pleased to note that those persons with little faith in the honesty of projectors who believed 'that this diving engine was an instrument only to pick pockets with, have failed in their conjectures'. The diver was encased in a suit of waterproof armour, according to a description in the *Exeter Mercury*. 'It was made of leather with glass eyes in such a manner as the use of his hands and feet were entirely preserved. For conveniency of air a long pipe was fixed from the engine to a vessel, and at the top of the pipe was a man planted, who by that contrivance could discourse with the diver the whole time.'[10]

Such equipment, similar to the semi-atmospheric apparatus invented by Overing and others in the 1690s, was still being used in the 1730s and 1740s though, by then, the head-piece and body armour were usually made of copper, while the arms and hands as well as legs and feet were covered with leather hose. A strong convex glass enabled the diver to see and there were two leather pipes through one of which air was sent down by bellows from the surface while the other served to remove the exhaust. The diver was let down by a rope round his neck which also prevented him falling over. There are, in fact, few examples of such equipment actually being used and it must have been incredibly unwieldy to work in. It also suffered from the usual problems of machines and engines which relied on air blown down a tube from the surface. The experts thought that it was only possible to use in very shallow water, though one critic was kind enough to note that it was 'at shallow depths that ships are usually cast away'.[11]

Some months before Becker conducted his demonstration on the Thames, an even odder contraption had been unveiled before a small audience of friends and neighbours in an orchard near Newton Abbot in Devon. The date was 22 April 1715, and it was one of destiny for this was the day of the long predicted and much feared total solar eclipse. The man who defied the stars by choosing not just the day but the very hour of the eclipse to conduct his experiment was John Lethbridge, an impoverished 40-year-old wool merchant with a large family who, according to his grandson, 'was possessed of a strong idea of living under water'.

This was a rather strange idea to have, for John Lethbridge was a landsman with no practical experience of the sea. He had, however, seen and given much thought to contemporary diving practice and was convinced that the attempts made by Becker and others to rely on air from the surface were doomed to failure.

Lethbridge therefore determined to invent a diving engine, 'without communication of air from above'. The first step was to see how long he could remain in a small enclosed space breathing just the air which was trapped inside it. He did this by climbing into a large barrel or hogshead which was 'bung'd up tight' by his friends who then stood around in his orchard while the sun went into eclipse. Half an hour later a tap from within the barrel signalled that Lethbridge was ready to emerge and his career as a diver had begun. A further test showing that he could breathe for the same time, or a little longer, when his barrel was submerged in water was sufficient to convince Lethbridge of the efficacy of his invention and he set off to have a prototype made for him by a London cooper.[12]

The cooper produced a slightly tapered cylinder made of oak, six foot long and two and a half feet diameter at the head and rather less at the base. It was hooped with iron to guard against the water pressure and weighted with lead sufficient to sink it. Two holes were cut for the diver's arms to go through and these were fitted with waterproof leather gauntlets similar to those employed in the 1690s by the Cornishman Joseph Williams in his 'diving tower'. [13] Visibility was provided by a glass window, four inches in diameter and one and a quarter inches thick, which was set in a direct line with the eye as the diver lay down on his chest in the barrel. Lethbridge used to 'go in with my feet foremost and, when my arms are got thro' the holes, then the head is put on, which is fastened with screws'. There was a large rope fixed to the back by which it was lowered to the sea bottom with the diver lying horizontal, and there was a signalling line within easy reach of the diver's hand by which he could communicate with his colleagues on the surface. Such divers will be described here as barrel divers. This was not a term used by contemporaries, but it will be helpful to distinguish them from other types of divers, such as bell divers or natural divers.

It must have taken a very brave (or unimaginative) man to go down in these claustrophobic wooden coffins. There must also have been absolute trust between the divers and their support teams. A bell diver had the chance of scrambling out of the bottom of the bell if disaster struck, but there was no way out for a barrel diver except by being hauled to the surface by his colleagues. Nevertheless, Lethbridge's barrel worked and he and other divers were to use the contraption with varying degrees of success for the next forty years or so, after which improvements to the diving-bell were to make diving barrels and the 'wreckmen' who dived in them redundant.

There were some fairly obvious problems involved in diving with the barrel. Time on the sea bottom was limited by the amount of air trapped in the barrel and, in most accounts, half an hour was the maximum before the diver had to be raised. Once on the surface, the foul air could be released through one cock and fresh air introduced through another if the diver wished to descend again and continue working. The barrel was also impossible to use in any but the calmest of waters and, even then, it was clumsy to manoeuvre to the right position above a wreck. John Lethbridge also seems to have had serious trouble with his equipment leaking, possibly through poor cooperage but more likely as a result of not being able to make the join between the sleeves or gauntlets and the structure completely watertight. Twenty years after his first development of the diving barrel, he told his grandson John that he 'had been very near drowning in the engine five times', while another grandson, Captain Thomas Lethbridge RN wrote that 'no danger ever annoy'd him while he was at work on the wreck of a ship, with the water up to his chin and his breath expended'. He really was a hero! And, finally, there were serious constraints on the depths at which the diver could work as a result of his body being subject to atmospheric pressure inside the barrel while his arms were affected more and more by the ambient water pressure as it was lowered. This caused a severe constriction on the arms which was very uncomfortable at ten fathoms (sixty feet) and could be fatal at greater depths. Nevertheless, most wrecks lay in depths under sixty feet and so the diving barrel was to prove a valuable addition to the existing range of equipment.[14]

John Lethbridge does not often appear in the English official records and it is necessary to piece together the bald story of his career from a rather odd assortment of sources. These include a letter written by him to the *Gentleman's Magazine* in 1749 (the main source for the description above of his invention), a silver tankard discovered in 1879 with 'two very curious engravings' celebrating his barrel and one of his greatest achievements with it, a board dated 1736 with an inscription in gold letters summarizing the wrecks on which he had dived 'by the blessing of God', two letters written sixty years after his death by his grandson Thomas to an antiquary, and an intriguing entry for 11 December 1759 in the parish register of Wolborough near Newton Abbot: 'Buried Mr John Lethbridge, inventor of a most famous diving-engine, by which he recovered from the bottom of the sea, in different parts of the globe, almost £100,000 for the English and Dutch merchants which had been lost by shipwreck.'[15]

Such success was to be some time in coming. There is little evidence as to the nature of Lethbridge's early work with his barrel, but he seems to have done most of it in Cornwall where, in July 1717, he got authorization to dive for wreck from a local landowner. The next year he was diving on an unnamed wreck at the Lizard when he met a man called Nathaniel Symons, a Devonshire carpenter who had come 'to see my engine, which he liked so well, that he desired to adventure with me on some wrecks near Plymouth, where we adventured together without success'. Symons did not dive again with Lethbridge, but he had seen sufficient of the barrel to use his carpentry skills to make one for himself and many years later he was to claim that he had invented it, thus prompting Lethbridge to write a letter in self-justification to the *Gentleman's Magazine* which provides the historian with the best description of his invention.[16]

Lethbridge suffered from a double disadvantage as a diving entrepreneur. Like most divers, for example, William Phips, he lacked the capital necessary to fit out an expedition for himself and so was forced to seek backing from investors who were likely to make a hard bargain with him. He was also one of the very few divers discussed in this book who was a landsman and so unable to navigate a ship to a wreck site or sail and command a vessel at sea. This inevitably placed him in a poor negotiating position and restricted the amount of money he could make from his invention.

'Had he been bred a seaman and could have conducted his own expeditions', wrote his grandson Thomas, 'he would have been enabled to realize wealth beyond the dreams of avarice.' Lethbridge's bargaining position improved with time and experience and 'his most laudable endeavours were so far crowned with success that he was enabled not only to maintain his family, but to purchase the estate of Odicknoll in the parish of Kingskerswill'.[17]

After his early diving exploits in Devon and Cornwall, Lethbridge came up to London to try to get merchants who had lost property in wrecks to back him and his invention, but 'they were apprehensive he could not perform what he proposed'. Obviously, the answer to this was to demonstrate his skills, like many before him, by diving before an audience in the Thames. This he did on three successive days at the end of March 1720. 'Mr Lethbridge of Devonshire, the famous diver', reported *Read's Weekly Journal*, 'was let down into the Thames, near White-Hall Stairs, in an engine, and kept under water half an hour; he took with him meat and drink and had his dinner under water; he had also fire in the engine, and bak'd a cake, bor'd several holes in a piece of wood, besides other performances, in a small quantity of air, without the use of air-pipes.' If John Lethbridge had not been a 'famous diver' before, he surely was after this amazing piece of journalistic licence. No diver in the 1690s had ever thought of baking a cake under water to prove his skills, no doubt because such a performance would have very rapidly exhausted the air in the barrel if the fire had not already made a hole in it.[18]

It was shortly after this demonstration that Lethbridge formed a relationship with Jacob Rowe, another Devonian who is the subject of the next chapter. Rowe was a well-educated man but also a practical sailor and inventor who, in June 1720, petitioned for a patent to cover his new invention of 'a machine for diving, more practicable and in greater depths of water then any other yet in use'. Rowe's device was also a diving barrel, very similar to that invented by John Lethbridge, but the latter had never sought to claim his rights to the equipment and so could do nothing to challenge Rowe's claim of originality which was accepted by the authorities who granted him his letters patent on 12 October 1720. Rowe, a man of higher social class and much greater entrepreneurial skill than Lethbridge, was then able with colleagues to set up a well-financed company to exploit his invention. Their first target was to be the East-Indiaman *Vansittart* which had been wrecked on the Isle of May [Maio] in the Cape Verde Islands in April 1719. This expedition will be discussed in detail in the next chapter and all we need know here was that Rowe led a very successful expedition to the wreck where he and his divers worked from May to August 1721.[19]

All writers on John Lethbridge assert that he took part in this expedition, but none of them gives any references so it is difficult to discover where they acquired the information. In fact, John Lethbridge's name does not appear in any of the main sources connected with this expedition and is not in the crew list which was attached as a schedule to the papers of a lawsuit later fought between Rowe and the East India Company. However, his name does appear in another schedule of expenses attached to the same action. Here we find 'To paid Lethbridge in account per order . . . £10.0.0 . . . To paid Lethbridge his quarteridge £10.0.0 . . . To paid Mr Lethbridge's daughter per order £10.0.0.' These payments could be a royalty for Rowe's use of the diving barrel, but they are much more likely to be a salary of £40 per annum paid quarterly. Several years later Rowe referred to Lethbridge as a former servant and this was the sort of salary that a senior and trusted servant might expect to receive at this date. It was hardly wealth beyond the dreams of avarice, but it was reasonable pay since it would have included free board on the expedition and the chance to learn at first hand how to conduct such a venture.[20]

Shortly after the return of Rowe's expedition from the Cape Verde Islands, the 40-gun naval ship *Royal Anne Galley* was wrecked on Sunday 18 November 1721 on the Stagg Rocks near the Lizard in Cornwall. This was a horrendous disaster in which well over two hundred people lost their lives and only three were saved – a quartermaster, a musician and a boy. These survivors lay untended on the rocks, 'battered, bruised and bleeding', while the local inhabitants rifled the bodies of their dead shipmates. One newspaper dramatically reinforced the popular image of evil Cornish wreckers. 'Upon the first notice of the misfortune, the people on the sea-coast ran out of the churches, armed with their hatchets etc. to the sea-side in quest of plunder.'[21]

Early in 1722 Rowe's two ships were reported on their way down to the Lizard to engage in that more genteel form of plunder called salvage by diving on the *Royal Anne Galley* and other wrecks in the vicinity. They were accompanied by a Treasury observer and his accounts show that diving was being carried on at the Lizard between 12 January and 28 March 1722. They also show that the diving was unsuccessful. Lethbridge was certainly in this party for he is recorded as receiving on 5 January his £10 quarterage 'on account before he went to the Lizard'. But, after this, his name vanishes from the records and it is difficult to discover exactly what he was doing for the next two and a half years. He may have done some more diving in England, but probably went to work on the continent, the most likely place being the Low Countries. It was in any case during these years that he parted company with Rowe on unfriendly terms and became his 'former' servant who had 'invaded' his patent by diving in the barrel for which Rowe had exclusive rights 'all over the King's Dominions . . . till the year 1734'.[22]

The next definite information we have about John Lethbridge is in the archives of the Dutch East India Company which was to make considerable use of the skills of English and Scottish barrel divers in the 1720s, 1730s and 1740s. This company was by far the largest of the various European East India Companies, sending well over twice as many ships to the east in the early eighteenth century as the English and six or seven times as many as the French. General management of the Company was conducted by a governing body called the *Heeren* or Gentlemen Seventeen, but the building and ownership of the individual ships was in the hands of regional chambers of which those of Holland and Zeeland with depots at Amsterdam and Middelburg were much the most important. These magnificent ships were loaded with metals, textiles and other European goods for their long voyages to Ceylon or to Batavia (Djakarta) in Java, the headquarters of the Dutch in

Asia, and most ships also carried substantial quantities of bullion to pay for the Asian goods in demand in Europe.

In the first half of the eighteenth century, the outgoing ships did not normally take the most direct route through the English Channel, but sailed instead by the 'backway' north of Scotland and around the Shetland Islands, a route which was usually easier given the prevailing westerly winds. They then sailed south, often calling at Madeira for wine and provisions, and then through the Cape Verde Islands which lay right in their track before picking up winds which would carry them to Cape Town, 'the tavern of two seas'. The Dutch colony had been founded in 1652 as a place where the ships could replenish their stores and, by the early eighteenth century, provided a wonderful place of 'refreshment' for sailors from all the East India Companies.[23]

The Dutch were to suffer many shipwrecks along this route and one of them, the *Slot ter Hooge*, was to make Lethbridge's name known throughout the contemporary maritime world. This outward-bound ship belonged to the Zeeland Chamber of the Company and set sail for Batavia in 1724 with four tons of silver ingots and four chests of coin. She was struck by a terrible storm as she sailed south and on the night of 10 November was flung ashore on the north coast of the small island of Porto Santo, some forty miles north-east of Madeira. Only thirty-three of the 254 passengers and crew survived, but these included the First Lieutenant who managed to get to Lisbon where he reported the wreck to the Dutch consul, giving his estimate that she lay in ten or twelve fathoms of water. The English presence was very strong in Lisbon at this time and the consul would certainly have known of the successful salvage of the *Vansittart* three years earlier by English divers using the newly invented barrel. His letter home reporting the wreck was very optimistic. 'I know not how well acquainted the Dutch are with the machines, but the English are most certainly capable of fishing all [the treasure] up.'[24]

The authorities in the Netherlands acted on the consul's advice. John Lethbridge was invited to demonstrate his equipment to the directors of the Company and the result was a contract drawn up at the end of April 1725 between Gerard Bolwerk van Londen, the agent of the Zeeland Chamber, and John Lethbridge of Newton Abbot, *dujker* [diver]. Lethbridge agreed to sail to Porto Santo on a ship supplied by Bolwerk and there 'dive and bring up the silver goods . . . as well as he can'. He did not receive a share of the treasure recovered, as most contemporary divers did, but was to be paid a salary of £10 a month and all his expenses. This was good pay, roughly equal to that of the captain of a large merchant ship at this date and three times what Rowe had paid him. He was also to be rewarded with a 'free gift' for 'his extraordinary trouble'.[25]

Despite the fact that most of the treasure lay at about sixty feet, near the limit for a barrel diver, and in a very awkward position, Lethbridge was incredibly successful. On his first expedition in 1725, he recovered 349 of the 1500 lost silver bars, most of the pieces of eight, a significant amount of smaller coins and two cannon. 'The rest I will fish, too, and easily', he wrote to the Company, 'if I would be lucky enough to have twenty or thirty days of calm weather next year.' He was as good as his word and on his second expedition in 1726 he recovered more silver bars and coins, salvaging in all well over half of the treasure which had been shipped in Middelburg. To celebrate his achievement he had a silver tankard engraved with a delightful picture of his support boat just about to lower the barrel into the sea and also a sketch of Porto Santo with the church and houses of the port on the south coast and cliffs and a ship foundering on the north coast. The tankard was discovered in 1879 and the engravings were reproduced in an article written about Lethbridge in the following year, two striking images which inspired the Belgian diver Robert Sténuit, not only to rediscover the wreck of the *Slot ter Hooge* in 1974, but also to dive a few years later in a replica of the barrel, an experience which filled him with admiration for this courageous and resourceful eighteenth-century diver.[26]

The success of Lethbridge in Porto Santo naturally encouraged the Dutch East India Company and its servants to think of other unsalvaged wrecks with treasure aboard on which he could dive. Much the worst disasters in recent years had been at the Cape of Good Hope in Table Bay, a notoriously unsafe anchorage during the southern winter when northerly and north-westerly gales lashed the exposed roadstead. On the "sorrowful and disastrous day" of 16 May 1722 such a storm destroyed eleven ships including six belonging to the Company and over six hundred Dutch and English sailors were drowned. There was some salvage and a lot of looting, despite the savage punishments inflicted on those who were caught, but it was estimated that there was over £50,000 worth of treasure left below the waters of Table Bay.[27]

The Governor of the Cape wrote home requesting that the Company 'send such machines as have lately been invented and employed in England' and negotiations were conducted with Lethbridge who was now in a better position to obtain a good contract. It was agreed that from the time he left London he should be paid 110 guilders a month (just over £9), and this time he was also to receive a share of the treasure recovered, six per cent, almost identical to the one-sixteenth given to Captain Phips from the treasure of the *Concepción* and Phips received no salary. Lethbridge had now arrived, landsman or not, and the Company sent orders to the Cape that he and his men should be well fed and lodged and treated with respect. 'Lethbridge has given us great satisfaction. Please supply him with everything he needs for his work . . . He is a man of mild, discreet and fairly peaceful nature . . . best kept at work by kindness.'[28]

John Lethbridge arrived at the Cape in a Dutch ship in October 1727. He was accompanied by an English-speaking Dutch naval officer and four assistant divers, one of whom Peter Richards we shall meet again. The English divers were provided with three diving tenders, a pontoon and twenty Dutch sailors to assist them. By this time it was possible to tow the submerged barrel and one writer describes Lethbridge 'cruising about the shallows in his barrel just above the sand', similar but not quite the same to a modern diver towed on an underwater sled. Visibility and weather were good and Lethbridge and his men made a respectable harvest from the bottom of the bay, seven cannon and two hundred bars of silver from the wreck of the *Rotterdam* and some 2,000 silver ducatoons from the *Zoetigheid*. But then diminishing returns set in and it was decided that they might do better diving on another target.

The wreck chosen was the *Meresteyn*, another outward-bound

ship with treasure aboard which had been lost at Jutten Island in Saldanha Bay in 1702, some sixty or seventy miles further north along the Atlantic coast of South Africa. The ship had quickly gone to pieces and it was reported that the stern in which the treasure chests were kept lay in fairly deep water up against a rock in the heaviest part of the surf. 'Regarding the recovery of the specie, we believe it to be impossible. The obstacles are the great and violent waves coming from the open sea.' Undaunted, Lethbridge, his son and his Dutch minder, Pieter de Graaf, set out for this awesome place on 28 January 1728, but their expedition merely proved that the experts were right. This was no place to dive in a barrel. Neither on this occasion, nor on a second visit in April, was it possible to recover the lost treasure of the *Meresteyn*, so heavy were the seas that crashed down on her wreck site.[29]

After this failure, Lethbridge and most of his party sailed back to the Netherlands from where he returned to England in August 1729. His achievements in South Africa caught the public attention and were recorded in a somewhat inaccurate but interesting report which appeared in several newspapers at the end of September. Lethbridge and a colleague were not named, being described as 'the two famous English divers living at Weymouth, having been three years in the Dutch East India Company's service, and had been sent to fish upon the wrecks of some ships of theirs in India [*sic*] . . . Their first trial was upon the wreck of a Dutch East India ship that had been lost off Cape Coast [i.e. Cape Town] in six fathoms water, in which they succeeded so well that they brought up at several times £36,000 in silver. They dived also upon another wreck in eight fathoms, and brought up some bars of silver and gold, and several brass guns. When one went to the bottom, his companion stay'd on board to pull him up as occasion offered, for they would not trust foreigners. Their diving-engine they contrived themselves in England, which was made of wood, six hundredweight of lead being affixed . . . the glasses before their eyes were three inches thick and their hands were at liberty to grope and fasten hooks to chests and such other things as they had a mind to get up. Notwith- standing the largeness of the engine, which terrify'd most of the inhabitants of the deep, there was one large fish that would often make at them; but to guard against him they carried in one hand a little sharp lance, with which they prick'd him, then he scoured off. They never dive but in the summer time, and then only on calm, serene and sun-shiny days . . . The bottom of the sea where they had been, look'd like a fine garden.'[30]

After his return from his South African exploits Lethbridge disappears from the records for over three years. The next we definitely know of him is in June 1733 when he contracted with the Dutch East India Company to dive on one of their ships which had wrecked a year previously on the Isle of May (Maio) in the Cape Verde Islands. The name of this ship was, by one of those awkward historical coincidences, the same as that of the wreck on which he had worked in Porto Santo, the *Slot ter Hooge* (*slot* meaning a castle in Dutch and Hooge being a place in Belgium). Lethbridge, in fact, contracted to dive on both these wrecks on very generous terms which suggested that the Company did not expect him to find much of value. He was to bring home any goods recovered at his own expense and the proceeds were to be split, 85 per cent to the English diver and just fifteen per cent to the Chamber of Zeeland. A letter of 1737 shows that he did recover something from both these wrecks, namely a bar of silver, some coins, lead, iron, anchors and cannon, but nothing to get really excited about. 'Mr Lethbridge came back with less than one could have hoped for', an agent of the Dutch Company reported, 'but still with a reasonable success.'[31]

The *Slot ter Hooge* on the Isle of May was not far from the *Vansittart* on which Lethbridge had worked with Rowe in 1721. So it was natural for him to check out this old wreck and, although he never said so, he must have discovered that time and the waves had shifted the wreckage so that now more of the *Vansittart*'s treasure was visible on the sea bottom. This was Lethbridge's great opportunity to make his fortune and he made the most of it. In December 1734, he wrote to the English East India Company, telling them that he was diving at the Isle of May for the Dutch and, since he was going to be there anyway, offering to dive on the *Vansittart* on the same terms. To his delight the Company accepted his terms and a contract was signed on 28 February 1735 which entitled Lethbridge to keep 85 per cent of what he recovered.[32]

A sloop called the *Happy Return* which had been fitted out at Dartmouth, arrived in the Cape Verde Islands in May 1735 and was back in Dartmouth on 10 October, from where Lethbridge's local agent Arthur Holdsworth wrote that 'he has had pretty good success in diving on the wreck of the *Vansittart*'. This was something of an understatement as can be seen from the detailed accounts 'of the treasure and other effects taken up'. These show that Lethbridge and his team got off to a slow start, three bars of silver on 24 May and then nothing until 27 June when a few coins and some old iron were raised. But from then on a bonanza began with treasure raised on 22 of the next 39 days, another twelve bars of silver but mainly coins, often several thousand in a day and over 100,000 coins in all. When this was all weighed in order to calculate the division with the Company, Lethbridge's share came to about 25,000 ounces of silver which, at about four ounces to the pound sterling, must have seemed a very attractive dividend to the 'silver fisher from Devon'.[33]

However, Lethbridge's exploits in his diving barrel had taken their toll on his health. He was now sixty years of age and he wrote to the Company in December 1735 saying that he was not fit enough to dive on the wreck the next season. But he had 'hired two able divers to proceed in my room'. These were Roger Boone, one of the divers who had been in South Africa, and Abraham Buckle and they were to have rather more modest success in the diving seasons of 1736 and 1737, bringing home some 5,000 ounces to be divided between themselves and Lethbridge in 1736 and about half as much in 1737. The *Vansittart*, which most people thought had been stripped of treasure by the 1721 expedition, had turned out to be a nice little earner.[34]

John Lethbridge now settled down to restore his health and enjoy his good fortune. He bought an estate with his dividend from the 1735 diving season and in 1736 he had his famous board prepared with an inscription in gold letters stating that 'John Lethbridge, by the blessing of God, had dived on the wrecks of four English men-of-war, an English East-Indiaman, two Dutch men-of-war, five Dutch East-Indiamen, two Spanish galleons and two

London galleys, all lost in the space of twenty years; on many of them with good success'. It can be seen from this list that he dived on many more wrecks than have been described in this chapter which covers only the six East-Indiamen and one of the English warships. Lethbridge must have dived on the others in the years for which there is not much information, 1715–1720 when he was diving on unspecified wrecks in Devon and Cornwall which might well have included some English men-of-war and London galleys, the middle of 1722 until April 1725, years which could have seen him working in the Netherlands diving on Dutch warships, and September 1729 to 1733 when it is possible that he went to the West Indies to dive on Spanish galleons. He certainly went there at some time in his career for, in his 1749 letter to the *Gentleman's Magazine*, he wrote that he had dived 'in the West Indies, at the Isle of May, at Porto Santo (near Madeira) and at the Cape of Good Hope'. There is then still much to be discovered about this remarkable man.[35]

It would be a reasonable assumption that this was the end of the diving career of John Lethbridge, surrounded as he was by children and grandchildren and noted throughout the European maritime world as a 'famous diver'. But such an assumption would be wrong, for in 1743 Lethbridge was enticed out of retirement by the Dutch East India Company after the outward-bound *Hollandia* wrecked in July on the Scilly Islands. She was holed after striking one of the outlying western rocks and sank with the loss of all aboard when she failed to make the safety of the island of St Agnes. The agent of the Dutch company made contact with Lethbridge and an expedition set out to dive for the ship's treasure in September. This time, however, he was not to enjoy the success he had had in the Cape Verde Islands, as was reported by Captain Robert Heath, an officer in the Scilly garrison who published 'a Natural and Historical Account' of the islands in 1750. He attributed Lethbridge's failure to 'the tide running strong at bottom, and the sea appearing thick [so that] the diver could not see distinctly through the glass of his engine'. Poor visibility and a dangerous current would obviously make diving difficult, but even in the most favourable conditions it is unlikely that Lethbridge would have been successful as, when the wreck was discovered by modern divers in September 1971, it lay at ninety or a hundred feet, well beyond the maximum practical depth for a barrel diver which was twelve fathoms or seventy-two feet.[36]

Captain Heath appears to have actually seen Lethbridge at work with his barrel for he provides one of the best surviving descriptions of the equipment. 'The figure of the diving-engine (made of thick planks, bound together with iron hoops, and headed at the ends) was a tapering vessel in which the diver was plugged up, with as much air as could be blown into it with a pair of bellow at the time of his going down. His naked arms went out at a couple of round holes next the biggest end; being exactly fitted to them, wrapt round with neats-leather [i.e. cow's leather] to keep out the water. Lying flat on his face, with his legs buckled down with straps to keep him steady, he looked through a piece of round glass, fixed right before him in the side of the engine, of about six inches over and two in thickness. Thus he descended by the force of weights fixed to the under parts of the engine. He carries a life-line in his hand which he pulls hard upon when he feels too much pressure or wants to be drawn up . . . The biggest end of the engine, where the diver enters, is made to take off, being fitted with cross-bars and screws to support it when duly fixed. A plug-hole at the upper convexity lets in fresh air when the diver is drawn up, for at being opened the confined air rushes out. This plug saves the trouble of taking off the head of the engine to give fresh air at each time of drawing it up.' It seems then that Lethbridge's diving barrel had changed very little in the three decades since it had been invented. The gauntlets for his arms and hands appear to have been dispensed with and the straps holding his legs steady seem to have been new, but otherwise the barrel was as it had always been.[37]

This was probably the last time that Lethbridge descended in his diving invention, though the barrel itself was to survive for another half century or so, rotting away on the premises of the Holdsworths, Lethbridge's former agents at Dartmouth. But, despite his advanced age, there is no doubt that he yearned to dive again, as can be seen in the correspondence of the English East India Company. In March 1755, when Lethbridge must have been about 80 years old, they received a proposal from him 'for fishing of the wrecks of the *Vansittart* and *Princess Louisa* lost some time since near the Isle of May, he rendering the Company the proportion of what shall be recovered as is usual in the like cases'.[38]

Presumably his main interest was in the *Princess Louisa* which was lost in April 1743, the same year as the *Hollandia,* with twenty chests full of pieces of eight which the Company believed were impossible to salvage. But Lethbridge may also have still been interested in the *Vansittart* for he had asked the Company in December 1735 for 'an account of what quantity of treasure etc. the *Vansittart* carried out from England'. Such an account should have enabled him to calculate that, despite the silver saved by his own expeditions in the 1730s, by Rowe in 1721 and by the efforts of the captain and crew at the time of the wreck, there were still about 15,000 ounces of silver not yet recovered. However, such calculations would have been 'academic', for Lethbridge was to learn that the salvage of both these wrecks, together with that of the *Duke of Cumberland* which had been lost in 1750 on the African coast, had been granted to another diving company headed by a Mr John Mills about whom little is known.[39]

Even then John Lethbridge's shipwreck fever was not assuaged. On 8 June 1757, the *Public Advertiser* and other papers carried the sad news of the loss nearly two years previously of the Company's ship *Dodington* on some remote rocks off the coast of Algoa Bay near the modern Port Elizabeth in South Africa. Eleven days later Lethbridge was writing to London from Newton Abbot to tell the Company that he was 'ready to serve the East India Company in the recovery of the treasure lost'. He asked them to supply him with information regarding the treasure lost, the distance that the wreck lay from the Cape and other details. And just in case they should not know who he was he told them that 'I am the person that waited on you in March 1755, in order to contract for a diving expedition to the Isle of May, but was prevented by a contract subsisting with one Mr. Mill [sic], which contract, I apprehend, expires next spring.' The Company wrote back to tell him that they did not plan to salvage the *Dodington* as they had shipped no treasure on her. However, on the expiry of their contract with Mr

Mills they would be ready to treat with him on fishing for the treasure lost on the *Princess Louisa*.[40]

Whether Lethbridge really intended to dive himself on these wrecks or was simply acting as a front man for younger divers in his employ we will never know, for he was to die before he could be put to the test and, as has been seen, was buried at Wolborough near Newton Abbot on 11 December 1759. Over four decades of mixed fortunes had passed since that fateful day of the great eclipse in 1715 when he had first put to the test his truly 'extraordinary method to retrieve his misfortunes'. His grandson Thomas claimed in 1821 that John Lethbridge's invention had 'now become one of the most valuable discoveries of the modern day . . . He was a man highly esteemed for honour and integrity and seemed to have been born for the express purpose of the discovery.' The last part of this encomium certainly seems to have been true. But alas loyalty expressed by his grandson in the first part is inaccurate, as no one seems to have used the diving barrel after Lethbridge's death. Nevertheless, one can only agree with Robert Sténuit, his greatest modern admirer, that John Lethbridge deserves to be remembered 'as a brave and accomplished diver'.[41]

Chapter Nine

Jacob Rowe and the Wreck of the Vansittart

Chapter Nine

Jacob Rowe and the Wreck of the Vansittart

"Captain Jacob Rowe . . . lies in the Downs, waiting for a fair wind to proceed on his expedition of fishing on wrecks; and 'tis believ'd he will exceed those who have attempted the like."[1]

Jacob Rowe, like John Lethbridge, was a man of Devon but, apart from a passion for diving, they shared few other characteristics. Rowe was no landsman and was usually referred to in documents as 'Captain', a man who was able to command the ships fitted out for his various wreck-hunting expeditions. He was also a well-educated man whose scientific knowledge and skills in research and development enabled him to invent and patent a variety of devices with potential value in navigation, pumping and the reduction of friction in vehicles. His was quite a common West Country name, but he is almost certainly the same Jacob Rowe who was appointed schoolmaster to HMS *Charles Galley* in 1713 and to HMS *Shoreham* in 1715. Naval schoolmasters naturally varied in quality, but the best were fine mathematicians who not only taught navigation to the midshipmen and boys aboard ship but also practised navigation themselves. Captain Thomas Howard of the *Shoreham* had a very high opinion of Rowe and begged the Admiralty to let him remain on his ship, 'he having put himself to considerable expense in providing himself with books, instruments etc for the voyage and extreamly diligent in his imploy'.[2]

Rowe was later to command ships in the merchant service, but his years in the navy were valuable in providing the opportunity to develop various improvements in his navigational instruments. They also enabled him to make some useful contacts which were to prove very important in promoting his treasure hunting schemes. The courting of the good and the great were vital skills for those who wished to thrive in the early eighteenth-century world and Jacob Rowe had the social confidence and smooth tongue to promote himself not just in the familiar milieu of London and the navy, but also in the very different environment of the Scottish aristocracy.

His inventive and networking skills were ready to be put on public display in 1719, when he set out to promote his invention of a new type of quadrant for taking altitudes at sea in order to determine latitude more precisely. He presented his ideas to the Admiralty in October and they arranged for the quadrant to be inspected by the officers of Trinity House, the chartered corporation which had a general watching brief over everything to do with the merchant service. They were impressed and believed that the quadrant 'may tend to the improvement and benefit of navigation', but thought that it should be tried out at sea. The Admiralty appointed Admiral Sir John Jennings and a committee composed of Royal Navy captains and the Master Attendant of Chatham Dockyard to make a practical examination of Rowe and his quadrant. They too were most impressed, after 'seeing several observations made with it' and believed that it 'answers what it contrived for, far beyond any other instrument that I have seen'. Sir John Jennings recommended that Rowe should be reimbursed for his expenses in developing the quadrant and also rewarded for his 'experiments for the improvement of navigation'. This was, in fact, done by royal order in April 1720 when the King ordered the Admiralty to 'reward the said Mr. Rowe in such a manner as you shall judge most suitable to the merit of his said invention'. Impressing the King, the Admiralty and the influential Admiral Sir John Jennings was obviously a good career move.[3]

While Rowe had been working on the quadrant, he had also been perfecting 'a machine for diving, more practicable and in greater depths of water than any yet in use'. In June 1720 he petitioned for letters patent for both of these devices. The Attorney General recommended that he be granted them since invention should be encouraged and the public was not in any danger of loss, since 'it is at the hazard of your petitioner both as to his expense and trouble whether the said invention will have the success he expects or not'. And so, on 12 October 1720, Jacob Rowe was granted a fourteen years' patent for these two inventions and proceeded to try to make some money from them. It could hardly have been a more inauspicious moment to start a new initiative, since the share price of the notorious South Sea Company had just collapsed and with it the whole system of credit, leading to economic confusion in the last three months of 1720 which, according to a historian of the South Sea Bubble, 'has perhaps no parallel in the history of England'. But this does not seem to have worried Jacob Rowe.[4]

The best description of Jacob Rowe's diving machine was written by the inventor himself in an undated and unpublished manuscript called 'A Demonstration of the Diving Engine' which was probably written in the 1730s.[5] The manuscript was beautifully illustrated and shows that Rowe's invention was based on the same principal as John Lethbridge's barrel but did differ in a number of ways. Rowe's machine was made of copper or brass rather than wood and, instead of being straight-sided, it was curved about two-thirds down where the diver's knees would be, this according to Rowe making 'it the more convenient for going between rocks or great stones and for the ease of the diver in working'. Rowe like Lethbridge was convinced that the only way to work underwater was flat on his stomach. 'As do fishes and all water animals, so must men in engines act on their bellies or otherwise would be liable to be thrown up and down with every little set of sea tide or current.' From this prone position Rowe had improved visibility by having the front cover of the machine fitted with a much larger glass, 'from which the diver can wipe the dew or steam with his nose upon occasion'. The diver wore no gauntlets and his arms emerged through tight-fitting metal sleeves which were 'defended by a soft quilting to prevent the arms from hurt by pressure'. And, when he was working in deep water, there was provision for him to have a saddle on his back which was designed to prevent his arms being forced back into the 'barrel' by the pressure of the water.

Otherwise, Jacob Rowe's diving engine was much the same as John Lethbridge's and it had the same disadvantages, namely only about half an hour of bottom time before having to be raised to the surface and supplied with fresh air and unbearable pressure on the arms at any depth below ten fathoms or sixty feet. There has been some dispute as to whether Rowe's machine was really made of expensive brass or copper rather than wood or whether this was just an ideal introduced into his manuscript. He probably did use cheaper wooden barrels on occasion, but there is no doubt that he used machines made of metal as well. In November 1721, for instance, he contracted with two London locksmiths to make and repair his 'engines or machines' for a salary of £40 each per year and 'a further £5 to each of them for every new engine or machine for diving'. It seems unlikely that they would have been employed to make something out of wood. And in the accounts of the expedition to the Cape Verde Islands, which will be discussed later, there is a payment to a copper-smith of just under £25 recorded 'for one engine'.[6]

During the winter of 1720–1 Jacob Rowe was very busy promoting a company to exploit his diving invention, 'the chief use, end and design of the said engine or machine being for fishing on wrecks and getting up treasure and goods that have been sunk in the sea'. Rowe's main associates in setting up the company were two prominent London businessmen, Edward Hughes and Edward Harrison. They decided to divide the patent into forty shares and, so great was thought the potential for Rowe's invention, they had no trouble in selling these shares despite the desperate economic climate. There were to be thirty proprietors, ten of whom, including Rowe and his two key partners, held two shares each, though Rowe was later to sell his own to the other proprietors for a lump sum of £2,500. Nearly every member of the syndicate was a man of considerable contemporary distinction and there was in particular a very strong naval element with four admirals, including the country's current naval hero Sir George Byng, who had utterly destroyed the Spanish fleet off Messina in July 1718, and Sir John Jennings, who had been the first to appreciate Rowe's worth, three other commissioners of the Admiralty and two Royal Navy captains. Other proprietors included Charles Delafaye, Under-Secretary of State, Sir John Eyles, a Director of the Bank of England, and Thomas Pitt, 1st Earl of Londonderry, son of 'Diamond Pitt', the incredibly wealthy East India merchant who invested his mercantile gains in a huge diamond which he sold in 1717 to the Regent of France. The numbers were made up by other members of the establishment such as aristocrats, civil servants and businessmen. There had never before been a treasure hunting syndicate which could match the range of talent, interest and wealth represented by the 'proprietors of Mr. Rowe's diving engine'.[7]

The first business of the partnership was to acquire a grant of an area in which to search for wrecks. This required negotiations with other holders of such grants, such as the assignees of the grant to Edward, Lord Harley, but, with so many senior government officers in the syndicate, the resolution of such problems did not prove too difficult. And so the King was eventually 'pleased to condescend' to give them a fourteen-year 'grant of wrecks and goods derelict . . . between the latitude of 10 and 53 degrees north' in return for a ten per cent royalty on all goods recovered. This huge area, which covered both sides of the Atlantic, included the Cape Verde Islands off the coast of Africa in the east and the whole of the Caribbean, the Bahamas, Bermuda and the American coast as far north as Newfoundland in the west. 'The proprietors of Mr Rowe's diving engine' were in business.

The company had plans for a major treasure hunting cruise in American waters, but their first objective was to be the *Vansittart*, an East-Indiaman on her maiden voyage, which on the night of 2 March 1719 had struck a rock and been wrecked on the north-west point of the Isle of May in the Cape Verde Islands. At first the East India Company was hopeful that the ship could be salvaged, since Michael Gee, the chief mate and the first senior officer to report back in England, said that in his opinion a great part of the ship's treasure could be recovered. Negotiations were set in motion to hire a ship and divers to go out to the wreck, but then came to a halt when Robert Hyde, the captain of the *Vansittart*, reported to the Court of the Company on 22 July 1719.[8]

Hyde had stayed on the island after the ship had been lost and supervised salvage of the wreckage, being successful in recovering two chests of silver coins, more loose coins and bars of silver and a considerable quantity of cloth, most of which was washed and 'cured' and sent out on the next ship to India. But he was very pessimistic about any further success, believing that only the guns and some of the lead from the cargo could be recovered. 'The chests of treasure were broke and the peeces came on shore, but the treasure could not be found. And it was believed the same is in the holes of the rocks which are very deep.' The East India Company was run by practical men who had no wish to lose more money by sending out a salvage party to recover lead and guns whose value was likely to be much less than 'the charge of sending a ship with divers etc.'. So they abandoned the *Vansittart*, though they still claimed a legal right to their silver lying at the bottom of the sea. This, however, was hardly likely to deter treasure hunters, such as the Jamaican sloops which *Applebee's Weekly Journal* reported on 4 July 'going out thence to fish for the riches of the *Vansittart*', from trying their luck.[9]

Rowe's syndicate knew everything that went on in the Council of the East India Company, for some of the proprietors such as Edward Hughes were also directors of the Company. By the same token they also knew exactly what had been shipped on the *Vansittart* namely lead, cloth, 'petty merchandize' such as gunpowder, cordial waters and looking-glasses and, most importantly, the 'treasure', forty chests of silver in coins and bars, a total of 141,000 ounces which were valued in the Company's ledgers at just under £40,000. Captain Hyde had saved less than a tenth of this, so that what remained provided an exciting opportunity to try out Captain Jacob Rowe's diving machine.[10]

The early 1720s were a period of great potential danger from pirates, one of whose favourite haunts was the Cape Verde Islands, so the syndicate took care that their investment was well protected. They had a ship of 380 tons and 36 guns called the *Audrey* built for them and also bought as her consort the *Jolly Batchelor,* a smaller brigantine of 20 guns which was to be commanded by Rowe's brother John, two 'ships of force' which were provided with commissions to attack and seize 'all pyrates, free-booters and sea rovers together with their ships and vessels, goods and merchandizes'. Just to be on the safe side, they petitioned successfully to have the forty-gun Royal Navy frigate *Launceston* protect them as well. This ship was about to engage on a surveying voyage in the Cape Verde Islands and then in the West Indies and her captain, Bartholomew Candler, was ordered not just to protect the ships of the syndicate while they were fishing for treasure, but also to try out Jacob Rowe's navigational instruments in the course of his surveying. Captain Candler may well have been a friend of Rowe, but it was thought wise to ensure his loyalty by the gift of a share in the syndicate.[11]

The two ships and their naval escort were ready to sail from Spithead late in April 1721. The syndicate's ships carried between them 143 men, including a Captain of Marines in command of thirty men, so they were well equipped to see off all but the most powerful attack. They were also well supplied with what was necessary to find the treasure of the *Vansittart,* 'proper engines, machines and men skilled in the art of fishing and diving for treasure', five machines in all being shipped together with two engineers to repair them. And, just to ensure that they did not waste too much time when they arrived at the Isle of May, they had hired the cooper and other mariners from the *Vansittart* to show them 'the place where she met with her misfortune and encouraged them so to do with great rewards, gratuities and promises'.[12]

Among the surviving papers relating to this treasure hunting voyage are the orders given by the syndicate to Captain Jacob Rowe, their 'Commander-in-Chief'. This is a unique document which is full of interest and surprises. Clause One, for instance, is not quite what one would expect. 'You are to take care that God Almighty be duly worshipped on board your ships once every day by the whole ship's company according to the liturgy of the Church of England, and that blasphemy, drunkenness, swearing and profaneness be discountenanced and restrained as much as possible.' What follows is more predictable. Rowe was to sail via Madeira to the Isle of May 'and endeavour with the engines by you invented to recover lost treasure on some rocks near the said island'. He was then to follow in the wake of the great divers of the past by proceeding 'to the Plate Wreck of Sir William Phipps near the Bahama Islands' and from there to engage in a more general treasure hunting voyage in the West Indies and the Straits of Florida, making 'strict enquiry after such wrecks as have been lost' and sending home 'the most exact account you can of bearings, distances etc. as often as you have opportunity'. This was to be a long voyage in dangerous waters and Rowe was ordered 'to preserve the most cordial affection and harmony among your officers and company'. In a mercenary world the obvious way to do this was to dangle rewards before the sailors and divers and so 'the owners have agreed to give as an encouragement five per cent over and above their pay on all such treasure and effects as shall be taken up. As also that every person that continues under water an hour shall have twenty shillings sterling for an hour and so in proportion for a greater or lesser time to be paid out of the effects which shall be recovered.'[13]

Security was obviously an important issue and this was addressed in a number of clauses in the orders. Treasure recovered was to be sent home on Royal Navy ships or on powerful merchant ships, 'not exceeding £30,000 on board any man of war or £10,000 on any merchant ship'. Very great care was to be taken of the machines which were to be kept aboard the *Audrey* when not in use, 'that they may be in less danger of falling into the enemyes hands. And should any such accident happen as to put you in eminent danger of being taken, in such extremity we direct you to throw the engines over board.' No foreigner was to have a chance to use Rowe's invention. The proprietors certainly expected trouble – 'be as much on your guard as in time of war' – and the orders contain clauses which would not be out of place in the articles of association of a privateer or even a buccaneer. To encourage the men to fight, provision was made for a scale of compensation for those who were maimed which was almost identical to that used by the buccaneers in the West Indies, 200 dollars for the loss of an arm or a leg, 100 dollars for an eye and so on. And, if anyone was killed, they were 'to receive 400 dollars out of the effects taken up by diving or from any enemy and, in case of the capture of an enemy, one half to the owners, the other to the captains, officers and company as distributed in the privateers gone to the South Sea'. The privateers referred to were the *Speedwell* and the *Success* which had been commissioned to attack Spanish shipping in the Pacific during the short war against Spain which began in 1718. It is perhaps no surprise to discover that the principal partner in the Gentlemen Adventurers' Association which backed this notorious voyage was none other than Edward Hughes, Rowe's most important partner who was the managing agent, or ships' husband, for the treasure hunting voyage, receiving a commission of 2½ per cent on everything that was spent in the fitting out and conduct of the voyage. He certainly had an eye for the main chance. [14]

Captain Candler in the *Launceston* and the two treasure hunting ships arrived at the Isle of May on 29 May 1721 and soon afterwards the divers and engines were sent in the brigantine to the wreck site off the north-west point of the island. No details of their work have survived, though it is clear that it was fairly uneventful and it was certainly remarkably successful, given the pessimistic report from Robert Hyde, the *Vansittart's* late captain. The salvage work was completed on 2 August, too late in the season to make an expedition to the West Indies practicable. Rowe asked Candler to escort him clear of the Cape Verde Islands, 'having reason to believe there may be some pyrates hereabouts, those islands being seldom without'. This was done and, on 21 August, the *Audrey* parted from the *Launceston* and set sail for London. She had 27 chests on board containing just under 75,000 ounces of silver in coins and bars from the *Vansittart*, 868 slabs of lead, 64 iron guns and eleven anchors. This was over half the treasure originally loaded on the ship and, in all, the goods recovered were worth some £20,000, less than a tenth of what Phips had brought home in June 1686 but an awful lot more than any treasure hunting expedition had returned with since then. [15]

Jacob Rowe was later to give a general description of the salvage which emphasizes the difficulty of the task. 'After severall fruitless trials [they] did with the help and by the means of the said engines or machines . . . with great difficulty and hazard of the lives of the persons who worked . . . take and fish up divers quantities and parcells of treasure or silver which lay at the bottom of the sea, the greatest part of which silver or treasure was found loose and intermixt with the soil and sand at the bottom of the sea in four and five fathom water and under a violent surge and swelling water.' By contrast, Charles Delafaye, Under-Secretary of State and one of the proprietors, made it sound easy in a letter attempting to solicit Spanish participation in the treasure hunting company. Ever since Captain Phips had had to abandon the wreck of the *Concepción*, he wrote, 'the virtuosos' had been trying to contrive 'an engine to perform . . . more than can be done by natural diving'. Now Jacob Rowe had devised such an engine and in it 'our people have wrought in six fathoms and may do it in twenty, continuing there half an hour at a time, and having the free use of their arms and hands so far as to dig up chests of money that were bury'd in the sand. In short they brought us home the money which is a sensible demonstration.'[16]

The money thus brought home was unloaded into the longboat of the *Audrey* and carried up-river through London Bridge to Charing Cross where it was deposited in the vault of Andrew Drummond, a wealthy goldsmith-banker who was a member of the syndicate. Here, Sir Isaac Newton, Master of the Mint, and John Sydenham, the Treasury observer who had sailed with Rowe to watch out for the King's interest, saw the King's tenth part of the silver weighed and delivered to them. Newton had it brought to the Mint where it was 'converted into the current coyn of this Kingdom', which after melting costs and wastage amounted to £1,842 15s 0d which was paid into His Majesty's Privy Purse on 5 December 1721. There is no record as to what King George I spent this windfall on, but no doubt he thought it was well worth the employment of one of his ships for several months. Meanwhile, the lead, guns and anchors had been delivered to the wharf of William Harrison, another member of the syndicate, and from there taken to Lloyds' Coffee House in Lombard Street to be sold at auction 'for £800 or thereabouts'.[17]

Once this important business had been concluded, the Rowe brothers, Lethbridge, the *Jolly Batchelor* and a new vessel called the *Henrietta Yacht* were free to set off on a wreck-hunting jaunt along the south coast of England, not at all daunted by the fact that it was now the middle of winter. They first looked for an unnamed wreck off the Sussex coast during the last eleven days of December 1721. This was probably the *Guinea Frigate* which had attracted so much attention from Edmond Halley and others in the 1690s. Few divers could sail past Sussex without trying their luck with this wreck, as will be seen in the next chapter. Then, on New Year's Day, Rowe's two ships sailed down to the Lizard and were to stay there and elsewhere in Cornwall until 28 March 1722. Their first objective, reported in most of the London newspapers, was to fish on the wreck of the Royal Navy ship *Royal Anne Galley* 'with a new-invented diving-engine'. By mid-February they seem to have given this up and were now focussed on 'a galleon that was lost there many years ago. It seems the persons concerned flatter themselves with success in this undertaking, as having a man with them who was at the taking plate out of that wreck about twenty years ago.' But this venture, like the others on this cruise along the south coast, was to prove completely unsuccessful, as we learn from the papers of John Sydenham, the Treasury agent appointed 'to inspect into the wreck fishing'. He had nothing to report but his unpaid expenses.[18]

While Rowe was diving fruitlessly in Sussex and Cornwall, the East India Company was preparing to sue him and his partners for fishing up 'their' silver from the wreck of the *Vansittart.* They put the business into the very competent hands of Mr Woodford, a legal troubleshooter who, in a long career, was to solve many problems for the Company. He opened proceedings by demanding the return of the Company's 'proper goods and effects' and, when this had been predictably refused, opened proceedings against Rowe's syndicate in the Exchequer Court. The case was weak and rested mainly on their assurance that their men had only left the wreck 'for want of proper engines' and planned to return later when they were better equipped. This was easily proved false by the syndicate's lawyers, since the decision to abandon the wreck was clearly minuted in the Company's records. The defendants were also able to confuse the issue by stating that the Company had no proof that what had been recovered actually came from the wreck of the *Vansittart* and not from the many other wrecks, English, French and Dutch, which littered the north coast of the Isle of May. Their final clinching point was that the Court of Directors of the East India Company knew all about the preparations for Rowe's expedition and had made absolutely no objection. 'On the contrary several of the Directors . . . desired to be concerned in the said undertaking.'[19]

On the face of it, the East India Company did not have a chance of victory. But the process of law was always slow and expensive and decisions in the equity courts very difficult to predict, so that those concerned in the 'Adventure of Rowe's Expedition' proposed that the matter be referred to the arbitration of two men chosen by each side. Such mediation was governed by an Act of Parliament of 1698 but not very many people made use of this law, preferring to employ the more informal and cheaper extra-judicial arbitration, as in this case. The dispute was then fairly quickly brought to a close on 18 January 1723 with the agreement by Captain Rowe's syndicate to pay the Company £1,000 in return for 'a release of all claims and demands . . . relating to any silver or goods fisht up at the Isle of May by the ships *Audrey* and *Jolly Batchelor*'. This was only about five per cent of what had been recovered, but it was seen as almost a victory by the Company which believed this compromise would provide 'a good handle to intitle the Company to a demand in case of any the like unfortunate occasions'. Woodford was thanked profusely and presented 'with a warrant for three hundred guineas' as a gratuity and his two clerks got twenty guineas each 'in consideration of their extraordinary diligence and service to the Company'.[20]

Jacob Rowe himself was not present to take part in this lawsuit. On 5 May 1722, his syndicate informed the Admiralty that 'encouraged by their late success in the Isle of May', they had fitted out the *Henrietta Yacht* and the *Dover Sloop*, 'under the direction of

Captain Rowe to proceed forthwith to the West Indies to fish on wrecks in the Gulf of Florida, the Bahama shoals and in other parts'. Since these were pirate-infested waters, they asked for naval protection 'as opportunities shall offer'. This was duly promised and, on 11 May, Rowe set out on what turned out to be a very unsuccessful voyage.[21]

The bald outline of this expedition was provided by John Sydenham, the Treasury agent, who once again was claiming without much success for his expenses. His petitions to the Treasury show that the two ships went again to the Isle of May, where they recovered some more lead from the *Vansittart*, and then to the Gulf of Florida and 'other places in America'. Here Sydenham claimed that 'he suffered very great hardships' which lasted until 8 September 1723 when they returned 'without success', the last statement being supported by his accounts which show just a small amount of gum elemi, a resin, and logwood, a dyestuff, 'taken up in the Gulph of Florida' and absolutely no treasure at all.[22]

A letter from Jacob Rowe, written on 20 February 1723 from the Bahamas to an unknown correspondent in England, provides some more information, most of which was bad news for the recipient. He had delayed writing, 'in hopes I should soon be able to give you an account of some good success, but badness of weather, unseasonableness of the year and great quantities of sand being thrown on the wrecks lying on the coast of Florida has baulked my expectation'. He gives no indication as to what wreck or wrecks he was looking for, but the coast of Florida was littered with Spanish ships at this time following a terrible fleet disaster in July 1715 in which ten ships had been shattered along some forty miles of reefs, a thousand men drowned and a fortune in silver coins and bullion lost in the sea. Much of this was recovered by Spanish salvors and by sloops from Jamaica, Bermuda and the Bahamas, but there was still a lot left, some of which was to be discovered and salvaged in the twentieth century. It seems probable that it was these wrecks that Rowe was after, though the only ship he specifically mentions in his letter was 'the petatch' which he hoped to find on the Bimini Bank, 'if any part remains above the sands'.[23]

Rowe was quite optimistic about finding this ship, though it was unlikely to be all that profitable since *petachio* is merely Spanish for an advice ship which rarely carried much if any treasure. The general tone of the letter was, however, one of deep depression, the joy of his success just eighteen months earlier forgotten in his current failure. He berates himself for losing his sense of judgment in the wreck business and apologizes that his bad decisions have caused his correspondent to lose money. 'What adds most to my sorrow, is the thought that you have been a sufferer by my follies; but for the future I hope to stand the surer and I shall always ground my opinion on something more solid than superficial appearances and empty sound of words.' What exactly Rowe meant by this sensible resolution is not spelled out, but it would seem that his folly lay in leaving such near certainties as the wreck of the *Vansittart*, whose value and location were known and from which the syndicate had made so much money, for the tantalising but ultimately ruinous lure of Spanish treasure ships. It all made him very miserable. He closed his letter with 'my most humble service to your Lady and to my good friend Mr. Strahan', one of the shareholders. 'The latter with your self I may depend on to be my fast friends, but don't flatter myself of a third in the world except my brother and nephew to whom likewise pleased to remember my love and service.'[24]

On his return to London, Rowe decided to abandon wreck-hunting for the time being and renew his previous interests in navigation and invention. In 1725 he published *Navigation Improved*, book one of which described the quadrant which he had first demonstrated to Sir John Jennings and others six years previously, and book two was 'An Essay on the Discovery of the Longitude', a very popular subject for inventors since a 1714 Act of Parliament offered a prize of £20,000 to anyone who could devise a method of determining it to an accuracy of half a degree. In his introduction, Rowe apologized for the delay in publication, claiming that he had 'been hindered by my undertaking two expeditions on wrecks, which . . . I could not avoid'.[25]

The Admiralty, which had welcomed Rowe's new quadrant for determining latitude, now approached the octogenarian Sir Isaac

Newton for his opinion on this longitude innovation. Newton was beginning to lose patience with such demands, since he was quite certain in his own mind that true longitude could only be found by very complicated astronomical calculations relating to the motion of the moon or the innermost satellite of Jupiter. He was therefore predictably unimpressed by Rowe's attempt to solve the problem by constructing a more accurate hourglass. Nevertheless, he thought that 'the hour glasses of Mr Rowe made with sand of tin are a very good piece of art' and might be used to replace hour-glasses using common sand when calculating the ship's speed. He also found Rowe's instruments for 'taking altitudes at sea . . . well contrived, and deserve to be tried at sea for finding the latitude.' All of which was pretty high praise from such a great man, even if it did not secure Jacob Rowe the longitude prize.[26]

Jacob Rowe continued in inventing mode into 1726, taking out two more patents, for pumping and raising water, but in 1727 he was gripped again by the treasure hunting bug which was to take him this time to the far north, to Fair Isle, the remote and very rugged island that lies halfway between the Orkneys and Shetlands. These northern islands had always been the graveyard of ships whose wrecks at this time were the perquisite of the Earl of Sutherland. No doubt he or one of his agents had heard of Rowe's success with his diving engine in the Cape Verde Islands and invited him to contract to dive on what was potentially the most valuable wreck under his jurisdiction. This was *El Gran Grifón*, a Spanish Armada ship which was mistakenly believed to be 'the Grand Admiral of Spain . . . mounted with 130 brass guns or there-about' and carrying a great treasure. This was, alas, quite untrue, the ship being merely a very large cargo ship and what treasure she had aboard safely secured after she wrecked, but Rowe of course did not know this and he was hooked. In March 1727, he gained permission from the Earl to dive on the wreck, giving him one-fifth of what he recovered as a royalty.[27]

Rowe chose as partner in this venture William Evans, a ship's carpenter from Deptford with experience in diving and the construction of diving barrels who had helped him with one of his inventions. They agreed to share costs and profits equally and to fit out 'a ship with the proper engines, instruments, materials, provisions and meanes for diving upon and recovering a wreck supposed to be lying near the island called Fair Island in the Orkneys'.[28] The partners arrived at the island in the summer of 1728 and had no trouble in finding the 140-year-old wreck whose location was part of local lore and well known to the islanders who believed that it was 'now converted into a rock and covered with sea weed'. The ship had smashed to pieces against the overhanging cliffs of Stroms Hellier in the south-east corner of the island and the wreckage lay some fifty feet deep in underwater caves and amongst the rocks.

At the end of July, a local agent wrote an optimistic letter to the Earl of Morton who had replaced the Earl of Sutherland as Admiral of Orkney and Shetland. 'The company of divers at Fair Isle have found the wreck . . . and have got two or three brass cannon and talk of a great prospect they have here of no less than £40 or £50,000 sterling.' Such prospects were utter nonsense of course and these two guns and 'some other articles of a less value' were just about all that Rowe and Evans recovered from the wreck of *El Gran Grifón*. This was not for want of trying. Where they believed more guns and the treasure lay was covered with wreckage, rocks and seaweed all cemented together so, to the horror of modern marine archaeologists, they tried to clear the site 'by forceable drudges or draggs removing the crusted rubbish', a labour which not only revealed no treasure but resulted in the death of one of their men.[29]

It must then have been with great pleasure that they read letters from Edinburgh dated 26 July 1728 offering them alternative employment. These were written by Alexander Mackenzie of Delvine, a lawyer who amongst many other offices was Admiral Depute for the Western Isles (i.e. the Hebrides) which gave him rights over wrecks similar to those of the Earl of Morton in the northern isles. Mackenzie, who was to develop a ruinous enthusiasm for treasure hunting, had learned of the shipwreck in March of that year of a Dutch East-Indiaman, the *Adelaar* (Eagle), on the island of Barra at the southern end of the Outer Hebrides and so within his jurisdiction. He sent his brother-in-law Eugene Fotheringham to investigate and he did a very thorough job. He

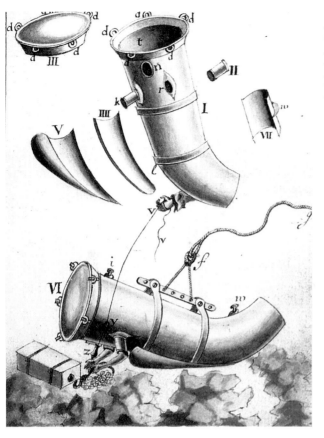

1. Jacob Rowe's diving engine. Illustrated from his unpublished manuscript 'A Demonstration of the Diving Engine' now published in a facsimile edition by the Historical Diving Society (2000).

2. 'An English East-Indiaman, c. 1720' by Peter Monamy. The East-Indiaman *Vansittart* which wrecked in the Cape Verde Islands on her maiden voyage in 1719 would have looked very similar.

3. Working the tongs from a small boat. Illustrated from the logbook of William Evans. The man in the bows is looking at the sea bed through a glass in order to direct operations.

In this manner, the Water, Smoake, and peeces of the Ship, appeard aboue after it was fired vnder,

V.

4. Blowing up a wrecked collier in the mouth of the Tyne before a huge crowd in 1673. Engraving by Wenceslaus Hollar of Edmond Custis's dramatic underwater explosion.

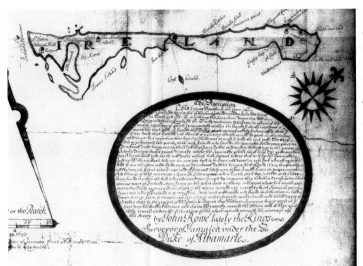

5. The supposed location of the treasure buried by the Spaniards on Ireland Island, Bermuda, from the survey carried out by John Rowe in 1693. The dotted line leads to the 'yellowood tree' where 'people do imagine they hid their treasure.'

6. The VOC wharf at Middelburg from an aquarelle by J Arends. William Evans worked for the Company here during his winters in Zeeland.

7. Captain Thomas Dickinson's 158ft long derrick built in 1831 to enable divers to work directly above the wreck of HMS *Thetis* at Cape Frio, Brazil. Sadly, it was only in operation for one week before being completely destroyed in a storm.

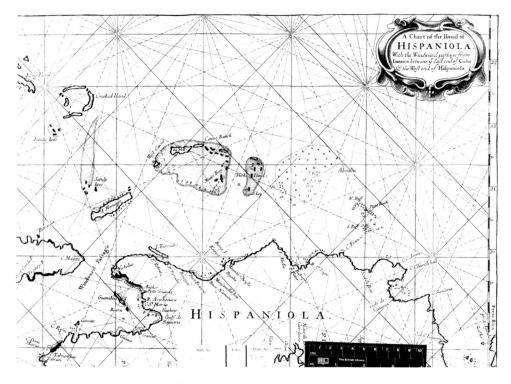

8. Chart drawn in 1687 for *The West-India Pilot* showing the 'Plate Rack', ie the wreck of the *Concepción* which had been discovered by the expedition led by William Phips earlier in the same year.

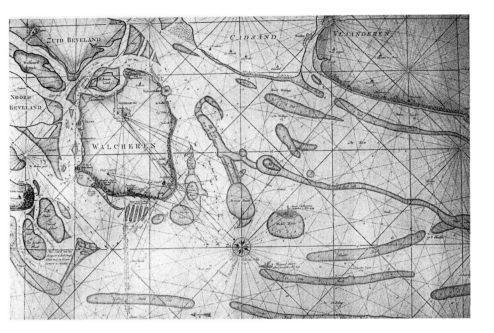

9. Chart drawn for the VOC to show the location of the wrecks of the *Vliegent Hart* and *Anna Catharina* which were lost amidst the sandbanks of the estuary of the Westerschelde in 1735. William Evans and his men dived on these wrecks.

10. Engravings on a silver tankard made to celebrate John Lethbridge's success in salvaging treasure from the Dutch ship *Slot ter Hooge* which wrecked at Porto Santo near Madeira in 1724.

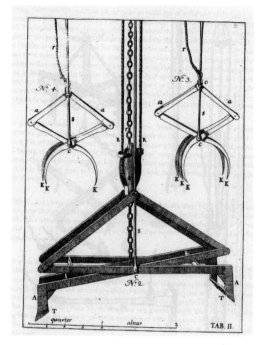

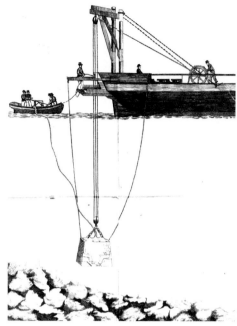

11. Divers' tongs of various sorts drawn in 1734 for Märten Triewald's book *The Art of Living Under Water* (English translation 2004).

12. John Rennie's improved diving bell from S W Smith's *Observations on Diving* (1823). This type was used by Isaac Dickson's expedition to Vigo Bay in 1825-6.

13. Semi-atmospheric diving apparatus made by William Tonkin for John Braithwaite to work on the wreck of the *Earl of Abergavenny*. Illustration from the frontispiece of the *Monthly Magazine*.

14. Portrait of Sir William Phips (artist unknown).

15. Detailed chart showing the wreck site of the *Concepción* probably drawn for Sir John Narborough's expedition in 1688.

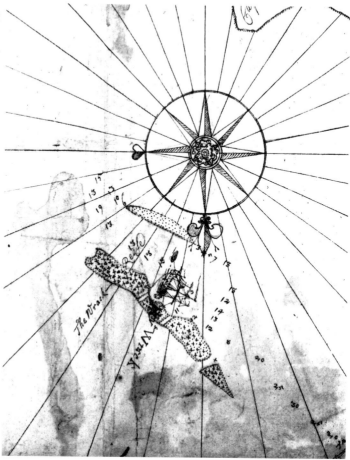

16. Edmond Halley's diving bell of 1691 showing how the bell was supplied with fresh air from a barrel (C) and also 'the travelling diver' (F) who was supplied with air from the bell to his 'capp of maintenance'.

17. Swedish diver working with tongs on the guns of the royal warship *Vasa* which sank near Stockholm in 1628. The first of over fifty brass cannon was recovered using a newly designed diving bell in 1664.

18. Royal Navy Sailors working from a diving platform slung from suspension cables above the wreck of HMS *Thetis*. Drawing by Captain de Roos of HM sloop *Algerine*.

noted the dangerous location of the wreck, 'all surrounded with steep rocks', but believed that in fine weather it should prove possible to dive on the wreck which lay in only four to six fathoms of water. And this would be worth doing, since amongst papers recovered from one of the corpses was a receipt signed by the Dutch ship's former captain for the treasure in silver bars and coins which had been loaded in seventeen numbered chests.[30]

All that was needed were skilled divers and, by good chance, such men were present in the Orkneys, conveniently on the way from Edinburgh to Barra. 'This is to inform you', wrote Mackenzie to William Evans, 'that a Dutch East India ship outward bound was wreckt on the island of Barra in the end of March last and, as we have power to fish thereon, we are of opinion that it would be worth your time and pains to goe there. The wreck lyes in four to six fathom water, for we have had a person at it already sounding the depth. We know also the extent of the treasure which she had on board . . . This project is well worth the entring upon.' No doubt Rowe and Evans, labouring fruitlessly on Fair Isle, agreed.[31]

Mackenzie fitted out a sloop, the *Grizel* of Leith under the command of John Hay, an old acquaintance of Evans who was to remain on Barra to watch over Mackenzie's interests. Hay sailed for the northern isles at the end of July and was accompanied by Fotheringham whose visit to Barra had given him so great a hope of success that he put up most of the original working capital in return for a fifth share in the enterprise. He had instructions to engage the 'skillfull dyvers who were then working on a wreck at Fair Island . . . on such terms as [he] should learn to be the practice in the like cases'. The divers were in a position to ensure that their services were not acquired cheaply and on 19 August they signed a favourable contract with Fotheringham. After one-fifth had been deducted for the Duke of Queensberry, High Admiral of Scotland, they were to get a third 'of all gold, money, silver, copper, brass or goods of any kind whatsoever recovered from the wreck'.[32]

Rowe, Evans and Hay now sailed from the Orkneys to Barra in the *Grizel* and in the divers' own sloop *Charming Jenny*. Rowe promised to come back and winter in Fair Island and to continue work on *El Gran Grifón* in the spring and, in the meantime, he arranged for a gang of local men to continue to clear 'the ground on ye west side of the reef where I am well assured the greatest part of the wreck lyes'. Later he also wrote to an unknown correspondent with Spanish contacts whom he believed would be able to locate in Spain the papers of survivors from the wreck and so 'learn from their journals what quantity of treasure was lost', finding such papers being a perennial dream of treasure hunters. But, as it turned out, Jacob Rowe never did return to Fair Isle and was to spend the summer of 1729 searching for another non-existent Spanish treasure as will be seen.[33]

Rowe and Evans were beset by storms and crosswinds in their voyage to the Outer Hebrides and they did not arrive at Barra until early September. What happened there will be discussed in the next chapter which is about the diving business run by William Evans of Deptford. It was Evans who did nearly all the very dangerous diving on Barra and he stayed there much longer than Jacob Rowe who sailed back to the Scottish mainland in early October and, after doing some business in Edinburgh, spent the rest of the winter in London. Rowe had plenty to think about during this period. The initial salvage in Barra had been astonishingly successful with over £20,000 worth of silver in coin and bars brought up by Evans and one of his crew in just four days in September. But it seemed very doubtful whether Rowe would be able to retain his substantial share of this bounty. He learned in Edinburgh that the Dutch East India Company was suing Mackenzie in the Scottish Admiralty Court, an action which gave rise to several other lawsuits between the various people involved in the salvage of the *Adelaar*, including Rowe and Evans. The suit in the Admiralty Court was not decided until July 1729, but it was clear from the outset that the Dutch company had a much better case than had the English company when they sued Rowe and his syndicate over the salvage from the *Vansittart*. The Dutch successfully claimed that they had not abandoned the wreck and were simply waiting for their best divers to return from the East Indies. Nevertheless, they had to accept that salvage was due to Rowe and Evans and that Mackenzie's expenses in recovering their treasure should be met.[34]

The only real winners in this lawsuit were as usual the lawyers and the main losers were Mackenzie and to a lesser extent Rowe. Mackenzie's reaction was that of a gambler rather than a respectable Edinburgh lawyer and Rowe's was also misguided, suggesting that he had not truly learned the lessons of his unprofitable voyage to the West Indies. Earlier in 1728, before he had sailed for Fair Island, Rowe had contracted with the Duke of Argyll to dive on that long-standing chimera, the so-called treasure of the Tobermory galleon, Rowe to have three-quarters of what was recovered and the Duke the other quarter. Now, on 4 June 1729, Rowe brought Mackenzie in to finance this venture in return for one-eighth of his contracted share. Other backers included the Duke himself and Duncan Forbes of Culloden, the Lord Advocate of Scotland. Rowe may have been guilty of choosing bad targets, but he had lost none of the powers of persuasion necessary to bring in great men to pay for his folly.[35]

It had been some forty years since the last serious attempt to salvage the Tobermory galleon, but the wreck had lost none of its allure in the meantime. It was still believed to be the Admiral of Spain, as Rowe had been informed by Lord Pembroke, a noted antiquarian who also told him of the great treasure that was there to be found. 'I did believe the wreck to be very rich and so rich that I was in hopes that holding but a small share to myself would be sufficient.' And so Rowe financed his venture by giving away most of his original three-quarters share to 'several noblemen and gentlemen in England and Scotland' in return for promises of monthly payments of working capital. With this money and a loan from Mackenzie, Rowe was able to buy a suitable salvage vessel in London, the *Princess Mary*, purchase equipment and stores and hire a crew whose loyalty and effort was ensured by promising them five per cent of what was recovered, a percentage which seems to have been the norm on Rowe's expeditions.[36]

Rowe set sail back to Scotland in June 1729 and he arrived in Mull some time in August or early September. His progress there can be followed by letters he wrote to Alexander Mackenzie in Edinburgh and also letters reporting his activities written by Richard Graham, a Glasgow businessman who arranged for food, drink and equipment to be shipped to him in Tobermory as occasion demanded. These letters, like most written by treasure hunters to their backers, are full of optimism as to the ultimate success of the venture, but such ebullience soon becomes rather forced as month followed month with no success and money problems built up, since this same lack of success led many of Rowe's backers to stop sending him his monthly payments.[37]

Previous attempts at salvage and the passage of time had ensured that the wreck site at Tobermory was in a real mess by 1729 which made searching for treasure chests and other valuables very difficult. Preliminary investigation had led to the discovery 'under the ballast of the wreck . . . [of] a large platform covered with boards under which we discover a great number of casks and chests, but they being cemented hard together we have not as yet been able to take up a specimen to prove whether ye same be treasure'. Rowe naturally thought that such a specimen would be sure to be positive and promised to send an express letter 'upon the first certain discovery of treasure'. Mackenzie and Graham were, however, to wait in vain for this express as Rowe spent the late summer and winter of 1729 trying to clear away all the rubbish on top of the 'treasure'. 'We have had very few opportunities for diving since my last', he wrote in November, 'but we have been making as large a progress by way of dragging or clearing the wreck as if it had been summer season, so that in the spring season when the water is most clear and fittest for diving we shall have nothing more to do than clearing of wood and taking up guns and treasure.'[38]

By February 1730 his men had cleared the whole length of the wreck and he felt certain he would be able to discover 'the platform of treasure' once he had 'any fair weather to work with our engine'. He also hoped to find most of the guns which he believed had been thrown out of the ship by the explosion which wrecked her in 1588. Early in May Graham reported to Mackenzie that he had had no recent letter from Rowe, 'but am told he was never in such great expectations. He has got through the platform . . . and was in hopes to lift the whole great lump of treasure they had in view.' This optimistic letter was followed by a long silence which was not broken until 21 November 1730 when Rowe admitted to Mackenzie that he had not written because of 'want of good success, as not being willing to break in on your time with only the bare account of fruitless labours.' On the same day he wrote a rather more informative letter to the Lord Advocate, one of his backers. The divers had, he wrote, cleared right down to the platform at the bottom of the wreck, but in breaking it up they had found no treasure. Nevertheless, both these letters end on an optimistic note. He did not doubt that he would recover the 'guns and treasure in the summer' and so end 'this tedious affair with a prosperous event'.[39]

By the summer of 1731, after two years hard labour, Rowe no longer had much confidence in finding anything of value within the wreck which he had now cleared down to the floor timbers. His hopes now rested in the waters outside the ship where the divers had found 'severall banks of hard semented matters' which he was sure must contain either guns or treasure. Rowe had invented a secret weapon to break up these concretions, 'our loaded steel dart which in four days did effectually perform its office on a heap lying close to the sternpost of the wreck whereby next week (the tydes falling out then for our diving) I shall be able to give you an account what it contains'. What the steel dart was loaded with and how it worked is not explained, but it was certainly very effective and several more 'banks' were broken up. However, nothing much of interest was discovered, though 'there still remains some hard banks that are large enough to contain all the treasure that I could wish to find'.[40]

This was just wishful thinking and now, as the summer of 1731 changed to autumn, Rowe was becoming desperate as no treasure was forthcoming and his money problems multiplied. In October he was so short of cash that he dismissed half his men and sold his ship, the *Princess Mary*, in order to keep the other half 'working on the wreck during the winter, having a sloop for the purpose'. Rowe himself left for London, telling Mackenzie that he planned to return to Scotland in the spring. If this was true when he wrote it, he soon changed his mind and decided to stay in London. He had had enough and was never to return, so leaving the unfortunate and soon to be ruined Mackenzie to be sued by the depleted and now unpaid salvage crew. 'We are poor seamen', they claimed in court, 'all, except one, strangers in this Kingdom [i.e. Scotland], destitute of sustenance, and wanting even clothing, and therefore expect dispatch.' And so ended the sad story of 'Captain Jacob Rowe and Company, Fishers Adventurers on the Spanish Admirall's Wreck'.[41]

Anyone who has read Jacob Rowe's letters from Mull would be surprised to learn that his was not the last attempt to find the Tobermory treasure. He was so thorough and had cleared so much of the wreck in his destructive but efficient way that the possibility of there still being undiscovered treasure seems very remote. And indeed the knowledge of Rowe's failure seems to have discouraged any further serious expedition until the twentieth century. But, from 1903 until the early 1980s with breaks for the two World Wars, there were nearly continuous attempts to locate the wreck and, more importantly, its reputed treasure. Company after company was established with names like the 'Pieces of Eight Syndicate' or the 'Tobermory Galleon Salvage Company'. The best divers using state-of-the-art equipment were hired, including in the early 1950s Royal Naval frogmen and, in 1982, some of the team who recovered the gold from the wreck of HMS *Edinburgh* in the Baring Sea, perhaps the greatest of all treasure hunting successes of modern times.[42]

Some of these expeditions made interesting finds – there was after all a sixteenth-century wreck at the bottom of Tobermory Bay – but none of them recovered anything that remotely resembled treasure. And none of them seem to have bothered to read Jacob Rowe's letters which are readily available in the National Library of Scotland, let alone the documents in Croatia and Spain which have enabled historians to discover that the Tobermory galleon was, in fact, the *Brod Martolosi*, a large cargo ship from Ragusa (Dubrovnik) which was known to the Spaniards who hired her as the *San Juan de Sicilia*. This same research has shown that this ship did not carry 'plate, jewels, gold and silver to the value of several millions', as claimed by those promoting expeditions to work the wreck; on the contrary, the Tobermory galleon carried no treasure at all, though even now there are some who refuse to believe it.

The collapse of Jacob Rowe's Tobermory dream led him once

more to abandon diving and the sea and to devote himself to mechanical invention and writing. In 1734, he published *All Sorts of Wheel-carriage Improved*, an attempt to reduce or remove the friction of wheels, which he claimed to have written seven years before with the assistance or at least the encouragement of his former diving partner William Evans. It was also about this time that he wrote his unpublished manuscript, 'A Demonstration of the Diving Engine'. The delightful illustrations were designed to appeal to the treasure hunter, showing as they did divers attaching hooks to promising chests or scrabbling about in large piles of pieces of eight.[43]

The main purpose of the manuscript was to provide a detailed description of Rowe's version of the diving barrel, but there are several other sections or chapters describing techniques for locating wrecks and working on them. Some of these seem to be theoretical, and indeed impractical, such as the 'lamp for burning under water' or his method of igniting gunpowder with a clockwork fuse encased in a watertight box, 'such a machine any clock or watchmaker is capable of making'. Others seem more practical and were probably used, such as his instructions for keeping the engine stationary over a wreck when working in rapid tides or currents or his 'method of finding wrecks' which involved going to the general area where one had information of a wreck and then setting up a grid search. There was nothing very new about this, nor indeed in his instructions as to what to do if no wreck is found in the search area. 'If the bottom proves sandy, so as to imagine the wreck or any part of her treasure to be buried: besides searching with the engine we make use of spits fasten'd to poles of a convenient length, and when discovery is made, make use of sand drudges [i.e. dredges] for that purpose.' This was very much the same technique employed by Robert Willis in the 1650s when he was searching for the guns of the *Liberty* in the shifting sands off Harwich.[44]

Using the power of the tide to raise or break up a wreck was a skill long known to divers and we will see in the next chapter just how difficult it was to achieve. Rowe describes a method of doing this which seems practical, though there is no evidence that he ever used it in his diving expeditions. A wooden frame was fitted with rows of empty barrels lashed down so they would not float away. Cables were then attached to the four corners of the raft and made fast 'to the most convenient part of the wreck.' At low water all the slack would be taken in and, in theory, the tide would raise the ship or rip away its deck or whatever else it was planned to do, though in practice something usually went wrong, such as the cables snapping.

Rowe also included a 'method of blowing up rocks and ships' decks etc. under water' which was very similar to that used by Edmond Custis underneath the Tyne in March 1673.[45] This involved a leather pipe, strengthened by a metal worm or spiral inside to prevent it being squeezed by the water pressure, which went down from a small raft on the surface to a barrel of gunpowder in an appropriate position underneath the wreck (or rock). The pipe was connected to the barrel by a brass cylinder containing a fuse. The fuse was then ignited by dropping 'a little red hot bullet' down the pipe 'which will not fail of setting fire to ye fuze (the space of many fathoms from the surface) which must be made to burn long enough for the boat & executors of this performance to get out of danger of the blow'. Rowe never mentioned using gunpowder on his expeditions, but he may have done so in clearing away the wreckage at Tobermory. He certainly had some aboard the *Princess Mary*, but this could, of course, have been for the ship's guns. No one was likely to engage in treasure hunting in this piratical age without the means of defending themselves.

Although Rowe's manuscript is untainted by corrections and elegantly written in a fair copy, it was clearly not finished as originally planned, as it ends with 'an incomplete sentence, 'and therefore make proposals of the utmost improvements thereon as follows . . .'. He also fails to deliver a promise to the reader to say how he first invented his diving engine, 'which shall be thoroughly explained in its proper place', an explanation which would be certainly welcome. This failure to complete and publish the first English manual or monograph on diving is rather strange, since Rowe was certainly not a man who was frightened to appear in print. But it is unlikely that we shall ever know the reason, for

Jacob Rowe, after being so much in the public eye in the 1720s and early 1730s, completely vanishes from the records thereafter except for a cameo appearance in 1743.

The occasion for this was yet another wreck on the Isle of May in the Cape Verde Islands, the scene of Rowe's triumphant salvage of the *Vansittart* in 1721. The victim this time was the *Princess Louisa*, another out-bound East-Indiaman which set sail from Portsmouth on 20 March 1743 with a cargo which included twenty chests of Spanish and Spanish-American pieces of eight, a total of 69,760 ounces of silver. Sailing in company with the *Winchester*, she sighted the Isle of May at midnight on 17 April and about an hour later fired her guns as a signal of danger. Shortly afterwards, the *Winchester* saw her sister ship 'in or very near the breakers', just in time to save herself from the same fate. Attempts to launch boats to rescue survivors were defeated by very high seas and the *Winchester* reluctantly sailed away. 'I am afraid', wrote her captain, 'there is not a man alive of them to tell their tale.' This was too pessimistic as can be seen from a letter written by Stephen Lightfoot, the surgeon of the *Princess Louisa*. Some forty men saved themselves by swimming or clinging to wreckage, but '74 very cleaver fellows drowned' and nothing was saved from the ship. Both survivors and corpses were stripped of their valuables by the islanders, the naked and badly sunburned surgeon being relieved of a diamond ring and a pair of gold buttons which he had hoped to save from the scavengers by carrying them in his mouth.[46]

Reports on the condition and location of the wreck convinced the East India Company that salvage was unlikely to be successful, though it was prepared to sign a contract on terms that were very favourable to the salvors with a syndicate headed by Thomas Hall, a well-known merchant and shipowner who was the stricken ship's husband or managing agent. Hall and his partner, James Pearce, were to retain 80 per cent of what they recovered up to a value of £6,000 and 75 per cent thereafter. On 19 September they agreed that the actual diving should be done by Jacob Rowe who had already written to the Company offering his services. His contract must have been a sore disappointment after the good terms he had negotiated for working on the Scottish wrecks or indeed on the

Vansittart. He was to receive a salary of £6 a month, '£5 as an allowance for liquors' and 'a farther gratuity if meet success on his expedition'.[47]

Whether Rowe actually sailed to the Cape Verde Islands on this venture is not clear but, if he did, he was soon replaced, for another copy of the contract in the voluminous Hall papers has his name crossed out. This second expedition, consisting of a galley and a sloop fitted out 'in a warlike manner', certainly did set out with the aim of combining the salvage of the *Princess Louisa* with slave-trading and privateering. They were, however, unsuccessful in all three ventures and one of their vessels was captured by the French and taken into Bayonne, thus leaving the treasure of the *Princess Louisa* to be discovered by the Portuguese-based company Arqueonautas two and a half centuries later.[48] Why Rowe was replaced is not explained in the Hall papers, but the most likely reason is that he was dead. No further reference to him can be found after September 1743, though one would have thought that somewhere there must have been some obituary or appreciation of a man who had once been so famous. He seems to have been completely forgotten by all those dukes and admirals and other great men who had once courted him as the man with the diving engine who was going to make them rich.

Chapter Ten

The Evans Logbooks

Chapter Ten

The Evans Logbooks

"By what means do you get your living?"
"This deponent uses the art of diving for taking up wrackt goods from the bottom of the sea."
Deposition of William Evans, March 1739.[1]

The main business of the High Court of Admiralty in the eighteenth century consisted of actions brought by disgruntled sailors suing for their wages. One such case was brought in February 1739 by mariners from the *Kitty* sloop 'against the said ship' and her master William Evans. Such a trivial case would not normally be of much interest, but on this occasion serendipity was to make a welcome appearance. For, on 22 May 1739, 'three ship's books marked A, B, C' were deposited as evidence in the Registry of the Court. These three documents have survived and, to this researcher's amazement, turned out to be the logbooks of the diving company run by William Evans covering some five years of the period between September 1728 and January 1739. They suffer from the defects of most logbooks in that they do not tell the modern reader everything he would like to know but, for all that, they provide an unique contribution to the history of English diving in the eighteenth century.[2]

William Evans was a ship's carpenter from Deptford, near London, who first appears on the diving and treasure hunting scene in 1727, as the partner of Jacob Rowe in his expedition to locate and salvage the Spanish Armada wreck, *El Gran Grifón,* on Fair Island. Since Rowe made Evans his equal partner he probably had diving experience before this date, though no positive evidence of this has been discovered. There are hints in the logbooks, but nothing more, that Evans was familiar with the Cape Verde Islands, and so perhaps with the many wrecks in those islands, and, when hired in 1736 by the Dutch East India Company, he was described as 'a veteran diver who had worked before with the English and Swedish East India Companies'. No details were forthcoming, however, and so we are forced to rely on the logbooks themselves for the little that can be discovered about William Evans.[3]

These show that, as well as being a carpenter and diver, he was a seaman who acted as master of his own diving vessels, usually sloops with a crew of some seven or eight men and boys. He was a very practical and competent man who himself carried out much of the repairs of equipment aboard and was quite capable of building a diving-engine for himself, as he did one winter in Zeeland. Evans was a family man, whose wife, and at least one daughter, remained at their house and garden in Deptford when he was away on his diving expeditions, while his brother Samuel acted as mate and his young son William Jr, who wrote up most of the logbooks, was engaged as a boy and later as an adult sailor. Evans was prone to sickness, being quite seriously ill on at least four occasions during the period of the logbooks, but this does not seem to have been related directly to his diving and he was always back at work as soon as possible.[4]

The logbooks start on 10 September 1728 with Evans and his men about to begin work on an unnamed wreck on an island in the Hebrides. It is clear from the context, however, that the island was Barra and the wreck that of the *Adelaar* which, as seen in the last chapter, Evans and Jacob Rowe planned to salvage in partnership with Alexander Mackenzie of Delvine, the Admiral Depute for the Western Isles. This magnificent Dutch East-Indiaman had last been seen by the Minister of the island of North Uist on Saturday 23 March 1728, sailing proudly to the southward in no apparent distress, though she did seem to be keeping closer to the western shore of the island than was thought wise. The following day the wind shifted further into the west and continued so until night when a great storm blew up and the vessel was seen no more. On the Monday morning the villagers of Greian (also spelled Green and Ghrein) in the north-west of Barra went down to the shore to see if the storm had brought them any harvest and were amazed to find the great ship 'intirely beat to pieces, and a great number of the bodies and some goods floating on the beach'.[5]

The local men and their laird, Roderick MacNeil of Barra, tried to keep this bounty to themselves but news of the wreck soon reached Alexander Macdonald in the island of South Uist, some ten miles north of Barra. Macdonald was Mackenzie's 'substitute admiral' in the islands and he set out with three boats full of his armed kinsmen to investigate. On arrival at the wreck site he found that there had been no survivors and saw 'about 240 bodies stript on the beach'. MacNeil of Barra refused to order his men to bury the corpses unless he was given a share of the booty and, after some undignified haggling, was granted a third, though, in fact, there was not much to share out as the goods washed ashore and the 'body pickings' had been spirited away to secret places in the hills by the Barra men. Macdonald reported all this to his superior Alexander Mackenzie in Edinburgh and so set in motion the process which brought William Evans and Jacob Rowe to try to recover the sixteen chests of silver bars and coins and anything else of value which had been loaded on the *Adelaar* at Middelburg in Zeeland.[6]

On the face of it this was not likely to be easy. The wreck lay in only four to six fathoms of water, so was easily within reach of a barrel diver, but in such an awesome place that one shudders to imagine anyone descending into it in a barrel. It was a terribly dangerous location, a cove on the northern side of Greian Head, Barra's north-western headland, open to wind, surge and wild seas coming from the north and west and studded with jagged rocks and the exposed reef called Mollachdag, the 'Cursed Rock', on which the unfortunate ship had been beaten to pieces. Given calm weather, this destruction would have been an advantage since there was unlikely to be any need to rip up decks to get at the cargo. But one can wait a long time for good weather in Barra and, the longer

the divers waited, the more likely the treasure would be washed out
into deeper water beyond their reach.

Barra was said to be 'famous even in the Highlands for being
barbarous' and the islanders were notorious wreckers so that, if the
treasure was successfully recovered, the small crew employed by
Evans and Rowe would be quite incapable of defending it from
marauders. Mackenzie and Macdonald wasted no time in fore-
stalling this problem, ordering 'all the gentlemen in the Countrey
of South Uist with their travelling weapons and their servants to
the number of 150' to proceed to Barra to protect the wreck site and
the salvors and 'to hold courts and make enquiry of the goods
ashore and taken up by the inhabitants'. Since there was little love
lost between the men of the two islands, this was an agreeable duty
and made more so by the prospect of a payment of £1,500 when the
treasure was recovered, riches indeed in the cash-hungry Hebrides.
These gentlemen of South Uist were in holiday mood as they lined
the shore to watch the divers prepare for their work. 'We have had
ever since we arrived here several gentlemen and lairds with their
servants to the number of a hundred', Evans' son reported in the
logbook on 10 September, and three days later he wrote, 'we have
still the same number of gentlemen and servants as before,
continually feasting'.[7]

'On the 14th of September we began our search', wrote Jacob
Rowe in a letter to a correspondent in Edinburgh, 'and on the same
day we discovered some of her guns, and continuing our search
(with the greatest hazard of our lives) on the 18th we discover'd
some chests with treasure lying in eight fathoms of water; which
chests, with great difficulty, hazard and more than ordinary skill we
have fished up . . . The chests we found hanging by ropes (fastened
to each other) on the side of a steep rock, so that the winter storms
must of necessity have broke them loose and tumbled them into 25
fathoms of water.'[8] This is as dramatic a description of a great
treasure hunting feat as one could desire but, strangely enough, it was
a feat in which Rowe seems to have played no part at all. Rowe was
in Barra at this time, but Evans' logbook does not even mention him
and certainly gives him no credit for the recovery of the treasure.
Evans and his men had arrived at the wreck site on 10 September

and spent the next few days getting their equipment ready and arranging for accommodation ashore. Every day the weather got slightly better and, on 14 September, the sea was reported 'much abated and water pretty clear'. On this day they recovered three small brass swivel guns from the surface and 'by diligent search', probably through a glass, 'we discovered all the treasure . . . but night coming on we could make noe further progress'. Next day was Sunday and, in good 'Whiskey Galore' tradition, they chose to respect the Sabbath and did not go to work on the wreck, even though it was 'very fine weather'.

On Monday, 16 September, it was fortunately still 'exceeding fine weather. At 6 a.m. we went to the wreck in our sloop and moored the same about 8. And my father went down in the diving engine and, with a sharp knife that he had with him, he cutt loose two chests of money and made fast ropes to the same, which we hauled up and took aboard, and then Robert Hunter went down and cut loose two more and made fast ropes to the same which we hauled up and took aboard and then returned hence.' Next morning William Evans went down in the engine again and cut two more chests of money loose, but the sea got up in the afternoon and they were forced to quit the wreck. But on Wednesday morning it was calm again and Evans descended in the barrel once again and cut three more chests loose and then, on Thursday 19 September, they beat all previous records. 'Good weather. We went to the wreck as before and recovered seven chests of money, one brass gun and a chest of hard wares ... and then returned home and put all the money ashore in our tents.'

All sixteen treasure chests recorded in the manifest of the *Adelaar* had thus been recovered in just four days' work. Five contained a hundred silver bars each and the other eleven held bags of coins, 160 bags containing 32,000 silver ducatoons and 150 bags containing 450,000 double stuyver copper coins. In one of the chests there were, in addition to ten bags of ducatoons, the keys of all the other chests and six bars of gold which are rather suspiciously not mentioned in the logbook.[9] It was a truly remarkable achievement which demonstrated what could be done by a brave, skilled man in a diving barrel, given fair weather and good visibility. Inevitably what followed was rather an anticlimax. On Friday they recovered the ship's bell and two casks full of assorted ironmongery, but then more typical Barra weather set in, 'a great sea, could not work on wreck', and the crew were put to the fairly congenial task of 'telling [i.e. counting] of the money which we recovered' and 'packing up of the money in order for Mr Alexander Mackenzie to carry with him to Edinburgh, which was all put in new canvas bags and sent aboard his sloop which then lay at Eriskay, a small island about six miles off'.

Jacob Rowe joined Mackenzie when he set off for the mainland early in October, but it was agreed that Evans and his crew should stay in Barra for the winter since 'more money and other valuable effects . . . might be recovered, the rather that they observed quantities of money then lying on the rocks below water in much the same depth out of which they had recovered the other treasure'. On 5 October 1728 Evans received his instructions at Eriskay, the small island which lay between Barra and South Uist. 'You are to embrace all opportunities of weather for fishing on the wreck . . . when the wind is off shore and the weather pretty moderate.' Faced with the 'melancholy prospect' of a winter on Barra, he was able to get good terms both for himself and for his crew who were to receive ten shillings a month per man additional to their former wages, with a bonus of five per cent of the value of everything they brought up for the divers, and £5 sterling of 'bounty money' for each man at the end of the voyage, 'which encouragement doth nevertheless depend on their good behaviour and due obedience'. It was also felt necessary to keep some check on the good behaviour and obedience of Evans as well as his men, so John Hay, an Edinburgh shipmaster who was Mackenzie's man, was left on Barra to keep an eye on him.[10]

The surviving Evans logbook covers only the first few weeks after Rowe and Mackenzie left for the mainland but, fortunately, John Hay's journal which covers the whole period up to their departure from Barra in May 1729 has survived. Since both Evans and Hay were later accused of embezzlement of treasure these documents have to be treated with a certain caution, though these accusations seem malicious and even ridiculous, such as the claim that Evans had 'all the while been living extravagantly with his crew', something that would have been virtually impossible in a Barra winter in the early eighteenth century. John Hay's accounts show that they were reasonably well fed with fresh vegetables, cows for milk and cheese, sheep, hogs, chickens and fish supplied by MacNeil of Barra and by Alexander Macdonald. They rented a couple of houses which they could heat with load after load of peat at twopence a load, but the 'lodgings were not as commodious as we would wish, by reason ye weather has hitherto been so very cold and disagreeable'. All in all, it does not sound as if they were living very extravagantly.[11]

Poor weather allowed just six days' work on the wreck in October, but on these days they recovered a couple of brass guns and nearly all the rest of the treasure that they were to find, six boxes containing 3,000 ducatoons, a silver coin worth five shillings and sixpence, as well as a number of loose coins. There then followed another three weeks of bad weather, 'very hard at times with a great sea', one of many frustrating periods which was to be enlivened by the news from Uist that Peter Richards, 'a diver belonging to the Dutch', was on his way to Barra to inspect what was left of the *Adelaar* on behalf of the Dutch East India Company which had just begun to challenge Alexander Mackenzie's right to profit from the wreck in the Scottish Court of Admiralty. Evans' men 'immediately put all the things out of sight which we had recovered, by building them in a stack of wood which we had split up for burning'.

On 12 November, a very rainy day, Richards arrived in Barra. He was described in a letter to Jacob Rowe as 'a gentleman of your acquaintance', but it seems that he was also a gentleman of John Lethbridge's acquaintance, since a diver with the same name, not a very common one, was one of those who had sailed with him to Cape Town in the previous year. Richards' visit to Barra, in atrocious weather, lasted just two days, during which he 'saw the foulness of the coast, took a draught of the west side of the island Barra [actually drawn for him by Evans] and then returned without making further inquiry'. The next we hear of him is in September of the following year when he was in Glasgow on his way to join

Jacob Rowe in Tobermory. Mackenzie's Glasgow agent, Richard Graham, reported that Richards had 'been in Venus Garden', by which he meant that he had contracted a venereal disease, but he assured Mackenzie that he had 'put him in good hands, who promise to make him a sound vessel', and a month later he wrote that Richards was on his way to Tobermory 'and is now I hope a sound vessel'.[12]

William Evans and John Hay were to spend nearly six months on Barra after Richards' departure, but this was not a very productive period as they were beset by gales and onshore winds, driving rain, snow and every other sort of foul weather which one might expect in Barra in winter. They worked just two days in November, four in December, none in January, eight in February, two in March and eight in April and, on these working days, they managed to recover from the wreck and from the shore some sheets of copper and brass, several pigs and rolls of lead, assorted iron-mongery, a cask of salt pork deemed 'unserviceable . . . though the country people take it up', and just over two hundred more ducatoons. On 27 April 1729, they decided to call it a day. 'We have searched the coves and all places that could be expected to receive any part of the wreck', wrote John Hay in his journal, 'finding the coast . . . from Sloughnay to Claide to be entirely clear of all goods.' 'Sloughnay' is probably Sligeanach, on the west coast about a mile and a half south of the wreck site, and 'Claide' must be Cliaid which has a sheltered beach, just over a mile east of the last resting place of the *Adelaar*. This is a very rugged and exposed stretch of coast and they had done well to have searched it so thoroughly in winter.

Early in May Evans broke up his camp and sailed via the Orkneys to London. An attempt was made to get him and his men to Tobermory to work with Jacob Rowe, but Evans was not interested and thought (correctly as it turned out) that 'it would not avail a farthing'. His intention was to get home to Deptford and there 'refresh himself for some time'. He had sailed away from Barra 'with the share of goods that were justly his own after he found no more was to be recovered', and he had no wish to stay in Scotland and argue his right to do this, as the lawsuits between the various people involved in the salvage of the *Adelaar* multiplied. Evans occasionally signed depositions relating to these matters, vehemently denying the charge of embezzlement and seeking to come to an understanding with Jacob Rowe, but three years after his return he had still not 'settled my accounts with Captain Rowe'.[13]

Meanwhile he set his diving career in motion once again. He had a new sloop built in Deptford, equipped with everything necessary for diving as well as small arms and six brass swivel guns for defence against predators. The sloop was christened the *Eagle*, a very suitable name since this was the English translation of *Adelaar* whose riches had provided the wherewithal to build it. On 28 May 1730 the Evans logbooks begin again with the departure of the *Eagle* from Greenwich, bound on a voyage to the coast of Sussex where they were to remain for fifteen months working on the wreck of the *Triumphant*, a French ship whose cargo was mainly linen, silks and other expensive textiles. Once washed and dried, these still had considerable value, despite their soaking in sea water, sufficient to attract thieves both at sea and on land. On the night of 2 July 1731, while they were lying at anchor in Pegham harbour, they were 'robbed of ten pieces of brocaded silk, the men being all ashore except the butcher'. And, a couple of weeks later, they saw two boats anchored on the wreck. 'Wee immediately bore down upon them and saluted them with a shott, they rowing away we fired again and then they lay by till we came up with them.' The boats were searched, but nothing was found and it was assumed that the interlopers had sunk the evidence of their guilt.

William Evans was to receive £3 for every bale of textiles or mercer's goods recovered, according to a contract he made with David Chauval, the agent in Portsmouth for the French owners of the goods. This was obviously not as profitable as hauling up silver coins and bars, but Evans and his men did pretty good business, recovering in all about three hundred bales or their equivalent, which earned them enough to pay and feed the men, maintain the sloop and still provide a decent profit. Nearly all of this was brought up without diving, with creepers, tongs and hooks operated from the surface, tools and techniques which will be described in more detail below. This was standard practice for contemporary salvors, but what was unusual in the case of the *Triumphant* was a valiant attempt to raise the wreck completely or at least to shift her into much shallower water.

Evans set about this task in company with Captain Denis, the Master Attendant of the Portsmouth Dockyard who provided men and two powerful brigs to help with the work. All the diving was done by Evans who descended in his barrel on 24 July 1730 to fix cables from the brigs to the wreck which were then hove taut at low water, the idea being that the rising tide would lift the *Triumphant* out of her muddy berth. But, on this occasion and many others, either the cables or the parts of the wreck to which they were attached gave way and the work had to start all over again. Evans was down again fixing cables on 6, 7, 9 and 11 August, and at noon on 12 August all the cables 'were hove very taut and we found the wreck to be lifted from the ground six or seven foot. At about 4 p.m. we got a four-inch rope under her bottom in order to draw through an eighteen-inch cable', all of which sounds very promising. They soon found out, however, that only the forepart of the *Triumphant* had been hoisted free, 'her after part remaining still in her old dock [i.e. the mud]'. On another occasion, the foresail and foretopsail of one of the brigs were set and an attempt was made to sail the ship out of the mud which held her tight, 'but that took noe effect, we supposing her after part not to be forced from the ground'. And so eventually, after nearly a month of effort, they had to give up the attempt to weigh the wreck. Captains Evans and Denis seem to have gone about this exercise in a correct and sensible manner and they were just unlucky that the *Triumphant* was held so fast. Other salvors had better fortune, the most famous being those who worked on the *San Pedro de Alcántara*, a Spanish man-of-war with a huge treasure aboard, which wrecked after striking a rock at Peniche in Portugal in February 1786. Divers were attracted to the site from all over Europe by the very generous pay and bonuses offered by the Spaniards, but the work was made much easier from 19 June onwards when the hull of the *San Pedro* was suspended from launches and tide-lifted ashore, using an almost identical method to that employed by William Evans on the

Triumphant half a century previously. The *San Pedro* carried over seven million *pesos* of treasure and all but a small fraction of this was recovered.[14]

Barrel-divers were sources of immense public interest and Evans and his men were often required to put on a show to entertain curious visitors of rank. On 12 August 1731, for instance, while anchored in Pegham harbour, they took on board the French agent 'Mr Chauval and several other gentlemen and ladys to shew them the nature of diving, and put down in the engine Mr Chauval's man; about 6 they went ashore and we saluted them seven guns'. A month earlier they had been ordered to the naval anchorage at Spithead to receive even more distinguished visitors, Admirals John Balchen and Sir Charles Wager, on the eve of departing for a cruise in the Mediterranean. They came aboard for a short visit on the afternoon of 12 July 'to see ye engine and nature of diving'. Admiral Wager had been one of the syndicate who backed Jacob Rowe's expedition to the *Vansittart* and he was no doubt interested to see Evans' version of the diving-engine. Wager clearly liked what he saw for, the next morning, a shipbuilder from Portsmouth visited the *Eagle* to take 'the dimentions of the diving engine in order to make a moddle for the Sir Vayer [Surveyor] Generall'.

Evans conducted his salvage of the *Triumphant* from anchorages in Arundel, Littlehampton, Pegham and Selsey, places where he soon learned, if he did not know before, that he was close to the wreck site of the *Guinea Frigate*, the Royal African Company ship which sunk with gold and ivory aboard in April 1691 and had been dived on by Edmond Halley amongst others. Searching for this wreck seems to have been a pet project of the English diving community, possibly because they believed incorrectly that the £20,000 in gold aboard had not been salvaged, and Evans was keen to succeed where his former partner Jacob Rowe had failed in December 1721.[15] On 20 May 1731, Evans welcomed aboard 'Old Mase', a fisherman from Bognor who directed them to where he believed the wreck lay and showed them how to find it by lining up landmarks which he had memorized. But Evans and his men 'saw noe speciment of itt' and returned to work again on the *Triumphant*. Three months later they decided to have another go and a section of the logbook is confidently headed 'remarkable occurrences on board the *Eagle* while in quest of the *Guinea Frigate* wreck on the coast of Sussex'. But, in fact, nothing very remarkable happened. They brought their 'marks to bear'; they swept the bottom with a cable to see if they could snag the wreckage and, on 17 September, they seemed to have done so. 'We directly gott our sloop over the same and put Thomas Baker down in the engine but could not discover anything of a ship, but said it was nothing but a heap of hard mudd.' Modern divers who have checked anomalies on the sea bottom detected by electronic equipment will sympathize with the frustration of the crew of the *Eagle* as they decided to abandon the search and lay the sloop up for the winter. The wreck of the *Guinea Frigate* and its forty-two tons of ivory remained hidden in the Sussex sand.

Evans had agents and correspondents, possibly partners, in London and elsewhere who kept him informed of wrecks which might repay his interest, if a suitable deal could be arranged with the owners of the ship and goods. In the middle of December he received such a call, to work on an unnamed general trader from Holland which had wrecked in November on the Whiting Sand near Orford, Suffolk. There was no problem in finding this wreck since her masts were above water and, by Christmas, Evans was off the Suffolk coast ready to salvage what he could when weather permitted. This was freezing cold work and not very successful, with a total of fifteen days work on the wreck producing a mixed bag of whale fins, elephants' teeth, soap, molasses, paper and stockings before salvage was abandoned on 27 February 1732, 'the wreck being sanded up'.

The highlight of this voyage to the east coast was an unexpected foray into local politics by the *Eagle* and her crew which nicely illustrates the almost celebrity status of these strange men who could dive to the bottom of the sea. On 18 January they anchored at Aldeburgh and next day, in a hard frost, one of the divers went down in the barrel to do a demonstration dive in six fathoms 'in the presence of Captain [George] Purvis and the gentlemen of the Corporation'. Purvis was a captain in the Royal Navy and a protégé of Admiral Sir Charles Wager whom the crew of the *Eagle* had met at Spithead. He was now standing as parliamentary candidate for Aldeburgh, in the government and especially Admiralty interest, and was clearly a useful man to cultivate, so they lent him their six brass guns and their 'union flagg' to make a fine show at the election. This proved sufficient to do the trick. On 21 January, the weather not being 'fit for work on the wreck, we stayed to see the election. Captain Purvis being chosen, he was carried on four men's shoulders thrice round the cross and thence to the sign of the Swan to dinner, the guns being fired several times.'[16]

Back in Deptford, Evans overhauled his sloop and then, on 10 April 1732, set out on a fresh voyage. Before he left he wrote an interesting letter to William Irvine, a fellow barrel-diver who had worked with Rowe and Evans in Fair Island and was now developing his own diving business in the Orkneys and Shetlands. Evans was clearly a good friend to Irvine and had arranged for a 'diving engine' to be made for him in London which was almost ready 'to be put on board the vessell according to your directions', together with written instructions on how to use it. Evans had been in two minds as to where to spend the summer season, the best time of the year for diving, 'on which you know our businesse wholly depends'. He had finally decided to go 'south about England and Scotland and shall stop at two or three places that I have now in view, and if they don't answer according to expectation I shall proceed to Shetland'.[17]

The voyage of the *Eagle* 'south about England' in the summer of 1732 was very similar to the wreck-hunting jaunt undertaken by Captain Rowe ten years before, visiting some of the same sites and turning out to be equally unprofitable. They sailed via Pegham in Sussex, where they had left some equipment after the *Triumphant* salvage, and then made their way to Portland where Evans took 'on board an old man to show him the marks for the Pembrook wreck sunk in this bay 66 years ago'. This would seem to be HMS *Pembroke*, a 28-gun frigate which had foundered after being rammed by another warship in May 1667.[18] The old fisherman was given half a crown for his help and he certainly knew where some large wreck lay, *Pembroke* or not, for after getting his marks to bear and sweeping they managed to snag a wreck and haul up two large

anchors, one of them 'all cimented with oysters', a piece of the
wreck and a couple of guns. They spent about a week over this and
then followed up two other nearby possibilities mentioned to them
by locals, some brass guns reputed to belong to a Dutch man-of-
war cast away off Chesil Beach 'about forty years ago' and a vessel
laden with tin which had been wrecked near Portland lighthouse
twenty-six years before. Neither wreck proved of any value. The
brass guns turned out to be iron, so rusty as to be valueless, and
they were assured by someone who had worked on the tin ship that
'all the tinn was saved, but only one block of it which dropt out of
the tongs'.

By now it was the middle of June and their summer was being
frittered away. It was time to sail to their main targets at the Lizard
in Cornwall. Here they planned to dive on two wrecks, the 40-gun
man-of-war *Royal Anne Galley* lost on the Stagg Rocks in
November 1721 and a wreck at Bumble Rock, 'that being the place
designed and for which we fitted out'. These were the same two
wrecks dived on by Rowe and Lethbridge in 1722. The latter,
described as a galleon by Rowe, was probably that of the Genoese
ship, *Santo Christo de Castello*, which had sunk in October 1667
with much silver aboard and had been the target of hopeful divers
ever since.[19] The voyage of the *Eagle* down to Cornwall was
interrupted near Plymouth by the impressment of four of her men
by the First Lieutenant of HMS *Yorke*. Even in peacetime, this was
a hazard for which sailors had to be prepared, but in this case the
men were soon cleared after the production of the necessary
paperwork and perhaps a drink for the lieutenant.

William Evans' men worked very hard for the five weeks they
spent at the Lizard. But great rocks and masses of seaweed obscured
the wrecks and the returns to their efforts were pitiful, large
numbers of cannon balls, 'three moidores [a gold coin] . . . a brass
candlestick without a foot . . . a pewter plate intirely spoiled and a
silver tea spoon' from the *Royal Anne Galley* and from the wreck at
Bumble Rock not even that much, just ballast stones 'and a small
piece of iron the substance of which was all eat up'. This was
proving a very unprofitable summer and desperate men seek
desperate remedies, in this case the solution sought being a voyage

to Vigo in Galicia where huge treasures from a Franco-Spanish fleet destroyed by the English and Dutch in 1702 were reputed to lie.

No details about the organization or financing of this voyage have survived, but it seems probable that Evans was acting for a syndicate of investors who were themselves in partnership with Juan Antonio Rivero, a Spaniard who had a royal patent to work the Vigo wrecks at this date. Several English and possibly Scottish names are mentioned in the logbooks in connection with this voyage, some of them familiar ones, such as Captain John Rowe, Jacob's brother, Mr Delafaye, the politician who had invested in the salvage of the *Vansittart*, and 'Mr Alix' or 'Allix'. Could this have been Alexander Mackenzie of Delvine making another unwise investment? It was this Mr Allix who sent orders on 1 August 1732 for their departure and so, on the next day, the *Eagle* 'weighed from the Lizard and made saile for our intended voyage by God's help to Corunna in Spain and from thence to Vigo to work on the ships sunk in ye river in ye year 1702'. Discussion of this voyage will be deferred until Chapter Twelve where it will be compared with another voyage to Vigo made a century later.[20] All that need be said here is that Evans was still in Galicia on 3 December 1732 when the logbook comes to an abrupt halt and that, at least up to that date, the voyage had been just as unprofitable as everything else that Evans and his crew had attempted in 1732. The days of their successes on the *Adelaar* and *Triumphant* must have now seemed distant memories.

There are no logbooks or other material relating to the career of William Evans for the years 1733 through to 1735 and we have to wait until early 1736 when he received a letter from the Dutch East India Company, dated 30 January in Zeeland, before taking up the story again. The Company was seeking experienced English divers to work on two of its outward-bound ships, the *Flying Hart* [*Vliegent Hart*] and the *Anna Catharina* which had been lost in the treacherous waters of the estuary of the Westerschelde on 3 February 1735, the very same stormy day that they had unwisely set sail from Zeeland for Asia. The smaller *Anna Catharina* had struck one of the many sandbanks and her entire company was lost as the ship was beaten to pieces by the waves, but the *Flying Hart* had gone down more slowly and in deeper water so that there was thought to be a good chance that her valuable cargo, which included three treasure chests with gold and silver coins, could be recovered.

The Company wrote first to Captain James Bushell, a diver from Frinton in Essex, whom a Swedish writer described with some exaggeration as 'known all over Europe for recovering Spanish galleons'. He demanded that a chart be prepared to enable him to find the *Flying Hart*, a copy of which has survived and helped modern divers to rediscover the wreck in 1981. Bushell, however, declined the offer and so the Company turned to Evans, having 'bin informed [that] you with much suckses have fisht on racks lost by bad weather'. Evans was offered what he called 'no purchase no pay', 'he bearing the charge and risque of his vessell and materials' in return for one half of everything he recovered. This seemed a reasonable deal and, on 24 March 1736, he set sail from Rotherhithe in a new sloop, the *Catharine* (or *Kitty*), for 'Middelburg in Zeeland and there to fish and dive for a wreck and from thence to Vigo to dive for other wrecks and elsewhere and back to London'. As it turned out, only the first part of this programme was to be achieved.[21]

By the evening of 3 April, Evans had made himself known at the Company headquarters at Middelburg, acquired a local pilot and an interpreter and surveyed the wreck of the *Flying Hart* which could be found easily enough without a chart as her mast was above water at low tide. He nailed part of an old topmast onto the protruding mast, so that he could find the wreck at high water, and, by sounding, determined that she lay at about ten fathoms at low water, near the limit for barrel divers. William Evans and his men then got their equipment ready for their attempt to salvage the sunken East-Indiaman, a pretty dispiriting job which was to occupy them for three successive summer seasons. Nearly all this work was done on the *Flying Hart*, though the *Anna Catharina* was surveyed, sounded and buoyed.[22]

The wreck was not just rather deep, but it was a complete jumble of ropes, sails, timbers, and bits and pieces of the cargo, much of it covered in silt. The water was muddy and stirred up by tides and strong currents and visibility was nearly always very poor, making use of the diving barrel almost pointless. As a result nearly all the work was done from the surface using tongs and similar tools. Given the conditions they brought up an astonishing quantity of stuff but, because the visibility was so bad, they generally did not know what was in their grasp until it cleared the surface. They were literally grappling in the dark. On 10 July 1736 there was great excitement as they recovered 'an iron chest' which everyone thought must be one of those three treasure chests but, when it was opened under Company supervision in Middelburg, it turned out to contain 'nothing but 9 keys'. This was just one of many similar frustrations and in the end all the treasure recovered was four silver ducatoons, worth just over £1 sterling.[23]

In terms of value their best recoveries were probably four brass guns and 856 bottles of wine – hock, claret, canary and others, 300 bottles being raised in just one very large chest. Otherwise it was pretty similar to what had been recovered from the *Adelaar*, with the important difference being that there was no treasure for the men to count and place in canvas bags. Pieces of the ship and her equipment such as cables, sails, cannon balls, spoiled gunpowder and 'an ensign of the colours of Holland' were mixed up with standard items of an outward-bound East Indiaman's cargo such as copper, lead, iron, barrel hoops, cloth, leather, candlesticks, tobacco and tobacco pipes and 'one spoiled Cheshire cheese cased up in lead'. By 11 October 1736, when Evans ceased operations for the season and went to settle accounts with the Company, he must have been heartily regretting that he had entered into a 'no purchase, no pay' contract. His recoveries were valued at only £350, and half of this 'did not answer the charges and expenses'.

The officers of the Dutch East India Company must have had a high regard for Evans though for, once they learned that he was getting into financial trouble, they treated him with great courtesy and generosity. His debts were paid off and he and his crew were taken into Company pay, while he was still to retain half the value of what was recovered, 'the Company to find all my men in wages and victuals and to share according to the first contract'. Working on the wreck now became just one of many tasks performed by the crew of the *Kitty* sloop, as they followed the orders of their Dutch paymasters. 'Waiting on' the East-Indiamen took up a lot of their time, a job which involved looking out for incoming ships and taking pilots to them and sometimes leading them through the treacherous sandbanks. More mundane tasks included sweeping for lost anchors. On 16 June 1738, they had orders to go to the assistance of the incoming East-Indiaman *Reigersbroek* which was in trouble off the coast of Westkapelle at the mouth of the Schelde, but they could do nothing to help as the ship drove ashore in strong gales, 'but 30 men saved and the rest drowned'. Much of this ship's cargo was pepper, which became a noxious hazard as it was washed ashore. Removing this 'foul pepper' and taking it out to sea to dump in deep water was one more job for the *Kitty*, an unpleasant duty which the crew can hardly have expected when they signed on to dive for treasure.

There were some consolations and amusements to be had in Middelburg and Vlissingen (Flushing) – the wedding of one of the crew 'to Miss Mary of a very agreeable fortune' and the safe delivery of their daughter eight months later, the celebration of King George II's birthday each 30 October, smoking the sloop 'to kill the rats and lice', the noisy merrymaking of the great July *kermis* or fair at Flushing and, on just one occasion, watching Evans and two other men dive 'nacked' on the wreck. But, overall, these were tedious days for the crew of the *Kitty* and they must have been glad when, in August 1738, William Evans decided to quit Zeeland and 'fit the sloop out for the islands of Shetland in order to work on the wrecks there'. He had probably been encouraged to make this expedition by his former colleague William Irvine, a diver who had been working in Shetland and Orkney since the late 1720s. Evans had sent Irvine a diving-engine from London in 1732, described as 'a barrel with glass ports and armholes', and had originally planned to sail to join him in Shetland after his summer cruise along the south coast of England. But he had been sidetracked by Vigo and then the Dutch wrecks. Now the plan was to work on the wreck of the outward-bound Danish East-Indiaman *Wendela* which had been lost on the island of Fetlar in the Shetlands in December 1737 with a cargo 'of silver bars and coined money', as Irvine reported to the Earl of Morton, whose jurisdiction covered wrecks in the northern isles.[24]

This certainly sounded more promising than the pitiful returns from the *Flying Hart*, but, in fact, Evans never sailed north and may have been put off by a letter he received from William Sinclair, a former colleague from Scottish days who was currently in London. Sinclair confirmed the wealth of the *Wendela* which was said to have 150,000 dollars aboard, but some of this had 'already been recovered (by Mr Irvine and others in the country)'. The Earl of Morton had agreed with the Danish Company that it should keep seven-twelfths of anything more found and he should have five-twelfths, 'so that he has it in his power to make what bargain he pleases with the divers'. Sinclair advised Evans not to work on the wreck unless he had 'a signed contract and then you know upon what terms you stand'. And he warned him not to expect too much, for the terms given by the Earl of Morton were likely to be 'little to ye advantage of ye savers'.[25]

So, on 28 September 1738, when Evans and the *Kitty* set sail from Flushing, they headed not for Shetland but for Dunkirk where a promising wreck had been reported. However, on arrival, Evans discovered that he had been pre-empted by some French salvors and so sailed down to his old haunts at Portland and Weymouth where he learned of the wreck of yet another Dutch East-Indiaman, *De Boot*, which had been lost near Dartmouth on 20 October. The local agent for the Dutch company was Arthur Holdsworth, the same man who handled John Lethbridge's business while he was salvaging the *Vansittart*. Evans 'agreed with Esqr. Holdsworth for ye recovery of ye goods lost', but very few goods were, in fact, recovered as 'ever since my agreement there hath been continual bad weather and southerly winds' which had broken the wreck apart and driven all the bale goods ashore, where they were picked up and hidden away by the 'country men . . . notwithstanding ye King's officer and Esqr. Holdsworth's servants are continually there'. The people of Devon were clearly just as efficient wreckers as those of the remote and barbarous island of Barra.[26]

It was, then, a somewhat disconsolate and rather broke William Evans who was to receive a nasty surprise as he lay at anchor in Salcombe on 23 December 1738. An officer arrived from the High Court of Admiralty and nailed a warrant to the mast of the sloop.

This dramatic gesture meant that the sloop was arrested in the cause of 'Peter Richards and Coy v. Kitty Sloop' and, to ensure that the vessel stayed where it was, her sails were seized and carried ashore where they were locked up in a storehouse. This was a nuisance, but was standard procedure in cases in the Court of Admiralty, the arrested sloop providing security for payment if the plaintiff should be successful. The sloop and its equipment were soon freed when Evans produced sureties in the amount of £150 and the Court was then ready to judge the case in its usual extremely leisurely way.[27]

Peter Richards, in whose name the action had been brought, thus makes yet another appearance in the story, the same man who dived for Lethbridge in South Africa, appeared in Barra on behalf of the Dutch East India Company, caught a venereal disease in Glasgow and later worked for Jacob Rowe at Tobermory. In 1732 Richards had returned to South Africa but had little luck there and, in March 1736, he was destitute in London where he begged Evans to take him on the expedition to Zeeland. This Evans did, but he seems to have thoroughly disliked him and was only too pleased when Richards deserted in Zeeland in August 1738. He was now suing for some unpaid wages. Witnesses for Evans described Richards as 'an elderly man upwards of fifty years of age', whose only service on the sloop was 'at the winch and sometimes shaving the mariners and cooking the kettle'. This seems purely malicious and witnesses for Richards claimed rather more credibly 'that he understood the business of diving . . . was well acquainted with the Dutch East India Company and understood their language', which should have made him a useful member of the crew, regardless of his age. Richards did, in fact, win the case, but he had to wait five years for the £6 17s 6d which the Court granted him, a somewhat pyrrhic victory. More important from our point of view was the fact that the logbooks deposited by Evans in support of his case were never reclaimed and so have survived to provide the basis of this chapter.

It is impossible to say whether William Evans was an archetypal diving entrepreneur of this period, for no comparable logbooks of any other diver or diving company have survived. One suspects that he was typical in the swings of fortune which he encountered, a feature of diving and treasure hunting through the ages, and he was probably also fairly typical in not making much money out of diving overall. It really was a pretty chancy occupation. The mixture of salvage work on contract, as on the *Triumphant* and the Dutch wrecks, with more speculative forays into pure treasure hunting, such as the search for the *Guinea Frigate*, the sunken 'galleon' at Bumble Rock and the Vigo Bay wrecks, may also have been characteristic of early eighteenth-century divers. It was very much the way that Jacob Rowe and John Lethbridge operated.

William Evans' logbooks do not spell out in detail the techniques used by divers in his day. They did not need to since anyone who read them would be very familiar with such matters. But they still add a lot to our knowledge of the way in which barrel-divers operated. The most striking point, and rather a surprise, is that they did not, in fact, use the famous barrels very much. The logbooks cover some 1,650 days in all, but just under five hundred of these were actually spent working on wrecks. Time was spent fitting out and sailing to and from wrecks and, when in the vicinity of a wreck, bad weather often stopped work for days or weeks, sometimes for a whole winter, and like most sailors not at sea they rarely worked on Sundays. The diving barrel was only used on about sixty of these five hundred working days, most often by William Evans Sr himself, but sometimes by other crew members, such as James Lardant, a Frenchman who dived on the *Triumphant* to check that Evans was not cheating the French agent Chauval. He obviously enjoyed the experience since he later joined Evans' crew.

The most common reason to use the diving barrel was to survey a wreck or to check out the nature of something which had snagged their cables when they were dragging the sea bottom. At Bumble Rock, for instance, William Evans junior reported that 'my father went down several times to take an exact view of the place'. If the water was clear, the glass window in the barrel gave a good close-up view, much better than peering down from the surface. But visibility was often so poor that they could see virtually nothing at all, especially during their work in the Schelde on the *Flying Hart* where the water was so thick and dark that they hardly used this method at all. The barrel was also invaluable in carrying out really delicate work, such as cutting loose the treasure chests in Barra or attaching the cables to the *Triumphant* in the failed attempt to raise the wreck. Such jobs needed those precision instruments, human hands, if they were to be done properly. Similar skills were required at Portland where James Lardant 'went down in the engine three times and gave an account of severall guns heapt up and covered over with oysters'. A couple of days later Evans 'went down with a hammer in his hand to try if they were iron or brass guns . . . by knocking off some of the oysters from one, could perceive it was iron and then we hoysted him in'.

This comparatively modest employment of the diving barrel did not arise from any intrinsic fault in the equipment, though its use in even moderately rough weather or deep water was out of the question. No injuries to William Evans and his divers are reported in the logbooks and they do not seem to have suffered from the problems encountered by John Lethbridge who, it will be recalled, told his grandson that he 'had been very near drowning in the engine five times' from water seeping into the barrel. There are only two references to leaking in the logbooks, both in barrels which had been out of the water a long time. On 17 May 1736, they borrowed the Dutch Company's 'machine', their own having been 'brok all to peeces' when they tested it unmanned at fifteen fathoms (90 feet), an indication that the barrel was not a purely English instrument. A few days later the Dutch barrel was tried and they 'found it to be a little leakey'. The cure was simple. 'We hoisted him in and then put it over ye side into ye water to soak.' Almost exactly a year later the same thing happened again. 'We thought to have wrought the engine . . . [but] when the master had been lowered down about three feet he found the engine (being shrunk) to make water so we get it on board again.' A nuisance, but no more, and nobody was 'very near drowning'.

The barrel was sometimes used for making recoveries from wrecks as well as for surveying them. But this was unusual and the vast majority of recoveries were made by men operating from small boats on the surface. One of these men would be the 'eyes' of the others, leaning overboard and peering down through a 'surface glass' or a 'glass bucket' to direct the operations of the others. These had access to a variety of tools to assist in lifting, most important of which were tongs, scissor-shaped instruments with claws which could be manoeuvred round an object on the bottom and then snapped shut. Once something was held fast in the claws of the tongs, the instrument plus its purchase would be raised the fifty feet or so to the surface, sometimes quite small things such as bars of lead or even coins but often very large objects indeed, such as guns, chests full of hardware or wine and complete bales of linen or cloth. The logbooks only mention 'great' and ordinary tongs, but a wide variety were available to salvors, many of which are illustrated in two fascinating contemporary books by the Swedish engineer, scientist and diving entrepreneur Mårten Triewald whose work has recently been translated into English as *The Art of Living under Water*. Triewald always worked from a diving-bell and some of the instruments illustrated in his book, such as saws and drills, would not have been suitable for use from the surface, but many of them would be – various types of tongs, hooks, drags and drag bags. They made an awesome armoury for the diver to work with.[28]

William Evans Jr was quite a good marine artist. He wrote up the early logbooks and his journals are enlivened by sketches of warships and other vessels. There is also a delightful little drawing of a boat's crew working the tongs. One man is in the bows, leaning over in a very uncomfortable position, and peering through the glass at the wreck below, two men are amidships operating the tongs which are shown suspended above the surface, and two men are in the stern minding the boat, one of them armed with a boat hook to haul in their 'purchase'. As one might imagine, things were constantly going wrong with this method of recovery, cables broke, drag nets broke loose, tongs and hooks broke or buckled and objects had a disconcerting habit of slipping out of the claws of the tongs, sometimes when they were above water and almost within reach. On 29 April 1737, for instance, 'we tonged and had a great weight on them which employed us one hour to bring it to the surface of the water, when we had no sooner discovered it to be a brass cannon . . . but it slipt off'. All this equipment was very cheap and could easily be replaced or mended, by blacksmiths ashore or by Evans himself, if need be, as he was capable of working at a forge as well as on a carpenter's bench. Meanwhile, slowly but surely, recoveries were made, though, as has been seen, they were not necessarily very valuable.

Getting to the position where one could even try to raise a cargo often required considerable preliminary work. If a wreck had not broken up, it was necessary to rip it to bits, using the sort of violence employed by Jacob Rowe at Tobermory. The main tools employed were 'creepers', a sort of grapnel which would be dragged along the decks of the wreck until a firm purchase was achieved, and various types of hook which, once attached to deck timbers, beams, bowsprits, cables or whatever else they planned to break away, would be raised by the winch or windlass or often by the rising tide. Such activity often brought frustration as one might imagine, 'by the unhooking of the hooks' or by the lack of sufficient force to break the timbers free. At low water on 21 May 1731, for instance, 'we hookt two hooks to ye upper deck of the wreck [the *Triumphant*], which we hove taut, but as the tide riss one of the hooks broke and the cable of the other parted'. Next day they had better luck, fastening cables to 'ye beams of ye upper deck which were hove taut and by the flowing of the tide riss itt right up . . . Went to work with our tongs and recovered linen . . .'.

Many wrecks were obscured or completely covered by seaweed and rocks. Weed could be cut by hand from the barrel, but was usually hacked away from the surface, using weighted axes, crescent-shaped knives on long poles and other fearsome instruments, some of which are illustrated in Mårten Triewald's books. The worst wreck involving rocks of those documented in the logbooks was the one at Bumble Rock near the Lizard in Cornwall. Work started on the rocks on this wreck site on 24 June 1732, at first using 'the great tongs . . . but the stones or small loose rocks being so bigg that the tongs would not take them in, we hooked a large double hook under them and by heaving at the windlass turned them'. More drastic measures were necessary later. A pair of slings were made out of a six-inch hawser, a tackle rigged from the top of the Bumble Rock, and then Evans went down in the engine to place the slings round a large rock 'which we computed to be near three tons'. The slings slipped off the first and second time but they were lucky with their third try, the slings held, the cable from the windlass held and 'we hove it out and dropt it at a distance . . . The place is now pretty clear for to work with the drudge.' Weather prevented work for a couple of days, but then 'James Lardant went down in the engine in the place where the stone was taken out, but perceived nothing but only some ballast, and having searched in several other places without success, we hoisted him in'.

Such combinations of triumph and disappointment are typical of the lives of divers and treasure hunters, then as now, and this story of the rocks can serve as a fitting place to leave William Evans whose career has been traced from his triumphant cutting-out of the treasure chests of the *Adelaar* late in 1728 to the disappointments of his Dutch venture and the eventual disappearance of his logbooks into the Registry of the High Court of Admiralty early in 1739. What happened to him afterwards is not certain since William Evans is quite a common name, but the most likely scenario is that he gave up his diving business and returned to his former trade as a ship's carpenter on HMS *Rupert* during her fitting-out and launching at Sheerness Dockyard in 1740. During his 'leisure opportunities', he hired a vessel and 'with my diving engine' attempted at his own expense to raise a lighter which had sunk in twelve fathoms of water. He was defeated by the depth, the tide and 'the suction of the mud', but this carpenter sounds very much like the William Evans that we have come to know.[29]

Chapter Eleven

Bellmen and Braithwaites

Chapter Eleven

Bellmen and Braithwaites

"Our late famous Professor Dr. Edmund Halley improved the old diver's bell so much as to have perfected the art of living under water . . . whoever will be at the trouble and expence to have a bell made with his improvements, may send his divers down to any depth with safety."[1]

The barrel-divers, or 'wreckmen' as they were often called, provide a colourful and almost incredible interlude in the history of diving. The very idea of being lowered to the bottom of the sea in a sealed barrel is enough to make not just the claustrophobic shiver. Despite their many successful recoveries of treasure and other valuables from wrecks, this interlude was to be a comparatively short one. John Lethbridge first tested the possibilities of the diving barrel in 1715 and the next thirty years or so was the heyday of the barrel-divers. And then they quite suddenly vanish from the historical record some time in the 1750s, a good example of one of the wrong turns that invention and innovation often take.

Meanwhile their main rivals, the bell divers, had continued to ply their trade, working on wrecks and perhaps, even more, on the underwater work necessary for the construction of the bridges and harbour works being erected in increasing numbers as Britain entered the early years of the Industrial Revolution. The bells used were nearly all based on the model of the one developed by the astronomer Edmond Halley in the early 1690s, the most important feature of which was his system of supplying fresh air to the bell from a pair of weighted barrels which 'rise and fall alternatively, after the manner of two buckets in a well'.[2]

In September 1716, Halley decided to draw attention once more to the excellence of his improved bell by publishing in the *Philosophical Transactions* of the Royal Society a paper with the memorable title of 'The Art of Living Under Water'. This added very little to his 'Relation of the Diving Bell' which had been read to the Society exactly twenty-five years previously. Nevertheless, it revived interest in the bell and this was sustained by a demonstration in the Thames. 'Mr. Halley and four other persons went down in the bell to a depth of nine or ten fathoms and stayed there for an hour and a half. Although the top of the bell contained a glass through which could enter sufficient light to enable him to read and write, he nevertheless allowed a candle to be lit which was to burn for as long as he wished. He released the warm air, which always occupies the upper part of the bell, through a tap in the top of the bell [and in its place] . . . he could admit as much fresh air as he wished by means of two barrels which were alternately hauled down full of air.'[3]

Our knowledge of Halley's public entertainment comes from the work of Mårten Triewald, the Swedish engineer whose books on diving were mentioned in the last chapter. Triewald 'had the good fortune to witness' the descent into the Thames of Edmond Halley, 'my friend and patron', and on his return to Sweden ten years later he acquired exclusive rights to the use of Halley's diving-bell and set up a diving and salvage company to exploit his monopoly. Triewald also improved the bell in two important ways. Halley's bell was large, heavy and required a sizeable vessel and many hands to work it, making it rather an expensive tool to use in Sweden where most cargoes to be salvaged were 'of a far less value than the loadings of Spanish galleons'. He therefore devised a smaller bell made of copper and lined with tin inside to reflect light, and at the same time he worked out a way of making better use of the air trapped in the bell. This air tended to be cool, even cold, at the bottom of the bell and virtually unbreathable at the top. Triewald attributed this to the heat generated as the diver, or divers, exhaled but, as has been seen, the problem was more likely to have been caused by the air becoming foul as the divers continually breathed the same air at the top of the bell. Whatever the cause, Triewald devised an ingenious solution to the problem. This involved fitting a tube into the bell which took in cold air from the bottom, spiralled round the sides and ended in a mouthpiece through which the diver could take in the cooler and unbreathed air from the bottom of the bell.[4]

Further improvements to Halley's design were made by Charles Spalding, a merchant from Edinburgh who was the greatest loser when the trading ship *Peggy* wrecked in December 1774 on the Farne Islands off the coast of Northumberland. He was appointed by his fellow merchants to do what he could to 'collect what could be of the cargo and vessel'. Instead of contracting with one of the many salvage companies that existed by that date, Spalding decided to take the business into his own hands, going so far as to consult 'every author I could find on this subject of diving and the diving-bell'. By June of 1775 he had built his own bell and, after test dives in Scottish waters, he sailed south to Bamburgh which lies opposite the Farne Islands, arriving there at the beginning of September. When weather permitted, Spalding sailed out to where he thought the wreck lay and descended ten fathoms in his bell, from which he 'happily alighted on a flat part of the rock within a small space of a dreadful chasm'. Spalding's delight was not shared by his boatmen and pilots who were terrified by his antics in such dangerous waters and 'brought me up very precipitately before I had in any degree examined about me'. He did manage to dive again but had no success in finding the wreck, partly because of the rocky and dangerous conditions and also because of dense weeds which covered much of the seabed. He describes walking along the bottom of the sea with a cutting knife and hook 'breaking down some and cutting the tougher weeds'.[5]

Spalding must have been a man of some social significance or at least charm since, during the long periods when bad weather made searching for the wreck impossible, he was made welcome as a guest by Dr Sharp, Archdeacon of Northumberland, who lived with his family in Bamburgh Castle, one of the great sights of the magnificent Northumberland coast. Also staying at the castle was Granville Sharp, the Archdeacon's brother and a leading figure in the movement to abolish slavery. Like many learned gentlemen of his day, he was intrigued by technology and, having observed 'with great anxiety the extreme danger to which [Spalding] daily exposed himself by using a diving-bell', he was determined to devise a better and safer piece of equipment. The main aim was to enable the bellmen to control their own bell by means of a central weight which could be lowered or raised by the divers. The correspondence between Spalding and Sharp on this innovation shows that Spalding, while flattered by the attention of such a great man, thought that the philanthropist's designs were impractical and over-elaborate and he proceeded to make a simpler version.[6]

The main scenario in which it was envisaged that this equipment would be used was a failure of signals between the bellmen and the surface crew, so it is tragic that it was in just such a situation that Charles Spalding and his nephew were to lose their lives in the summer of 1783, while diving on an East India wreck on the Kish Bank in Dublin Bay. The inquest believed that the accident was caused by 'a highly noxious effluvia', arising either from putrid corpses in the wreck or rotting ginseng which was part of the cargo. But no distress signals were received by the support boat, nor did Spalding use 'the power of raising or falling his bell on any emergency', so the two men were found dead from suffocation when the bell was eventually raised to the surface. Granville Sharp showed himself to be only too human when he wrote a letter of condolence to Alex Small, Spalding's kinsman and assistant. He attributed the accident entirely to the stubbornness of Spalding who had not followed the design which he had prepared for his use. 'I may therefore the more lament that he did not adopt my plan; for if he had, he might (according to all human probability) have been still alive!' Sharp offered to send a copy of the design to Small on two conditions, that a share of any profits ensuing should be paid to Charles Spalding's widow and seven infant children and 'that no work whatsoever shall be performed with the machine on the Lord's Day'.[7]

Charles Spalding's bell was supplied with fresh air from barrels on the Halley model, but this rather clumsy system was soon to be superseded. The solution had been suggested in 1689 by Dr Denis Papin, a French physicist, who devised a method of supplying a diving-bell with fresh air through a pump. But theory was ahead of practice and the mechanism in Papin's day was not strong enough to deliver air very far below the surface. The eighteenth century was, however, a great era for the improvement of pumps, particularly for raising water to fight fires or drain mines, and some attention was paid to their use in diving machines. In 1754, for instance, Dr Richard Pococke, traveller and divine, watched 'the curious manner of diveing' being employed on the wreck of HMS *Assurance* which had been lost on the Needles in the Isle of Wight in the previous year. 'They are let down in a machine made of leather, strengthened at the knees and shoulders, and if I mistake not on the head with brass', equipment which sounds similar to the semi-atmospheric apparatus demonstrated in the Thames in 1716 by Colonel Andrew Becker. But whereas Becker's machine was supplied with air by bellows, the one seen by Pococke had two tubes made of leather – 'one for the air to go down and to speak by, the other to pump out the air'.[8]

This description is rather ambiguous and it is unclear whether the air was pumped in as well as out but the real breakthrough was to be made by John Smeaton, inventor, instrument maker and the first of Britain's great civil engineers who constructed canals, bridges and harbour-works and was perhaps most famous as the designer and builder of the third Eddystone Lighthouse. Smeaton first used a diving-bell supplied with air from a pump while building a bridge across the Tyne at Hexham in 1777–8, 'a very handsome bridge of nine arches' which was swept away by flood water in the spring of 1782. It was Smeaton's only failure in an illustrious career. This disaster, however, was nothing to do with the bell and Smeaton was to develop an improved version in June 1788, during work on Ramsgate Harbour.

The two men in the newly designed bell 'were supplied with a constant influx of fresh air, without any attention of theirs, that necessary article being amply supplied by a forcing air pump in a boat upon the water's surface'. Constant fresh air enabled Smeaton to do away with the traditional bell shape which had helped to slow up the rise of water within as the machine descended. His 'bell' was a much more convenient square cast-iron chest, four and a half feet high, four and a half feet long, three feet wide and open at the bottom. This chest shape was to become the norm, though the name of 'bell' was retained, 'as in conformity to custom'. On 24 August 1789, Smeaton 'had the honour' to take the Chairman of the Harbour Trustees 'down to the bottom of the sea; upon which we could stand and work in the dry. In this situation the Chairman, finding himself perfectly at his ease, and very comfortable, staid full three quarters of an hour', so long indeed that his friends on the surface 'were beginning to be apprehensive that something might have happened to us'.[9]

Shortly before the Chairman's visitation, the harbour-works and diving-bell had been inspected by the Scotsman John Rennie, Smeaton's successor as Britain's leading civil engineer who was to become particularly famous as a bridge builder. He was told by Henry Cull, the man in charge of the works, that the bell answered its purpose very well. 'The method for supplying this machine with air', he wrote in his notebook, 'was by means of an air pump of ten inches diameter and ten inches stroke worked by two men which forced the air down to the bell. Light is admitted by means of circular glass windows of about five or six inches diameter and the air, if they keep pretty closely pumping, could be kept fresh and not above three inches of water admitted into the bell.'[10]

According to Henry Cull, the main drawback of the new bell was that it would never work properly in more than twelve feet of water, so when Rennie himself became the engineer of Ramsgate Harbour he decided, when repairs became necessary in 1813, to make improvements to Smeaton's bell. He made it bigger, increased the size of the windows and kept it constantly filled with air by means of a much more powerful pump, a double air-pump worked by four men on the surface. Rennie's bell was widely used in underwater engineering works and a good description of it can be found in a book written by S. W. Smith who was in charge of works in Plymouth Dockyard from 1817 to 1820. The bell at Plymouth became quite a tourist attraction and many visitors were taken down in it, including a Mrs Morris who wrote a poem to her father from the bottom of the sea.

> 'From a *belle*, my dear father, you've oft had a line,
> But not from a BELL under water;
> Just now I can only assure you I'm thine,
> Your diving, affectionate daughter.'[11]

The most famous employment of Rennie's bell was after his death when, in 1827, Isambard Kingdom Brunel used it during the inspection and repair of the breach which had been made in the roof of his father's Rotherhithe Tunnel. On one occasion the young chemist Michael Faraday accompanied Brunel to the bottom of the Thames in the bell and noted that Brunel was able to leave the bell, holding his breath, for two minutes at a time. So it looks as though Edmond Halley's concept of 'the travelling diver' supplied with air from the bell had been abandoned, if it had ever been used, though something similar in principle is employed in modern bells, such as those used in the North Sea, from which divers can go out to work provided with an 'umbilical' to carry their oxygen, communications cable and a means of heating their diving suit.[12]

While Smeaton's and Rennie's bells were used in engineering projects, improvements were also made to the equipment used by divers engaged in salvage and treasure hunting. The most successful of these developments were those made by William Braithwaite and his two sons, John and William Jr. Their expertise lay in the manufacture of pumping equipment and they ran a business making fire engines among other things in Soho in London. As a sideline this family of pump experts turned their minds to diving and, by 1783, they had developed a system of pumping air down to divers working in a bell. How this worked they did not say exactly, since they had no wish to give a present of their innovation to competitors. The best and deliberately vague description appeared in an interesting 'Account of Messrs. Braithwaite' published in the *Universal Daily Register,* forerunner of *The Times,* in September 1786. 'The father conceiving that a chamber supplied with atmospheric air by means of a hose or leather tube would answer the purpose of exploring wrecks better than Dr Halley's diving-bell

... by a very ingenious contrivance devised a method of working on the wreck which he keeps secret.'[13]

The first employment of this equipment was on the wreck of the first-rate warship *Royal George*, the pride of King George III's navy, which capsized and sank at her moorings at Spithead on 29 August 1782, while being heeled over to effect some repairs. This was the last British man-of-war to be armed mainly with valuable brass rather than iron guns, the 28 brass 24-pounders and 28 brass 12-pounders being valued by the Ordnance Board shortly after the shipwreck at nearly £17,000. Since the Board was prepared to contract with salvors that they should retain 'one-half of the real value' of all guns and other ordnance stores recovered, it is no surprise that the authorities were bombarded with over a hundred proposals for salvage, some indication of the growth of the diving and salvage business, though many of these applicants seem to have been cranks.[14]

First onto the sunken ship was Thomas Spalding, brother of Charles, who on 10 September 1782, less than two weeks after the wreck, reported a series of dives on the *Royal George* conducted by himself, from which reconnaissance he had 'not the least doubt but my brother may very easily get up all the guns, and likewise all her stores'. Charles worked on the wreck for most of October and the beginning of November. Things were not quite as easy as his brother envisaged and he had quite a lot of trouble, with bad weather, with the swell which crashed the bell into the wreck or knocked over divers standing on the decks, with hoses getting pulled out of the air-barrels, with rotting corpses (nearly a thousand people died in the wreck), with the general clutter and with his black diver, John Winer, 'who has been very usefull in cutting the breaching of the guns and slinging them, an excellent seaman, but quite a buccaneer'. His efforts and those of the other divers succeeded in raising seventeen of the guns of the *Royal George*, mostly the smaller brass 12-pounders and the even smaller iron 9-pounders from the quarter-deck, before they left off for the winter.[15]

Charles Spalding had planned to return in the spring, but in the event he went to work in Irish waters where he tragically died. His place was taken by William Tracey, a local Portsmouth man, who started work in May 1783. His ambitious plan was to raise the *Royal George* in its entirety, in a cradle of chains and stout cables, a plan which Spalding thought unlikely to succeed. 'I doubt the possibility of weighing so great a ship with all her stores in', he wrote to Granville Sharp, and this was to prove correct despite Tracey's heroic attempts. Like almost everyone who worked on the *Royal George,* Tracey had trouble with the Navy and Ordnance Boards and with the Portsmouth dockyard officers and, on its termination in May 1784, his contract was not renewed, being handed, together with all the equipment assembled for raising the wreck, to William Braithwaite and his sons. Their contract was for three months, but during the first half of this period the weather was so bad that they were unable to do any work on the wreck. When they did get going in July, they recovered some guns and one of the warship's great anchors but, like Tracey, they too suffered from the arguments between the various government departments involved and were glad when their contract expired and they were free to seek warmer waters in which there were even more brass guns lying at the bottom of the sea than in Spithead.[16]

During the American War of Independence, which ended in 1783, the British had been at war with nearly every navy in Europe and the Spaniards had scented a great opportunity to recover Gibraltar which had been lost in 1704. The British naval base was besieged by land and sea for over three and a half years, the climax coming on 13 September 1782 when ten 'battering-ships' were towed within cannon range of the garrison. These had been created specifically for this operation, using old men-of-war which had been massively reinforced and made supposedly fireproof on the one side where all their guns were mounted. They were anchored in a line broadside onto the Gibraltar batteries and at about ten o'clock in the morning they opened fire. At first it seemed that these floating batteries would live up to their reputation for invincibility but, once the British started using red-hot shot, the fire from the garrison's batteries began to take its toll. By nine o'clock in the evening, every Spanish ship was in flames and 'one of the most tremendous bombardments in history' was over as the last enemy gun was silenced. The night was punctuated with terrific explosions, as fire reached the powder magazines of the anchored ships, and in the morning the victorious British could see that all ten ships had either blown up and sunk or been burned down to the waterline. And some two hundred guns, many of them brass, had found a new home on the seabed.[17]

It was to Gibraltar then that William Braithwaite sailed in 1785 and, although some of the guns had been recovered easily enough by the navy, there were plenty left for him and his sons to dive on. 'We are informed', reported the *Universal Daily Register* in November, 'that Messrs. Braithwaites have, by means of their diving machine, been very successful in getting up many of the brass guns belonging to the Spanish floating batteries off Gibraltar.' Some were sold privately, some were taken into the Gibraltar garrison, and others were sent to Algiers, Morocco and Sallee where they provided convenient presents for the Moslem rulers, such as the Emperor of Morocco who was said to be 'remarkably pleased with the late present of some brass pieces he received from Gibraltar. They were fished up from the Spanish wrecks and are 32-pounders of the most elegant workmanship.' William Braithwaite himself took some of these guns to Sallee, a port on the Atlantic coast of Morocco which, since its main function was to make piratical attacks on Christian shipping, was always glad of a few more guns. 'In the name of the Almighty God', wrote the Governor of Sallee to the Governor of Gibraltar, 'I am to inform you that the diver William Braithwaite (an Englishman) arrived at this port with eight guns and 280 shot; I received him with great hospitality.'[18]

The turn of events that had taken the Braithwaites from Soho to Sallee had broadened their horizons and given them a real taste for diving and treasure hunting. They were now famous divers with a reputation throughout Europe for their professional skills. In June 1786, the Braithwaites received an invitation from the Chamber of Commerce at Cadiz to work on the fabulously rich Spanish treasure ship *San Pedro de Alcántara* which had wrecked at Peniche in Portugal a few months earlier. They were naturally keen to join in the bonanza enjoyed by divers working on this wreck, but an accident to their ship delayed their departure from Sallee and, by the time they set sail, all the treasure had been recovered. Nothing daunted, they sailed to Dublin instead to dive on the *Belgioso*, the East-Indiaman wreck where Charles Spalding had died three years previously. Here they were also to be frustrated, being threatened with legal action by another diving company which claimed to have contracted with the insurers for the sole rights to work on the wreck. Two such disappointments must have been depressing, but the luck of the Braithwaites was about to change as a result of a contract they made in August 1787 with the English East India Company to salvage its outward-bound ship *Hartwell* which had wrecked on the island of Bonavista (Boa Vista) in the Cape Verde Islands.[19]

At 938 tons the *Hartwell* was the largest ship yet built for the service of the East India Company, but she was not to serve it for long. Her disastrous maiden voyage under the command of Captain Edward Fiott began at Portsmouth on 1 May 1787. All went serenely until the evening of Saturday 19 May when, as was the Saturday night custom in East-Indiamen, most of the crew not on watch were gathered in the forecastle, singing, drinking, 'making a great noise' and generally having a good time. When it was time for lights out, the Chief Mate went down and ordered the rowdy sailors to desist 'and go to hammock'. Most went quietly but three of the men refused to obey and their leader, one Thomas Adams, knocked the mate down and 'called the ship's company to assist him against the commander and the officers.' He received little support and the three men were clapped in irons for the night.[20]

On Sunday morning Adams asked for permission to go to the heads and relieve himself. This was granted but, once released, he broke away from his escorts and threatened anyone who came near him with a knife. Captain Fiott himself went forward, armed with a brace of pistols, and with some assistance put Adams back in irons. He then called the crew on deck and, as was customary, read divine service before dismissing those not on watch. An uneasy calm followed until four in the afternoon when Fiott was presented with a 'round robin' signed by fifty of the sailors, demanding in 'a

threatening and mutinous manner' the release of the three men
without further punishment. The Captain was by now thoroughly
alarmed. He armed the officers and petty officers, loaded the
quarterdeck guns with grapeshot and swivelled them round to face
forward towards the men's quarters, ready to deal with the slightest
sign of trouble during the night.

On Monday morning an officers' meeting decided to try to
calm matters down by releasing two of the miscreants, but Adams
was seen as too guilty to be pardoned and so was sentenced to
receive a dozen lashes and remain in irons. While he was being
flogged, Adams was 'extremely troublesome and used much
abusive language' and many of the sailors were 'likewise very
insolent'. By the evening the situation was looking very nasty.
Most of the crew were in the forecastle, 'very tumultuous and
noisy, singing very daring songs and defying all orders from the
officers', while the officers themselves and other loyal crew
members remained armed and on watch, as 'they walked the
quarterdeck all night'. Next morning the officers summoned up
the courage to put an end to this ridiculous stalemate. They
moved forward, arms in hand, and quashed the mutiny in a
determined manner, seizing nine of the ringleaders who were
punished at the gangway with two dozen lashes each and then left
in irons. Since it was still a very long way to China, where the ship
was bound, a decision was made to rid the ship of the mutineers
by marooning them at the first suitable place.

This was determined to be Santiago, the most important of the
Cape Verde Islands about two or three days sail away, and the ship's
course was altered accordingly. On the evening of Wednesday 23
May they sighted land which, 'after diligent consultation, was
conceived to be the island of St Nicholas [São Nicolau]; and
accordingly, leaving it, they shaped their course for St Jago [i.e.
Santiago]'. This was a serious error in navigation since the island
they had sighted was, in fact, Sal, a hundred miles further east.
Confident in his course and desperate to get rid of his bad apples,
Captain Fiott sailed south into the night under full sail, unwise in
any circumstances in darkness in the midst of islands, and a fatal
decision in this case, since the island of Boa Vista, or Bonavista as

the English called it, lay directly in their path. At half past three in the morning the *Hartwell* struck a reef of rocks which ran out to sea from the north-east of this island and within fifteen minutes the water had risen above the lower deck. It was time to abandon ship. The mutineers were released and all but one of the crew got safely ashore in rafts and the ship's boats, but 'it was not possible to save any of the Honourable Company's or the private treasure that was in the bread room and which was filled with water'.

At first the shipwreck was blamed in England on 'the mutinous behaviour of the crew' and Captain Fiott was praised for his firm handling of the dangerous situation. The Company was to change its mind, however, when it heard the evidence of Gregory Jackson, the fourth officer who, independently of the other officers, had sailed with twenty-three sailors in the ship's longboat to the West Indies and so back to England in a merchant ship. His evidence has not survived, but it is clear that it laid the blame fair and square on the three most senior officers, for 'their total inattention to the safety of the ship after passing the island of Sal'. 'Nine of the mutineers were in irons', thundered the *Universal Daily Register* in a report on the verdict of the Company's Committee of Shipping. 'The officers were properly armed, the ship in good condition – and yet she was unaccountably driven with all her studding sails bent on the reef of rocks on which she unfortunately struck.' Captain Fiott and his Chief Mate were dismissed from the Company's service and the second mate was suspended, while Gregory Jackson came out of the affair smelling of roses. He was 'a young man barely of age' and the shipwreck and later salvage of the *Hartwell* was to greatly accelerate his advancement in the Company's marine service.[21]

Mutiny was quite common in East-Indiamen, but it rarely occurred so early in a voyage, being mainly the product of very long passages at sea, heat, boredom, drink and short commons. The business was normally fairly trivial, a drunken refusal to obey orders, a set-to between some of the men and the officers, and then a reluctant climbdown as a measure of peace was reinstated. At first the mutiny on the *Hartwell* seems to fit this scenario, but it was believed in England that it was more serious than this. Indeed it was thought to be part of a deliberate piratical plan to make 'eight and twenty of the officers and their adherents walk over board', prior to taking possession of the ship in order to seize the 'very large quantity of specie that was on board'. The official treasure consisted of sixty chests of silver belonging to the Company, worth £53,642, three more chests belonging to the ship's owners and 'several packages of private trade'. This was a pretty big treasure for an English East-Indiaman, but it was to get much bigger in the pages of the London newspapers. The *London Chronicle*, for instance, reported that the *Hartwell* was carrying 'dollars to the amount of £150,000 sterling, cases of jewellery to at least the same amount; and the entire cargo of the *Belvidere* which lost her passage'. The *Belvidere* did lose her passage, since she was a new ship and not ready when the fleet was due to sail. But her cargo was, in fact, split between the *Hartwell* and the *Nottingham*, another ship in the fleet, and one suspects that everything else in this newspaper report was similarly exaggerated. Nevertheless, one can imagine that such rumours might have excited the sailors and they probably made the Braithwaites a bit enthusiastic as well, since there were 'great hopes that by employing skilful divers most part of the treasure may yet be saved'.[22]

William Braithwaite senior was now in his mid-fifties and he was to run things from the London end, while his sons John and William Jr did the actual diving on the wreck. The salvage contract they signed was not all that generous, but would be satisfactory if sufficient treasure was recovered. The Braithwaites were to receive one-eighth of the value of everything collected and 'if that should not amount to £250, the Company to pay the difference'. They were also to receive freight and all expenses for their sloop *Elizabeth* and to be maintained themselves during the expedition, so they would be at no cost. The *Elizabeth* was to be accompanied by the brigantine *Lark*, which had been hired by the Company, and overall command of the expedition would rest with Gregory Jackson, the former fourth mate of the *Hartwell*, assisted by the splendidly named Clotworthy Upton, the former fifth mate. Exquisitely polite requests for assistance were successfully made to the Portuguese authorities in Lisbon and the Cape Verde Islands and naval protection was provided in the form of the sloop-of-war *Bull Dog*, commanded by Captain Robert Fancourt.[23]

Captain Fancourt was back in Falmouth from the Cape Verde Islands on 30 January 1788 and his report shows that the Braithwaite brothers had not done too well during their first expedition to the wreck of the *Hartwell*. Fancourt first saw their sloop *Elizabeth* on 4 November 1787, driven ashore on the island of Sal and, although she was got off three days later, she was in such a leaky condition that it was a couple of weeks before she was repaired sufficiently to start 'fishing' on the wreck. And, even then, they had only recovered three chests, containing 12,000 dollars, by 4 January when he left the islands. This rather small harvest was, he was told, the result of 'very strong sea breezes having prevailed which continue to blow till the month of May when the inhabitants give me to understand that the weather becomes moderate'. However, the Braithwaites, like all divers, were optimistic that they would 'be able to recover a great part of the treasure as soon as the weather is moderate', and the officers of the Company too were far from displeased. They found Gregory Jackson's conduct 'very commendable' and were 'greatly pleased with the success the Braithwaites have already met with, and the encouragement they give of recovering a much greater part of the cargo'. So a flood of letters were sent out, thanking everyone for their assistance and arranging that everything would be ready to go ahead once the weather improved in May 1788.[24]

Despite these fond hopes, the Braithwaites were even less successful in the 1788 season than they had been in 1787. Captain Fancourt and the *Bull Dog* again acted as their naval escort and, on his arrival in the islands on 12 May 1788, he reported progress up to that date to Philip Stephens, Secretary to the Admiralty. 'Messrs. Braithwaite have been able to act but once with their diving machine which was so much agitated by a grand swell that they only got 630 loose dollars; all the chests being destroyed which will make the business tedious and difficult.' They did not think it prudent 'to risque the machine till the weather becomes more favorable, which the inhabitants say will be in the months of August and September, when they are in hopes of making greater progress'.[25]

Progress however was not very great as Fancourt reported on his return to Spithead on 9 November. Since his previous letter the divers had recovered only 1,600 more dollars and on 2 September 'they gave up the idea of fishing any longer on the wreck of the *Hartwell*'. The Braithwaites planned to return to London for the winter and there 'construct a new diving machine and other apparatus calculated for the reef'. Once again the Company was not too disheartened. Jackson and Upton were praised again and promoted. Captain Fanshaw was presented with the Company's thanks 'and 200 guineas or the value thereof in plate' while the want of success of the Braithwaite brothers 'was owing to the weather during their continuance at Bona Vista being uncommonly unfavourable'. Arrangements were made for a third expedition and this time the Braithwaites were able to improve the terms of their contract. Instead of receiving one-eighth of every-thing recovered, as in the previous two seasons, they were now to get 'one fifth salvage on all bullion and one half on such other goods and stores as may be recovered', terms which were later to be improved even more to a very attractive one-third on bullion, so providing a real incentive to try even harder in the 1789 season.[26]

The Braithwaites sailed from Portsmouth on 12 May 1789 in two sloops, the *Endeavour*, captained by the elder brother John, and the *Elizabeth*, captained by William. They arrived in Bonavista on 23 June and spent a week or so testing their equipment, including the new diving-bell which was lowered into the sea with William inside, who 'found it to answer'. On 2 July they went out to the wreck site and laid down moorings and then, firmly anchored directly over the *Hartwell*, they sent the bell down and were immediately successful, sending up over 10,000 loose dollars [i.e. pieces of eight] in the first two days. Only a few more days (ten in all) were calm enough to work the bell, but on every one of these they brought up loose dollars, nearly 19,000 on 15 July, their best day, and a total of just over 100,000 dollars, worth about £20,000, by 8 August, the last day on which they dived. On a few days it was calm enough to work on the wreck with tongs but not the bell, and on these days they brought up pigs of lead and blocks of tin. The cynical might think it a bit suspicious that the Braithwaites should do so much better once the terms of their contract had been improved, but this would probably be unfair. The wreck site was continually disturbed by storms and high seas brought in by the prevailing north-easterly winds and it was just good luck that so many of the coins carried by the *Hartwell* were adequately exposed and the weather sufficiently fair to enable them to prosper on this expedition.[27]

This voyage is recorded in the surviving logbook that John Braithwaite kept. It did not provide many technical details, although one interesting fact emerges. In 1786 William Braithwaite Sr had informed a journalist that it was 'his general practice . . . to remain at work under water for six hours consecutive'. But this was far from being the general method of his sons who sometimes made as many as a dozen descents between them in a day while working on the *Hartwell*. On 21 July 1789, for example, Braithwaite records 'after breakfast moored over wreck, brother went down four times, sent up two boxes [i.e. circa 6,000 loose coins], after dinner self went down four times, sent up allmost two boxes, Richard Parry [the only other diver] went down twice, sent up one box, the sea beginning to rise obliged us to give over for this day, unmoored and sailed into our old station'. The practice thus shown is rather strange on two counts. Bell divers normally worked in pairs, for safety and for convenience in working at the bottom, but the Braithwaites clearly dived alone. And their bell did not stay much longer on the bottom than a barrel-diver would have done. That this was indeed a bell is clear from the logbook and other sources. The answer to this apparent puzzle is probably that the Braithwaite pump was not as powerful as they would have liked people to believe. It will be recalled that John Smeaton's pump, which he invented for use in Ramsgate harbour at exactly the same date, was not capable of working properly in more than twelve feet (two fathoms) of water. The *Hartwell* lay at depths ranging from five to seven fathoms and it was no doubt necessary for the Braithwaites to supplement the air delivered by their pump by fairly frequent visits to the surface to replenish and refresh their air.[28]

The East India Company had thought that it was 'not absolutely necessary to have the protection of a sloop of war' for the 1789 expedition. This was to underestimate the efficiency of the information service that carried news back and forth across the Atlantic. The wrecking community in the West Indies and the Bahamas were well aware that a fortune in silver lay on the reefs off the north-east of Bonavista. When they learned that this treasure was no longer protected by a British warship, these 'Moon-Cursers' as the *Times* called them, half pirate, half wrecker, hurried to fit out sloops and schooners and hire negro divers to work on it. The first intimation of trouble ahead came on 14 August when the Braithwaites saw a small schooner 'behaving suspiciously'. This soon became three and then five vessels in all, based at the nearby island of Sal and hardly bothering to conceal their intention of diving on the *Hartwell*. 'I hailed the largest of them and asked him what he wanted on the reef', wrote John Braithwaite in his journal. 'He said he came for some of the money and was determined to have it, if he lost his life in the attempt.' These piratical vessels completely outgunned and outmanned the crews of the Braithwaites' two sloops and, after a couple of weeks of argument, bluster and threat, they summoned up the courage to open fire and, on 29 August, drove the Braithwaites off the reef for the rest of the 1789 season. 'After we left the wreck saw all the schooners and sloops bear down for reef and send their boats on the wreck', and they were to see this wretched sight for several more days before John Braithwaite left for England to get more guns and some naval assistance, leaving his brother to keep an eye on things in the islands. Gregory Jackson, the Company's agent, had taken the precaution of digging a large pit underneath his house on Bonavista where he could keep the proceeds of the season's diving safe, but he believed that the arrival of the pirates had deprived them of 'ten chests more this season'.[29]

In October 1789 Captain Henry Savage of HMS *Pomona* decided to leave his station on the West African coast and sail to Santiago in the Cape Verde Islands to 'refresh' his men who were suffering badly from various tropical diseases. On his arrival, the Portuguese Governor sent him a letter addressed to 'The

Commander of any of His Britannic Majesty's ships or vessels to whose hands this may come.' This had been written in Bonavista on 26 August by Clotworthy Upton, Jackson's assistant, and asked for help against the pirates. Captains in the Royal Navy were instructed to respond to such pleas if at all possible and Savage wasted little time in doing so. Three days later he was off Bonavista and on the following day, 29 October, he chased and captured a sloop which turned out to be the *Brothers* from the Danish West Indian island of St Thomas, a notorious haunt of pirates. The sloop was well armed and her crew consisted of the master, Thomas Hammond of New York, the mate, two white sailors and seven black men.

Savage had little trouble in getting a frank admission of what they had been doing in the islands, the Scottish mate, for instance, saying that the sloop had been fitted out to work on the wreck of the *Hartwell* and that 'they had procured seven negroes divers for that purpose, which negroes were the men now on board'. A search revealed that these black divers, with no bell or any other equipment to assist them, had been very successful and had recovered 20,000 dollars. The crew of the *Brothers* also reported on the success of some of the other vessels that had been diving on the reef and had now gone home. The schooner *Mary* had got 10,000 dollars, the *Swift* 8,000, 'but had lost his best diver on the reef', and a sloop with Swedish colours whose name they had forgotten had also got 8,000 dollars. This was pretty depressing news for the Braithwaites, 46,000 dollars and no doubt much more unrecorded lost to the Moon-Cursers, enough to fill fifteen chests rather than the ten which Jackson thought the pirates had cost them.[30]

Captain Savage stayed only a few days at Bonavista but, a month after his departure, two other British warships, the *Adventure* and the *Fairy* sloop, arrived at Santiago and were informed that there were now five more armed schooners with Dutch colours at the island of Sal intending to go on the wreck of the *Hartwell*. The *Fairy* chased these intruders away and later the two royal ships cruised through 'all the islands in search of them' without making any captures. They then prepared to go about their normal business, but not before meeting up in Santiago with HMS

Termagant, a sloop under the command of Captain Walter Gwennap which had been sent out from England to protect the wreck and to bring home the treasure and other effects recovered in the 1789 season. He arrived in the islands at the end of December and stayed a couple of months, some of which he spent 'cruizing in quest of [the pirates] . . . but have every reason to suppose that on their hearing of my arrival, that they are gone off, as at present I cannot gain the least intelligence of them'. This is what normally happened when naval officers chased pirates, but at least his presence kept the wreck free from attention until he sailed home with the contents of the pit under Gregory Jackson's house, '25 chests of dollars, said to contain 21,000 pounds [sterling], 77 pigs of lead and 24 blocks of tin'. His arrival at Falmouth was reported in the *Public Advertiser* on 26 April 1790 with typical journalistic exaggeration. 'The *Termagant* . . . has brought home upwards of one hundred thousand pounds worth of dollars saved from the *Hartwell*', some five times the actual value.[31]

Both the East India Company and the Braithwaites believed it would be worthwhile spending a fourth season on the *Hartwell* though, with less left to dive for, the Company was forced once again to improve the Braithwaites' cut to two-fifths of all bullion and half of anything else. John Braithwaite in the *Elizabeth* sailed from the Thames on 22 March and arrived back at the harbour of English Road on the sheltered western side of Bonavista on 27 April 1790 and was told that 'my brother at the North Side, all well'. But matters were not to be all well for very long as, before they had even begun to work on the wreck, they could see a piratical sloop and a schooner acting suspiciously near the reef. The Braithwaites had been promised a sloop of war to protect them, but this had not materialized, so they found themselves in the same position as in the previous year though they now carried a few more guns.

Towards the end of May the situation became increasingly tense as pirate vessels tried to work on the reef but were warned off. On 28 May, for instance, a schooner came close and her captain said that he 'wanted us to let him try his divers as he had not tried them'. John Braithwaite said that 'if he did he should fire at him'.

Next day much the same happened, but all was to be resolved on 3 June when five sail of pirates closed in on the reef where the *Endeavour* sloop lay at anchor with the two Braithwaite brothers and another nine men aboard. One of the pirate vessels, braver than the rest, 'hoisted a black flag' and opened fire, at first with muskets and then with swivel guns. 'Immediately all the vessels fired upon us from all quarters, when our men began to fire our carriage guns at them as well as small arms.' Such determined resistance may have surprised the pirates; it certainly had the desired effect, and 'after a close action of two glasses [one hour], the pirates sheered off different courses, and were pursued for two hours, but the *Endeavour* having been so long at sea was very foul and could not come up with them'. Apart from a few minor alarms, the Braithwaites and their men were now left to get on with their business for the rest of the diving season. John Braithwaite noted in his journal that they had received several shot on board and through their sails, two shrouds had been severed, 'but none of us either killed or wounded'. It was a great day that neither he nor his brother was ever likely to forget.[32]

Such close attention from the pirates meant that very little was done on the wreck until the successful battle left them free to dive and work as they wished. Even after the battle, the need to repair the sloop and stand at arms stopped anything much being done before the last week of June. But, from then until they packed up in September, they were able to get in about thirty working days on the reef. Just five of these involved descents in the bell from which they sent up another 4,000 or 5,000 loose dollars, practically all that had been left by the pirates. The last day for dollars was 19 August when John 'went down several times . . . and took up most of the dollars we could find. This day and yesterday the smoothest we ever had here.' On the other working days, they operated from the surface with their glass and tongs, the main target being 'pigs' or ingots of lead. The Company had loaded 2,815 pigs of lead in England which were valued at just over £4,000. Each weighed about 150 pounds, so to raise a hundred in a day from depths of thirty or forty feet, as the Braithwaites occasionally did, must have been extremely hard work, so hard indeed that on two occasions their specially designed 'lead tongs' broke and had to be repaired at the forge. Altogether, they recovered just under 2,000 pigs which, at fifty per cent, were worth some £1,400 to the salvors, together with 47 blocks of tin, some iron and bits and pieces, so it had been worth winning the battle of the Hartwell Reef, as the wreck site was to be called on future charts, some of which also distinguished Braithwaite Island.[33]

The Braithwaite brothers demonstrated skill, perseverance and considerable courage during their four seasons working on the *Hartwell*, but they were fortunate that the local people were 'perfect well wishers to the undertaking', as the *Times* later reported, both at the time of the shipwreck and during the salvage operations. When the British thanked the Queen of Portugal for the 'humane attention' of her people in the Cape Verde Islands, she replied that she 'was very pleased to learn that her subjects in a part of the world so unconnected with the civilized manners of other nations' could behave so well. The Governors of both Bonavista and Santiago were always ready to help, while the black soldiers of the garrison on Bonavista provided armed protection for the treasure during the times of threat from the pirates and were also useful in rounding up deserters from the Royal Navy ships (for a fee). Members of the crew made friends with the islanders during their Sunday shore leaves, none more so than John Braithwaite himself who met and courted Eliza Doyle, the 17-year-old daughter of an Irish trader, a treasure indeed who was to bear him seven sons. He brought her home with him after the *Hartwell* was finally abandoned and they were married on 3 June 1794, the fourth anniversary of the battle.[34]

On their return to London, the Braithwaites toyed with the idea of working again on the *Royal George*, but once more encountered difficulties with the officials involved. So they abandoned diving and the sea and resumed their engine-making business which became a partnership between John and William Jr when their father died in 1800. Two years later William was followed to the grave by his younger son, and so it was John alone who made the decision to return one more time to the profitable business of diving for wrecks. The occasion was the shipwreck of the outgoing Indiaman *Earl of Abergavenny* on 5 February 1805 which, at five in the afternoon, struck the Shambles, a shoal of coarse sand and shingle off Portland Bill. After a couple of hours of pounding on the shoal, she floated off with the tide and an attempt was made to beach her on Weymouth Sands. But she was so badly holed that desperate efforts with pumps and a bucket chain failed to keep her from sinking further and further into the water. At about eleven o'clock in the evening she finally settled on the sea bottom, with her main and mizzen masts above water. By then the wind was blowing very hard and the sea was breaking in short, violent waves, a terrifying sight for the passengers, crew and soldiers aboard. A few got off in boats, many leaped into the sea and swam or clutched onto wreckage and some of these were later saved, while some two hundred clung desperately to the masts and rigging. As the night went on, their numbers were gradually reduced to about seventy men who were rescued by boats in the morning. Some were swept off by the swell, while others 'from the piercing cold were unable longer to retain their hold'. Altogether, about 260 of the four hundred people aboard lost their lives in this disaster.[35]

Among the dead was the ship's captain, John Wordsworth, and it is because of his death that this shipwreck is most often remembered. For John was the much loved younger brother of William Wordsworth, the poet, who described him as 'meek, affectionate, silently enthusiastic, loving all quiet things, and a Poet in every thing but words', unusual characteristics for a ship's captain. John's death was 'a tragedy which darkened [William's] life' and some critics attribute a decline in William's quality as a poet to this disaster. William's affection was reciprocated by John, who saw the main purpose of his labours to earn enough money to support their sister Dorothy and to enable William to concentrate on his writing. And on this voyage, his third as captain of the same ship, he believed that he would at last make his and their fortune as, after much lobbying, he was granted 'a voyage far beyond my expectation, I had almost said my wishes'. This ideal voyage for an East India captain was to sail to China via Bengal where the £20,000 investment which he and members of the Wordsworth family had put together could be used to purchase opium for the Chinese market. This very profitable trade was illegal but condoned, by both the British and the Chinese, and no one at the time thought any the worse of Captain John Wordsworth for investing the family money in such an evil business.[36]

Writers on this tragedy concentrate on how it affected the Wordsworth family and their friends, including other writers such as Charles and Mary Lamb and Samuel Taylor Coleridge, and on John's behaviour during the catastrophe. John was quickly acquitted of blame, leaving the pilot to bear responsibility, though there was a later and more charitable view that he had been unlucky as the 'wind suddenly died away and the tide set her into the breakers'. There was also the question of whether it would have been better to abandon ship and try to reach shore with the boats, though it was generally felt that the sea was too tumultuous to do this with any hope of success. The Wordsworth family were also worried about John's bearing and behaviour during the shipwreck and this was something which particularly concerned Charles Lamb who actually worked in East India House and so was able to interview survivors. At first he thought that William Wordsworth, up in his Lake District home, would like to hear that his brother had died in a spirit of noble self-sacrifice. 'Perhaps he might have saved himself', he wrote on 18 February, 'but a captain who in such circumstances does all he can for his ship and nothing for himself is the noblest idea.' But he quickly realized that this was not at all what the Wordsworths wanted to read and later emphasized that 'it does not at all appear that your brother in any absence of mind neglected his own safety'.[37]

Literary historians do not really approve of the heroes of this book, men who loved profit more than poetry, so it is perhaps not surprising to find them described in the most recent and best account of the wreck as 'various individuals and firms who were already ghoulishly applying for the job of salvaging the ship'. But there was no room for sentiment in the salvage business. The *Earl of Abergavenny* had aboard a quarter of a million ounces of silver specie, worth about £70,000, together with much private treasure such as that invested by the Wordsworths, and the usual outward-bound cargo of cloth, lead, tin, copper and so on which has been seen in previous East India shipwrecks. The wreck was surveyed and found to lie in about ten fathoms (60 feet) of water, with '27 feet of water on her upper deck'. Captain Wilkinson, commander of the Customs cutter *Greyhound* who was guarding the wreck, reported on 23 February that she 'still remains a whole and . . . thinks it impossible in her present state to get out any part of her cargo unless she is weighed or the decks blown up'. This was the commonly received opinion, reported in newspapers and elsewhere, and there were plenty of people who believed they had the skill and resources either to weigh up or blow up the *Earl of Abergavenny*. The Court Minutes of the East India Company record a dozen separate applicants, but there were probably many more than this since the names do not include the two who later did dive on the wreck.[38]

Not very much was done in the way of salvage in 1805. Various objects from the wreck were washed ashore as were many bodies. More corpses, including that of John Wordsworth, were recovered by dragging. During the summer a man called Tucker dived on the wreck, but he did not succeed in recovering very much, just some masts and rigging and bits and pieces. The absence of any serious competition may have been one factor in persuading John Braithwaite, now 55 years old, that it would be a good idea to return to his old profession of diving. He teamed up with a man called William Tonkin who had invented a most extraordinary diving machine which was described and illustrated in the *Monthly Magazine*. 'The machine . . . consists of a body of copper with iron boots and joints, as in coats of mail. The whole is then covered with leather, and afterwards with canvas painted white, to distinguish it in the water. The arms are made of strong, water-proof leather, and the place for sight is about eight inches diameter, and glazed with glass an inch thick.' Tonkin's semi-atmospheric diving apparatus looks incredibly unwieldy and one wonders if John Braithwaite actually used it very much. He certainly took with him a tried and trusted diving-bell as well when he sailed down to Weymouth from the Thames in September 1805, having contracted with the Company to retain one-eighth of all specie recovered, the same share as in his first two voyages to the wreck of the *Hartwell* seventeen years previously.[39]

The winter was spent planning and preparing for the salvage operations which began in earnest at the end of March 1806. John Braithwaite knew exactly where the treasure had been stowed and, since the wreck was still intact, his main task was to clear a route to this room. This involved taking up quite a bit of cargo from on top of it, for example, lead, cloth, skins, books, silk handkerchiefs and 'a quantity of great coats for hot countries', as well as sails, cables and bits of the wreck. On 21 April he was ready to blow his way into the store room, so he dived and 'prepared for explosion' and next day he 'exploded with a small charge, about 18 pounds powder'. This seems to have done the trick, though there was still work to do before he could get at the money. More cargo had to be shifted and he also needed to expand the hole made by the explosion by breaking up the deck around it, as well as hooking up and removing 'the tiller, being very much in our way in clearing the way to the dollars'. But, on 30 April, that way lay clear and he was able to send up nineteen chests of dollars and another sixteen on the first three days of May. More chests were to follow, whenever the weather permitted, and on 17 May John Braithwaite was pleased to record in his journal the raising of the last chest, 'making in all 62 chests. I believe about £1,200 in each chest.' 'Last night', reported the *Gentleman's Magazine* on 18 May, 'was landed at the Customs-House in Weymouth the last chest of dollars from the wreck of the *Earl of Abergavenny*, which completed the 62 chests recovered by Mr Braithwaite who, with much perseverance and ingenuity, has succeeded. The total of the 62 chests is about £70,000 value. He is going to proceed immediately on the cargo.'[40]

The key to John Braithwaite's success was clearly his skill at conducting underwater explosions and it is fortunate that he described his method of doing this at the end of his short journal about the salvage of the *Earl of Abergavenny*. The gunpowder was put in a copper pipe, four to six inches in diameter, which was placed horizontally against or under the part of the wreck which was to be blown up. Into the centre of this 'powder magazine', as he called it, was fixed a vertical section of half-inch lead pipe through which the quick match was carried down to the powder. And on the surface, one is glad to see, there was 'a fuse or slow match put in the pipe to give time to get away'. This ingenious device did not work every time. On one occasion the powder got 'into the match conducting pipe, choked the match' and on others the match was defective or had got wet. But these explosions were successful more often than not and Braithwaite proceeded in May and June systematically to blow up the wreck, bit by bit, so that he could break up and raise to the surface the decks and sides of the ship and so get at the cargo. The biggest bang of all came on 30 May when he 'exploded with a charge of triple proof powder, 75 pounds, the largest charge we ever used, that was to cut through the wale of the ship's side, six inches thick oak plank'. Although John Braithwaite does not mention it in his journal, his equipment also included a saw worked by four men on a raft. This was designed to provide the 'means of sawing apart the deck of a ship under water' and, according to his obituary, 'evinced the perfection to which his discoveries had attained'.[41]

The rest of the salvage was just hard work, mainly with hooks and tongs, getting up the huge and multifarious contents of the very large sunken Indiaman, guns and gun carriages, lead and more lead, packing cases containing looking glasses, leather, perfumery and millinery, glassware and hundreds of other things. Braithwaite himself was ashore for a week at the end of June, 'but they came regularly to work on board, taking up general cargo, lead, tin, copper, iron and all sorts, keeping a schooner and large 10-ton boat going to bring goods to shore, the upper side of ship pretty well cleared away [so] had full scope for work'. This labour went on, weather permitting, until November when they packed up for the winter, but it resumed on 28 March 1807. John Braithwaite summarized the 1807 season briefly in his journal. 'Fixed the windlass and other machinery, then we went to work and had a prosperous summer, worked as long till the cargo got so thin, not worth getting up. After succeeding in breaking up the ship "Earl of Abergavenny" by the assistance of gunpowder and weighing the cargo as above, and settling all things at Weymouth, we returned in the "Endeavour" to London', arriving on 23 December. He was said to have recovered £75,000 in dollars, 'the whole of the tin and other valuables, worth £30,000'.[42]

Some of that 'thin' cargo, 'not worth getting up', has been retrieved by scuba-diving enthusiasts in recent years, but overall John Braithwaite's salvage of the *Earl of Abergavenny* must rate as one of the most thorough and successful diving expeditions ever undertaken up to his day. But John was never tempted to try it again. He was now a rich man, able to join the gentry and buy a gentleman's house at Westbourne Green near Paddington. When he died in 1818, he left £30,000, worth several millions today, to be shared between his seven sons, almost certainly more than the fortunes left by any of the other divers considered in this book.[43]

Chapter Twelve

Enterprise in Vigo Bay

Chapter Twelve

Enterprise in Vigo Bay

"It was here [in Vigo Bay] that the united flags of Holland and England triumphed over the pride of Spain and France; when the burning timbers of exploded war-ships soared above the tops of the Gallegan hills, and blazing galleons sank with their treasure chests."[1] George Borrow, *The Bible in Spain*

The treasure of Vigo Bay is probably the most famous (and certainly the most sought after) of all the treasures considered in this book, not least because it was periodically visited by Captain Nemo in the *Nautilus* when he had need of more funds to finance his extravagant lifestyle. The narrator describes the underwater scene on one such visit. 'The sandy bottom was clean and bright. Some of the ship's crew in their diving dresses were clearing away half rotten barrels and empty cases from the midst of the blackened wrecks. From these cases and from these barrels escaped ingots of gold and silver, cascades of piastres and jewels. The sand was heaped up with them.' Jules Verne was of course writing fiction when he wrote these words in 1869, but such is the stuff of treasure hunters' dreams.[2]

The story starts in the summer of 1702, at the beginning of the War of the Spanish Succession, when the English and their Dutch allies had to decide how to employ their fleets. They quickly came to the conclusion that the best strategy would be to capture the nineteen galleons in the Spanish treasure fleet which had sailed for

Europe from Havana early in June under the escort of twenty-three French warships. This would be the most fabulous prize, for no treasure had been shipped across the Atlantic for four years and the gold and silver in the ships were described in the *Gaceta de Madrid* as 'the richest that had ever come from America . . . more than twenty million pieces of eight', a fantastic sum that was repeated and sometimes exceeded in other newspapers throughout Europe. The allied plan was to send an Anglo-Dutch fleet under Admiral Sir George Rooke to capture Cadiz, the normal destination of the galleons, thus forcing them and their French escort to seek refuge in another port on the Atlantic coast of Spain or France where a second fleet under the command of Admiral Sir Cloudesley Shovell would be waiting for them.[3]

Such ambitious plans, requiring amphibious descents on foreign ports, very often went seriously wrong and this one was no exception. The attempt to capture Cadiz was a complete failure, characterized by poor planning, indecision, dissension between the expedition's leaders and disgraceful behaviour by the soldiers who, once ashore, confined their activities to drinking, looting and desecrating churches. After a month or so of this ineffectual campaigning, it was resolved at a Council of War 'that we take the first opportunity and make the best of our way with the fleet to England' and so, on 19 September 1702, they headed for home in 'shame and confusion'. There would be no great victory over Spain that year.[4]

Meanwhile the Spanish treasure fleet and their escort of French warships had been sailing uneventfully across the Atlantic until they were near the Azores where they received accurate information on the current naval situation in Europe. War had broken out, an Anglo-Dutch fleet was besieging Cadiz and another one presented a dangerous obstacle somewhere off the Atlantic coast of France. The French Admiral Château-Renault wanted to make for a French port, now that Cadiz was barred to them, but the Spanish felt certain that once their treasure was in France it would stay there. After a long debate a compromise was reached and it was decided to make for the port of Vigo on the Atlantic coast of Spanish Galicia. It was not a very good choice, however, since the port lacked strong fortifications and a powerful garrison to protect the fleets.

The French and Spanish fleets arrived at Vigo on 22 September and immediately made preparations to defend themselves if necessary. The Bay, or *ría*, of Vigo is a long inlet of the sea, running inland for some twenty miles. It is a very picturesque place, surrounded by mountains and similar in appearance to a Norwegian fjord or a Scottish sea-loch, though the surrounding mountains are lower and greener. As in many sea-lochs, the *ría* is divided into inner and outer sections by a narrow stretch of water called the Straits of Rande, and Rande is, in fact, the name given by the Spanish to both the battle and the treasure. The Franco-Spanish plan was a simple one. The galleons were anchored in the bay of San Simón and near the town of Redondela in the south-eastern corner of the innermost part of the *ría*, from where it would be comparatively simple to unload their cargoes. The straits, which were 'a musket shot over' or about three-quarters of a mile, were defended by 'a very strong boom made up of masts, yards, cables, top-chains and casks, fastened together with ropes, several yards in circumference'. On the south side of the narrows, the crumbling fort of Rande was repaired, garrisoned and given extra guns from the fleet, while on the north side, at Corbeyro, a gun platform was erected and placed in similar readiness. Directly inside the boom, many powerful units of the French fleet lay anchored in a half-moon ready to fire on anyone so foolhardy as to approach. Further defence was provided on the southern shore by several thousand men of the local militia who had been taken by force from their homes in the mountains and brought down to the seaside on the orders of the Prince of Barbanzón, Captain-General of the Kingdom of Galicia. These militia were later described as 'a confus'd heap got together' but, even so, the men in the galleons and the French fleet must have felt pretty safe, especially when they were informed that Admiral Rooke and the Anglo-Dutch fleet had passed the Cíes Islands [Bayona Islands to the English] which protected the mouth of Vigo Bay and were headed northward.[5]

The luck of the Dutch and English was, however, just about to change. Three ships of the fleet sailing north from Cadiz stopped off at Lagos in southern Portugal to take on water. The chaplain from one of them, a French speaker from Jersey, went ashore to stretch his legs and fell into conversation with the French consul who was unable to resist this opportunity to mock the English for their failure at Cadiz. 'He told him that their designs upon the galleons were likewise disappointed, seeing they were arrived safe into Vigo in Galicia.' The whereabouts of the treasure fleet was hitherto unknown to the English, so this was very welcome news and the chaplain quickly passed it on to his commander, Captain Hardy of the *Pembroke*. This ship was fortunately one of the fastest in the fleet and on 6 October, despite bad weather, she caught up with the rest of the fleet off Cape Finisterre. Admiral Rooke and his colleagues were overjoyed with the news, seeing at once that here was a chance to eradicate the bad memory of their failure at Cadiz. He sent out a scouting vessel which captured a launch off the mouth of the *ría*, the prisoners confirming the information provided by the chaplain. Three days later, the Anglo-Dutch fleet sailed into Vigo Bay, passed the town on the southern shore of the outer bay in 'a favourable fog' and came to anchor within sight of the boom and the French fleet.[6]

Next morning, 23 October 1702, the English and their Dutch allies attacked. The Duke of Ormond landed with two thousand guardsmen and marines about halfway between the town of Vigo and Fort Rande. As his men marched towards the fort through a rocky and wooded defile, the Galician militia scattered like sheep before them, 'frighted with the echo of the English and Dutch cannon among the mountains'. The defenders of the fort itself put up slightly more of a fight, but not for very long as the English soldiers clambered onto each other's backs to scale the walls and then leaped down into the fort and 'took it immediately, sword in hand'.[7]

Meanwhile the Anglo-Dutch fleet approached the boom in four divisions of six ships each, led by Vice-Admiral Sir Thomas Hopson in the *Torbay*, a guided missile 156 feet long and 1,200 tons in weight. To left and right of the leading division, two powerful ships of the line had orders to bombard the batteries on each side of the straits while the rest poured through the centre. The wind was fitful as they drew near, sudden gusts, then calms, but at noon was sufficiently strong for Rooke to order Hopson to slip his anchor and push for the boom which the French 'thought impossible to be forced; but they soon found their mistake', as the momentum of the *Torbay* forced an opening 'with more facility than was expected'. But, at this critical moment, the wind fell again and the *Torbay* was in great danger, becalmed while the French fleet pounded her with their guns and a blazing fireship was laid along her side. The moment of danger soon passed however as the breeze freshened once more and the English and Dutch ships could follow their flagship through the gap in the boom.

Admiral Château-Renault and his ships were now trapped in the inner bay by the much more powerful Anglo-Dutch fleet and he could see at once that the day was lost. Rather than let the allies capture his entire fleet, he gave orders to set fire to his flagship and signalled the rest of the captains under his command to follow his example. Not all were successful and six of the French ships of the line were, in fact, captured by the English and the Dutch, sometimes after heroic bravery in quenching the fires, but the rest were either burned or scuttled. Nine of the Spanish galleons were also captured, four by the English and five by the Dutch, leaving another ten to be sunk or set on fire. Several blew up as fire reached their gunpowder stores and the scene was truly terrible, corpses, cargoes and ships' timbers being flung high into the air by the explosions, while those still alive tried desperately to flee the burning vessels. The fires illuminated the road for the Duke of Ormond, as he marched that evening to seize and plunder the town of Redondela in the south-eastern corner of the inner bay, 'being well lighted in his way by the enemies' ships in flames, which yielded a pleasant though dismal spectacle'. And so ended the astonishing battle of Vigo Bay which saw the destruction or capture of every single French and Spanish ship. It was described by the naval historian Sir Julian Corbett in 1904 as 'one of the most complete victories in British naval history', though few have heard of it, there being an unspoken rule of the national historical memory that no naval victory need be remembered if the British fleet was not commanded by Admiral Lord Nelson.[8]

The English and Dutch remained in Vigo Bay for just over three weeks after the battle, commanded first by Rooke and then by Sir Cloudesley Shovell who quit the Spanish port with the last allied ships on 5 November. Their task was to make the most of their astonishing victory by ensuring that the captured ships were sufficiently seaworthy to sail back to England and Holland and to salvage what they could from the others. Spanish treasure was the stuff of English sailors' dreams and they went about these tasks enthusiastically. Both nations were reported to have sent divers down on the wrecks and these men recovered large numbers of guns, particularly the valuable brass ones, and quite a lot of silver and other goods. Everyone in the fleet was busy trying to recover what they could, as can be seen from the petition of the masters of twelve transport ships employed in the royal service. They successfully begged to be able to keep the hides, snuff, cochineal and indigo which they had hooked up 'by creepers . . . from the bottom of the river in three and four fathoms water'.[9]

Most of the fleet set sail for home with their prizes under the command of Admiral Rooke on 26 October but, on this same day, an unfortunate accident was to reduce substantially the value of the booty taken back to England. For, while passing through the channel between the Bayona Islands at the mouth of the bay, the *Nuestra Señora de Maracaibo*, richest of the captured galleons, struck a concealed rock and sank. Nearly everyone was saved from *Monmouth*'s prize, as she was known in honour of her captor, but most of her valuable cargo was lost. But there were still eight others which the English and Dutch could parade in triumph before their cheering fellow countrymen, an amazing sight which had not been seen since Elizabethan times.

The victorious allies had taken as much French and Spanish treasure as they were able to capture or salvage in the limited time available, but no one believed that they had located all the treasure in the sunken ships. So how much was left? This question has been debated from the time of the battle itself right up to the present day, and there has been a paradoxical tendency for estimates of the value of the sunken treasures of Vigo Bay to grow in tandem with the accumulation of evidence that there is, in fact, very little, or no, treasure to be found, except possibly in the wreck of *Monmouth's* prize. The treasure of Vigo Bay is thus very similar in reputation to the treasure in the Tobermory galleon. The more it seems certain that there is nothing left to find, the more the optimistic will believe that just one more day's diving will reveal those chests of gold and silver and jewels which were recovered with such ease by the divers employed by Captain Nemo in the *Nautilus.*

The problem is that none of the variables necessary to calculate the amount of treasure at Vigo can be estimated with any real confidence. In essence one needs to know how much was loaded in the West Indies, the amount that was unloaded in the month between the fleet's arrival at Vigo and the battle and the total that was captured or salvaged after the battle. No one would be happy to accept the official figure of twenty million pieces of eight brought from America in the 1702 fleet, since there was certainly much more brought clandestinely, some of this being found hidden in cargoes by the English and Dutch. But estimating secret cargoes is, of course, simply a matter of guesswork. There was always some, but how much could only be determined when a ship wrecked and was totally salvaged and it was discovered that there had been two or three times as much treasure aboard as was on the register.

There are also many ambiguities about the degree to which the treasure was unloaded at Vigo. It seems certain that the King of Spain's silver was unloaded and carried into the interior on the 1,500 ox-carts summoned for the purpose, figures of ten to fifteen million pieces of eight or three million pounds sterling saved in this way often being quoted. But there was also a large amount of silver carried on behalf of merchants and other individuals, as well as such valuable cargoes as cochineal and logwood. Some say that none, or very little, of this was unloaded because the Consulado of Seville, the official body which organized the treasure fleets, refused to allow anything to leave the galleons unless the proper officials were there to prevent smuggling and other irregularities. Other writers say that some of the private treasure and cargo was removed, but then put back on the galleons when news came from Cadiz that the allied fleet was on its way home. The remaining commentators say that the English made a very serious error when they allowed their scouting vessel to be seen from the castle high above Vigo four days before the battle. Now that it was clear that the fleets' hideaway had been discovered, merchants and officials ceased to argue with each other and concentrated on unloading the galleons in frantic haste right up to the last moment.

This last scenario sounds the most likely, but it still does not tell us how much was, in fact, removed. Nor does it tell us how much was actually taken home by the English and the Dutch, in the captured ships, in goods and treasure salvaged from the sunken galleons and warships, and from the loot taken at Redondela and elsewhere ashore. Whatever the figure it is likely to be much higher than the official estimates, since there was certainly much embezzlement. The truth is that all parties had valid motives to exaggerate the amount of treasure that lay in the sunken ships. The more the King of Spain could claim to have lost, the more he could seize from his subjects in compensation. The more the French had lost, the greater the indemnity they could claim from the Spanish crown. Merchants overstated their losses in order to swell insurance claims and to improve their bargaining power in getting concessions to ship goods on other fleets. And the English and Dutch inflated what was left at the bottom of Vigo Bay in order to excuse what was seen as a relatively small prize after such a great victory.

Given so many variables and such good reasons for deceit, it is hardly surprising that no two writers can agree on the value of the treasure lying under the sea. The range of estimates is huge. Henry Kamen, a much respected economic historian with a special interest in Spain and the treasure fleets, but no interest in treasure hunting, believed that the evidence showed that virtually all the treasure was unloaded from the galleons before the arrival of the allied fleets. Contemporaries who addressed the matter generally assumed that there was some treasure left in the wrecks, but few would put the value at more than five million pieces of eight, a huge figure but trivial in comparison with the extraordinary estimates made in more modern times. Avelino Rodríguez Elías, 'the official chronicler of the city of Vigo', believed in 1935 that immense riches still remained sunk in 'la ría de Vigo'. His absolute minimum estimate of these riches, on the most pessimistic assumptions, was fifteen million pieces of eight. His 'probable minimum' was fifty-four and his most optimistic estimate was seventy-nine million pieces of eight. If that seems rather a lot, one should note that it was a great deal less than the Italian Carlo Iberti thought was lying at the bottom of the bay in 1908. At the end of several pages of elaborate calculations, he summarized his findings. 'There is not the least doubt that the treasure in gold and silver still lying in the galleons of Vigo Bay amounts to not less than 113,396,085 pieces of eight, or £24,651,323', a figure which he rounded up to £28 million to take account of inflation.[10]

Readers will no doubt be suspicious of such very large valuations of sunken treasure, especially when made by people trying to raise capital to fund a treasure hunting expedition. And indeed the truth is that there was probably not very much treasure in the galleons of Vigo Bay, and that most was recovered long before the Spanish government started handing out concessions to private diving companies. Consider the situation. The location of all the galleons and warships sunk in Vigo Bay was known exactly to the French and Spanish authorities, most of them being visible from the surface and some still marked by masts or even superstructure above water. These same authorities and the merchants aboard, most of whom survived the disaster, also knew what had been taken out of the ships and what remained. The wrecks themselves were close to shore and in fairly shallow water, most of them in less than thirty feet, some much less, and the deepest in fifty or sixty feet. Such depths were easily accessible to the divers of the day, as has been seen, and both the French and Spanish had divers who could and did salvage the wrecks, either immediately or within a few years of the battle.

As soon as the allies had left the Bay, the Prince of Barbanzón arranged for divers to go down on the wrecks and they were reported to have recovered 'a not negligible quantity of silver'. This inexact figure is normally interpreted by treasure hunters as implying that there was plenty more not yet recovered, but it could of course mean that there was not much there to find, though the *Gaceta de Madrid* reported news from Vigo on 5 December 1702 'that they are proceeding with success in the raising of the precious burden belonging to the Capitana and Almiranta of the silver fleet'. Spain was rich in divers and no doubt many more would have been sent to Vigo if it had seemed worthwhile to do so. The French, too, were quick to work on the wrecks once the coast was clear. The English newspaper *Flying Post* reported a letter from Madrid which said that Château-Renault and several thousand men were returning to Vigo 'to fish up the merchandize and cannon that were sunk . . . and for that end several divers are gone thither'. A couple of weeks later the same paper quoted a letter from Vigo which praised the care and diligence of the Viceroy and the Admiral. 'They have already taken up many cannon and a great quantity of merchandize out of the burnt galleons and put it on shoar and there was great likelyhood, if the sea remain calm for some time, they would easily recover the rest.' This sounds like bravado, but the French certainly did recover material from the wrecks and were to do so for some years into the future. The French Vice-Consul in Vigo had orders to contract with divers to recover guns and other effects. His efforts led to the salvage of large numbers of cannon, some of which were sold to the Spanish, but seventy-six guns, together with anchors and other effects were sent back to France in 1705.[11]

Such evidence suggests that, with the exception of *Monmouth*'s prize whose location was not exactly known and was almost certainly in quite deep water, the wrecks of Vigo Bay had been quite thoroughly worked over, first by the English and Dutch and then by the French and Spanish, and that most goods of value sunk in them had been recovered within a few years of their loss. Reason therefore suggests that it would not be a very good idea to spend a lot of money diving in the muddy waters of Vigo Bay. But in treasure hunting reason plays little part and the 'immense riches' were to draw in optimistic adventurers right up to the second half of the twentieth century. Indeed, the treasure was still a major attraction when the tercentenary of the battle was celebrated in 2002.

Carlo Iberti, who has been quoted above, claimed that there were so many concessions to work on the wrecks granted between 1702 and 1723 'that even to enumerate them would be a lengthy task', and that there were another seventeen concessions between 1723 and 1748. Like much else in his book, this would seem to be a slight exaggeration, since most other accounts state that the first serious concession for private salvage work was granted in 1720 (or maybe 1722) to a Swede called Wolter de Sjöhelm. He was granted a royal privilege to work in the bay for three years, using a diving machine of his own invention, on payment of one-third of what he recovered to the Royal Treasury. This was a generous contract by Spanish standards, and presumably reflects the authorities' view of what de Sjöhelm was likely to find. He certainly does not seem to have recovered very much, but he found some iron guns, seven large anchors and 'an unknown quantity of gold and silver in coin and bars', this 'unknown quantity' being presumably a small one, like the 'not negligible quantity' salvaged by the divers working for the Prince of Barbanzón.[12]

This Swedish enterprise was followed in 1726 by a concession to a Spaniard called Don Juan Antonio Cosca, about whom nothing is known, and then in October 1728 by a patent granted to a French sea captain called Alexandre Goubert who was to search for wrecks intermittently in Vigo Bay for the next ten years. He is credited with locating almost all the sunken ships, but he focussed his attention on a wreck which lay close inshore. Goubert believed this to be the *almiranta* or vice-admiral from the silver fleet, but it turned out to be one of the French warships. After much effort, his men succeeded in dragging the wreck ashore, but they were to be disappointed with what they found inside, which included ballast stones, water jars, cannon balls, spoiled cables and rigging, logwood, fourteen iron cannon and four *marcos* of silver, a *marco* weighing half a *libra* or 230 grams, all this proving to be a poor return for an expenditure which was estimated at two million francs.[13]

Overlapping Goubert's concession was one granted to the Spaniard Don Juan Antonio Rivero in February 1732. Rivero's contract was the same as that granted to de Sjöhelm ten years previously, one third of recoveries to the Treasury, and he was to continue working in Vigo Bay for six years, by which time he had exhausted most of his great fortune, directing divers to move from wreck to wreck in continually disappointed hopes of at last finding the big one. Juan Antonio Rivero is, however, of interest to us, for he was the patentee who arranged for William Evans and John Rowe to come and dive on the wrecks in late August 1732, as was seen in Chapter Ten above. The first four months that they spent in Vigo is covered by the surviving logbook which ends on 3 December when they were still in Spain. During this period at least, the English divers appear to have enjoyed harmonious relationships with the patentee and indeed with all the Spanish authorities, but the exact contractual arrangements between Evans and Rivero are not specified in the surviving documents.[14]

'Brought the water on board, a hogg and other necessaries. Weighed from the Lizard and made saile for our intended voyage by God's help to Corunna in Spain and from thence to Vigo to work on the wrecks sunk in the River in ye year 1702.' William Evans sailed from the Lizard on 2 August 1732 and arrived ten days later at Corunna after a slow passage in which for a while they were completely lost and had to ask their way from a fishing boat. Over a month was now spent in Corunna, taking in provisions, claret and brandy, paying their respects to the English consul and to the patentee Juan Rivero who came over from Vigo to visit them. This long delay can be explained in part by a severe illness which kept Evans sick ashore for a couple of weeks. The sloop was also overhauled and the 'engine', which in this case was a diving barrel, was brought up out of the hold and tested.[15]

At last, on 17 September, they set sail round Cape Finisterre and three days later 'sailed in between the Bayonne [Cíes] Islands and the main land and at 5 [o'clock] we anchored above the town of Vigo over against the Consul's house'. Next day they sailed up the *ría* to La Portela, at the entrance of the channel to Redondela, 'where the wrecks are and anchored there about 6 o'clock'. For most of the rest of what survives of the logbook, they worked on the wreck of a ship which they called 'the Spanish Admiral', presumably the *almiranta* of the treasure fleet. Her name was actually *Jesús, María, Joseph,* but these and other proper names were never used for the wrecks which instead were given names made up by the local fishermen, many of whom considered particular wrecks to be their own family's privileged fishing ground. The *Spanish Admiral* lay deepest of all the ships in San Simón Bay; when Evans sounded on her he found nine and ten fathoms of water. A few days were spent sounding, sinking stones with buoys for markers and fitting out a launch belonging to the patentee. This was to be used to work the 'engine' and an iron gun was put in the launch to counterbalance the engine's weight as it was lowered and raised.

On 26 September, everything was ready. The patentee, Juan Antonio Rivero, and Don Martín, the King of Spain's local agent, came aboard, and the launch was anchored over the wreck. 'About eleven o'clock my father [i.e. William Evans] went down in the engine on the wreck of the Spanish Admiral in 10 fathom water. Her starboard side overhangs and is not above 7 fathom on her top timbers. He saith that it is very dark and could not but with difficulty see the timbers. He brought up a few oysters and a small piece of wood. He went down three times.' Captain Rowe went down in the barrel a couple of days later, but he too 'could not discover anything', the bottom of Vigo Bay being notoriously muddy and visibility therefore poor or non-existent. In such water there was little point in making much use of the diving barrel and it was not until over a month later, on 30 October, that it was used again, when 'my father went down in the engine seven times and Thomas Baker three, but it is so dark under water that they could not do or see anything'.

In such circumstances, William Evans and his men had no choice but to work the wreck using cruder tools such as great and lesser tongs, sweeps, drudges and drudge bags [dragnets] and hooks. It is clear from what was recovered that this wreck had been thoroughly worked over in the thirty years before Evans' arrival, for they brought up no rigging, sails or other equipment of the ship, no cannon-balls and just two broken pieces of a gun, no casks, no wine or foodstuffs or any of the thousand other things that one might expect to find in a wreck if it had never been salvaged. What they did recover on the days when weather permitted them to work were lots of pieces of timber and, once this had been cleared away, ballast stones, up to three tons in a day.

The timber was brought up mainly with tongs or the hook and ballast in the dragnet. This was then worked through on deck for hidden treasure and, although most days were marked by 'no success', some attractive bits and pieces were found, hardly enough to fully sustain their enthusiasm but some reward for effort, 'a small china image entire, being a man on an elephant', 'a lump of reals and half reals united together', 'three china chocolate cups and three callabash cups all intire without the least fracture'. Tuesday, 21 November, was one of these fairly good days. Don Martín, the King of Spain's agent, 'found among the ballast one double royall [a coin] and in the evening we found another, and miraculously brought up in the drudge in three several times eight entire china chocolate cups like those of Saturday last. We have worked later than usual being that we drudged in a good place.' These chocolate cups would have been of Chinese manufacture, brought across the Pacific by the Manila galleon and so to Europe on the treasure galleons. Several have been discovered by modern salvors and they are very beautiful, but a few Chinese cups, a handful of coins and an awful lot of ballast were not really a very good return for the patentee who presumably had to meet Evans' expenses.

While Evans concentrated mainly on the *Spanish Admiral*, he and his men did occasionally look at other wrecks to see if they should bring better luck. A couple of days were spent on a wreck found by chance, which was thought to be 'a Dutch ship who sunk there'. Some time was also spent trying unsuccessfully to find 'a certain launch [which] was sunk with vast quantity of treasure on board', according to Don Kelly, a local man who contracted to show them the marks for 6½ per cent of any recoveries. Rather more effort was put into working on a wreck known as the 'French Admiral' which was lying in five fathoms or thirty feet. Divers went down on her on 10 November, 'but could see nothing but her timbers sticking up out of the mudd, some four some five foot some less'. This wreck did not look too promising, and so they were perhaps not too bothered when told by the King's agent to suspend their salvage work until a dispute had been resolved with the captains of four French ships who were waiting at Vigo for a royal patent to work on the French wrecks. This dispute was decided in favour of Rivero and Evans, the latter being told he could 'work without fear of any obstruction', though, in fact, he continued to work on the Spanish and not the French Admiral for the last few days of the surviving logbook.

When Evans finally quit Vigo is not known, but one fears that the rest of his stay was no more profitable than what has been described above, since the total recoveries made on behalf of Don Juan Antonio Rivero were said to be worth just 3,068 *reales* or 383 pieces of eight. The very poor returns to the patents of Goubert and Rivero did not however discourage other companies from trying their luck in Vigo Bay, maybe another six in the eighteenth century, though the documentation recording these efforts is scarce. We will therefore move ahead to 1825 when a very well documented expedition set out for Vigo from the Thames. The entrepreneur in charge was Isaac Dickson, a wine and spirit merchant who had once held a commission as a major in the Spanish army and still maintained many contacts in Spain. He claimed to have first become interested in the Vigo treasure when a gentleman from Galicia, of good repute and education, had 'expressed much surprise that the English, who were so enter-prising a people, had never attempted to raise such immense treasure'. The well-read Galician suggested to Dickson that he consult Tobias Smollett's *Complete History of England* for further information. Smollett, in fact, concluded his description of the battle of Vigo Bay by remarking that 'the value of fourteen million of pieces of eight, in plate and rich commodities, was destroyed in six galleons that perished'.[16]

Dickson asked a Mr Steele, 'an intimate friend', to do some further research on the treasure in other books and documents and it is nice to see that he did this in the British Museum, then as now some sort of guarantee that the researcher is a serious person. Steele, in fact, concluded that it was 'impossible to guess at the amount from the materials to which he had resorted', but such honest hedging did not deter the faithful who believed that what Smollett wrote must be true, especially when Dickson in his prospectus used creative arithmetic to improve Smollett's fourteen million pieces of eight (circa three or four million pounds sterling) to a more exciting £13 million sterling. Encouraged by the general interest, Dickson set about establishing the Vigo Bay Company. He successfully negotiated with the Spanish Ambassador to obtain a contract and this was confirmed during a visit that he made to Madrid. The Spanish Crown was to receive one half of everything recovered, Dickson a quarter and the other quarter was to be divided equally between eight gentlemen managers. Dickson and the managers then subdivided their entitlement into 800 shares and proceeded to try to sell them to cover their investment of £10,000 in the venture. 'One sixteen hundredth share in the Vigo Bay undertaking' was sold on Dickson's behalf on 1 November 1825 for £150, a very nice profit on an investment of £12 50s, and, by January 1826, after the insertion of numerous 'Bull articles' in the newspapers, the *Morning Herald* estimated that the shares had been 'got up to the price of £1,000 instead of the price originally fixed by the Company of £100'. This is almost certainly an exaggeration, but it is still hardly surprising that one of the shareholders should later consider himself 'the victim of a bubble scheme'.[17]

Most of this tricky stockjobbing took place after Dickson's expedition had set sail for Vigo, bullish reports of immediate success obviously being more convincing if they were not sent from London. The expedition itself was, however, a very different matter from the puffery of the stock-market promotion, an earnest, honest and very hard-working venture which is well documented in its logbook which is now held at the National Archives. This starts on 1 September 1825 when the brigantine *Enterprise*, captained by W. S. Brown, was fitting out in Dawson's Dock in London. The brig was armed with twelve guns and had a crew of thirty-three men which included such specialists in the work at hand as bellmen, armourers and engineers to maintain and repair the equipment, as well as the normal range of maritime tradesmen to be found on any sea-going vessel. The diving-bell was hired from Ramsgate Corporation where it had been used in the construction of a pier and was presumably similar to those developed by Smeaton and Rennie, that is square rather than bell-shaped and made of iron rather than wood. It was large enough to carry three men, though two was the normal load, and it was supplied with air from either 'the small air pump' or 'the double air pump', a piece of equipment which required up to ten men to work it. This again sounds like Rennie's pump, though it was never properly described. Fairly early on in the expedition something went wrong with the double air pump, which was not delivering as much air as it should. Several trials and comparisons with the small pump were made until the double pump was eventually 'greased and put into a case in the hold, being unserviceable'. However, the small pump proved to be a satisfactory replacement until another double pump was delivered, provided at a cost of £108 by G. & J. Rennie, and this was quite capable of keeping the bell full of air and free of water. The bell was tried out in the City Canal on 30 September, a trial which nearly ended in fatality as the men on deck mistook the signals of the bellmen. This never happened again, though working with the bell had to be abandoned on several occasions when strong breezes, choppy water and surface noises prevented the men on deck from hearing the signals, which were a certain number of blows with a hammer on the bell to signal the surface team to raise or lower the bell, to deliver more air or whatever.[18]

The *Enterprise* came out of the Canal in the first week of October 1825 and arrived in Vigo on the 26th of that month. The Captain and his clerk made the rounds of the Commandant of Marine, the King's Pilot and other officials to get their 'permission to survey and sound in the bay of Vigo', this being granted on condition that there was a Spanish officer on board while they were working on wrecks. A couple of weeks were now spent consulting with fishermen and other knowledgeable locals and surveying and buoying wrecks in San Simón Bay, the inner part of the *ría*, before they started working with the bell on their first wreck on 12 November. The *Enterprise* was to spend nine months in Vigo Bay and in this time they dived and worked on twelve different wrecks, three of them twice, as well as doing a lot of exploratory sweeping, sounding and buoying of other wrecks both in the area of the 1702 disaster and elsewhere in the Bay.

The first four wrecks on which they worked were in

comparatively shallow water. These included the wreck called the *Chaternau* at a depth of thirty or forty feet, presumably a corruption of Château-Renault and hence the French flagship, and two wrecks called *Sotelo* and *Toxo* or *Tojo* close inshore in twenty feet or so. These and the other names were those used by the fishermen and bear no resemblance to the real names of the lost warships and galleons, so that it is usually impossible to identify the ships which had been wrecked. In early February 1826 they moved into deeper water and dived on the *Tambour* and *Cruceta*, both in six or seven fathoms and probably French warships as the guns recovered from them were later identified as French. Early in April they started work on the *Almiranta*, the same ship that William Evans had concentrated on, which was described as being in ten or eleven fathoms. They then looked for the *Andreya* which was supposed to be lying nearby, but without success, finally giving up on 4 May 1826, 'no longer believing in the existence of the *Andreya*', and so on to the *Espiche*, maybe also a French warship, and then back again to do some more work on the *Tambour*, *Chaternau* and *Tojo*. Finally, they looked at two wrecks, the *Madeira* and the *Telleyro* in very shallow water just south of the San Simón Islands, but these were soon abandoned when an old fisherman told them that 'it has been handed down in his family that the vessels [in this area] were merchant vessels who landed their cargoes in boats at the time of the action'.[19]

The routine of work on the wrecks was soon established and can be analysed fairly exactly, since the journal records the name of everyone who went down in the bell and how long they stayed below. After a wreck had been located, surveyed and buoyed, the brigantine was anchored over it and work with the bell began. This involved very much more bottom time than William Evans and his colleagues had spent in their diving barrel. The *Enterprise* spent a total of 307 days in Vigo Bay and the bell was sent down on 116 of these. Work was much more intense during the peak period of April, May and June 1826, in which months the bell was sent down on nineteen, twenty-five and fifteen days respectively. Only two days were lost to repairs or bad weather in May, since the crew of the *Enterprise* never dived on Sundays which were devoted to washing and mending, prayers in the morning and liberty ashore for some of the crew after dinner. The bell might be lowered as many as five times in a single day, the length of each descent ranging from half an hour or so to a maximum of four hours at the bottom on 18 March when they were working on the *Cruceta* in some six fathoms of water. There were many occasions during the long daylight hours of the summer when the bell remained lowered for more than eight hours in all, the record being 12 July when the bell was sent down for ten hours and fifty minutes in four separate descents on the *Tojo* in just over twenty feet of water, being first lowered at five in the morning and finally finishing for the day at half past four in the afternoon. The bell could not of course go down in rough weather, but such figures indicate the huge gain in potential productivity achieved with working from a bell rather than a barrel.

A total of fourteen men, nearly half the crew, went down in the bell at some time or other, including one descent by the entrepreneur Isaac Dickson who stayed in Vigo for about a month before returning to England in mid-December 1825. But the bulk of the work was done by just a few men, the busiest being Thomas Wood, described as 'bellman', and John Little, at first joiner, then bellman, who descended in the bell on ninety-six and ninety-five days respectively. These two men did practically all the diving until April, when longer daylight hours and good weather meant that much more time could be spent on the bottom. The two 'bellmen' were now often 'spelled', the work usually being split between two pairs of men, each of whom would go down one or two times in the day. The most important of these extra divers were John Wigton, one of the two carpenters, and Thomas Bennett, the boatswain, who descended on forty-six and thirty-eight days respectively.[20]

These four men thus spent a lot of time below the waters of Vigo Bay, but they do not seem to have suffered very severely for it. The *Enterprise* usually had two or three men on the sick list, sometimes more, but bellmen were not particularly prone to illness. Thomas Wood was off sick for a couple of weeks in May, but worked fairly regularly for the rest of the campaign. John Little hurt his arm, but this did not keep him away from work for very long. Most of the wrecks were in less than forty feet, often much less, so decompression does not seem to have been a problem or at least there is nothing in the journal to suggest that it was. Potentially the most dangerous wreck was the *Almiranta* which lay in ten fathoms or sixty feet and on which they worked for the first three weeks of April 1826. Sixty minutes at sixty feet is a diving rule of thumb to indicate the threshold of danger from decompression. However, descents of over two hours on this wreck were commonplace and no ill effects were reported in the journal. The only serious sickness problem was encountered in diving on the *Espiche* which lay at about fifty feet. On 11 May, the journal reported that 'all the bellmen complain very much of their eyes and heads being affected down in the bell today, a thing which has never occurred before', though this did not stop them working. The same problem was reported a couple of weeks later, one man not being able to work, 'his eyes being so sore from going down in the bell'. This is never explained, but was presumably because of some noxious effluvia stirred up when working on the wreck.

The work that the bellmen did at the bottom of the sea was exhausting, boring and very dirty. Some twenty-five guns were recovered, mainly from the French warships, all iron and all in terrible condition, the valuable brass guns having long been raised, mainly by the English and Dutch immediately after the battle. But, with the exception of the guns, there was very little of interest in the wrecks, just ship timbers, ballast and mud and a certain amount of corroded and worthless metal artefacts, such as cannon balls. The writer of the journal reported of the *Telleyro* on 5 July 1826, 'I think she has been well searched before', but he could have written this about any of the twelve wrecks on which they worked. Nevertheless, the divers and crew of the *Enterprise* worked efficiently and effectively on what was found in the wrecks, however unpromising. Timbers, some of them huge pieces of the fabric of galleons or warships, were fixed to chains and raised by the brigantine's crane. Sometimes more power was needed, as when they raised the stern-post of the *Almiranta* on 4 April. The crane failing to lift it, 'we made all fast and let the brig raise it as the tide flowed'. Most of these timbers were rotten after 120 years in the sea, but there were some sound pieces and these, together with some big anchors that were found, were taken ashore to be sold at public auction and the proceeds divided with the Spanish.

The main purpose of raising these timbers was however to clear the bottoms of the wrecks so that they could shift the ballast and mud to see if they concealed treasure or other valuables. This was laborious work, but was done patiently and efficiently. Locally made baskets were purchased and reinforced with strips of canvas. These were then filled by the bellmen, raised to the surface, tipped into a punt or a cutter and taken ashore to be turned over 'in order to ascertain if any specie was amongst it'. Local men helped in this work, and also assisted in working the air pump, a dozen or more Spaniards being employed on many days. The journal sometimes records the number of baskets lifted in a day and the figures seem quite astonishing when one thinks of the likely problems of filling baskets with mud from a bell at the bottom of the sea, presumably in zero visibility. On the *Almiranta*, for instance, from which the greatest volume was taken, they often raised over forty and sometimes over fifty baskets of mud in a day. On 20 April, they recorded the weight as well as the number, '39 baskets of mud each weighing 220 pounds', a total of nearly four tons.

Sooner or later, a decision had to be made to give up on each of these worthless wrecks, and the results of these 'consultations' provide a sad refrain of futility and failure through the journal. On 17 January 1826, work on the *Tojo* was abandoned when a meeting of bellmen and officers decided 'that it was only wasting time making any further attempts, as they had thoroughly searched her nearly fore and aft'. Just nine days later work ceased on the *Sotelo*, 'it being all our opinions that nothing was to be expected from the wreck'. And so it went on. They left the *Tambour* on 10 February, it being only 'a waste of time remaining any longer on this wreck'. The *Cruceta* was abandoned on 18 March and the *Almiranta* on 21 April, 'not thinking it worth while to send the bell down again'. On 26 May it was time to leave the *Espiche*, 'having worked down to the ballast without finding anything worth our notice, so we thought it prudent not to send the bell down again'. And, on 13

June, an end came to the second stint of work on the *Chaternau*. 'We have got down to the bottom of the wreck and I think there is no hopes now.'

These and similar observations make depressing reading and so does the (very short) list of objects of possible value which were recovered from these wrecks, providing in all an even worse return for the effort than that experienced by William Evans and his men nearly a century previously. The very first (unnamed) wreck they dived on produced an empty earthenware jar and a silver plate, but such high productivity was not to be maintained. Some of the wrecks contained absolutely nothing but rotten timber, barrel staves, firewood and other such useless articles. A few had something of interest to put in the log, 'a jar of white earthenware clean and in perfect condition', glass bottles, parts of a copper saucepan, oil jars 'all full of mud', the ship's bell (broken) of the *Chaternau*, 'a box with some chocolate cups in it, some perfect and some of them broken', from the *Tojo* and the next day some plates from the same wreck. These caused a dispute between Captain Brown and a Spanish observer, the Captain quite sure that the plates were silver and that he had at last got something of value, the Spaniard equally certain that they were only pewter which sadly proved to be the case when they were inspected by an expert in Vigo.

The last few months that the *Enterprise* was in Spain, it is clear that Captain Brown and his crew were getting fed up with this futile work, as indeed were the Spanish observers whose summary journal of proceedings becomes sparser and sparser as the months went by and nothing newsworthy happened. During this period, the main interest was in survey work, often done in conjunction with Spanish pilots and other experts and usually involving consultation with the all-knowing fishermen. Some of this was general survey work, operating with two launches provided by the Spanish and sweeping the bottom with two hundred feet of weighted line, checking anomalies through a glass from the surface or quite often by sending the bell down and traversing the bottom. Surveys of this kind were carried out not only in the inner bay where the wrecks of the ships that were lost in 1702 lay, but also near Rande in the narrows where the Englishmen were shown the marks in the rock left by the chains which held the boom, and in the outer bay, off Cangas on the north shore opposite Vigo and off Bouzas, west of Vigo on the southern shore.

There were also searches for specific wrecks, such as two British men-of-war, the *Stag* lost in 1800 and the fifty gun *Jupiter* which was lost on a reef on the north side of the bay in 1808, and a large number of supposed 'wrecks' reported by fishermen who had snagged their nets on them. Sometimes the fishermen would be taken on board to guide the Englishmen to the correct spot, one of them taking the searchers to the place where he had fished up an octopus which was inside an earthenware storage jar. The bell was lowered and seventy similar jars were recovered, but there was no sign of any wreck. More often it was a question of lining up marks on the shore, 'the high tower of Bouzas Church on with the second cypress tree over it' or 'a white house in the upper part of the fish market on with the highest house in Vigo'. Such activities did not produce anything much of value, many of the 'wrecks' turning out to be anchors or 'nothing but a large rock'. But the survey work of the *Enterprise* certainly improved official knowledge of the bottom of Vigo Bay.

The verdict of the locals was that the men of the *Enterprise* had done a thorough job. 'The fishermen inform us,' the journal reports on 8 August, 'that they do not know of anything but what we have been down upon.' It was time to pack up and leave, though not before one more venture 'to ascertain how far we could go down and distinguish the signals. At 10 [o'clock] lowered the bell down and at 11 [o'clock] hove up again, having been down 13½ fathoms [81 feet] and heard the signals quite distinctly. The British Consul with a party of friends was on board to see the bell go down.' They then returned to Vigo, settled up with the Spanish, prepared the brigantine for sea and on 29 August set sail. On 6 September they came to an anchor in Margate Roads and four days later hauled into the City Canal and discharged the crew.

Many people have found it impossible to believe that an expedition to look for the fabled treasures of Vigo Bay, which worked so efficiently and searched twelve separate wrecks so thoroughly, could have been so completely unsuccessful. There has been a persistent rumour, repeated in book after book, that the officers and men of the *Enterprise* were dishonest men who concealed from the Spanish the treasure they had found. The bellmen were said to have worked, not just by day as reported in the logbook, but also at night when there were no Spanish observers aboard. Such nocturnal activity eventually made the Spanish suspicious and the *Enterprise* had to slip out of the Bay clandestinely one night, before she was searched and the silver hidden in her hold discovered. Back home, the managers disappointed the investors by reporting that nothing had been found, but Dickson was said to have retired to Scotland where he lived out the rest of his life in luxury in a substantial mansion appropriately called Dollar House.

This story seems to originate with Hippolyte Magen, a French banker who acquired the concession to search for the Vigo Bay treasure and published a book called *Les Galions de Vigo* in 1873. Magen did a lot of research on the wrecks, including talking to the local fishermen who seem to have been the source of this story. Old fishermen remembered or had been told by their fathers that only Englishmen went down in the bell and saw the wrecks, and that the Spanish acting as observers, working on the pumps or unloading mud and timber all went home when the bell came up for the last time in the afternoon. From there it took only a little Galician imagination to see the wicked men of the *Enterprise* working by lights all night, some old fishermen claiming to have actually seen on deck silver ingots and pieces of eight all blackened by their long immersion in the sea. Such a story would seem to be complete nonsense; to fabricate the logbook in the way required would have been an immense task and there is certainly no evidence that the *Enterprise* left Vigo secretly and suddenly at night. At sunset on Sunday 27 August 1826, a gun was fired and 'the signal for sailing' hoisted. Monday was spent clearing the ship for sea and at eight in the evening Captain Brown came on board with orders for sailing. At 5 a.m. on Tuesday 29 August, the ship's clerk came aboard with 'the ship's clearance. Weighed and proceeded to sea with the wind from the southward at 6 a.m.' Not much sign of a clandestine departure there, but it is easy to see why treasure hunters like

Magen and those who followed him should want to believe the story. For, if what the logbook reported was the truth, they were clearly wasting their time and their money in going to Vigo.[21]

No one back in England suggested that the expedition had cheated the Spanish, but there was a lot of muttering that it had somehow cheated the shareholders, who were understandably upset to lose their money. A meeting of the shareholders was held at Dickson's office on 26 September 1826, where reasonable accounts of what had happened were given by Dickson and by Captain Brown who provided a succinct summary of the expedition. 'They worked at twelve galleons that were sunk in the bay', he said, 'and took a great quantity of mud out of them. They found nothing of any consequence in them, although they examined them from aft to the mainmast.' Most of those present seem to have been satisfied that every exertion had been made, but a sizeable minority led by one Edward Polhill was not prepared to leave it at that. They set up a committee with Polhill as chairman and demanded to be allowed to see the company's papers. The managers were quite happy to comply since these were not incriminating; if anything they reinforced the picture of hard work and endeavour which they wanted to convey. Still not satisfied and still hoping to recover his investment, Polhill opened an action in the Court of Chancery in February 1829 against Dickson and his eight managers.[22]

Polhill had two main lines of attack. He claimed, or rather his lawyer claimed for him, that the brig, the diving equipment, the personnel employed and the method of search were all inadequate for the job in hand, Captain Brown being dismissed as a captain from the coal trade who knew nothing about surveying and the skilled artificers aboard as men who knew nothing about diving equipment and had been trained as chairmakers. More pertinently, he suggested that the price of shares had been artificially boosted by puffery and rumour. He referred to the newspaper campaign in late 1825, in which success at Vigo was regularly reported, and he also claimed that the defendants had put it around that application had been made to the Secretary of the Admiralty to send ships of war to Vigo to pick up the treasure and for waggons to be ready to

bring it from the coast to the Bank of England. Polhill claimed to
have been very impressed by this evidence of quick success and so
applied for shares, but had at first been put off as they 'represented
the same to be much too valuable to be disposed of'. This was of
course just another ploy to raise the price and eventually Polhill was
sold ten shares for prices of £150 and £160, the going rate when he
bought them in November and December, but quite a bit higher
than in September and October 1825 when shares were being sold
for £50 to £100.

More information about share dealing can be found in the
'Answer' that Isaac Dickson submitted to the Court of Chancery in
December 1829. It will be recalled that the total investment by the
partners in the Vigo Bay scheme was £10,000. Dickson was due to
put up half of this and he, in fact, borrowed the necessary £5,000
from his eight co-directors. He and his agents then proceeded to
sell over half of his four hundred shares between the middle of
September and November 1825. He provided very rough accounts
for these transactions in a schedule attached to his Answer. These
show that he received between £25 and £250 for these shares,
bringing in a total of over £17,500. Dickson then repaid the £5,000
he had borrowed from his co-directors and put the balance of
£12,500 in his pocket, a huge profit from dealing in shares which
may well have financed the luxurious lifestyle that he was supposed
to enjoy in Dollar House.[23]

The accusation of fraudulent promotional activity was therefore
largely true, though hardly exceptional in the stock-market culture
of the day, but it would have been difficult to lay the blame firmly
with the defendants who had signed no newspaper articles. So the
defendants simply denied everything that could not be proved and
made the most of what could be shown to be untrue, such as the
criticism of Captain Brown who turned out to have served in many
other trades as well as the coal trade, knew all that could possibly
be known about surveying and was, according to Dickson, 'an
active, prudent, honourable man of great experience and
professional knowledge [who] well knew the proper mode and
manner of using the diving-bell'. The fact of the matter was, as one
defendant put it, that there was no certainty of success in such a

project, and 'they always considered such an undertaking to be a very doubtful speculation'. They had been attracted to the business because of the mention of huge amounts of treasure in historical accounts, 'but, since the searches made by the persons employed in the same undertaking, they believe the fact to be that there was not any specie or treasure in the galleons'. All this was obviously true and so, like many other cases in Chancery, the action petered out and nobody won but the lawyers.

No one who reads the journal of the *Enterprise* could be anything but amazed that this expedition was not the last to search for the 'treasure' of Vigo Bay. But, human nature and the lure of treasure being what they are, this was far from being the case. Avelino Rodríguez Elías recorded ten new concessions and several renewals of old ones between the departure of the *Enterprise* in 1826 and 1935 when he wrote his book, these optimists coming from France, Italy, Spain, England and the United States. Some of these companies recovered bits and pieces of interest, one even found some silver, but basically they all shared the frustrating experience of the *Enterprise*. Between them they employed increasingly sophisticated and powerful equipment to reduce what was left of the Vigo Bay wrecks to a few pieces of timber sinking deeper and deeper into the mud. But interest in the treasure still continued after the Second World War. The American John D. Potter Jr and his colleagues in the Atlantic Salvage Company started work in Vigo in 1955 and these 'hombres-ranas' or frogmen were later joined by the Belgian diver Robert Sténuit. These divers found that there was virtually nothing to be seen of most of the wrecks worked on by the men of the *Enterprise*. Only the *Tambour* remained sufficiently intact to make it seem worthwhile excavating the mud which lay inside her.[24]

While they were in Vigo they received a letter from Count George Khevenhüller in Austria. He had been in Vigo in 1928–9 with an Italian expedition and he told Potter that they had cleared the wrecks to the bottom, using a dredging machine, and did not find a trace of silver or coins. It was therefore his opinion 'that precious metal is not any more existing in the seven galleon-wrecks which are lying in the bay of Redondella'. Potter felt compelled to agree, as his continued excavation of the mud in the *Tambour* showed that it contained nothing but ballast and disintegrating iron artefacts such as cannon-balls. He therefore decided to focus his attention on the wreck of *Monmouth*'s galleon in the Cíes Islands, though that too was to elude him. So one fears that, unless something strange happens or some remarkable new information emerges, those who seek the treasure of Vigo Bay will have to do so on the board of a game called 'Vigo' which was invented in 1994. 'Players sail the high seas searching for treasure; more specifically, the remnants of treasure chests. The idea is to locate these remnants and reconstruct complete chests.' It sounds rather fun and should certainly be easier than digging in all that mud.[25]

Chapter Thirteen

The Salvage of the Thetis

Chapter Thirteen

The Salvage of the Thetis

"A mere handful of men have performed a work which I believe may be placed on the list of the greatest undertakings performed by the British Navy and which British seamen alone could have accomplished."[1]

One of the most valuable perks available to captains in the Royal Navy was the freight which they personally earned if their ship carried bullion or specie for merchants or other private individuals. This could be very profitable for captains returning from the West Indies or West Africa, but at no time was there more to be made than on the South American station during the 1820s and 1830s when the Wars of Independence first opened the area to international trade and the defeated royalists were desperately trying to get their money out. Many English naval ships carried half a million dollars, some much more, and, since the rate of freight was two per cent (with deductions for the Admiral on the South American or 'Brazils' station and for the upkeep of Greenwich Hospital), it is not surprising that service on this station was much sought after.[2]

One such ship was HMS *Thetis*, a large frigate whose captain, Samuel Burgess, had taken command in Rio de Janeiro after the death of Captain Bingham, the previous captain, on the coast of Ecuador. The *Thetis* had sailed from Callao, the port of Peru, on 24 September 1830 and was bound from Rio for England with a cargo of treasure valued at 810,000 dollars [worth nearly £200,000]. The weather had been poor since Captain Burgess left Rio and he 'had not seen sun, moon or stars from the time of our departure', but he was not unduly worried about this as he rested in his cabin on the evening of Sunday 5 December. He had estimated by dead reckoning that there were twenty-four miles of sea-room between the *Thetis* and Cape Frio, some seventy miles east of Rio, the last land before he headed north-east across the South Atlantic. The captain had served forty-one years in the Navy and was no doubt looking forward to spending his freight money, as his fine ship gobbled up the homeward miles at over ten knots.[3]

It was quarter past eight in the evening when the captain's long record of blameless service came to an abrupt end. His cabin door flew open and a boy burst in, crying 'Land ahead, Sir.' As Captain Burgess rushed on deck, the bowsprit crashed into cliffs rising high above the ship and all three masts snapped off with the impact. Some forty men managed to jump onto a shelving, projecting rock about twenty feet above the sea; others failed to make the leap and were lost between the ship and the rocks; while the ship herself and the remaining crew ricocheted along the coast, striking against rocks and cliffs several times before being driven into a cliff-girt cove, later to be known as Thetis Cove, where she struck on rocks and rapidly began to sink. Fortunately, there was help at hand. The men who had jumped ashore had scrambled over craggy precipices and through woods to keep up with their ship as she drifted into the cove. They were now available to catch a rope flung by the brave and acrobatic boatswain balancing on the stump of the bowsprit and, when this had been made taut, 'every man who presented himself . . . hauled through the surf upon a rough craggy rock . . . all were landed just as daylight came, except twenty-five who perished'.

News of the loss of the *Thetis* and her immensely valuable cargo reached Rear-Admiral Sir Thomas Baker, commander in chief on the 'Brazils' station, on the day that he had invited one of his captains to dinner, Thomas Dickinson of HM sloop *Lightning* which was being refitted in Rio. This meal might have been entertaining to an eavesdropper since these two men were to be the chief architects of the salvage of the *Thetis*. Baker was a man of about sixty who had progressed efficiently, but without very great distinction, through the ranks of the Royal Navy. Thomas Dickinson, the somewhat flawed hero of this chapter, had by contrast had a rather disappointing career. He joined the navy in 1796 when he was nine and was commissioned Lieutenant in 1805 after showing conspicuous bravery at the battle of Trafalgar. So far very good, but further promotion eluded him until 1814 when he was promoted to Commander and there he stuck. He was still awaiting promotion to Post-Captain when he joined Admiral Baker's command and he was said to be not just disgruntled but very short of money. Dickinson then was a man in his mid-forties who was desperate for riches and promotion, a man who might welcome 'a noble opening for acquiring honourable distinction and fortune'. Such an opening lay in the salvage of the *Thetis* if it were at all feasible, but first it was necessary to inspect the wreck and the cove in which she lay to determine what might or might not be possible.[4]

Admiral Baker went overland to Cape Frio and arrived there on 16 December 1830, eleven days after the *Thetis* had wrecked. The desolate scene was hardly encouraging. The surviving crew were suffering badly from cut and bruised feet, wounds inflicted as they clambered about in the rocky cove. They were also very hungry as the local people had been reluctant to supply them with food without any guarantee of payment. Such problems were soon resolved as the Admiral had despatched two ships with food and clothing whose captains had orders to bring the survivors back to Rio. He had also arranged for a third ship, the *Algerine*, to guard the wreck.

The problem of the wreck and its possible salvage did not look as though it would be so easily resolved. Cape Frio is a mountainous and heavily wooded island, about three miles long by one wide, separated from the mainland of Brazil by a narrow stretch of water known to the English as the Gut. The cove where the *Thetis* wrecked is on the south-western side of Cape Frio. It is rectangular in shape, about two hundred yards in depth and somewhat less in width. On three sides it is bordered by nearly perpendicular cliffs, from eighty to two hundred feet high, and, on the fourth, it is open to the full fury of the Atlantic whose huge rollers were swept directly into the cove by the prevailing south-westerly winds. The depth of the cove varied from four to twenty-four fathoms and was strewn with huge, irregular rocks whose pattern was changed daily by the Atlantic swell. It was, in short, not a very encouraging place to contemplate diving.

The wreck of the *Thetis* lay in the eastern corner of the cove, in some five or six fathoms of water. Baker had been unable to get hold of any local divers in Rio, but it was clear from his own observation and from information provided by the survivors that the wreck had not yet broken up and that the decks were completely covered with sails, rigging and pieces of spars which would have to be removed before anything else could be done. The salvage of the *Thetis* was clearly not going to be easy, but it was certainly worth attempting since, apart from the honour and distinction of recovering a treasure which everyone in Rio deemed to be 'irrecoverable', there was money to be made. For although the men who salvaged the *Thetis* were in Admiralty pay, and so might be thought merely to be doing their duty if they worked on the wreck, there were strong precedents that in such circumstances they would be entitled to salvage money. And it was widely believed (though not, in fact, true) that such salvage would be at a standard rate of one-third of the value recovered, a potentially huge sum to be shared very disproportionately between the Admiral, the captains involved, and the men who 'were stimulated to such exertions in the same manner as in time of war the seamen in HM's service are encouraged by the hope of prize money to engage in arduous and daring enterprizes'.[5]

Admiral Baker and Captain Dickinson were later to be at daggers drawn, but in the early stages of planning the salvage they behaved well enough and indeed worked as an effective team. Baker was to claim, sarcastically, that he had appointed Dickinson to take charge of the salvage because he 'felt that the Commander's needy circumstances peculiarly qualified him to search for treasure with avidity'. This may have been true, but Dickinson had other qualifications for the job. He had an inventive streak which had earned him a gold medal for his skill in mechanics from the Society of Arts in 1825 and this was recognized by Admiral Baker and others in Rio, such as the master of the *Lightning* who believed his captain to have 'a very considerable nautical and mechanical skill'.[6]

At an early stage it was recognized that successful salvage would require a bell, but enquiry quickly established that there were no diving-bells in Rio and it was clear that they would have to make one for themselves. Dickinson later claimed credit for the idea of the bell (and everything else), but it probably owed more to the chance presence in Rio of an engineer, John Moore, who was employed by the Brazilian government and who later claimed with justification to have been 'the only person at the time capable of constructing a diving-bell in this part of the world'. It was also fortunate that there were two men in the crew of HM sloop *Clio*, George Dewer and John Littlejohn, who 'were the only persons here [at Rio] who had previously been employed in diving-bells' and so were able to make 'sensible and experienced observations on the construction, capabilities and peculiarities of such machines'. It was later discovered that George Fisher, a sailor on HMS *Warspite*, was also 'rather an expert diver', suggesting that such skills were quite widely dispersed in the navy by this date.[7]

The solution to the problem of making a diving-bell in remote Rio de Janeiro was simple, ingenious, and demonstrated the lateral thinking that was likely to lead to success. Diving bells by this date were, as has been seen, square or rectangular and made of iron. Someone, probably Dickinson though others including Baker laid claims, realized that the raw materials for such a machine existed in every one of His Majesty's warships in the form of their water-tanks. And so, on 29 December 1830, the captain's log of HM sloop *Lightning*, which was still anchored at Rio, records the receipt of 'two large tanks from HMS *Warspite*, per order of the Commander in Chief, to make a diving-bell'. Carpenters and armourers set to work to convert them and, three weeks later, the completed bell was lowered into the water from the bows of the *Warspite* 'and found it efficient at the depth of 5¾ fathoms with four men in it'. This first bell was very large, being constructed from two tanks each four feet square which were cut and converted into a bell six feet high by four feet each way. There were seats inside and hooks to suspend tools from and a suitable forcing pump was constructed to supply the men with air and keep them dry. Visibility was provided by six patent deck illuminators, two on top of the bell and one on each of its four sides, rendering it so light that 'the men say they could see every object about them with great ease'.[8]

The *Lightning*, her crew reinforced by men from other ships, especially the *Warspite*, now sailed with her bell for Cape Frio where she dropped anchor on 30 January 1831, ready to try to salvage the wreck of the *Thetis*. Preliminary reconnaissance had indicated that it would rarely be possible to operate a diving-bell from a boat, so heavy was the surf in the cove. 'The principal difficulty, therefore', Admiral Baker explained to the Secretary of the Admiralty, 'was to contrive a point of sufficient strength and steadiness whence the bell could be suspended over the wreck.' There were two main solutions suggested, both replete with problems and difficulties, a huge derrick anchored by the cliffs and reaching out over the water or a network of cables strung across the cove from cliff to cliff. In either case the idea was that a platform should be hung over the wreck to provide work space for the support team who operated the air pump and raised and lowered the bell which would hang below the platform.

Dickinson's orders from Baker were rather ambiguous, but it is clear that he had no intention of trying the cable option, partly because he could see more glory in the magnificent derrick option, but also because cables were the preferred choice of Admiral Baker. Dickinson behaved respectfully towards his admiral while still in Rio but, once ensconced in his lone command at Cape Frio, he became increasingly insubordinate, not just to Baker, whom he seems to have despised, but also to Captain Gavin Hamilton and others who took command of the station for several months in the second half of 1831 while Baker was in Mauritius and the Cape of Good Hope. Anything that Baker suggested was sure to be condemned, mocked or ignored by Dickinson. For instance, on his first visit, Baker had noted that the cove shelved steeply to seaward and thought it would be a good idea to construct a stop-net to prevent treasure being washed out into deeper water. On

3 February 1831, Dickinson laid down such a net and, when he inspected it three weeks later, he 'found it good'. But that was the last good word he had to say on this subject. In October, he examined the net and claimed that 'it does not appear to have been of the slightest use', and in his narrative of the salvage he said that 'the preventer net was about as much use as a gossamer net to stop an elephant'. But all this seems to have been just part of his resentment against the Admiral, since Captain de Roos, who replaced Dickinson at Cape Frio in March 1832, praised the net and its effectiveness. 'I happened to be in the bell and can testify to the quantity of heavy articles which have been arrested by this means.'[9]

Dickinson's first task on arrival at Cape Frio was to establish a camp and work base. He anchored the *Lightning* in a sheltered place about two miles from the wreck site and kept a quarter of his crew aboard who were replaced by another quarter every three or four weeks. The rest of the crew established a camp near the beach on the northern side of Cape Frio Island which was only about half a mile overland from the top of the cliffs above the wreck site, though the access was very steep. Most journeys to the wreck or elsewhere to do the necessary work were carried out in boats, an arduous passage over a bar and against a powerful current through the Gut which wasted a lot of time every day. The men were lodged in tents made of sailcloth at first, but these were soon replaced by huts made from local wood and thatched with dried grass. The camp was described by Dickinson as 'a small village' and he tried to maintain some similarity to shipboard life by building a hut eighty feet long for the crew which was criss-crossed by poles at the height of above six feet from which they could sling their hammocks. Separate huts were built for officers and for midshipmen and to serve as storehouses, workshops, guardhouses and so on. Fresh supplies and any necessary equipment and stores were brought in regularly from Rio by the royal schooner *Adelaide*, but it would be wrong to think that the sojourn at Cape Frio Island was one long holiday for the men. The huts leaked, the men were afflicted by great heat, torrential rain and sand storms, by a wide range of unpleasant insects, diarrhoea, rheumatism, ulcers from jiggers which bored into their feet, and they were 'unremittingly

employed', according to the surgeon of the *Lightning,* 'in arduous
and laborious services far exceeding the ordinary duties of
shipboard both in respect of fatigue and personal danger'. The
salvage crew were not even free of that excessive love of flogging so
characteristic of the early nineteenth-century Royal Navy. On 29
October 1831, for instance, 'all hands came on board [the *Lightning*]
from the island, read the Articles of War and punished Thomas
Glover, marine, with 48 lashes for stealing spirits, getting drunk
and neglecting his duty as acting corporal of the middle watch on
shore in the island of Cape Frio, also John Roberts, able seaman,
with 48 lashes for stealing spirits and getting drunk on shore in the
island of Cape Frio.' And exactly one hour after their arrival on
board, 'all hands returned to the island', no doubt suitably subdued
after having witnessed such excessive punishment.[10]

The first of the laborious services that these hands had to fulfil
at Cape Frio was to locate and survey the wreck. Commander
Martin of the *Algerine,* which had been left at Cape Frio to guard
the wreck, had reported as early as 11 January that severe south-
westerly gales had struck the cove and 'we could perceive from the
hills above that the wreck was rapidly breaking up', information
that did not dishearten Admiral Baker. 'On the contrary, I consider
the breaking up of the wreck as a circumstance materially
facilitating our success.' Dickinson confirmed that the wreck had
broken up, but at first had difficulty in finding it. 'Launches
creeping . . .', he noted in his salvage journal on 4 February 1831,
'but no sign of wreck, swell increased and could not continue.' A
few days later, the men in the launches struck wreckage with their
grapnels and were able to get up rigging, scraps of sails and so on,
but it was obvious that it would be much better if they could dive
down and get a closer look.[11]

Working with the launches in the cove had shown that, although
there was a near permanent swell, there were days when it might be
feasible to work a diving-bell from a big launch. But the bell made
in Rio weighed four tons and would be much too heavy for this so,
on 16 February, they started to turn another water tank into 'a small
diving-bell'. This was about half the size of the large bell, could take
two men and was ready in the first week of March. After several

trials and much tinkering, it was 'found to answer perfectly in every respect', a slight exaggeration since the swell was such that it was impossible to use the bell more often than not and, when they did use it, the launch sometimes surged 'so much that the bell swung eight or nine feet'. Nevertheless, they now had the means of inspecting the wreck and bringing up treasure if they could find it, while they waited for the work on the derrick to be completed so that they could use the larger bell made in Rio.

Admiral Baker in Rio was naturally pleased that the small bell had been successfully tested, but he also had hopes of using native divers to assist the men from the Royal Navy. But this proved to be difficult. Such men did exist in Brazil, but they had been put off by 'absurd rumours about the danger to be apprehended from voracious fish and entanglement in the wreck'. However, early in March, his enquiries at last met with success and a Colonel Guasque, Chief of the Imperial Academy of Engineers at Rio de Janeiro and a man with experience in salvaging wrecks, set off for Cape Frio with seven native divers. Baker was full of confidence when he informed the Admiralty. 'From their being accustomed to continue under water for a much longer time than our own people, they may probably be found of great service in sallying from the diving-bells at the bottom, and attaching the necessary tackling to objects for the purpose of drawing them up.' But this scenario was never to take place. Colonel Guasque later said that Dickinson had 'thwarted him in every possible way and afforded him no facilities whatever', while Dickinson said that the native divers were 'ineffectual' and unable 'to remain under water for a longer period than two thirds of a minute', despite being promised money if they could stay down longer. What exactly caused a showdown is obscure but, whatever it was, the Brazilians quit after just six days, having achieved nothing. Thomas Dickinson claimed to be surprised at their leaving, but one suspects that he had made himself deliberately unpleasant in order to get rid to them. He now had the means for his own men to dive on the wreck in the small bell and he had no intention of sharing his glory with native divers, especially if they had been acquired as a result of the efforts of Admiral Baker.

On the last day that Colonel Guasque was at Cape Frio, Sunday 13 March 1831, the strong swell which had persisted for the previous three days died down and, instead of a gale, there were 'light airs from the southward', a perfect day for working the small bell. Observers from the cliff tops believed that the bell-divers had previously been searching too far out into the cove, so the launch was hauled further inshore and the bell sent down. Shortly afterwards, the bellmen floated up to the surface a piece of board on which they had written 'We have found the wreck' and, by the end of the day, they had a very good idea of how the wreck was lying and had even 'walked along the kelson'. When Dickinson reported to Baker, he said that Colonel Guasque and his divers 'were jealous at our people having found the wreck without their assistance', so maybe it was this jealousy that led to their departure in a huff the next day.

The next four days after finding the wreck were frustrating for the men of the *Lightning*, for the swell was too high and dangerous to work the bell, but on 18 March they were able to spend all day in the bell, 'in search of the wreck, buoying the various parts as they were found'. Captain Dickinson never went down in the bell himself, but he was able to produce a chart of how the wreckage lay from the information brought up by his divers. There was as yet 'not a particle of the treasure to be seen', he wrote to Baker, 'but it appears to me that it is in the large heap in the after part of the ship, but so covered up with confused fragments of every description of stores that the bottom cannot be seen'.[12]

It was a whole week before it was possible to work the bell again and to begin to clear away the heap to see what lay beneath it. Again they had just one day of good weather and then had to wait yet another week, until 31 March, before moderate breezes and fine weather set in from the north-east and the swell in the cove subsided. Dickinson wrote to Baker this day, enclosing a copy of his sketch of the wreck site, and said that they were now quite sure 'that the heap (*vide* sketch) is that part of the wreck in which the treasure is stowed', being above the afterhold and spirit room where the treasure was reported by the survivors to have been kept. 'If it is there we will have it.' Dickinson was writing this letter in the camp, but decided to visit the cove before sending it off and as a result was able to send an exciting postscript. 'I have the happiness of informing you that our efforts are crowned with success. We have taken up about three thousand dollars, and are continuing to do so as fast as one man can separate them from the rubbish and between the rocks. They are very much scattered but at present the men do not see the termination of them.' Once again, the bellmen had sent the news up to the surface on a tally board. 'We are now over some dollars', they wrote. And the proof of this was soon visible to everyone, 'when they came up with their caps full of dollars and some gold and there were three hearty cheers'.

The weather in April was much better than in March, allowing the small bell to be used on fourteen days, although on two of these the swell got up and forced them to quit before anything had been accomplished. On the other twelve days, they recovered dollars, from just under a thousand to nearly eight thousand a day, together with bars of silver and a small quantity of gold, some fifty thousand dollars and over a thousand pounds of silver in bars in total, all recovered it should be noted from a bell suspended from a launch, a technique deemed to be impossible in the conditions of Thetis Cove before they started. The treasure was not all lying about in places where it was easy to pick up. Much was covered by ship's stores or by rotting provisions which had to be dug through 'to the depth of several feet to obtain the treasure mixed therein', the resulting foul stench causing much distress to the bellmen. This and other rubbish, timbers and general clutter had to be cleared away, some of it lifted and sent out further to sea, some of it brought up to be sifted on the surface in canvas buckets made by the sailmaker.

On a few days they made the most of good weather by continuing their work after sunset, using torches mounted on the launch, pinnace and cutter to give 'a very strong light' through the water, and a lighted wax candle in the bell itself, though this 'consumed the air so fast that it was necessary to extinguish it as soon as the bell-men got a fair sight of the place they were to work'. They worked by torchlight for five hours on the day they first found treasure, but only on two other nights, so presumably it did not work all that well and no doubt the exhausted men did not like this extra labour very much. For the work was very tiring and even when they had finished their 'very laborious and dangerous day's work', the bellmen had to suffer the indignity of a strip search, taking off their frock-coats and trousers made from blankets and having them examined by officers when they came up from the wreck.

During all this period of modest success with the small bell, the work of making the derrick continued. This amazing artefact took a full two months to construct and was completed on 8 April 1831. It was 158 feet long and had been made from some twenty separate pieces of masts and yards recovered from the wreck of the *Thetis*. While the derrick was being made at the camp, a large party under the command of Mr Moore, the engineer, was busy preparing the cliffs to receive the derrick and its complicated rigging of cables, guys and topping lifts. Explosives were used to blow out a step for the foot of the derrick about ten feet above the water, the tops of the cliffs, nearly two hundred feet above, were levelled, holes were drilled to sink bolts to hold the guys, and a 'roadway' made to enable the men to move more easily up and down the cliffs as they did their work, all arduous labour which combined the skills of sailors and quarrymen. There were many accidents as men fell or were struck by rocks, but to everyone's surprise there were no fatalities, though one man who was knocked senseless when he was washed off the rocks 'had a very narrow escape of his life'.

Early in April, Admiral Baker despatched an extra one hundred men to Cape Frio to assist in the launching and suspension of the derrick, though he had long been doubtful of the project and was 'not altogether sanguine of success'. On 9 April, a day of moderate swell, the derrick was launched from the beach near the camp and towed out to the cove, but 'our utmost efforts to heave it up [into its step] were exerted in vain and, at sunset, we reluctantly relinquished further attempts and left the cove to tow it back . . . a most arduous and fatiguing day's work'. Next day they returned to their task, this time with success and managed to get the foot of the derrick fixed in its step and the head raised above the sea. This was a fantastic achievement, given the 'enormous weight, length and great pliability' of the derrick, and had utterly exhausted both the men in the boats and 'the sixty to seventy employed over the cliffs, some suspended by ropes and others not so, and all exposed to the constant falling of loose fragments of rock'.

This was far from being the end of the affair. It was found that refinements had to be made to the large bell which had been lying idle since its manufacture in Rio. And a lot more work had to be done clearing the cliffs, drilling holes in the rock and setting up the rigging for the derrick and the bell. So it was not until 12 May, a month after the placement of the derrick, that the large bell was actually lowered from the derrick into the sea. This was done with no new problems and the bellmen were able to pick up some treasure, though their main work was drilling holes in several large rocks which had been too heavy to raise with the small bell. These holes were fitted with lewis bolts, expanding devices which gripped the rocks and allowed them to be lifted and swung away from the wreck site.

Two days after the first successful employment of the large bell, HMS *Eden* sailed into Cape Frio to collect and take back to England 124,000 dollars worth of treasure, 'saved from the wreck of his Majesty's late ship *Thetis* by the admirable, ingenious and stupendous contrivances and indefatigable labors of Captain Dickinson and the crew of His Majesty's sloop *Lightning*'. While at Cape Frio, Captain Owen of the *Eden* climbed the cliffs and had a good look round and was understandably impressed by what he saw. The derrick was stepped 'in a socket or excavation in the rocks' and its other end was supported by chain cables from the cliff-tops and could be raised forty feet above the sea. Suspended from the outer end was a platform large enough to hold sixteen persons and, below the platform, was the bell which was raised or lowered by ropes attached to a capstan on the summit and could be moved from side to side by guy ropes. The men in the bell signalled to their colleagues on the platform by pulling on a line or sending up messages on tally-boards and the men on the platform signalled to the team on the cliffs by semaphore. Owen believed that the 'works and operations do infinite credit to the talent, zeal and seamanlike tact' of Captain Dickinson and he felt certain that it 'could only have been performed by British seamen'.[13]

HMS *Eden* set sail for England at six o'clock in the evening of

18 May and that night a week of unusually good weather came to an end. Next morning, there were gales from the south-west and 'a dreadful and increasing sea in the cove, beating heavy against the derrick and shaking it violently, the sea beating over the cliffs'. At ten o'clock, a monster wave came in which struck the derrick and snapped it off about twenty feet from the step. The diving-bell, the pump and all the other equipment were lost in the sea and the derrick was 'in a very short time dashed into many pieces against the rocks by the force of the sea'. Captain Dickinson's astonishing construction which had worked so well the day before was no more. It had been in operation for just one week.

There was never any thought of replacing the derrick. When Dickinson reported the disaster, he kept quiet about its causes, except to say it was a very big wave, not being the sort of man who would admit to a design fault. Admiral Baker received the news with 'regret, but no surprise at this unfortunate termination to a contrivance in which I never had much confidence'. Indeed, one gets the impression that the Admiral was quite pleased about the disaster as it vindicated his judgment. Dickinson was instructed to switch to the suspension cables plan and this is what he did, starting on 27 May, just a week after the destruction of the derrick. These cables were a simpler and in the end more effective method of suspending a bell over the wreck, but their construction still met with many problems and it was not until the last day of September that a new large bell was slung over the wreck from the cables and two weeks more before it was operating efficiently. Meanwhile, salvage continued using the launch and the small bell.

This could not begin immediately since both the bell and the launch needed some repairs and, when they were ready, the priority was to try to recover the large bell and other lost equipment. They eventually managed to do this, only to find to no one's surprise that everything was 'too damaged to use'. Work could now focus on the wreck site where it was first necessary to remove 'a great quantity of rubbish washed in by the late heavy sea'. Recoveries of treasure were made on three separate days at the end of May, but then there was a break in the salvage work of two weeks until exceptionally good weather allowed six recovery days in a row, from 13 to 18 June.

Heavy squalls and fresh gales then set in again, but this short period had been very productive and, when HM packet-boat *Calypso* sailed for England on 21 June 1831, she was carrying slightly more of the *Thetis's* treasure than the *Eden* had done a month earlier, making a total of over a quarter of a million dollars worth recovered since the first success on 31 March, about one-third of the total treasure carried on the wrecked frigate.

This and earlier salvage was not achieved without human cost as well as wear and tear to boats and equipment. The divers were later to depose that they were 'constantly exposed to the most imminent danger by severe concussions of the diving-bell against the rocks occasioned by the motion of the boats'. They often had headaches and suffered sickness from the constant movement of the sea and from the 'indescribable stench' arising from rotting stores. They were nearly always exhausted and 'frequently came up totally helpless', but they did come up, though on occasion it was a close thing. On 26 May, the air pumps burst from the violence of the swell and the most experienced of the bellmen, George Dewar, had to duck under the bottom of the bell and swim up to the surface where he was taken into the launch 'in a very dangerous state'. Just a couple of days later, the launch was taking in so much water in a squall that her crew were forced to cut away the diving-bell to save themselves from swamping. A week was lost trying to locate it, only to discover that it had been dashed to pieces. So the armourers found themselves making not just a large bell to replace the one lost in the derrick accident, but also a small bell. They were getting quite good at this and the replacement small version was completed in five days, 'having worked all night'. It was not the last bell that they were to make.

The only fatal accident during the salvage of the *Thetis* occurred on 11 July 1831 when a longboat overturned in the surf. Three men were drowned, including the engineer Mr. Moore whose 'melancholy fate' much distressed Captain Dickinson who recorded that 'surely never was life more foolishly lost'. Successful attempts were made to drag for the bodies and, after divine service on Sunday 17 July, all three were interred in coffins made by the ship's carpenter in one common grave near the camp. A week later,

Captain Dickinson and the *Lightning* had orders to sail to Rio where brigands had seized some of the forts and there was general unrest. A party of sixteen men were left in charge of the stores under the command of the chief mate Frederick Read who had instructions to continue rigging the suspension cables, 'whenever the weather will permit, but not on any account to attempt the use of the diving-bell'.[14]

The trouble in Rio proved short-lived and the *Lightning* was back at Cape Frio on 25 August where Read and his party were discovered 'undisturbed . . . but suffering much from lameness by jiggers'. The huts needed a complete overhaul and work had to be done on the small bell and launch, so it was not until 2 September that work commenced once more on the wreck, the first task being the removal of rocks and rubbish which had accumulated during their month's absence. This done, treasure was recovered on five days in September and then a record sixteen days in October. Meanwhile the work on the suspension cables was nearing completion. This had involved much effort clearing the cliffs and sinking bolt-holes, but on 4 June the main cable had been successfully suspended from the north-west to the south-east cliffs, a distance of over 150 yards from cliff edge to cliff edge with a generous tail stretching inland to the anchors which held it firm. This cable spanned the wreck site, but in addition it was necessary to set up a two-hundred yard cross cable guy as well to give the network more rigidity. This sort of work and the rigging that had later to be set up was not challenging technically for sailors in the Royal Navy, but completion of the task was only achieved with immense labour, as Captain Dickinson informed Admiral Baker on 15 October when he reported that the large bell was now slung from the cables and ready for operation, nearly five months after it had last been slung from the derrick. 'The fastenings to the cliffs caused much greater obstacles than I could possibly foresee, the rocks being of that nature that (after a great deal of toil in excavating to get securities for the bolts and having fixed them in their places) a short period of exposure to the atmospheric air split them to pieces . . . It is now my intention to work both bells at once.'

Although some treasure was raised by the large bell, most of what was recovered during the rest of 1831 was, in fact, brought up by the tried and tested means of the small bell slung from the launch. The much greater lifting power available when using the large bell and the suspension cables was mainly used to remove large rocks and heavy pieces of equipment, such as the guns which were found to be 'so corroded and honeycombed by the action of the salt water as to be useless'. These cables and others slung directly from the cliffs could also be used to raise heavy objects which had been prepared for removal by the men working in the small bell. This was sensible enough, but the large bell had been designed with the recovery of treasure not guns in mind. Nevertheless, one way and another the amount of treasure raised had grown to a total of 520,000 dollars by 21 December 1831 when Admiral Baker reported to the Admiralty. This was beginning to be really impressive, nearly two-thirds of what had been carried on the ill-fated *Thetis.*

It did however seem that this was just about all that was going to be recovered. The crew of the *Lightning* was badly depleted by illness in November and December and a mood of despondency set in. On 5 November, Captain Dickinson himself fell seriously ill with a bronchial inflammation and then dysentery and was described five days later by the ship's surgeon as being in 'the most unfavourable state'. While in this weakened condition, he foolishly wrote a most uncharacteristically pessimistic letter to Lord James Townsend who was in command at Rio in Admiral Baker's absence. 'I do not think it at all likely that any considerable quantity more can be obtained, for the rocks at the bottom are of such immense magnitude that it is impossible to move them.' When Dickinson recovered, which he did shortly afterwards, he tried to excuse this letter by saying (probably quite truthfully) that his illness had 'in some degree affected my mind . . . I certainly did not know what I was about, and, in fact, everything that occurred at that period is now like an imperfect dream to me'. But the damage had been done, since his letter had been forwarded to the Admiralty. The situation was there discussed by the Lords Commissioners who decided on 6 January 1832 that enough was enough and directed their Secretary to write to Admiral Baker to arrange the recall of Captain Dickinson and the *Lightning* from the task on which they had so admirably laboured.

This might seem unfair, but the truth was that the situation at Cape Frio did not seem very hopeful. From the middle of December 1831, recoveries of treasure dwindled to very little, 200 dollars being a good day, and in January and February 1832 they collapsed altogether, with just one dollar being recovered in January and 170 during the whole of February. Admiral Baker was now back in command at Rio. He had not yet received the letter demanding Dickinson's recall, but he was alarmed by reports from Cape Frio and so decided to pay a visit to the wreck site, arriving there on 5 February. 'I entered into a minute examination of the state of the enterprise', he claimed with some exaggeration in a letter to the Secretary of the Admiralty, 'and found that for some time past the search after treasure had been abandoned', the only things raised being guns. He interrogated the bellmen 'and found them generally of opinion that little more of the treasure could possibly be recovered, as they had seen none for many days, and from their whole manner . . . they were disposed to give a disponding prospect of further proceedings'. Baker then lectured the salvage crew, admonishing them to do their duty and to renew their labours with energy, but he left Cape Frio on 14 February with little confidence in Captain Dickinson and his men. 'If they are unwilling to prosecute the adventure with vigour to the utmost, I will have no hesitation, indeed I shall feel it my duty, to replace the *Lightning* by some other vessel.'[15]

Decisions on this score had already been taken, as has been seen, and, as soon as Baker received the letter from the Admiralty, he issued orders for the recall of the *Lightning* and her replacement by HM sloop *Algerine* which arrived at Cape Frio on 6 March 1832. Dickinson later claimed that this was the first he knew of his recall and he was naturally unhappy not to be allowed to finish the job. He did however behave impeccably during the transfer, handing over his stores, arranging for men from the *Algerine* to be instructed in the use of the bell and lending his successor some of his most experienced men. On his last day, Captain Dickinson went down himself in the bell for the one and only time, 'to survey the bottom of the cove previous to giving up charge of the enterprise to the Honourable Captain de Roos of the *Algerine*. This was ironically quite a good day, since movement of the rocks had left treasure visible on the sea bottom, some of which was brought up, so bringing the grand total recovered by the *Lightning* to 588,621 dollars.

The Honourable Captain John Frederick Fitzgerald de Roos was a very different sort of naval officer to Thomas Dickinson. He was a scion of the Anglo-Irish aristocracy whose birth ensured rapid promotion and he was only 28 when he arrived at Cape Frio. Dickinson later grumbled that the task facing de Roos was merely routine. 'The work was now reduced to a mere plaything compared with what it had been.' But this was unfair and de Roos was to show himself to be an excellent (and obedient) officer who made very good use of the five months he spent at Cape Frio. He was far more hands on than Dickinson, regularly going down in the bell himself to survey the bottom and direct the work. He also did much to raise the productivity of the salvage crew. The *Algerine* herself was anchored much closer to the wreck than the *Lightning* had been, just off the encampment, in fact, 'to the great convenience of the service'. And he made much greater use than Dickinson had of 'the suspension cables, an invention as splendid in its conception as we have found it useful in its application'. Where Dickinson had used the cables mainly for raising articles of great weight, such as guns and rocks, de Roos after experimentation was using them for everything, with both the big bell and the more convenient and manoeuvrable small bell. This enabled them to dispense altogether with the use of the launch, and so with 'the anxiety, delay and danger' associated with it, and allowed them to work the bell 'during weather and swell which would formerly have rendered its employment impossible', a change which enabled them to double the number of days they worked on the wreck. It is hardly surprising that Baker should consider de Roos 'truly zealous and enterprising', with none of 'that unfortunate despondency by which Captain Dickinson afflicted himself and perplexed the whole proceedings'.

De Roos' approach to the salvage work itself was logical and very systematic. A week after his arrival, he had a careful survey made of the whole wreck site and discovered that all the treasure so far recovered had come from 'the spot where the spirit room had discharged its valuable contents when the ship fell to pieces', a section of the granite seabed forming an ellipse 'of which the major axis was 42 feet and the minor 30'. The seabed here was six or six and a half fathoms, deepening to eight fathoms on the seaward side, and nearly half of the area was covered by rocks. De Roos' plan, which he followed to the letter, was to clear out all the rubbish from this elliptical space and then to remove all the rocks within it, one by one, commencing with the smallest. This was hard labour, requiring the drilling and slinging of some very heavy rocks, but it worked. On 22 June, for instance, 'we succeeded in moving a large round rock of seven feet diameter the distance of about forty feet and discovered a large bed of treasure beneath it.' There were twenty-one rocks in all and each was given a name, such as the 40-ton 'Clump Rock' or the 50-ton 'Gun Rock' or 'The Shark's Mouth', biggest of them all, some fifteen feet long by seven wide and weighing an estimated 63 tons. There was, in fact, nothing underneath this great rock, 'but we had the satisfaction of knowing that no exertion had been wanting on our parts', and the bellmen found plenty of treasure under other rocks as they 'examined each hole and crevice at the bottom'. In all, the *Algerine* was to recover a further 161,590 dollars, making the total raised by the two sloops 750,211 dollars or fifteen-sixteenths of the whole, a remarkable achievement given 'the almost universal belief which prevailed, both in England and elsewhere, that her valuable freight was lost beyond the hope of recovery'.[16]

Four days after the removal of 'The Shark's Mouth', the last of his twenty-one rocks, Captain de Roos gave orders for the suspension cables to be taken down and stowed aboard the sloop, 'the enterprise being concluded'. And, on 31 July 1832, he sailed for Rio, leaving Cape Frio Island once more to the Brazilians after some eighteen months of British occupation. The salvage of the *Thetis* had been an astonishing success and was a great credit to the ingenuity and persistence of the officers and men of the Royal Navy. But, like so many other affairs involving treasure, the expedition to Cape Frio was to be followed by several years of dispute between the various claimants to salvage money. Dickinson's head had swollen since he got home, where he was much praised and at last received his promotion to Post-Captain, and he now thought that he alone should be given all the credit for the salvage, 'to the total exclusion of everyone else'. 'Surely, there never was a more vain little man', railed Admiral Baker, who told everyone who would listen that nothing had been done without his orders and was determined to press his claim for a share of the salvage.

On 12 January 1833, the High Court of Admiralty heard the case of 'the King in his office of Admiralty v. certain treasure saved from the wreck of the *Thetis*'. This case which drew on the expertise of eleven advocates, nearly the whole bar, was to determine the amount of salvage due and its distribution between the various claimants who included the officers and men of the *Lightning* and the *Algerine*, Admiral Baker, and a number of individual claimants such as the widow of the engineer Mr Moore and several divers, mechanics and others whose names had been put forward as deserving by the two captains. Judgment was given on 20 March 1833. The Court valued the gross treasure recovered at £157,000 and decided that one quarter would be an appropriate payment for salvage in this case. Deductions were made of £12,000 for agents' and legal fees and expenses and a staggering £13,800 claimed by the Admiralty for expenses and wear and tear to its ships. The legal arithmetic is impenetrable, but this apparently left a total of £17,000 to be awarded as salvage, out of which £1,000 went in small payments to individuals, £2,000 to Admiral Baker and the remaining £14,000 was distributed between the officers and men of the *Lightning* and *Algerine* pro rata of the treasure each sloop had recovered.[17]

This award satisfied no one but the Admiralty, though even they had tried to push a claim as 'sole salvor' since the officers and men had been acting under their orders. Everyone else thought it outrageous for the Admiralty to claim such a large sum for wear and tear, since the sloops had no more wear and tear than on any other service, less indeed as their alternative employment would have been battling round Cape Horn to the west coast of South America. Dickinson was to complain of this decision right up to

1854, the year of his death, but he had no success in changing the decision and the Admiralty hung on to their money. This and other matters of appeal were heard before the Judicial Committee of the Privy Council in June 1834. Dickinson appealed against the total amount of salvage, the award to the Admiralty and the grant to Baker of his Admiral's one-eighth. Baker appealed against the total only and De Roos did not appeal at all, having been advised that his gains were unlikely to exceed his expenses. Everything was mulled over by the lawyers once again, but the only thing changed by the appeal was the total amount granted as salvage, which was increased by £12,000. This was to be divided between Admiral Baker, Captain Dickinson and the crew of the *Lightning*, according to the prize rules specified in an Order of Council of 1827, i.e. one-eighth to Baker, two-eighths to Dickinson and the balance to the officers and crew of the sloop in prescribed proportions. The Honourable Captain de Roos got nothing more, since he had appealed for nothing, but in June 1835 the insurance underwriters who were now the owners of the treasure took pity on him and his shipmates and awarded him a vote of thanks and a piece of plate worth 100 guineas and a grant of £2,000 to be shared between him and his crew, 'being the amount they would have received had they been parties to the appeal'. Captain Dickinson was most upset about this, not about the £2,000 which he thought reasonable, but because the underwriters had not thought to give him a vote of thanks and a piece of plate as well. Some people are never satisfied.[18]

* * * * *

The salvage of the treasure from HMS *Thetis* provides a convenient point in history at which to bring this book to a close, for it was the last great recovery of underwater treasure using the technologies employed by the divers and treasure hunters whose exploits fill these pages. The diving-bell continued to be used for underwater building and engineering work on bridges, harbours and similar structures, but it quickly became redundant for salvage once a new technology had been perfected. This was being developed in

England and it was to fulfil what had long been the dream of the inventors of diving equipment, namely a safe and sure method of walking and working freely on the bottom of the sea.

The prototype of this innovation was established in 1829 with the invention by the brothers Charles and John Deane of the open diving helmet, a sort of mini-bell which covered just the head and shoulders while the rest of the body was protected by a waterproof india-rubber suit. The main problem with the open diving helmet was the necessity for the diver to remain upright lest his helmet fill with water. The answer to this was the close diving dress invented in 1838, in which the dress was attached to the helmet by air-tight and water-tight joints, air being supplied by pumps on the support vessel, and this gradually evolved into the standard helmet diving dress which is so familiar from illustrations of late nineteenth-century and early twentieth-century divers.[19]

The divers who have been the heroes of this book had many wonderful achievements, whether they dived naked and unassisted like William Phips' divers in the 1680s or with the greater bottom time made possible by the diving-bell and the barrel. But none of them could possibly have competed with the mobility under water which the new breed of helmet and hard-hat divers could achieve. And so they were consigned to history and largely forgotten, so much so that many people today are amazed to be told that there were men who could dive and recover treasures from the bottom of the sea in the seventeenth and eighteenth centuries. But there were, and it has been the aim of this book to celebrate their successes and, of course, their many failures.

Notes

The notes normally refer only to the surname of the author, or the first word or words of anonymous works, with the date of publication given for authors with more than one work listed in the Bibliography. For full details of references, see the Bibliography, pp. 359–370. For abbreviations see pp. 359–60.

Preface

1. Quoted (in Spanish) by Abilleira Crespo, p. 3.
2. Add. 25,374 fo. 157.
3. Hill, p. 13.

Chapter One: Sad Newes from the Seas

1. *Sad Newes*, *CSPV* 18 October 1641; *CSPD* 30 September 1641; Add. 27962 I (2) fo. 297.
2. htpp://www.divernet.com/wrecks/wrkqa198.htm.
3. Earle (1998) p. 110. About 3–5% in the 18th century, rather more in the 17th.
4. There are many works on the organization of the treasure fleets. See, for example, Linage; Haring; Chaunu; Parry.
5. The main sources for this section are AGI Contratación 5104; Fernández de Navarrete, vol. xxi, pp. 375–6, 429–32, 488–91; 509–10; Chaunu, vol. iii, pp. 44, 48–51, 54–5, 60, 64–5; Fernández Duro, vol. ii, pp. 465.

6. Ruidíaz y Caravia, vol. ii, p. 603.

7. Horner (1973) ch. 7 for an example of the Bermuda theory; also Potter (1973) p. 280.

8. Ruidíaz y Caravia, vol. i, pp. 46–7; Menendez de Avilés, p. 21.

9. For the lawsuit see AGI SD 128/106A; and for an account of Castillo see Fernández Duro, vol. ii, p. 493.

10. AGI SD 128/106A fo. 22; SD 119, 19 September 1600.

11. AGI Mexico 136, Ramo 1. My thanks to Victoria Stapells Johnson for directing me to this document. See also Linage, p. 267 for Cardona.

12. Serrano Mangas, p. 81; p. 84 has an almost identical application dated 1638.

13. This account rests mainly on Horner (1973) ch. 9 and research I did on this fleet some twenty-five years ago, the notes of which are no longer in my possession.

14. AGI SD 119, 14 January 1608; Serrano Mangas, p. 47; AGI Mexico 136, Ramo 1; Linage, p. 267.

15. Fernández de Navarrete, vol. x, pp. 251–2. The following description of the 1622 shipwrecks and the subsequent salvage attempts draws mainly on Fernández de Navarrete, vol. xii, pp. 255–68; Fernández Duro, vol. iv, p. 41; Horner (1973) ch. 10; Potter (1973) pp. 216–7; Lyon (1979); Mathewson.

16. Chaunu, vol. viii (2) p. 1846. This section is based on Earle (1979) chs. 1–7 where full references can be found.

17. Marx (1973) p. 1; Portichuelo de Ribadeneyra, p. 12; these two works, Horner (1973) ch. 12 and Horner (2002) chs. 4–10 are the main sources for this section.

18. Serrano Mangas, p. 109.

19. ibid., p. 73 fn. 20.

20. Martin & Parker, p. 236, see also pp. 234–44 for the Irish wrecks.

21. On the Armada and the wrecks see Martin & Parker and Martin (1975) pp. 266–79 for a list of the ships and the places where those which wrecked were lost.

22. McLeay, p. 11. The following relies mainly on this book.

23. ibid., p. 42.

24. Bodleian Rawlinson A. 189 fo. 432.

25. See McLeay, chs. 8 & 9 for the true identification of the wreck.

Chapter Two: Men Under the Sea

1. Homer, p. 271; cf. p. 197.
2. For the history of diving I have relied mainly on Davis pp. 536–642; Diolé; Marx (1968); Larsen; Syme.
3. Norton, p. 2; Syme, p. 17.
4. Winthrop, pp. 331–2, 399–400; Fardell.
5. Negri, pp. 93–6; Eng. trs. in Saunders, pp. 54–8; and see also Franzén, pp. 11–15.
6. Lyon (1979) p. 77; Serrano Mangas, pp. 121–2 and see above pp. 17–18.
7. Davis p. 606; Marx (1968) p. 36.
8. Linage, p. 183. The following section relies mainly on Serrano Mangas, ch. 5, "Los Buzos".
9. Serrano Mangas, p. 111.
10. Quoted by Roddie, p. 253. This article is the main authority for this section.
11. Roddie, pp. 262–3.
12. *CSPD* 1628–9, 17 August 1628; Roddie, pp. 267–9; SP 63/276/149; HCA 13/49/536–7, December 1631. My thanks to Geoffrey Harris for this and other references from HCA.
13. Roddie, pp. 256–7.
14. HCA 13/47/28; the wreck of the *Campen* was discovered in 1979, see Larn (1985).
15. For details on the change from bronze to iron guns see Caruana. Spanish warships retained bronze guns much longer; SP 18/104 #36, 9 February 1654–5. This section is pieced together from *CSPD* 1654–63 and see Cowan (1993) pp. 20–3.
16. Capp, p. 52; Hepper, pp. 1–3.
17. SP 18/112 #97, 24 August 1655.
18. SP 18/166 #9, 1 May 1657; #47, 9 July 1657; 18/171 #15, 4 September 1657; SP 18/191 #44, 7 June 1658; #101, 17 June 1658.
19. Bray, p. 245, 19 July 1661; Birch, i, 35, 194; ii, 13, 24–6, 55; Tomalin, p. 428 fn. 13.
20. *CSPD* 6 August 1663. Willis to Capt. Hicks, Deptford.
21. This section on the tin wrecks is based on *CTB* 1667–70, 1675, using the index heading "Tin wreck". For some biographical information on Custis see Lynch.

22. Rawlinson A. 185 fos. 41–2; Lynch, p. 18.
23. *CSPD* 1671–2 p. 94, 22 January 1671–2; 1672–3, p. 351, undated.
24. GB Patent #163; *CSPD* 1671–2 p. 124, 7 February 1671–2; pp. 351, 388, 20 & 28 April 1672.
25. The story is told in a series of letters to London from Anthony Isaacson, the Government agent in Newcastle; SP 29/319 #58 & #84, 21 & 24 December 1672; SP 29/332 #43, 63, 92, dated 7, 10, 14 January 1672–3; SP 29/334 #124, 8 March 1672–3; and also in Custis' own rather clumsily written account in SP 29/336 #310, fos. 295v–298 and in Custis.
26. Custis; and see the wonderful engraving by Wenceslas Hollar which accompanies his text.
27. SP 29/334 #124, Isaacson to Williamson, 8 March 1672–3; Custis; Serrano Mangas, pp. 124–5; Horner (2002) p. 142.
28. SP 29/361 #142. Lord Arlington to Lord Ogle, 18 July 1674.
29. See Earle (1979) ch. 8 for more on the subject of this section.
30. BL Egerton 2395, fos. 472–6. See Craton for the early history of the Bahamas.
31. *CSPAWI* 29 August 1682.
32. See pp. 18–21.
33. BL Egerton 3984 fo. 191.

Chapter Three: Captain Phips' Wreck Project

1. Defoe (1697) p. 16.
2. This chapter is based on ch. 9–15 of Earle (1979) where full references can be found.
3. Mather, p. 165. This contemporary biography of Phips has much useful material.
4. BL Egerton 2526.
5. This account is based on Stanley's Journal in Rawlinson A.300.
6. BL Egerton 2526; this journal kept by John Knepp is the main source for this part of the voyage.
7. Mather, pp. 20–1. Knepp had gone home by this stage of the voyage and Mather is the main source.

8. Defoe (1697) p. 16.

9. PRO C/10/227/63; John Smith *v.* Christopher, Duke of Albemarle et al. The papers of this lawsuit contain all the material relating to the business side of the project and the fitting out of the two ships.

10. Mather, p. 26. The next section is based mainly on the two logbooks, BL Sloane 50 (*James and Mary*) and Kent Archives Office, Maidstone, U1515/010 (*Henry*).

11. This quotation from Journal of *Henry*; there are other good descriptions of the finding of the wreck in de Beer, p. 29; Mather, pp. 27–8; Rawlinson A. 171, fo. 206v.

12. Mather, pp. 28–9.

13. Quoted in Lounsberry, p. 15.

14. Mather, pp. 31–2.

15. HMC *Downshire* i (1924) p. 245.

16. For details on the distribution of the treasure see Earle (1979) ch.15.

17. Mather, p. 34; Ronquillo quoted in de Beer, p. 29; BL Add. 25374 fo. 143v.

18. NMM LBK/1, Narborough's letter book. This document is the main source for the following passage, together with the logbooks kept by Stanley (ADM 52/35/2) and Lieut. Hubbard of the *Foresight* (NMM ADM/L/F/198).

19. Mather, pp. 32–3; NMM LBK/1, 14 April 1688, Narborough to Falkland.

20. NMM LBK/1 4 May 1688, Narborough to Falkland; 10 May 1688, Narborough to Pepys.

21. ADM 52/35/2 16 December 1687 & 15 February 1688; NMM ADM/L/F/198 27 January 1688.

22. Earle (1980) pp. 239–40 and see ch. 18 for a description of Webber's expedition which was aided by research carried out by the present writer. See also Grissim, p. 197.

23. John Taylor, "Multum in parvo or parvum in multo", iii, 758, 796. Taylor was a mathematician from Jamaica who visited the wrecksite and this manuscript is in the Institute of Jamaica at Kingston.

Chapter Four: The Great Treasure Hunting Boom

1. Sloane, p. lxxxi.
2. Add.25,374 fo. 157; *Angliae,* pp. 4, 20.
3. T 52/12 pp. 261–2.
4. NMM SOU/11 pp. 41–2; CO 37/1 fos. 202, 221; *CTB* vol. 8 (3) 7 February 1687–8.
5. NMM LBK/1 7 January 1687–8, 8 May 1688; ADM 52/35/2 29 January, 20, 25 March, 9 May 1688.
6. C8/436/92.
7. For the expedition see Sharpe; Burney, iv, 116–7; and for the maps Lynam (1953); William Hack, "West Coast of South America", BL MAPS.7.TAB.122, and BL Sloane 44, 46A, 46B, 47, and 239.
8. These quotations from Hack, "West Coast", maps 48, 60 and 68. See also Sloane 44 for similar observations.
9. Ringrose, p. 352 and see his MS journal in Sloane 3820 pp. 82–4. For a modern account see Potter (1973) pp. 193–4.
10. Capt. John Strong's journal is Sloane 3295 and there is another livelier account by Richard Simson in Sloane 672. See also Burney, iv, 329–37.
11. Horner (1973) ch. 11; Horner (2002) chs.1–3 & 14 and see above pp. 22–5.
12. See above pp. 12–15 for the story of the loss of Córdoba's galleons. The French side of this story is in AN C9a/2, letters of 5 March, 26 June 1689, 3 June 1690, 23 October 1691. For some information on de Graff's colourful career see Rogoziński, pp. 143–4.
13. NMM SOU/11/67, letters from William Musgrave, Attorney-General of Jamaica, dated May 1690; *CSPAWI* 6 July 1690, Earl of Inchiquin to the Lords of Trade and Plantations; T 64/88 pp. 324–5; T 27/12 pp. 370–1; PC 2/73 p. 525.
14. ADM 106/400 #384, Spragg to Navy Board, 7 July 1690.
15. Luttrell, ii, 97; NMM SOU/11/67; Sloane, p. lxxx.
16. AN C9a/2, 23 October 1691; Luttrell, ii, 640, 13 December 1692; Houghton, #94, 18 May 1694. Misteriosa Bank does exist; it lies about 150 miles west of the Cayman Islands.

17. McLeay, p. 47; Woodcroft, GB Patent # 210; T27/12 p. 79; Sacheverell, pp. 126–44.
18. SP 44/235 p. 184; SP 44/236 pp. 221–2; T 52/16 pp. 50–2, 86–7.
19. T 52/13 pp. 93–5.
20. T 52/13 pp. 93–5; T 27/12 p. 86; *CTB* vol.9 (3) p. 870.
21. On the *Santo Christo* see Larn et al. (1974–5) and on the 1619 Dutch ship see above p. 39; Larn & Carter, p. 103; HMC *Portland* vol. 5 (1899) pp. 350–1, Robert Davis to the Earl of Oxford, 20 October 1713.
22. SP 44/235 pp. 146–7; Scott, iii, 95.
23. SP 44/235 p. 169; T 52/16 pp. 19–23.
24. Thomas, p. 337.
25. C8/540/85, indenture dated 20 October 1687; NMM SOU/10 p. 103; T 64/88 p. 328; T 52/15 pp. 184–5.
26. SP 44/236 p. 247; T 52/15 pp. 333–5 and see above pp. 39–40.
27. Cape Clear SP 44/235 p. 192; Baden's patent T 52/16 pp. 50–2; SP 44/235 p. 184 (Wallop); *CTB* vol. 9(4) p. 1444 (name change).
28. SP 44/235 p. 199; T 52/16 pp. 238–41.
29. T 52/13 p. 315; T 52/16 pp. 253–5 and see T 52/16 pp. 338–48, 27 September 1692, for a lengthy summary of Neale's shipwreck grants up to this date. T 52/17 pp. 52–3.
30. CO 37/1 #16 contains most of the material about the Bermuda wreck project, but this is difficult to assess as it consists mainly of accusations made against Isaac Richier.
31. Rawlinson A. 305 fo. 45v; the story of the Ireland treasure is pieced together from the material in Rawlinson A. 305 fos. 1–47. See also Hayward (1928), pp. 137–8.
32. Rawlinson A.305 fos. 16–17. For more on Long see below, Chapter Six.
33. Thomas, p. 357.
34. Rawlinson A. 305 fo. 1; the affidavits are in Rawlinson A. 305 fos. 22–36 and also printed in Williams, pp. 301–23; see also Lynam (1937).
35. Sloane, vol. i. p. lxxxi.
36. SP 44/235 p. 279.
37. Rawlinson D.808 fo. 11.

38. T 64/89 pp. 122–6.
39. Carswell, p. 7.
40. Hill, p. 13.

Chapter Five: Diving-Engines of Divers Kinds

1. *Angliae,* p. 20.
2. Houghton, #98, 15 June 1694; Defoe (1697) pp. 4–6.
3. Macaulay, iv, 320; see also Scott, i, ch.18; Davies, pp. 277–81.
4. Davies, p. 275; MacLeod (1986) p. 558; *Angliae,* p. 23; and, see, in general, MacLeod (1986) and (1988) on the patent boom.
5. Van Dulken, p. 2; see also Davenport; MacLeod (1986 & 1988) and Woodcroft for useful material on the patent system.
6. Van Dulken, p. 62; Davenport, p. 42; Hayward (1987), i, 195–207.
7. MacLeod (1988) p. 20.
8. GB Patent #56 in Woodcroft; Marx (1968) p. 21.
9. SP 44/235 p. 490; 44/236 pp. 329, 332; 44/343 p. 545; GB #256.
10. GB #210, 4 March 1680-1.
11. PC 2/73 p. 194, 22 July 1689.
12. PC 2/73 p. 229.
13. SP 44/338 p. 468; GB #279; *CTB* vol. 9 (2) p. 835.
14. *LG* 14-17 March 1691-2; *CTB* vol.10 (2) p. 996, 18 April 1695; SP 44/240 pp. 39–40, 28 November 1702. For other patents for lifting equipment granted during this boom see GB # 311, 17 January 1693, to George Nation et al. and GB # 321, 27 April 1693, to John Bushnell.
15. PC 2/73 p. 229; Marx (1968) pp. 29–32; Davis, p. 550.
16. SP 44/235 p. 358; SP 44/341 p. 394; GB patent #302 granted 20 September 1692.
17. Kerr & Duncan, p. 35; Luttrell, ii, 589, iii, 88.
18. Luttrell, ii, 559,561 and see iii, 176 for another exhibition of the engine in September 1693.
19. *LG* 16-19 January 1692-3; the invention of Ralph Alexander Jr. seems similar to that of Overing though the description is even vaguer, "an engine for diving with newly invented screws and pipes, which convey air eight fathoms deep, enabling a man to

continue two hours under water, and yet have the use of his ears and eyes." SP 44/236 p. 334, 26 June 1693. The application seems to have lapsed as there is no patent recorded.

20. SP 44/235 p. 277; SP 44/341 p. 322 and GB # 298 on 31 May 1692; SP 44/235 p. 210, application of John Tyzack and Nicholas Finchley, 28 October 1691, no patent; SP 44/235 p. 435, application of John Stapleton, 13 January 1692-3 and GB # 318, 13 April 1693.

21. On Papin see below p. 253.

22. PC 2/74 p. 228, 20 August 1691; SP 44/341 p. 168, 29 August 1691; C8/556/79, Answer of Rice Jones.

23. PC 2/74 p. 232, 27 August 1691.

24. Defoe (1697) p. 14; C 6/499/41; C 7/373/22; C 8/556/79; Sutherland, pp. 283-4; Moore, p. 284.

25. C 8/556/79, Answer of John Skeate.

26. *LG* 2-6 February 1692-3; *CSPD* 23 December 1703.

27. SP 44/236, p. 326, 29 May 1693; SP 44/343 pp. 293-4, 13 June 1693; GB # 323, 10 April 1694.

28. SP 44/237 p. 14, 23 August 1693.

29. *LG* 27 April – 1 May 1693.

30. Quoted by Ronan, p. 86; MacPike, p. 144.

31. Hooper, p. 119.

32. Hooper, pp. 115-123; Desaguliers, ii, 211-22; Bachrach, pp. 9-11; Franzén, p. 13; Phillips, p. 15; Sinclair, pp. 169-72.

33. T 70/83 fo. 8; T 70/223 13 June 1691; Luttrell, ii, 186, 204.

34. Kerr & Duncan, p. 110 (the writer actually says that this bell was designed for work on the Tobermory galleon but both the date and the description fit Halley); Astle, pp. 136-7; Cook, pp. 236-43.

35. MacPike, pp. 150-2; Desaguliers, ii, 216.

36. MacPike, pp. 150-2; Huygens, x, 236-7, letter of 26 January 1692.

37. SP 44/235 p. 182; SP 44/341 p. 178; GB #279, 7 October 1691; CIII/192, Packet 41, deed of covenant between the partners, 17 November 1691; Houghton, #13, 21 May 1692; #93, 11 May 1694 and elsewhere; Scott, ii, 484.

38. MacPike, pp. 144–5, 153, 214, 224–5; Bevan, p. 29.

39. Sloane, p. lxxxi; T 70/84, fos. 67v, 72r, 85r, 89v; T 70/85, fos. 35v, 37r, 41v, 53v, 56r; Defoe (1963) p. 157.

40. Cowan (1993) pp. 17-20; Diolé; Davis, p. 613; SP 44/235 p. 180; SP 44/341 p. 259; GB # 308, 24 March 1693. A similar apparatus invented by John Hooke and partners had been granted letters patent on 19 October 1691. It was described as an invention "made of timber with glass windows, a door, and several air pipes, leather sleeves, and iron braces affixed thereunto." GB # 283.

41. C6/304/39; MacLeod (1986) p. 563; Cowan (1993) p. 19.

42. Defoe (1697) pp. 1, 34–5.

43. *Angliae*, p. 21.

44. Luttrell, iii, 508, 510; OIOC B/41 p. 17, 13 August 1695 and see index for further references.

Chapter Six: A Long Story

1. SP 44/204 p. 178.

2. *CTB* vol.10 (1) pp. 64–5, 25 February 1692–93; NMM SOU/10 p. 125; Rawlinson D.808 fo. 4.

3. *DNB*; Macky, p. 46; *CSPD* 30 July 1691; Rawlinson D.808 fo. 4.

4. See above pp. 115–6.

5. Rawlinson D.808 fos. 4–5; *LG* 27-31 July 1693; Luttrell, iii, 176; iv, 143.

6. *CSPD* 4, 6 May 1697; ADM 1/4085 p. 155, 8 May 1697.

7. Scraps of information on Richard Long in Rawlinson A.305 fos.10, 16–17; ADM 1/4085 p. 155; Long, p. 9; ADM 3/16 10 May 1701; Add. 61366 fo. 173; Add. 47,132 p. 49v; Pitcairn Jones.

8. T 1/46 fo. 179, 6 July 1697; for Phips see above p. 61.

9. Lyon (1993) p. 186; ADM 1/4085, p. 157.

10. ADM 106/520 17 January 1697–8; SP 44/204 pp. 170-1, 177-8; the main sources for Long's expedition are his letters to the Admiralty in ADM 1/2033/20, especially his report dated 17 June 1700, and the captain's and master's journals of the *Rupert Prize* in ADM 51/4325/10 and ADM 52/95/14.

11. Vázquez de Espinosa, pp. 332–4; Wafer (1903) pp. 56–7 (description of gold panning), pp. 85–6 (mines of Santa Maria); Dampier, pp. 91, 102–3; BL Sloane 3820 pp. 4–18 (Basil Ringrose's account of the raid on the mines).

12. Add. 47,132 fo. 54, Long to Duke of Leeds, 15 February 1699–1700; Hart, p. 220; Long; BL Maps. K. MAR. VIII. 3 is a map of Darien drawn by Long in 1700 and dedicated to King William III which gives a very good idea of what Long knew when he left Darien.

13. Dampier, p. 30; Add. 47,132 fo. 56.

14. ADM 1/2033/20, 19 May 1700.

15. Long, pp. 4, 8, 11, 12; SP 44/238 pp. 436–8, 1 July 1700; BL Maps K.MAR.VIII. 3&4.

16. I have relied mainly on Prebble for the Company of Scotland.

17. Some historians of the Company of Scotland do believe Long was a spy, e.g. Hart, pp.71–2 and, even more positively, Prebble, pp. 107, 161–3. But Prebble's generally excellent book is very hostile to the English and he reads more into the relationship between Long and James Vernon, the English Secretary of State, than is justified by the evidence. For an alternative view see Howarth, pp. 117–8.

18. Long, p. 8; Burton, pp. 70–1; Insh, p. 88.

19. ADM 106/528, 2 February 1698–9; Hart, pp. 220–3; Insh, pp. 100–6.

20. ADM 1/4085, p. 155, 8 May 1697. Practically all the information on Long's wreck hunt comes from his own and his master's journals. ADM 51/4325/10 and ADM 52/95/14.

21. For this fleet see above pp. 15–18.

22. ADM 1/2033/20, Long to Josiah Burchett, Secretary of the Admiralty, 19 May 1700; for Mel Fisher see Mathewson.

23. As before the main source is Long's journal, ADM 51/4325/10.

24. ADM 1/2033/20 Long to Burchett, Portsmouth, 19 May 1700; ADM 52/95/4, Twitt's Journal, 11 August, 9 September, 12 October 1699; ADM 1/2033/20, Long to Burchett, Spithead, 12 May 1700.

25. The map is BL Maps K.MAR.viii.3; CO 323/6 #60, affidavit of Richard Long, 17 May 1708.

26. ADM 3/16, 13 May 1701; ADM 52/210/1, journal of HM hulk *Lewis Prize*; ADM 1/2034/16, 18 September 1704; CO 324/9 pp. 182–4, 12 May 1708; Rodger, p. 165; Trevelyan, pp. 250–4.

27. Wafer (1704) pp. 265–83 & quotation p. 278; CO 137/45 #21 & #22; these last two reports, from the Governor and Judge Advocate of Jamaica, say that the privateers attacked the mines of Santa Maria but it is clear from Davis's account in Wafer (1704) that it was Canea; ADM 1/2035/8, 4 September 1706, Long to Burchett; CO 324/9 pp. 182–4, petition of Long to the Board of Trade, 12 May 1708.

28. ADM 1/2034/16, 22 November 1703.

29. ADM 1/2034/16, 18 September 1704; ADM 52/210/2, 12 September 1705.

30. ADM 1/2035/8, Long to Burchett, 4 September 1706; BL Maps K.MAR.viii.4, Long's map dated 12 September 1706.

31. CO 324/9 pp. 182–4, 12 May 1708.

32. Add. 61366 fos.139, 173, Long to Marlborough, 24 January and 22 April 1709. Long died in 1717 according to Pitcairn Jones.

Chapter Seven: Captain Hunter's Treasure Hunt

1. ADM 1/4086 p. 629, 13 November 1699, Secretary of State to Admiralty.

2. Dates from logbooks, ADM 52/25/8, *Dolphin* and ADM 51/4325/10, *Rupert Prize*.

3. ADM 1/1872/17, 16 April 1701, Hunter to Commissioners of Admiralty; 14 May 1701, Hunter to Burchett; Lyon (1994) pp. 26, 188.

4. ADM 3/14, Board Minutes, 14 July 1698; CO 31/5, pp. 393-5, petition of Champneys read before the Council of Barbados, 9 May 1699; ADM 1/1871/12, Hunter to Burchett, 11 May 1699.

5. ADM 3/14, Admiralty Board, 6 January 1698; ADM 1/4086, pp. 630–2, representation of the Earl of Macclesfield, 13 November 1699.

6. ADM 1/1871/12, 29 September and 27 October 1698; Luttrell, iv, 454; Earle (2003) p. 119, 149.

7. T 54/16, pp. 157–8, 17 January 1698–9, instructions for Oake; SP 44/204 pp. 201–6, instructions for Hunter; ADM 1/1872/17, 6 October 1698.

8. CO 31/5 pp. 393–5, 9 May 1699; ADM 1/1871/12, 6 & 28 June 1699. Thomas Allin was replaced as master by James Knowles on 25 June 1699.

9. ADM 1/5261, 4 March 1700–1; ibid., 11 May & 16 June 1699; Hunter p. 2.

10. Hunter, p. 3.

11. ADM 1/1871/12, 22 August, 22 September, 2 November 1699; Hunter pp. 3–4.

12. C5/287/7, John Breholt *v.* John Turner, for the *Carlisle*; ADM 1/1462/4, 11 August 1699, Jediah Barker of HMS *Speedwell* to Admiralty; CO 318/3, 28 October 1699, Benbow to Vernon. Breholt was probably hoping to locate the treasure galleons *N.S. de la Soledad* and *N.S. de las Mercedes*, both wrecked near Havana in 1695, though most of their treasure had been recovered by the Spaniards. Marx (1983) p. 352.

13. ADM 1/1871/12, 22 September; Hunter p. 4.

14. ADM 1/1871/12, 2,13 November, 7 December 1699; Hunter p. 5; ADM 52/25/8, master's log of *Dolphin*, 19 September – 1 December 1699; Hunter's own journal has not survived.

15. ADM 2/364 p. 5, Lords of the Admiralty to James Vernon, Secretary of State, 1 November 1699; ADM 1/4086 pp. 622, 629, Vernon to Admiralty, 6, 13 November 1699; ADM 3/15, Board Minutes, 1, 22, 25 November 1699.

16. ADM 3/15, Admiralty Board 22 November 1699, 27, 31 January, 15 February, 23, 27 March 1700; ADM 1/1435/2, Acton to Admiralty, 8 August 1700.

17. ADM 1/1871/12, 7 December 1699, 28 February 1700; Hunter p. 5.

18. Hunter pp. 5–6.

19. Hunter p. 7.

20. This section on the Turks Islands from Hunter pp. 7–9 and ADM 52/25/7, journal of the master.

21. ADM 52/25/8, 12 April 1700.
22. ADM 1/2277/4. Capt. Pickard to Admiralty, 18 April 1700, for some unknown reason he refers to Mills as Capt. Webb in this letter; Luttrell, iv, 656–7; ADM 1/1871/12, Hunter to Admiralty, 10 May 1700; Hunter pp. 9–10.
23. Hunter pp. 10–13; ADM 52/25/8.
24. Hunter p. 13; ADM 1/1872/17, 6 & 18 February 1700–1; ADM 106/546, Hunter to Navy Board, 24 April 1701.
25. ADM 1/1872/17, 16 April, 14 May 1701, 16 January 1701–2.

Chapter Eight: A New Way of Diving

1. John Lethbridge to *GM*, xix (1749) p. 412.
2. Harrison, p. 122; Karraker, pp. 87–91; CO 323/6 #91 (ii), dep. of Laurence Waldron, 17 May 1709; Add. 37682 fo. 155.
3. T 52/22 p. 134, indenture between the Queen and Lord Fairfax, 10 January 1703-4; Rawlinson C.451 fos. 22–32; Luttrell, v, 433, 463.
4. T 1/101 fos. 52, 54; T 54/20 p. 355; Add.37682 fos. 155-6; Harrison, pp. 122–3.
5. Rawlinson D.808 fo. 4v; this section on Weale is based on D.808 fos. 1–6, 10–18, 252.
6. Rawlinson D.808 fos. 13v–14v.
7. T 52/15 pp. 417–9 (Harley); T 52/24 pp. 403–4 (Randyll); T 52/27 pp. 58–60 (Sandys), 252 (Becker); T 1/233 fos. 140–3.
8. SP 35/1 #50-51, 1, 13, 16 November 1714.
9. Molloy, i, 387–9, 398–400; Abbott, part 3, pp. 381–403.
10. *St. James's Post* 27–30 August 1715; *Weekly Packet* 27 August – 3 September 1715; *Exeter Mercury* quoted in Amery, p. 495; Becker's patent was granted in February 1716 [GB#398].
11. Desaguliers, ii, 213–4; Clare, p. 169. For similar equipment in the 1690s see above pp. 115–8.
12. Add.9428 pp. 353–6; the other main sources for Lethbridge's biography are Lysons, ii, 568–70; Amery and *GM* xix (1749) pp. 411–3. Cowan (1978) is a modern biography.
13. See above p. 126.
14. Amery, p. 495; Add. 9428 pp. 353–6; Desaguliers, ii, 215.

15. Amery, p. 495; for the other sources see the references in Note 12 above.

16. Cornwall Record Office, AR/15/82/1; *GM* xix (1749) pp. 312, 411–3.

17. Add. 9428 p. 355; Amery, p. 495.

18. *Read's Weekly Journal,* 2 April 1720.

19. SP 35/21 #105, 11 June 1720, petition of Jacob Rowe; GB #431, Rowe's patent, 12 October 1720.

20. Cowan (1978); Turner, p. 91; PRO E 112/992/1014, third schedule; Cowan (1993) p. 47 says he was paid £50 for the whole expedition; NLS MS 1491 fo. 92v.

21. *Mist's Weekly* 18 November, 2 December 1721; *Applebee's Original Weekly* 25 November 1721.

22. *Mist's Weekly* 6 January 1721–2; *London Journal* 17 February 1721–2; T 1/239 #41, 12 April 1722; E 112/992/1014, third schedule; NLS MS 1491 fo. 92v, 20 November 1728.

23. Gaastra & Bruijn 188–97; Boxer, ch. 9.

24. This section is based mainly on Sténuit (1975); see also Green, pp. 21–2 and www.naufragios.com.br, a Brazilian web-site which has a piece on the *Slot ter Hooge.*

25. ARA VOC 11493.

26. Amery; Sténuit (1975); *HDT* #27 (2000) p. 27; *HDT* #29 (2001). There is a replica of Lethbridge's barrel at the Charlestown Shipwreck, Rescue and Heritage Centre in Cornwall.

27. The following section on the Table Bay wrecks depends mainly on Leibbrandt, pp. 288–90; Green, pp. 19–25; Turner, pp. 87–8.

28. Green, p. 24; Cowan (1993) p. 36; for Phips see above p. 61.

29. Leibbrandt, pp. 309–12; Green, pp. 26–8; Burman, pp. 44–50; Turner, pp. 113–5; Marsden (1976).

30. *Weekly Journal* 27 September 1729; *London Journal* 27 September 1729.

31. ARA VOC 4119 fo. 156; VOC 7259 fos. 391–2; Leibbrandt, pp. 337–8; Sténuit (1975) p. 267.

32. OIOC B/63 pp. 226, 275; OIOC E/1/27 #117.

33. OIOC E/1/26 #104, 105; OIOC B/63 pp. 459, 472, 481.

34. OIOC E/1/26 #199, 19 December 1735; E/1/27 #112, 1 September 1736; OIOC L/AG/1/1/17, EIC ledger, 1735-42 #154.
35. Amery, p. 495; *GM* xix (1749) p. 412.
36. Cowan (1975); Heath, pp. 150–1.
37. Heath, pp. 152–4.
38. Add.9428 p. 355; OIOC B/73 p. 324, 12 March 1755.
39. OIOC E/1/26 #199; OIOC B/71 pp. 325, 330, 6 & 13 March, 1750-1. For more on the *Princess Louisa* see below pp. 217–8
40. Allen, pp. 61–2; OIOC B/74 p. 411, 24 June 1757.
41. Add. 9428 p. 354; Amery, p. 495; Lysons, ii, 568; *HDT* #27 (2000), p. 27.

Chapter Nine: Jacob Rowe and the Wreck of the Vansittart

1. *Read's Weekly Journal,* 22 April 1721.
2. ADM 6/427 pp. 133,317; ADM 1/1879, Thomas Howard to Admiralty, 2 May 1715; Taylor, p. 165 thinks that Jacob Rowe was the son or nephew of Robert Rowe who wrote on the same navigational subjects and whom Jacob refers to in one of his works; there is a biography of Rowe in the introduction by Michael Fardell and Nigel Phillips to Rowe (2000) pp. 6–14.
3. SP 35/18 #54, 14 October 1719; SP 35/18 #68, 26 October 1719; ADM 1/4102 #118, 18 April 1720; for another very glowing opinion of Rowe's quadrant after it had been used in trials in the Channel in March 1720 see ADM 1/1826, Capt. Edward Gregory to Admiralty, 22 February and 6 March 1719-20.
4. SP 35/21 #105, 11 June 1720, 105 (i), 14 June 1720; GB #431, 12 October 1720; Carswell, p. 191.
5. Now published in facsimile by the Historical Diving Society; Rowe (2000).
6. Rowe (2000); Brown; NRO Holt 682, articles of agreement 1 November 1721; PRO E112/992/1014, Third Schedule; Desaguliers, i, 215 has a description of Rowe's machine but the shape is different from that in Rowe's manuscript, "a tub or truncated cone made in the shape of a Scotch snuff-mill".

7. Most of the information on the organization of the company here and later comes from Rowe's answers to the charges brought against him by the East India Company in PRO E112/992/1014 and E112/1003/1542.

8. OIOC B/55 pp. 297–9, 304, 308.

9. OIOC B/55 p. 329; D/96 18 June, 28 July 1719; E/1/10 #135; *Applebee's* 4 July 1719.

10. OIOC L/AG/1/6/8 p. 254; L/AG/1/1/14 #149.

11. ADM 1/4103 #43–4, 28 March 1721; ADM 2/50 pp.365–8, 13 April 1721, orders for Candler; for the pirates in this period see Earle (2003), chs. 9 & 10.

12. E112/992/1014; E112/1003/1542.

13. E112/992/1014, First Schedule.

14. Poolman, p. 1.

15. ADM 52/426/8, master's log of *Launceston*; ADM 1/1597/3, Candler to Admiralty, 21 August 1721; T 1/235 fo. 195, invoice of goods recovered.

16. E112/1003/1542; SP 35/30 #24, 1/12 February 1721–2, draught letter from Delafaye to Col. Stanhope.

17. E112/1003/1542; T1/235 fos.193, 245, 247.

18. T 1/239 #41, 12 April 1722; T 1/248 #54; on the *Guinea Frigate* see above pp. 122, 125–6 and below pp. 231–2; *Mist's Weekly Journal* 6 January 1721–2; *London Journal* 17 February 1721–2.

19. OIOC B/56 p. 489; E112/992/1014; E 112/1003/1542.

20. OIOC B/57 pp. 122, 140, 174-5, 235, 275, 279; on arbitration in this period see Horwitz & Oldham.

21. ADM 1/4104 #19, 5 May 1722; ADM 2/367 pp. 343-4, 7 May 1722; T 1/248 #54.

22. T 1/248 #11, #54; T 1/255 #59.

23. CO 23/13 fos.83–4, 20 February 1722–3; for the 1715 fleet disaster see Wagner and Burgess & Clausen.

24. CO 23/13, fos. 83–4.

25. Rowe (1725), preface, p. x.

26. Turnbull, vii, pp. 330–2, Newton to the Admiralty, 26 August 1725; Sobel, pp. 52–3.

27. GB #485 & 486; Colin Martin who led an expedition which rediscovered this wreck in 1970 has written several pieces on

El Gran Grifón, Martin (1972); Martin (1975) pp. 137–87; Martin (1998) ch. 2; NLS MS 1491 fo. 92v.

28. NAS AC 8/392.
29. Martin (1975) p. 162; SP 54/19/47 fo. 159; Sinclair (1925), p. 98.
30. On the *Adelaar* see Martin (1998) pp. 92–101.
31. Martin (1998) pp. 92-101; NAS AC 9/1202/26 & 77; NLS MS 1490 fos. 6–7, 234.
32. NAS AC 8/392; NLS MS 1490 fo. 16.
33. NAS AC 9/1182; SP 54/19/47 p. 159.
34. For details on the lawsuit see Martin (1998) pp. 99–101.
35. NLS MS 1490 fo. 39; for Rowe and the Tobermory galleon see McLeay, pp. 49–65.
36. NLS MS 1491 fo. 113; NAS CS 271/41058.
37. Most of these letters are in NLS MS 1491 fos. 73–119.
38. NLS MS 1491 fos. 96, 98.
39. NLS MS 1491 fos. 78, 99–101, 103.
40. NLS MS 1491 fos. 111, 115.
41. NLS MS 1491 fos. 111–9; McLeay, pp. 57, 64.
42. For this paragraph and the next see McLeay.
43. Rowe (2000).
44. See above pp. 41–4.
45. See above pp. 46–8.
46. OIOC L/MAR/B/643C; L/AG/1/6/12, March 1743; *London Evening Post*, 1-3 September 1743; *GM* xiii (1743) p. 493.
47. OIOC B/67 pp. 378–9, 382–3, 389, 391; PRO C111/190, Packet 31; for Thomas Hall see Gill.
48. C103/130; Cowan (1999); the *Princess Louisa* was rediscovered in June 1996 and the company recovered 20 cannon, 60,000 silver coins, three anchors, bars of iron and lead and ivory tusks. My thanks to Niki Sandizell for this information.

Chapter Ten: The Evans Logbooks

1. HCA 15/40.
2. HCA 3/72 fos. 269, 299; the logbooks are in HCA 15/40.
3. www.voc-shipwreck-vliegent-hart.org.
4. Most of this chapter is based on the logbooks which include a

few draft letters, scraps of accounts and pay lists as well as a brief day-by-day account of activities.

5. See above pp. 208–10 and Martin (1998) pp. 92–101 for the wreck of the *Adelaar*; NLS MS 1490 pp. 6–7 has the best description of the wreck.

6. See above pp. 209–10 for the organization of the salvage expedition.

7. Martin (1998) pp. 97–8; most of the rest of this chapter is based on the three logbooks in ADM 15/40 and no more references to these will be given.

8. SP 54/19/47 fos. 159–60, Rowe to unknown, Edinburgh, 8 November 1728.

9. For the inventory of the specie loaded see NAS AC 9/1202/74 and English translation in /77.

10. NLS MS 1490 fo. 9; NAS AC 8/393; NAS AC 9/1203/26.

11. NLS MS 1490 fos. 21–3; NAS AC 8/393; Hay's expenses in NAS AC 9/1142; NLS MS 1491 fo. 94, James Baker to Jacob Rowe, Barra, 3 February 1729.

12. In addition to the logbook and Hay's journal see NLS 1491 fo. 94, James Baker to Jacob Rowe, Barra, 3 February 1729 and ibid., fos. 73 & 66, Graham to Mackenzie, Glasgow, 25 September and 31 October 1729. See above p. 183 for Lethbridge and Richards.

13. NLS MS 1490 fo. 225, Evans to Mackenzie, Deptford, 17 December 1729; ibid., fo. 232, John Mackinnon to Mackenzie, Tobermory, 7 July 1729; NAS RH 15/38/16; Evans to William Irvine, Deptford, 11 April 1732, draught letter in logbook.

14. Potter (1973) pp. 350–1.

15. On the *Guinea Frigate* see above pp. 122, 125–6.

16. For Purvis see Sedgwick, ii, 377. Wager was also an MP, as well as a Commissioner of the Admiralty.

17. Evans to Irvine, draught letter dated Deptford, 11 April 1732, in logbook.

18. *CSPD* 13 May 1667, two letters from Weymouth describe the accident; Hepper, (1994) p. 6 says the accident happened in Tor Bay which would seem to be wrong.

19. On these wrecks see above pp. 89–90, 179–80, 203 and see Larn & Carter, p. 103.

20. For Evans in Vigo see below pp. 290–3.

21. A copy of the VOC's letter is in the logbook and there is some additional information in HCA 24/139, HCA 13/89 and HCA 13/138. On the loss of the two ships see Van der Horst, pp. 25–6; Weber, pp. 9–17 and the website http://www.voc-shipwreck-vliegent-hart.org. On Bushell see Triewald, p. 62 and Morant, i, 480. The wreck of the *Flying Hart* was rediscovered in 1981 and, over several diving seasons, many thousands of artefacts have been recovered. See Hildred for details.

22. Zélide Cowan, whose husband Rex played an important part in the rediscovery of the *Flying Hart*, wrote that the wreck lay at fifty feet, just over eight fathoms, so maybe it had shifted in the 150 years since Evans had dived on it. Cowan (1993) p. 59.

23. One of the treasure chests, complete with gold coins, has been recovered by the modern salvors. This chest, some of the gold and silver coins, and a wide variety of artefacts from the wreck can be seen in the Zeeuws Maritiem Muzeeum at Vlissingen.

24. NAS GD 150/2550 fo. 24, Irvine to Morton, Lerwick, 30 January 1737–8; Sténuit (1988) p. 286.

25. Undated letter from Sinclair to Evans copied into the logbook.

26. Quotation from a draft letter in the logbook from Evans to an unknown correspondent, dated Salcombe, 27 November 1738.

27. This section on the lawsuit is based on material in HCA 24/139, HCA 13/89 and HCA 13/138.

28. Triewald (2004) especially pp. 61, 73, 79–82, 85–7. The books were originally published in Swedish in 1734 and 1741, so are exactly contemporary with Evans.

29. ADM 106/926 #85, 86, 87.

Chapter Eleven: Bellmen and Braithwaites

1. Desaguliers, ii, 215.

2. See above pp. 121–4 for a description of Halley's bell.

3. Halley (1716 & 1721); Triewald (2004) p. 42.

4. Triewald (2004) pp. 23, 42–7; Triewald (1735-6) p. 381. For more on the hot air problem see above pp. 35–6. For a useful discussion of all the diving technologies in use *c.*1740 see Desaguliers, ii, 211–32. He considered the improved diving-bells to be the best.

5. GRO D3549 13/1/S1, "A relation of some attempts made with the diving-bell", Edinburgh, 15 February 1776.

6. GRO D3549 13/1/S21; there is a good description of Spalding's improvements to the bell in Smith, pp. 17–19.

7. *GM* liii, 542, 2 June 1783; GRO D3549 13/1/S16 & 13/1/F10.

8. Marx (1968) p. 37; Pococke, ii, 129–30; Hepper, p. 39; for Becker see above pp. 172–4.

9. Smiles, ii, 62–3, 69–70; Skempton, pp. 159, 163, 215; Smeaton, pp. 70–1,77; Davis, pp. 610–11. For Smeaton's designs for the bells and air-pumps used at Hexham and Ramsgate see his "Designs and Drawings" vol. iv, fos. 144–6 and vol. v, fo. 138 in RSL.

10. NLS MS 19833 fos. 18–19, Rennie's notebook #3, 3 August, 1789.

11. Smiles, ii, 219–20; Davis, pp. 611–2; Smith, p. 41.

12. Bevan, p. 29; Vallintine, pp. 151–3 and illustration #59; for Halley see above p. 125.

13. *Universal Daily Register*, 22 September 1786, 4a; Braithwaite (1986, 1992). My thanks to William Braithwaite, the direct descendant of the diving Braithwaites, for information on his ancestors and the chance to consult the two logbooks mentioned below.

14. ADM 1/4013, 27 November 1782, 3 May 1783; Johnson, p. 138; Uden, p. 56.

15. GRO D3549 13/1/S22. 13/1/B34, 13/1/S21.

16. GRO D3549 13/1/S21, Spalding to Sharp, 6 September 1782; Tracey; ADM 106/1282, 30 June 1784, Commissioner Martin to Navy Board; ADM 106/1281, 13 July 1784, William Braithwaite & Sons to Navy Board.

17. Drinkwater; MacGuffie, ch. 9.

18. *Universal Daily Register*, 9 November 1785, 2c; 18 November

1785, 2b; 21 September 1786, 3d; 22 September 1786, 4a; CO 91/32 12 May 1785; CO 91/33, 2 July 1786.

19. *Universal Daily Register* 14 April 1786, 3b; 14 July 1786, 2c; 22 September 1786, 4a; OIOC B/105 pp. 381–2, 22 August 1787.

20. The main sources for the mutiny are OIOC L/MAR/B/461A; BL Add. 47490 fos.63–66v; PRO FO 63/10, Sir John Hort to the Marquis of Carmarthen, 29 October 1787, enclosing three depositions about the mutiny taken in Lisbon.

21. For the shipwreck see the same sources as above, together with Fiott and some articles in the London newspapers, e.g. *London Chronicle* 9-11, 11-14 & 14-16 August 1787.

22. For mutiny on merchant ships see Earle (1998) pp. 174–82; official treasure in OIOC L/MAR/B/461A, log of *Hartwell,* 20 April 1787; OIOC L/AG/1/6/19, Commerce Journal, April 1787; *London Chronicle,* 11-14 & 16-18 August 1787.

23. OIOC B/105, pp. 367, 369, 381–2; E/1/225 pp. 37–42, instructions for Jackson; E/1/81 #85, Admiralty orders for Captain Fancourt.

24. ADM 1/1792, 30 January 1788, Fancourt to Stephens, Secretary of the Admiralty; OIOC B/106 p. 1071; E/1/226 pp. 430–1, EIC to William and John Braithwaite, 4 March 1788.

25. OIOC E/1/82 #153 & 203, Fancourt to Stephens and to EIC, 22 July 1788.

26. ADM 1/1792, Fancourt to Stephens, Spithead, 9 November 1788; OIOC B/108 pp.819–22, 23 December 1788; OIOC E/1/228 pp.102–5, EIC to Jackson and Braithwaite, 18 May 1790.

27. The Braithwaite logbook is the main source. See also ADM 1/3914 pp. 309–18, Jackson to EIC, 1 September 1789, enclosing accounts of recoveries.

28. Braithwaite logbook; *Universal Daily Register,* 22 September 1786, 4a; Heinke, p. 15; for Smeaton's pump see above pp. 253–4.

29. Logbook; ADM 1/3914 pp. 309–10, Jackson to EIC, 1 September 1789; "Moon-cursers" in *Times* 1 June 1790, 3b and the term explained in *OED.*

30. ADM 1/2488/12, Savage to Stephens, 27 May 1790, enclosing a "narrative of proceedings"; ADM 51/703/2, log of *Pomona.*

31. ADM 51/333/4, log of *Fairy* sloop; ADM 1/1988/5, Captain Inglefield of *Adventure* to Admiralty, 14 January 1790; *Times* 1 June 1790, 3b; ADM 51/976/8 log of *Termagant*; ADM 1/1840/15, 1 February and 21 April 1790, Gwennap to Stephens; *Public Advertiser* 26 April 1790.

32. Logbook and *Times,* 25 November 1790, 3d, an account based on a letter from Bonavista, dated 22 July.

33. The wrecksite of the *Hartwell* was rediscovered on 23 July 1996 by Arqueonautas, whose divers found guns, anchors and some more lead ingots. My thanks to Niki Sandizell for this information.

34. *Times* 5 January 1789, 2c; ADM 1/1792, Capt. Fancourt's journal, 1, 3 & 6 December 1787; Braithwaite (1992) p. 8.

35. For an excellent recent account see Hayter (2002).

36. For the shipwreck and the family connections see Hayter (2002) and for contemporary attitudes to opium see Hayter (1988), especially pp. 26–33; McAdam, pp. 240–1; Ketcham, pp. 146, 153; De Selincourt, pp. 438–9.

37. Marrs, pp. 152–3, 157–9.

38. Hayter (2002) p. 120; *Authentic Narrative* (1805) pp. 26–7; PRO CUST 59/24, Weymouth Collector to Board, 23 February 1805; OIOC B/140 pp. 1430, 1458, 1467, 1487, 1500.

39. *Monthly Magazine & British Register* vol. xxi, 1 July 1806; *Times* 5 May 1806, 3c, reporting his use of the bell and his percentage.

40. The main source is John Braithwaite's own brief journal covering the salvage. Many thanks to Bill Braithwaite for letting me look at this; *Times* 5 May 1806, 3c; *GM* lxxvi pp. 471–2.

41. Journal; *GM* vol.88 (1818) p. 644; the saw can be seen on the left of the illustration from the *Monthly Magazine* vol. xxi, 1 July 1806.

42. *GM* vol.88 (1818) p. 644.

43. Braithwaite (1992) pp. 8–9.

Chapter Twelve: Enterprise in Vigo Bay

1. Borrow, p. 263.

2. Verne, p. 189.

3. Fernández Duro, vi, 37; the main sources used for the description of the campaign and the battle were Corbett, ii, ch. 29; Owen, pp. 81–6; Burchett, pp. 626–31; de la Roncière, vi, 320–32; Touron Yebra; Browning; Boyer, pp. 130–6.

4. Browning, pp. 212–3; Markham, p. 56.

5. Ormond, p. 113.

6. Sources as above and also Lediard, p. 754; Uring, pp. 53–4; *Post Man,* 31 October – 3 November 1702.

7. *The English Post* 25–7 November 1702; Uring, p. 56.

8. Boyer, p. 136; Corbett, p. 225.

9. PRO PC 1/1/196.

10. Kamen, p. 171; Lediard, p. 757; Rodríguez Elías, pp. 17, 165; Iberti, p. 113.

11. Sténuit (1958) p. 52; Iberti, p. 91; *Flying Post* 28 November – 1 December, 12-15 December 1702; Calmon-Maison, p. 283 fn. 1.

12. For these and other concessions discussed below see Rodríguez Elías, pp. 56–62; Fernández Duro, pp. 42–5; Iberti, ch.10; Calmon-Maison, p. 283.

13. Fernández Duro, p. 43.

14. Fernández Duro, p. 43; the logbook is in HCA 15/40.

15. Some accounts have Evans working at Vigo later in the eighteenth century and using a diving-bell, but this is wrong and probably based on confused local memories like much else about Vigo.

16. *Times* 26 September 1826, p. 3a; Smollett (1759) ix, 288; C.13/1814/18, Polhill *v.* Stringer and others for Dickson's background. This lawsuit has many scraps of information about the expedition.

17. For the organization of the company see C.13/1814/18, Polhill *v.* Stringer; London Metropolitan Archives, F/ANG/141, sale of a share to Thomas Nettleship, 1 November 1825; prospectus in *Morning Herald* 10 December 1825, p. 2c; and for examples of "bull" articles see ibid., 10, 12, 17, 19 December 1825; for "bubble scheme" see *Times* 21 December 1829, p. 3b.

18. This section on the expedition of the *Enterprise* to Vigo is based on the logbook, PRO 30/26/49 and the Spanish

summary of proceedings in Rodríguez Elías, ch. 6; for more information on the wrecksites see Sténuit (1958) and Potter (1958). These two books describe the activities of themselves and their colleagues in Atlantic Salvage Company in Vigo Bay in 1955–7. There is a very useful chart showing the wrecks and the depths at which they lie on p. 159 of Potter's book.

19. The depths of the wrecks are given in the First Schedule of the lawsuit in C.13/1814/18, Polhill *v.* Stringer, which also gives the depths or supposed depths of mud on the wrecks, as much as sixteen to eighteen feet on the *Tambour* and *Cruceta.* Potter (1958) p. 159, also gives depths which are generally less as a result of silting up over the intervening years.

20. These numbers are my count from the logbook. The number of descents per diver is also given in the Second Schedule of C.13/1814/18. Counting from the logbook is quite difficult and we both made mistakes, but the same men are the most important in both counts and they make roughly the same number of dives, e.g. Wood 99 and Little 93.

21. Magen; Rodríguez Elías, pp. 72–3; Potter (1958) pp. 56–7; Sténuit (1958) p. 78; Bevan, p. 25.

22. See *Times* 26 September, 13 October 1826, 7 February 1828, 21 December 1829 and similar reports in other papers and also the papers of the lawsuit in C.13/1814/18.

23. C.13/1814/18, answer of Isaac Dickson.

24. Rodríguez Elías, pp. 180–1; Iberti, pp. 92–7; Sténuit (1958) pp. 78–83; Potter (1958).

25. Potter (1958) pp. 213–5; www.boardgamegeek.com.

Chapter Thirteen: The Salvage of the Thetis

1. PRO PCAP1 /4, 10 April 1832.

2. ADM 7/598, 12 December 1831, J. Woodhead to George Elliott, Admiralty.

3. Most of this chapter is based on documents in ADM 7/598, a volume of papers relating to the *Thetis*. Only references not in this will be noted here. ADM 1/5476, Court Martial of Burgess and the master of the *Thetis*, 15 March 1831; Burgess

was blamed in part for the disaster, but his long record was taken into account and he lost only one year's seniority. See also Dickinson, pp. 3–10.

4. Marshall, iv (1) pp. 251–2; O'Byrne, i, 287; ADM 1/38, 2 June 1832, Baker to Elliot.
5. Dickinson, pp. 22–4.
6. ADM 1/38, 9 April 1832, Baker's annotation of Dickinson's report; PRO PCAP 1 / 4, 29 October 1832, affidavit of Charles Pope.
7. ADM 1/38, 30 May 1831, John Moore to Baker; ADM 7/598, 14 August 1832, Baker to Robert Dewar.
8. ADM 51/3250/2, 29 December 1830, 22 January 1831; Dickinson, pp. 18–19.
9. Dickinson, p. 29; de Roos's narrative is in ADM 7/598, enclosed with a letter from Baker to Elliot dated 16 August 1832.
10. PRO PCAP 1 / 4, 24 October 1832, affidavit of Surgeon Dabbs; ADM 51/3250/2, 29 October 1831.
11. A copy of Dickinson's salvage journal is in PRO PCAP 1 / 4, the papers of the later appeal to the Privy Council.
12. ADM 7/598, Dickinson to Baker, 19 March 1831.
13. PRO PCAP 1 / 4, affidavit of Captain Owen, 19 November 1832.
14. PRO PCAP 1 / 4, Dickinson to Baker, 22 August 1831 re Mr Moore; ADM 7/598, 25 July 1831, Dickinson's instructions to Read.
15. ADM 1/37, Baker to Elliot, 26 February 1832.
16. ADM 7/598, Baker to Robert Dewar of Lloyds, 14 August 1832; for details of de Roos's time at Cape Frio, see his narrative in ADM 7/598 enclosed with a letter of 16 August 1832 from Baker to Eliot; see also the captain's log of *Algerine* in ADM 51/3040. There are two underwater charts drawn by de Roos showing the rocks and the ellipse before and after his activities in RSL, AP 18.7.
17. ADM 7/598, 20 March 1833, printed report of the case.
18. For the appeal see Knapp, pp. 390–410; for the underwriters see Dickinson, p. 173.
19. For the invention of the open diving helmet and later modifications see Bevan.

Bibliography

Abbreviations used in endnotes

Add.	Additional Manuscripts, British Library
ADM	Admiralty documents, PRO
AGI	Archivo General de Indias, Seville
AN	Archives Nationales, Paris
ARA	Algemeen Rijksarchief, The Hague
BL	British Library
C	Chancery documents, PRO
CO	Colonial Office documents, PRO
CSPAWI	*Calendar of State Papers, America and West Indies*
CSPD	*Calendar of State Papers, Domestic*
CSPV	*Calendar of State Papers, Venetian*
CTB	*Calendar of Treasury Books*
DNB	*Dictionary of National Biography*
EIC	East India Company
GB #	British Patent Number, as listed in Woodcroft (1854)
GM	*Gentleman's Magazine*
GRO	Gloucestershire Record Office
HCA	High Court of Admiralty documents, PRO
HDT	*Historical Diving Times*
HMC	Historical Manuscripts Commission
Hunter	Capt. Collin Hunter's account of his proceedings, ADM 1/1872/17, 18 February 1700/01.
IJNA	*International Journal of Nautical Archeology*
LG	*London Gazette*

Long   Report of Capt. Long to Admiralty, ADM 1/2033/20,
              17 June 1700
MM   *Mariners' Mirror*
NAS   National Archives of Scotland
NLS   National Library of Scotland
NMM   National Maritime Museum
NRO   Northants Record Office
NRS   Naval Records Society
OED   *Oxford English Dictionary*
OIOC   Oriental & India Office Collections, British Library
OLA   Orkney Library and Archive
PC   Privy Council papers, PRO
PRO   Public Record Office, The National Archives
PT   *Philosophical Transactions of the Royal Society*
Rawlinson   Rawlinson MSS, Bodleian Library, Oxford
RSL   Royal Society Library
SD   Santo Domingo section, Archivo General de Indias
Sloane   Sloane MSS, British Library
SP   State Papers, PRO
T   Treasury Papers, PRO
VOC   Verenigde Oostindische Compagnie [Dutch East
              India Company]

The works listed are those which have been referred to in the
Notes. Place of publication is London unless otherwise stated.
Where there is a second publication date in parentheses, the second
one has been consulted.

Abbott, Charles, *A Treatise of the Law relative to Merchant Ships and
     Seamen* (3rd ed., 1808)
Abilleira Crespo, Yago, *Los Galeones de Vigo* (Vigo, 2005)
Allen, Geoffrey & David, *Clive's Lost Treasure* (1978)
Amery, John S., "John Lethbridge and his diving machine",
     Transactions of the Devonshire Association xii (Plymouth,
     1880)
Angliae Tutamen: or, the Safety of England (1695)

Astle, Thomas (ed.), *Familiar Letters which passed between Abraham Hill, Esq. and several eminent and ingenious persons of the last century* (1767)

An Authentic Narrative of the Loss of the Earl of Abergavenny . . . by a gentleman in the East-India House [signed W.D.] (1805)

Bachrach, Arthur J., "The history of the diving-bell", *Historical Diving Times* (1998)

Bevan, John, *The Infernal Diver: the lives of John and Charles Deane* (1996)

Birch, Thomas, *The History of the Royal Society of London* (1756–7)

Borrow, George, *The Bible in Spain* (1842)

Boyer, Abel, *The History of the Reign of Queen Anne digested into Annals, year the first* (1703)

Boxer, C.R., *The Dutch Seaborne Empire, 1600–1800* (1965)

Braithwaite, William, "A New Line of Business: the pioneering Braithwaites", *Diver* (1986)

Braithwaite, William, "A Short History of the Braithwaites", *Family Tree Magazine*, vol.8 (September, 1992)

Bray, William (ed.), *Diary and Correspondence of John Evelyn* (Dent, London, 1920)

Brown, John, "A Description of the Diving Engine", *Universal Magazine* xiii (1753)

Browning, Oscar (ed.), *The Journal of Sir George Rooke, 1700–1702* (NRS, 1897)

Burchett, Josiah, *A Complete History of the Most Remarkable Transactions at Sea* (1720)

Burgess, Robert F. & Clausen, Carl J., *Florida's Golden Galleons; the search for the 1715 Spanish treasure fleet* (Stuart, Florida, 1982)

Burman, José, *Strange Shipwrecks of the Southern Seas* (Cape Town, 1968)

Burney, James, *A Chronological History of the Discoveries in the South Seas or Pacific Ocean*, 5 vols. (1803–17)

Burton, John Hill (ed.), *The Darien Papers* (Edinburgh, 1849)

Calmon-Maison, J.J.R., *Le Maréchal de Château-Renault (1637–1716)* (Paris, 1903)

Capp, Bernard, *Cromwell's Navy: the fleet and the English Revolution, 1648–1660* (Oxford, 1992)

Carswell, John, *The South Sea Bubble* (1960)

Caruana, Adrian B., *The History of English Sea Ordnance . . . 1523–1715* (Rotherfield, 1994)

Chaunu, Huguette & Pierre, *Séville et l'Atlantique* 8 vols. (Paris, 1955-6)

Clare, Martin, *The Motion of Fluids* (1735)

Cook, Alan, *Edmond Halley: charting the heavens and the seas* (Oxford, 1998)

Corbett, Julian S., *England in the Mediterranean* 2 vols. (1904)

Cowan, Rex, "Cape Verde: the new Mecca for wreck-hunters", *Diver* (Sept. 1999)

Cowan, Zélide, "The Dutch East-Indiaman *Hollandia* wrecked on the Isles of Scilly in 1743 – historical section", *IJNA* iv (1975)

Cowan, Zélide, *Early Divers: underwater adventures in the 17th and 18th centuries* (Great Yarmouth, 1993)

Cowan, Zélide, "John Lethbridge, Diver", *History Today* xxviii (1978)

Craton, Michael, *A History of the Bahamas* (1968)

Custis, Edmond, *A Brief Relation, and Exact Map of the harbour of New-Castle* (1673)

Dampier, William, *A New Voyage round the World* (1697, 1998)

Davenport, N., *The United Kingdom Patent System: a brief history* (Havant, 1979)

Davies, K.G., "Joint-stock investment in the later seventeenth century", *Economic History Review* 2nd ser. iv (1952) reprinted in E.M. Carus-Wilson (ed.) *Essays in Economic History* vol. 2 (1962)

Davis, Sir Robert H., *Deep Diving and Submarine Operations* (6th ed., 1955)

De Beer, G.R., *Sir Hans Sloane and the British Museum* (Oxford, 1953)

Defoe, Daniel, *Captain Singleton* (1720) (1963)

Defoe, Daniel, *Essay upon Projects* (1697)

Defoe, Daniel, *A Review of the State of the British Nation* (1704–13; facsimile ed., 1938)

De la Roncière, Charles, *Histoire de la Marine Française* vol. vi (Paris, 1932)

Desaguliers, J.T., *A Course of Experimental Philosophy* vol. 2 (1744)

De Selincourt, Ernest (ed.), *The Early Letters of William and Dorothy Wordsworth (1787–1805)* (Oxford, 1935)

Dickinson, Thomas, *A Narrative of the operations for the recovery of the public stores and treasure sunk in HMS Thetis at Cape Frio* (1836)

Diolé, Philippe, *Under-water Exploration: a history* (trs. H.M. Burton, 1954)

Drinkwater, John, *A History of the Siege of Gibraltar, 1779–1783* (1784, 1905)

Earle, Peter, *The Pirate Wars* (2003)

Earle, Peter, *Sailors: English Merchant Seamen, 1650–1775* (1998)

Earle, Peter, *The Treasure of the Concepción* (New York, 1980)

Earle, Peter, *The Wreck of the Almiranta* (1979)

Exquemelin, Alexander Olivier, *The Buccaneers of America* (1684–5; undated reprint by Broadway Translations)

Fardell, Michael, "Edward Bendall – America's first diver?", *Historical Diving Society Newsletter* ii (1992)

Fernández de Navarrete, Martin, *Colección de documentos* (facsimile ed., 1971)

Fernández Duro, Cesáreo, *Armada Española* vol. 3 (Madrid, 1897); vol. 6 (1900)

Fiott, John, *An Address to the Proprietors of East-India Stock . . . containing a narrative of the cases of the ships Tartar and Hartwell* (1791)

Franzén, Anders, *The Warship Vasa* (Stockholm, 1974)

Gaastra, F.S. & Bruijn, J.R., "The Dutch East India Company's Shipping" in Ibid. (eds.) *Ships, Sailors and Spices: East India Companies and their shipping in the 16th, 17th and 18th centuries* (Amsterdam, 1993)

Gill, Conrad, *Merchants and Mariners of the eighteenth century* (1961)

Good, J. Mason et al., *Pantologia* (1813)

Green, Lawrence G., *Something Rich and Strange: the story of South Africa's Treasures* (Cape Town, 1962)

Grissim, John, *The Lost Treasure of the Concepción* (New York, 1980)

Hackman, Rowan, *Ships of the East India Company* (2001)

Halley, Edmond, "An Addition to the Description of the Art of Living Under Water" *PT* xxxi (1721)

Halley, Edmond, "The Art of Living under Water", *PT* xxix (1716)

Hardy, Charles, *A Register of ships employed in the service of the Hon. the United East India Company* (1835)

Haring, C.H., *Trade and Navigation between Spain and the Indies* (Harvard, 1918)

Harrison, Fairfax, *Proprietors of the Northern Neck* (Richmond, Va., 1926)

Hart, Francis Russell, *The Disaster of Darien: the story of the Scots settlement and the causes of its failure, 1699–1701* (Boston, 1929)

Hayter, Alethea, *Opium and the Romantic Imagination* (1968, 1988)

Hayter, Alethea, *The Wreck of the Abergavenny* (2002)

Hayward, Peter, *Hayward's Patent Cases* (Abingdon, 1987)

Hayward, Walter B., *Bermuda Past and Present* (New York, 1926)

Heath, Captain Robert, *A Natural and Historical Account of the Isles of Scilly* (1750)

Heinke, J.W., *A History of Diving* (5th ed., 1876)

Hepper, David J., *British Warship Losses in the Age of Sail, 1650–1859* (Rotherfield, 1994)

Hill, Aaron, *An Account of the Rise and Progress of the Beech-Oil Invention* (1715)

Hildred, A. (ed.), *Report on the Excavation of the Dutch East-Indiaman Vliegent Hart, July-August 2000* (2001)

Homer, *The Iliad* (trs. Martin Hammond, 1987)

Hooper, W., *Rational Recreations* (1782)

Horner, Dave, *Shipwreck: a saga of sea tragedy and sunken treasure* (New York, 2002)

Horner, Dave, *The Treasure Galleons: clues to millions in sunken gold and silver* (1973)

Horwitz, Henry & Oldham, James, "John Locke, Lord Mansfield and arbitration during the eighteenth century". *Historical Journal* xxxvi (1993)

Houblon, Alice, *The Houblon Family: its story and times* 2 vols. (1907)

Houghton, John, *A Collection for Improvement of Husbandry and Trade* (1692–1703)

Howarth, David, *The Golden Isthmus* (1966)

Huygens, Christiaan, *Oeuvres Complètes* vol. x (The Hague, 1905)

Iberti, Carlo L., *The Treasure Hunt in Vigo Bay: a search for £28,000,000* (1908)

Insh, George Pratt (ed.), *Papers relating to the Ships and Voyages of the Company of Scotland . . . 1696–1707* (Edinburgh, 1924)

Johnson, R.F., *The Royal George* (1971)

Kamen, Henry, "The destruction of the Spanish silver fleet at Vigo in 1702", *Bulletin of the Institute of Historical Research* xxxix (1966)

Karraker, C.H., *The Hispaniola Treasure* (Philadelphia, 1934)

Kerr, Russell J., & Duncan, Ida Coffin (eds.), *The Portledge Papers* (1928)

Ketcham, Carl H. (ed.), *The Letters of John Wordsworth* (Ithaca, N.Y., 1969)

Knapp, Jerome William, *Reports of Cases Argued and Determined . . . before the . . . Judicial Committee of the Privy Council, August 1831 to June 1834* (1834)

Larn, Richard, "The wreck of the Dutch East-Indiaman *Campen* on the Needles rocks, Isle of Wight, 1627", *IJNA* xiv (1985)

Larn, Richard & Carter, Clive, *Cornish Shipwrecks: the South Coast* (1969)

Larn, R., McBride, P., & Davis, R., "The mid-17th century merchant ship found near Mullion Cove, Cornwall", *IJNA* iii (1974), iv (1975)

Larsen, Egon, *Men Under the Sea* (1955)

Lediard, Thomas, *The Naval History of England* (1735)

Leibbrandt, H.C.V., *Précis of the Archives of the Cape of Good Hope: Journal, 1699–1732* (Cape Town, 1896)

Linage, Joseph de Veitia, *The Spanish Rule of Trade to the West-Indies* (trs. John Stevens, 1702)

Lounsberry, Alice, *Sir William Phips* (New York, 1941)

Luttrell, Narcissus, *A Brief Historical Relation of State Affairs* (Oxford, 1857)

Lynam, Edward, "A Treasure Map", *Imago Mundi* ii (1937)

Lynam, Edward, "William Hack and the South Sea buccaneers" in Ibid., *The Mapmaker's Art: essays in the history of maps* (1953)

Lynch, James B., Jr., "Edmund Custis and his Wreck-Fishing Invention", *The American Neptune* vol. 50 (1990)

Lyon, David J., *The Sailing Navy List: all the ships of the Royal Navy . . . 1688–1860* (1993)

Lyon, Eugene, *The Search for the Atocha* (New York, 1979)

Lysons, Daniel and Samuel, *Magna Britannia . . . vol.6, Devonshire* 2 pts. (1822)

Macaulay, T.B., *The History of England from the Accession of James the Second* vol. 4 (1855)

McConnell, Anita, *The Salvage of HMS Thetis, wrecked at Cape Frio in December 1830* (Science Museum, July 1986)

MacGuffie, T.H., *The Siege of Gibraltar, 1779–1783* (1965)

Macky, John, *Memoirs of the Secret Services* (1733)

MacLeod, Christine, *Inventing the Industrial Revolution: the English patent system, 1660–1800* (Cambridge, 1988)

MacLeod, Christine, "The 1690s Patents Boom: invention or stock-jobbing?", *Economic History Review* 2nd ser. xxxix (1986)

MacPike, Eugene Fairfield (ed.), *Correspondence and Papers of Edmond Halley* (Oxford, 1932)

Magen, Hippolyte, *Les Galions de Vigo* (Paris, 1873)

Manucy, Albert, *Pedro Menendez de Avilés, Captain General of the Ocean Sea* (Sarasota, Florida, 1992)

Markham, Clements R. (ed.), *Captain Stephen Martin, 1666–1740* (NRS, 1895)

Marrs, Edwin W., jr., *The Letters of Charles and Mary Lamb* vol.2, *1801–1809* (Cornell, 1976)

Marsden, Peter, "The *Meresteyn*, wrecked in 1702, near Cape Town, South Africa", *IJNA* v (1976)

Marsden, Peter, *The Wreck of the Amsterdam* (1974)

Marshall, John, *Royal Naval Biography* vol. 4 (1833–1835)

Martin, Colin, "*El Gran Grifón*. An Armada wreck on Fair Isle", *IJNA* i (1972)

Martin, Colin, *Full Fathom Five: wrecks of the Spanish Armada* (1975)

Martin, Colin, *Scotland's Historic Shipwrecks* (1998)

Martin, Colin, "The wreck of the Dutch East-Indiaman *Adelaar* off Barra in 1728" in Roger Mason & Norman Macdougall (eds.) *People and Power in Scotland* Edinburgh (1992)

Martin, Colin & Parker, Geoffrey, *The Spanish Armada* (1988)

Marx, Robert F., *They Dared the Deep: a history of diving* (1968)

Marx, Robert F., *Quest for Treasure: the Maravillas* (Dallas, Texas, 1973)

Marx, Robert F., *Shipwrecks in the Americas* (New York, 1983)

Mather, Cotton, *Pietas in Patriam: the life of his excellency Sir William Phips, Knt.,* (1697) (New York, 1929)

Mathewson, R. Duncan, III, *Treasure of the Atocha* (1986)

McAdam, E.L. jr., "Wordsworth's Shipwreck", *Publications of the Modern Language Association of America* lxxvii (June 1962)

McLeay, Alison, *The Tobermory Treasure* (1986)

Menendez de Avilés, Pero, *Vida y Hechos* (trs. Anthony Kerrigan, Gainesville, Florida, 1965)

Molloy, Charles, *De Jure Maritimo et Navali* (1769 ed.)

Moore, John Robert, *Daniel Defoe: Citizen of the Modern World* (Chicago, 1958)

Morant, Philip, *The History and Antiquities of the County of Essex* (1768)

Negri, Francesco, *Viaggio Settentrionale* (Padova, 1700)

Norton, Trevor, *Stars beneath the Sea: the extraordinary lives of the pioneers of diving* (2000)

O'Byrne, William R., *A Naval Biographical Dictionary* (1849)

Ormond, James Butler, duke of, *Memoirs of the Life of . . .* (1738)

Owen, J.H., *War at Sea under Queen Anne, 1702–1708* (Cambridge, 1938)

Parry, J.H., *The Spanish Seaborne Empire* (1966)

Phillips, Nigel, "Edmond Halley and the age of the Diving Bell", *Historical Diving Times* (Summer, 2001)

Pitcairn Jones, C.G., *The Commissioned Sea Officers of the Royal Navy, 1660–1815* (n.d.)

Pococke, Richard, *Travels through England* 2 vols. (1888-89)

Poolman, Kenneth, *The Speedwell Voyage: a tale of piracy and mutiny in the eighteenth century* (Annapolis. Md., 1999)

Portichuelo de Ribadeneyra, Diego, *Relación del Viage y Sucesos que tuvo desde que salió de la Ciudad de Lima* (Madrid, 1657)

Potter, John S., jr., *The Treasure Diver's Guide* (1973)

Potter, John S., jr., *The Treasure Divers of Vigo Bay* (New York, 1958)

Prebble, John, *The Darien Disaster* (1970)

Ringrose, Basil, *The Dangerous Voyage and Bold Assaults of Captain Bartholomew Sharpe and others* in Exquemelin (1684-5)

Roddie, Alan, "Jacob, the Diver", *MM* xlviii (1962)

Rodger, N.A.M., *The Command of the Ocean: a naval history of Britain, 1649-1815* (2004)

Rodríguez Elías, Avelino, *La Escuadra de Plata* (Vigo, 1935)

Rogoziński, Jan, *Pirates: an A–Z Encyclopedia* (New York, 1995)

Ronan, Colin A., *Edmond Halley: Genius in Eclipse* (1970)

Rowe, Jacob, *All Sorts of Wheel-carriage Improved* (1734)

Rowe, Jacob, *A Demonstration of the Diving Engine: its invention and various uses* (Greenwich, 2000)

Rowe, Jacob, *Navigation Improved* (1725)

Ruidíaz y Caravia, E., *La Florida: su conquista y colonización por Pedro Menendez de Avilés* 2 vols (Madrid, 1893)

Sacheverell, William, *An Account of the Isle of Man . . . with a voyage to I-Columb-Kill* (1702)

Sad Newes from the Seas (1641)

Saunders, Roy, *The Raising of the Vasa* (1962)

Scott, W.R., *The Constitution and Finance of English, Scottish and Irish Joint-Stock Companies to 1720* (Cambridge, 1910)

Sedgwick, Romney, *The House of Commons, 1715–1754* (1970)

Serrano Mangas, Fernando, *Naufragios y Rescates en el trafico indiano durante el siglo XVII* (Lima, 1991)

Sharpe, Bartholomew, *Voyages and Adventures* (1684)

Sinclair, George, *The Hydrostaticks* (Edinburgh, 1672)

Sinclair, Sir John, *Statistical Account of Shetland, 1791–1799* (1925)

Skempton, A.W. (ed.) *John Smeaton, FRS* (1981)

Sloane, Sir Hans, *A Voyage to the Islands, Madeira, Barbados . . . and Jamaica* 2 vols. (1707)

Smeaton, John, *An Historical Report on Ramsgate Harbour* (2nd ed., 1791)

Smiles, Samuel, *Lives of the Engineers* (1862)

Smith, S.W., *Observations on Diving and Diving Machines* (Plymouth, 1822)

Smollett, Tobias, *A Complete History of England* 11 vols. (1758–60)

Sobel, Dava, *Longitude* (New York, 1995)

Southey, Robert, *Life and Correspondence* vol.2 (1850)

Sténuit, Robert, *Les épaves de l'Or* (Paris, 1958)

Sténuit, Robert, *Ces mondes secrets ou j'ai plongé* (Paris, 1988)

Sténuit, Robert, "The Treasure of Porto Santo", *National Geographic* vol. 148 (August, 1975)

Sutherland, James R., "Some early troubles of Daniel Defoe", *Review of English Studies* ix (1933)

Syme, Neville Ronald, *Full Fathom Five* (1946)

Taylor, E.G.R. *The Mathematical Practitioners of Hanoverian England, 1714–1840* (1966)

Thomas, J.H., "Thomas Neale, a 17th-century projector", unpublished Ph.D. thesis (Southampton, 1979)

Tomalin, Claire, *Samuel Pepys: the unequalled self* (2003)

Touron Yebra, "La Guerra de Sucesión en Galicia (1702–1712). La batalla de Rande", *Revista de Historia Militar* (1986)

Tracey, William, *A Candid and Accurate Narrative of the Operations used in Endeavouring to raise His Majesty's Ship Royal George* (Portsmouth, 1785)

Trevelyan, George Macaulay, *England under Queen Anne: Blenheim* (1930)

Triewald, Märten, *The Art of Living under Water* (1734, 1741) (Eng. tr. 2004)

Triewald, Mårten, "A Letter to the Reverend John Theophilus Desaguliers . . . concerning an improvement of the diving-bell", *PT* xxxix (1735–6)

Turnbull, H.W. (ed.), *Correspondence of Isaac Newton* vol. 7 (Cambridge, 1977)

Turner, Malcolm, *Shipwrecks and Salvage in South Africa* (Cape Town, 1988)

Uden, Grant, *The Loss of the Royal George* (1970)

Uring, Nathaniel, *Voyages and Travels* (1928)

Vallintine, Reg, *Divers and Diving* (Poole, 1981)

Van der Horst, A.J., *De Ondergang van het VOC-retourschip 't Vliegend Hart in 1735* (Amsterdam, 1991)

Van Dulken, Stephen, *British Patents of Invention, 1617–1977: a guide for researchers* (1999)

Vázquez de Espinosa, Antonio, *Compendium and Description of the West Indies* (written c.1620) (Washington, D.C., 1942)

Verne, Jules, *Twenty Thousand Leagues under the Sea* (1869, 1992) *The Voyages and Adventures of Captain Bartholomew Sharpe* (1684)

Wafer, Lionel, *A New Voyage and Description of the Isthmus of America* (1699, 1903)

Wafer, Lionel, *A New Voyage . . . to which is added Davis's expedition to the Gold Mines in 1702* (1704)

Wagner, Kip. *Pieces of Eight* (New York, 1966)

Weber, Wilbert, *Een Gezonken V.O.C. Schip 't Vliegent Hart* (Middelburg, 1987)

Williams, William Frith, *An Historical and Statistical Account of the Bermudas from their discovery to the present time* (1848)

Winthrop, John, *Journal, 1630–1649* (Cambridge, Mass., 1996)

Woodcroft, Bennet, *Titles of Patents of Invention, chronologically arranged* 2 vols. (1854)

Index